AMERICAN INSTITUTE OF CERTIFIED PUBLIC ACCOUNTANTS

THE GUIDE TO

INVESTIGATING BUSINESS FRAUD

BY THE PROFESSIONALS AT ERNST & YOUNG

Notice to Readers

The Guide to Investigating Business Fraud does not represent an official position of the American Institute of Certified Public Accountants, and it is distributed with the understanding that the authors and publisher are not rendering legal, accounting, or other professional services in the publication. This publication contains information in summary form and is therefore intended for general guidance only. It is not intended to be a substitute for detailed research or the exercise of professional judgment. Neither EYGM Limited nor any other member of the global Ernst & Young organization, nor the authors or publisher can accept any responsibility for loss occasioned to any person acting or refraining from action as a result of any material in this publication. On any specific matter, reference should be made to the appropriate advisor.

Publisher: Linda Prentice Cohen
Senior Managing Editor: Amy M. Stainken
Developmental Editor: Andrew Grow
Project Manager: Amy Sykes
Cover and Interior Design Direction: David McCradden
Copyeditor: Dan Streckert

About the Editors

Ruby Sharma, *Principal, Ernst & Young*

Ruby Sharma has investigative and forensic accounting experience in internal corporate investigations, white-collar fraud, damage assessment, accounting, and financial issues and contract disputes including inventory, contract accounting and pricing, purchase-price disputes, and financial statement accounting practices and procedures. She has provided analysis of financial, economic, and accounting issues in internal investigations, discovery, and pre-trial analysis, deposition preparation, and assistance in arbitrations.

Ruby has worked in industries such as entertainment, manufacturing and distribution, banking, and insurance. She has performed due diligence in management buyouts, IPOs, joint ventures, mergers and acquisitions, and company restructurings throughout Europe.

Ruby is a fellow of the Institute of Charted Accountants in England and Wales. She holds a bachelor's degree in economics from Delhi University in India.

Michael H. Sherrod, *Senior Manager, Ernst & Young*

Mike Sherrod is a senior manager in Ernst & Young's Fraud Investigation & Dispute Services practice. Mike was selected to lead the firm's efforts in the US in creating and delivering its anti-fraud service into the marketplace. Mike has led numerous fraud risk assessments, fraud awareness trainings and fraud response plan developments with numerous clients in various industries located in the US. In addition to Mike's work in dealing proactively with fraud, he also focuses attention in the area of fraud investigations, specifically on revenue recognition, embezzlements, audit malpractice and other internal investigations. Prior to joining EY, Mike was an external auditor for a large regional CPA firm. He primarily audited local government organizations as well as construction and manufacturing companies. Mike is a Certified Public Accountant and a Certified Fraud Examiner. He holds a bachelors degree in accounting from Virginia Tech.

Richard Corgel, *Executive Director, Ernst & Young*

Rich Corgel has more than 35 years' experience managing complex accounting, financial reporting, Securities and Exchange Commission (SEC) and auditing matters. He has directed and conducted financial, purchase and due diligence investigations, internal control reviews and other projects requiring financial and forensic skills.

Rich is an executive director in Ernst & Young's Fraud Investigation & Dispute Services practice. He has experience resolving complex financial issues by working with legal counsel on regulatory and litigation strategies. Rich's clients have included SEC registrants and private enterprises across a broad range of industries including telecommunications, energy, entertainment and professional sports, health care and financial services. He has advised numerous companies on the proper application of accounting principles, financial reporting and SEC compliance.

Rich has also assisted public company boards and audit committee members with the increasing complexity of their responsibilities by providing independent advisory services for audit committees.

Rich has a bachelor's degree in finance and accounting and a master's degree in tax accounting from Syracuse University. He is also a certified public accountant, licensed in California.

Steven J. Kuzma, *Americas Chief Operating Officer, Ernst & Young*

Steve Kuzma is the Americas managing partner of Ernst & Young's Fraud Investigation & Dispute Services practice—a group that offers accounting and financial advice to the corporate general counsel and retained counsel of global companies engaged in complex business disputes and investigative matters. The practice conducts fraud investigations and provides economic and damages analysis along with expert witness services to some of the world's largest companies and law firms. The practice is increasingly involved in helping companies investigate the integrity of financial statements, issue restatements and identify corruption and white-collar crime.

Steve has more than 30 years of experience providing *Fortune* 1000 companies and large law firms with investigative services; financial, accounting and economic analyses; valuation assistance; and complex commercial dispute resolution support. He has testified in deposition, arbitration, and in federal and state courts throughout the US.

Steve has significant experience across a range of industries, including retail, consumer and industrial products; health care; entertainment; real estate; agriculture; utilities; and technology. He advises on commercial disputes, fraud and forensic investigations and economic valuation and damages analysis.

Steve is a certified public accountant, certified fraud examiner and certified in financial forensics. Additionally, he is a senior member of the American Society of Appraisers with a focus on business valuation. Steve is recognized as being accredited in business valuation by the American Institute of Certified Public Accountants.

He holds a BBA from Florida Atlantic University and an MBA from Rollins College, both in finance and accounting. He completed postgraduate studies at Northwestern University's Kellogg Graduate School and Harvard Business School.

Contributors

Barb Lambert, *Manager,*
Ernst & Young

Barb has more than eight years of experience in litigation and advisory services across a broad range of industries, including financial services, manufacturing, energy, health care and professional services. Barb has worked on a number of large financial restatements, forensic accounting investigations and other regulatory investigations that involved issues such as revenue recognition, reserves and contingencies and derivatives and hedging activities. Barb is a certified public accountant and a certified fraud examiner. She holds a bachelor's degree in accounting from the University Michigan in Ann Arbor.

Ben Hawksworth, *Senior Manager,*
Ernst & Young

Ben has more than 18 years of experience in the provision of discovery services in a wide range of commercial and government litigation, antitrust, fraud, health care and intellectual property matters. Ben's practice focuses on legal technology services, including discovery response risk assessments; legal hold effectiveness assessments; legal hold design and implementation; processing of electronic information and online hosting and review; and discovery management advisory services. Ben earned his bachelor's degree in government from Cornell University. He is a certified project management professional and a certified fraud examiner.

Bruce Zaccanti, *Principal,*
Ernst & Young

Bruce has more than 19 years' experience in insurance risk and claim advisory services across a broad range of industries, including financial services, manufacturing, retail, real estate, energy, health care and professional services. He has served as partner on numerous insurance, claim, captive and advisory engagements as well as internal control reviews. He has also worked with clients on mergers and acquisitions due diligence, valuation and damage analyses. He has conducted fraud and forensic investigations for SEC registrants. Bruce is a holds a bachelor's degree in Enterprise Management from the Northern Illinois University.

Charles Owens, *Executive Director,*
Ernst & Young

Chuck serves as a leader in managing fraud and forensic investigations. Prior starting with Ernst & Young eight years ago, Chuck spent 25 years with the FBI where, as a senior executive, he had national responsibility for all FBI investigations and initiatives addressing financial institution fraud, health care fraud, governmental fraud, money laundering, computer crimes, securities fraud, insurance fraud and intellectual property crimes. Chuck holds a bachelor's degree in accounting from West Virginia University. He is also a certified public accountant.

Dale Kitchens, *Partner, Ernst & Young*

Dale Kitchens has more than 28 years' experience in litigation, audit and advisory services across a broad range of industries, including financial services, manufacturing, retail, real estate, energy, health care and professional services. Dale has served as partner on numerous financial statement audits and internal control reviews and he has worked with clients on mergers and acquisitions due diligence, valuation and damage analyses. Dale also has conducted fraud and forensic investigations for SEC registrants. Dale is a certified public accountant and holds a bachelor's degree in accounting from the University of Arkansas at Little Rock.

James McCurry, *Partner, Ernst & Young*

Jim has more than 10 years' experience in litigation advisory services and forensic investigations. He has assisted a diverse base of financial services clients, ranging from community banks to diversified financial concerns operating on a global scale. His engagements have included customer account analysis and reconstruction, historical, lost-profits calculations, surety claims, securities and shareholder class actions and investigations into market timing allegations. Jim is a certified public accountant and holds a bachelor's degree in accounting from Fairfield University and a master's in business administration from Columbia University.

Jennifer Baskin, *Manager, Ernst & Young*

Jennifer has more than seven years of experience providing litigation and advisory services for a variety of companies in the US and abroad. Her primary focus is financial investigations, particularly those related to the Foreign Corrupt Practices Act and other anti-corruption laws. In addition, Jennifer has participated on large accounting malpractice cases and complex accounting disputes. Jen is a certified public accountant and a certified fraud examiner. She holds a bachelor's degree in accounting and finance from Virginia Tech.

Jennifer Hadsell, *Senior, Ernst & Young*

Jennifer focuses her practice on forensic technology and discovery services. She has experience advising law firms on the collection, review and production of electronic documents. She has assisted large corporations through the electronic review process, and she has advised law firms on practices used in the management of electronic data. Jennifer also focuses on cost containment services related to legal departments and litigation; including project management of outside counsel and vendor costs, electronic billing and matter management solutions. Jennifer holds a bachelor's degree in English and textual studies from Syracuse University.

Jerry Hansen, *Senior Manager, Ernst & Young*

Jerry has more than 10 years of experience in forensic accounting investigations, purchase price dispute arbitrations and audit services. He also has more than 10 years of industry experience including a large multinational software company, a global telecommunications company, a general contractor specializing in insurance claims and mortgage banking. Jerry's experience in forensic accounting investigations and purchase price dispute arbitrations covers a wide range of industries including technology, energy, transportation, manufacturing, software and financial services. He is a certified public accountant and holds a bachelor's degree in finance from Southern Methodist University and a master's degree in accounting from the University of Virginia.

Joe Galanti, *Principal, Ernst & Young*

Joe has more than 10 years of experience working in the litigation environment. His responsibilities include preparing financial models, economic projections and sensitivity analyses used to determine financial damages. Joe focuses primarily on complex insurance claims and dispute services including breach-of-contract, antitrust, valuation, forensic accounting and health care fraud matters. He has experience working on first-party property and specialty claims involving property damage, business interruption, extra expense and employee theft, among others. Joe is a certified fraud examiner and a CFA(r) charterholder. He holds both a bachelor's degree in international affairs and an MBA from The George Washington University.

John Tsai, *Senior Manager,* Ernst & Young

John has more than 11 years of experience in the analysis of complex financial transactions and accounting issues, conducting independent internal investigations for companies and audit committees and assisting registrants through financial restatements and addressing SEC inquiries. John has advised clients on matters involving financial statement accounting practices and procedures, internal controls testing and remediation and the Foreign Corrupt Practices Act. He holds a bachelor of science in business administration and a bachelor of arts in economics and international relations from the University of Southern California. He also holds a master of science in accounting from the University of Virginia. He is a certified public accountant and has attained the certified in financial forensics credential from the American Institute of Certified Public Accountants.

Lynda Schwartz, *Partner,* Ernst & Young

Lynda has over 20 years of experience in accounting, auditing, fraud advisory, forensic investigation and dispute-related services. She frequently leads forensic investigations in to complex financial statement and fraud issues. An experienced expert witness in state courts, US federal court and alternative dispute resolution settings, she has testified on business valuation matters, solvency litigation in bankruptcy, complex contract litigation, financial reporting issues, embezzlement and fraud-related matters.

Lynda serves as a trainer to both Ernst & Young and client audiences on fraud risk, and is a frequent public speaker on these topics. She is active in several Ernst & Young firm-wide initiatives addressing the risk of fraud. Lynda is a summa cum laude graduate of the University of Massachusetts. She is a certified public accountant and is also certified in financial forensics.

Mike Savage, *Partner,* Ernst & Young

Originally from South Africa, Mike has experience in fraud detection, fraud prevention programs, whistleblower hotlines, forensic accounting investigations and dispute resolution. He has provided expert testimony at formal proceedings, including disciplinary hearings, arbitrations and criminal courts. He has investigated allegations of management fraud, asset misappropriation, corruption and financial statement frauds. Mike has trained and benchmarked investigative units at clients and regularly acts as a quality assurance partner on engagements. Mike is a chartered accountant and a certified fraud examiner. He holds a bachelor's degree in commerce and a higher diploma in accounting from the University of Natal, Pietermaritzburg in South Africa.

Jeanine Colbert, *Senior Manager,* Ernst & Young

Jeanine has more than 13 years of experience in litigation and advisory services across a broad range of fraud, compliance, regulatory, health care, arbitration and breach of contract matters. She has worked in a variety of industries including consumer and industrial products, pharmaceutical, manufacturing, energy, chemical, utilities, construction, and retail. Jeanine holds a bachelor's degree in accounting from Illinois State University. She is also a certified public accountant.

Rory Alex, *Senior Manager,* Ernst & Young

Rory has over seven years of experience providing services related to damages advisory, economic and market analysis, forensic analysis, accounting advisory, and related corporate finance matters. He has provided advisory services to companies in the retail, consumer and industrial, financial services, technology, and pharmaceutical industries. In addition, he has three years of experience in E&Y's audit practice providing assurance services to companies in the financial services industry. Rory holds a bachelor's degree in accounting from Sacred Heart University. He is also a certified public accountant.

SanDee I. Priser, *Partner, Ernst & Young*

SanDee leads forensic accounting and other internal investigations for global corporations. With over 15 years' experience in public accounting, she works with clients in corporate governance matters and investigations involving matters such as financial restatement, revenue recognition, the Foreign Corrupt Practices Act and corporate compliance. She has extensive experience providing services throughout Europe, Asia and the Americas. SanDee earned her bachelor's degree in accounting from La Sierra University, her master's degree in accounting with emphasis in accounting information systems from Northern Illinois University and her juris doctorate from the University of Wisconsin. She is a licensed CPA in Illinois and a member of the bar in both Wisconsin and Illinois.

Vincent Walden, *Senior Manager, Ernst & Young*

Vincent has more than 12 years of experience handling the information management and electronic discovery needs for large scale, complex litigations, investigations and proactive anti-fraud programs. He provides clients leading anti-fraud based innovation, research and analytics, including Fraud Triangle analytics, link analysis, text data mining, metadata analysis, entity extraction and cluster analysis. His work helps clients identify or predict fraud risk variables, data anomalies or data inefficiencies that can lead to unnecessary costs or enterprise risks. He is a certified public accountant and a certified fraud examiner, and holds a bachelor's degree in business administration from the University of Southern California.

Virginia Adams, *Senior Manager, Ernst & Young*

Virginia has more than nine years of experience in forensic accounting and corruption investigations, financial statement audits and various litigation matters. She leads global investigation teams and has extensive experience in emerging markets such as Kazakhstan, Poland, Brazil, China, India and the Philippines. She has testified as an accounting expert in a civil litigation matter. Virginia holds a bachelor's degree in business administration from the University of Georgia and a master's degree in accounting from the University of Virginia. She is a certified public accountant and a certified fraud examiner.

Preface

For the veteran fraud investigation professional, core concepts in business fraud investigations are embedded in everyday practice, firm policy, and procedure. Quite often, however, a fraud investigation reaches business professionals who are not familiar with how investigations are conducted, their role in an investigation, and possible outcomes. With frauds such as Enron, WorldCom, Tyco, Parmalat, Adelphia, Societe Generale, the Ponzi scheme recently perpetrated by Bernard Madoff, and the recent billion dollar fraud at Satyam in India, it has become even more important that business owners, controllers, and management understand how a fraud investigation is run. These cases are just a few examples of frauds that have occurred, resulting in devastating effects on their organization, employees, and investors. The continued onset of one of the worst global economic downturns in recent history has now created a robust environment for fraud. Based on these painful lessons learned in the past and the current environment, companies, regulators, and other key stakeholders are putting more emphasis into addressing their approach to fraud investigations and how they view fraud proactively and reactively. This book tackles the complex issues involved in fraud investigations and gives a detailed understanding of the many complex nuances that investigators and others who deal with fraud have to consider when faced with a fraud-related matter.

Background

The idea for this book was first conceived by the Fraud Investigation & Dispute Services practice within Ernst & Young. In developing the core concepts for this product, what emerged became not just another treatise on business investigation theory but a practical framework to approach a fraud investigation along a timeline. Several other published texts are devoted to this topic, but none of them approach this topic with a practical, business-minded approach. *The Guide to Investigating Business Fraud* is dedicated not only to the study of how business frauds are conducted but also to the understanding of how and why fraudulent activities occur.

Audience

The targeted audience for this book is, of course, business professionals who need to understand core fraud investigation topics, key considerations with-in a fraud timeline, and measurable outcome indicators at various stages in an investigation. Business professionals finding themselves involved in a fraud investigation at any level often need a broad understanding of how and why fraudulent activities occur. This text is written to serve as a reference for those professionals, as well as collateral employees who would benefit from understanding business fraud core concepts and considerations. Finally, students who enter accounting or business fields frequently will be enrolled in coursework that outlines business fraud. For those students, this text will serve as a primary source for understanding fraud and how business fraud investigations are conducted and the complexities that are dealt with when conducting these investigations.

Concept and Importance to the Profession

The fraud investigation framework found in chapter 1 of this text was one of the initial steps considered in the creation of this book. The ultimate benefit achieved by understanding the concepts in this book within this framework is coming away with a practical knowledge of how the various pieces of a fraud investigation work together and how those pieces change over the course of an investigation. The book is organized in a manner that is consistent with how issues arise during the course of an investigation.

It is critical that the reader understand that in these times, the demand for evidence-based practices and procedures is important for achieving desired outcomes in an investigation. This text has been designed and written by some of the leading experts in the fraud investigation field at Ernst & Young. These authors have conducted numerous investigations in different industries and countries throughout the world and, therefore, have dealt with the complex issues that arise during an investigation. We purposely selected subject matter experts within our practice to construct the various chapters included in this book. Their insights and abilities to relate this book to practical real-life scenarios and issues faced in an investigation make this book a tre-

mendous guide to gaining a deeper understanding of the issues faced during an investigation.

Organization

The book is organized to look at the concept of fraud holistically and the issues that are dealt with in fraud and fraud investigations. We have organized our thoughts to address the previous concepts in the overall design of the book (figure 1-1).

- Chapter 1 introduces the reader to the core concepts in a fraud investigation, introduces the fraud investigation framework, and outlines the steps that must be addressed throughout the course of every fraud investigation

  As noted in this diagram, it really begins with identifying the type of fraud involved in an investigation. The three main areas of fraud are misappropriation of assets, fraudulent financial statements, and corruption. In an effort to select what we feel are the most relevant and current schemes under these three main categories, we have organized the next three chapters to address those particular schemes.

- Chapter 2 deals with selected types of misappropriation of asset schemes. Misappropriation of assets entails any scheme that involves the theft or misuse of an organization's assets. These schemes could include fake vendors; theft of assets, such as cash, inventory, accounts receivable, and fixed assets; payroll; and travel and entertainment fraud.

- Chapter 3 deals with fraudulent financial statement scheme issues and what happens when the financial statements need to be restated as a result of a fraudulent scheme. A *fraudulent financial statement scheme* is the falsification of an organization's financial statements or other nonfinancial statements prepared by the organization to make the organization appear more or less profitable.

- Chapter 4 deals with the concepts involving Foreign Corrupt Practices Act (FCPA) violations, which are one of the most talked about and investigated forms of corruption in the market place today. It is gaining significant attention by the Securities and Exchange Commission and the Department of Justice and, therefore, is top of mind for companies trying to understand the issues involving compliance with this statute. This is one of the primary reasons we have focused a chapter specifically on this type of corruption scheme. Corruption relates to any scheme to which a person uses his or her influence to obtain unauthorized benefit contrary to that person's duty to their employer. These schemes could include FCPA violations, bid-rigging, and conflicts of interest. After gaining an understanding of the various types of fraud, the next area of an investigation is the planning and organizing of a fraud investigation when one of these fraud schemes is uncovered.

- Chapter 5 deals with the first 48 hours of an investigation. This is an overview into the complex issues that an investigation creates and how critical the first 48 hours are to an investigation once a fraud has been identified or uncovered.
- Chapter 6 deals with roles and responsibilities. Upon consideration of the complex issues in an investigation, it is helpful to determine the roles and responsibilities that different parties involved undertake.
- Critical to any investigation is the collecting and processing of documentation critical to gaining an understanding of the issues involved.

Chapters 7–8 deal with the complex issues of sources of evidence (chapter 7), the areas of documentation on which the investigation needs to focus, and the elements of electronic evidence (chapter 8) that need to be considered and how to gather that information once this determination has been made. Another key element described in these two chapters is gaining an understanding of the concerns that investigators face when conducting investigations outside of the United States and the complexities that this places on the data collection efforts of the investigation team.

In addition to the data collection concerns, throughout the duration of the investigation, organizations, investigators, and other key stakeholders need to worry about who is involved and where the investigation is being conducted and the ramifications of those issues to the overall success of the engagement.

- Chapter 9 deals with these cross jurisdictional issues. The globalization of business has increased the extent to which investigations are likely to be impacted by legal requirements from more than one legal jurisdiction. In addition, fraudsters have long known that moving their assets (and themselves) to a different location beyond the reach of the "long arm of the law" is an effective strategy. For ease of reference, we'll call these cross jurisdictional investigations. Differences and variations in laws, governing and regulatory bodies, accounting standards, business practices, governmental policies, litigation forums, and even language can make cross jurisdictional investigations quite complex.
- Once an investigation has started, one of the considerations that is made is determining when or if outside counsel is involved. In chapter 10, we deal with the concepts of working with attorneys on an investigation. The circumstances brought forth in an investigation raise a variety of intertwined business, legal, and financial reporting challenges. An understanding of the underlying facts will be the foundation of decision making regarding the best course of action. Accounting, auditing, and finance skills will be needed to help develop an understanding of the facts and determine the best course of action from a business and financial perspective. At the same time, these circumstances will drive a need for sound legal advice, and oftentimes, outside counsel is retained by an organization to deal with these issues.
- Another reason that makes investigations so difficult and the reason to obtain sound legal advice is that, oftentimes, parallel investigations are occurring on a particular matter. Chapter 11 deals with the complex issues of multiple investigations (for example, this might include multiple government regulators conducting an investigation at the same time).
- Upon completion of an investigation, it is almost as important to determine how to report the results as it is to conduct the investigation and compile the results. Chapter 12 deals with reporting after the investigation has been performed and data have been gathered. The

forensic accountants or those assigned within an organization to conduct an investigation have to determine how they want to compile and report the results of their findings. The objective of the written or oral report often is to present the findings and observations to the organization or the opposing party, or both, in a litigation matter.

- Upon completion of the report and presentation of the findings, organizations have oftentimes not considered or are not aware of the investigative protocols or potential recovery options, such as insurance. Chapter 13 deals with the various considerations that organizations should consider in dealing with these recovery options.

- Finally, once an investigation has been completed, board members, chairmen of the audit committee, or c-suite executives within an organization often try and determine what, if anything, the organization can proactively do to mitigate this occurrence or another occurrence of fraud within their organization in the future. Chapter 14 deals with the various elements of an antifraud program and what companies can do to mitigate against fraud and deal with fraud not only reactively but proactively.

Distinctive Features

- A comprehensive look at fraud investigations from the earliest stages all the way to identifying areas for remediation and consideration of measures to prevent or detect fraud in the earliest stages.

- A case study has been included to apply a hypothetical fraud scenario throughout the book to give a practical example to reiterate the concepts illustrated within the book.

- Subject matter expertise for each chapter was identified from within the Fraud Investigation & Dispute Services practice of Ernst & Young, and these individuals were asked to construct their respective chapters based on their extensive experience conducting investigations across various industries and countries around the world.

- The book is being published by the AICPA. Their collective knowledge on how best to construct and create a book and introduce it into the marketplace has taken a tremendous amount of information generated by Ernst & Young and polished it into a user friendly format that has not been created before, which is truly one of a kind thought leadership.

- An extensive key word list has been created to add clarity to the various terms and ideas discussed throughout this book. This list allows the users of this book to vary across different levels of experience in dealing with fraud and allows for a broader distribution of potential users.

Acknowledgments

The editors and authors would like to thank the following individuals for their invaluable contributions to this book:

William Titera

Sara Brandfon

Tracey Foley

Eric Yarger

Nikki Stern

Virginia Destro

Caitlin Mercier

Poonam Maharjan

Aaron Brehove

Fiona English

Ernst & Young SCORE team

William Paine, Wilmer Cutler Pickering Hale and Dorr LLP

Joseph Poon

Casey L. Collopy

Colin Huong

Ryan Collins

Jenna Voss

Jessica Cruz

Lauren A. Olson

Jessica Gecoy

Megan Burnside

Table of Contents

Chapter 1: Basics of Investigations

Chapter 2: Misappropriation of Assets

Chapter 5: The First 48 Hours of an Investigation

Chapter 6: Roles and Responsibilities: How Different Stakeholders Work During Investigations

Chapter 7: Sources of Evidence

Chapter 8: Electronic Evidence

Chapter 9: Cross-Jurisdictional Issues in the Global Environment

Chapter 10: Working With Attorneys: The Relationship With Counsel

Chapter 11: Working With Regulators and Parallel Investigations

Chapter 12: Reporting on Fraud

Chapter 13: Recovering from Fraud: Fidelity Claims and Directors and Officers Claims

Chapter 14: Antifraud Programs

Glossary

Introduction

This book is intended to provide the reader with knowledge and resources needed to understand and manage a fraud investigation. It is important not only to recognize and understand the underlying concepts that are typically encountered in a fraud investigation but also to apply those concepts in a practical setting. In this section, the reader will find a case example that outlines a fictitious company called Grand Forge Company. This case example is designed to provide the reader with practical background information about this company that is further referenced in selected chapters throughout this book.

The benefit to creating this hypothetical scenario is an attempt to generate real world type examples of issues that one may encounter when investigating a potential matter. The case study illustrates in various ways the issues and concerns that arise when conducting an investigation and complements the in-depth subject matter expertise portrayed throughout the book.

The reader will follow Grand Forge Company through the identification of an issue via the whistle-blower hotline to proactively addressing fraud through the creation of a holistic antifraud program to mitigate the potential for the fraud scenario occurring in the future. It is strongly encouraged that the reader becomes familiar with this case example and references it often as Grand Forge Company navigates through troublesome incidents introduced throughout the book. The case study starts with this overall example and uses the same names of executives and directors from important strategic positions from Grand Forge Company throughout for ease of use to the reader.

Grand Forge Company

Grand Forge Company[1] (Grand Forge), a Delaware corporation and a public company registered with the Securities and Exchange Commission (SEC),

---

1 Please note that Grand Forge Company and its specific circumstances are wholly fictitious, though the depiction of its situations falls broadly in line with events and circumstances from the authors' experiences.

is a global company that manufacturers precision components for steel processing. Grand Forge was founded in 1873 as a domestic manufacturer. In the 1970s and 1980s, Grand Forge went through several acquisitions of international steel companies to continue expanding in key international locations to improve its ability to serve key international customers.

Currently, Grand Forge's corporate headquarters is located in Pittsburgh, Pennsylvania. It has four manufacturing plants located in Shanghai, China; Sao Paulo, Brazil; Mumbai, India; and Siberia, Russia. Grand Forge also has global distribution centers in Australia, Puerto Rico, Spain, Singapore, Japan, South Africa, Argentina, the Philippines, and the United States.

Grand Forge employs over 12,000 personnel globally, with 57 percent of those employees located outside of the Untied States. Grand Forge is the third largest producer of precision components for steel processing in the world. Competitors to Grand Forge are structured similarly, and most of their manufacturing is conducted outside of the Untied States, due to cheaper labor costs in other countries.

As an organization, Grand Forge has prided itself on its ability to compete internationally while achieving a high level of safety in its operations. During the past 4 years, its global rate of recordable injuries has decreased by 48 percent, and days away from work cases have been reduced by 71 percent. Safety, along with a culture of integrity, are 2 of Grand Forge's most important values.

Roland Brasky is the chair of the audit committee, which comprises independent directors. The board of directors and the audit committee are experienced board members and understand their oversight responsibilities and duties.

The Internal Audit department is well trained and reports to the audit committee and the CFO. Given the international operations, the audit committee, management, and internal audit are concerned about Foreign Corrupt Practices Act (FCPA) compliance and considerations.

The following organization chart illustrates key board and management roles:

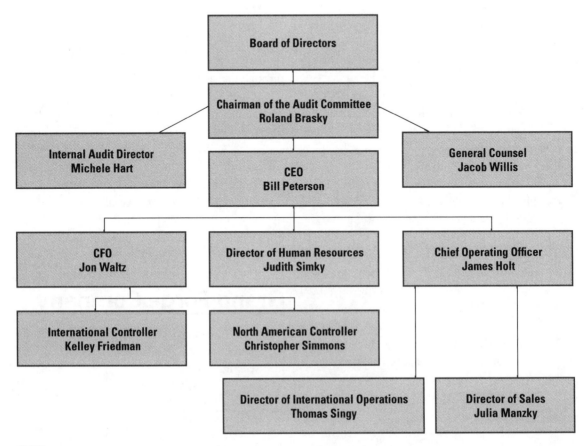

Grand Forge is audited by the independent accounting firm Handel & Smith LLP, which has been auditing Grand Forge for the last four years.

The following table presents selected financial information for the year ended December 31, 2008:

Statement of Operations Data (Dollars in Millions)	2008	2007	2006	2005
Net Sales	$11,187	$13,573	$17,154	$14,997
Income (Loss) from operations	$ (213)	$ 417	$ 1,304	$ 1,710
Net income	$ (817)	$ 1,101	$ 1,125	$ 997
Balance Sheet data—12/31				
Total assets	$14,011	$17,081	$22,053	$19,043

In 2008, Grand Forge experienced the second consecutive year of sales decline after nearly a decade of 10 percent to15 percent growth. The decline is mostly attributable to significantly higher product prices driven by the soaring cost of raw material. Grand Forge also posted a second consecutive annual net loss for the first time in the company's history. The reaction from industry analysts was significant, and, as a result, the stock price has declined 31 percent over the last 2 years. As previously illustrated, the company's earnings are declining, the cost of raw materials is rapidly increasing, and the demand for the company's product is suffering in the current global economic recession. Grand Forge is dangerously close to violating its debt covenants, and the 5 year outlook is gloomy.

Additionally, Grand Forge has recently experienced several circumstances, including the following:

1. **Cash Embezzlement**

   The controller of Grand Forge's facility based in Shanghai called corporate headquarters. The facility held about $2 million in cash balances at local banks. When the controller had recently followed up on vendor complaints of slow payments, the controller learned that the actual cash in the bank was almost zero. Upon scrutiny, the bank statements in the company's files look as if they may be inauthentic. One of the facility's cash clerks admitted to the controller that he had taken the cash. The controller also said that the clerk sounded suicidal over the discovery.

2. **Inflating Expenses**

   A Grand Forge employee made a report on the company's whistle-blower hotline alleging that her supervisor had been inflating his expense reporting to receive reimbursement in excess of the amounts actually incurred. Allegations of widespread abusive accounting practices from employees in its operations also have come through on the hotline.

3. **Stock Options Inquiry**

   Grand Forge recently received a seemingly routine inquiry from the SEC, which suggests some regulatory inquiry or scrutiny of the company's executives trading in stock and stock options.

4. **Revenue Recognition and Product Quality Issues**

   A significant overseas customer called to complain about the quality of a large volume of product that was recently shipped. They stated that the country manager routinely pressured them to take product in excess of their needs, especially at the end of the quarter. Now, they allege that the product they received is substandard, unusable, and outside their contract specifications. They allege damages to their company related to the substandard product.

5. **Cross Jurisdictional Issues**

   The attorney for Grand Forge has contacted Perusi & Bilanz LLP, independent accountants. The attorney reports that he received an e-mail over the weekend from a new accountant working in the procurement unit at a foreign distribution center of Grand Forge located in the Philippines.

a. **Inappropriate Procurement Practice**

The attorney stated that the accountant's e-mail reported concerns regarding inappropriate procurement practices at a remote production facility in another country. Goods were being purchased for cash under a cost plus arrangement from a particular vendor.

b. **Data Protection and Local Privacy Laws**

Upon receiving the call from Jacob, Perusi & Bilanz LLP quickly assembled a team, and, upon reaching the destination, the work began. The records storage facility is located within the European Union, and, therefore, the location falls under the jurisdiction of the European Commission's Directive on Data Protection (Directive 95/46/EC). The forensic accountants from Perusi & Bilanz LLP are subject to the local privacy laws and, therefore, draw upon the knowledge of those included in the team from the regional location to establish protocols for the review.

c. **FCPA**

It is apparent that there may be issues in the Philippines related to possible FCPA violations. However, because of privacy laws in the jurisdiction, the forensic accountants at Perusi & Bilanz LLP do not have access to the banking records of the implicated individuals.

Further, Perusi & Bilanz LLP has identified "shell" companies to which large assets have been transferred. Grand Forge is now dealing with a number of different issues:

i.   FCPA violations (bribery)
ii. Kickback
iii. Vendor fraud
iv. Illegal transfer of assets

d. **Investigative Team**

The investigative team from Perusi & Bilanz LLP consists of experienced experts in international investigations, including individuals who have conducted investigations in Asia. Although Filipino and English are both spoken in the Philippines, nobody on the U.S. team speaks or reads Filipino, nor are they familiar with the local customs, laws, or accounting standards.

6. **Earnings Management**

Grand Forge had another large issue come to light as other matters were being investigated. With the economy continuing to tailspin in a downward spiral, sales showing flat to negative growth, and the pressure mounting to show positive results, Bill Peterson, the CEO, determined that he needed to "adjust" some of the financial statement numbers.

a. **Manipulate Inventory and Reserves**

Grand Forge has accounts that require significant estimations each quarter and year-end and involve ultimate sign-off by Chris; his CFO, Jon Waltz; and the controller, Christopher Simmons. Bill devised a plan with the help of Jon and Christopher to manipulate the inventory and the reserves for bad debts because these areas typically had large month-to-month fluctuations in valuations, and Bill and his team thought they could get away with manipulating this area for the benefit of the company. The company, with the manipulated numbers, appeared to be turning the corner, and bonuses, which were the first in two years, were given to employees, based on the performance of the company.

In an effort to quickly resolve the issues, the board and senior management had directed Grand Forge's internal people to look into all the issues. As more information became known, it was decided that they needed an independent investigation by lawyers and forensic specialists. From management's perspective, the entire process seems to be outside their control and is costing more than they had ever expected. The financial people are still crunching the numbers and working on the disclosures. The company's employees are exhausted and are not able to focus on operations. The investors are skittish, and the stock price is down. Management wonders, if it were to be done all over again, what could have been done to prevent this mess.

Antifraud Program

Roland Brasky, the Chairman of the Audit Committee for Grand Forge, was becoming concerned with the large number of recent allegations and the previously identified issues. Roland was fearful that the prefect storm for fraud was brewing. The concern caused Roland to ask his Internal Audit Director, Michele Hart, what the company was currently doing proactively to address this potential increase in fraud in the current economy. Based on this directive from Roland, Michele wanted to develop an overall process to address fraud proactively and reactively. Michele contacted the company's preferred independent accountants, Perusi & Bilanz LLP, to determine options she should be considering to address fraud proactively, what these options might look like, and how to implement them.

Perusi & Bilanz LLP's recommendation was that Michele work to implement a holistic antifraud program for Grand Forge.

Basics of Investigations

Ruby Sharma, Partner/Principal
Dale Kitchens, Partner/Principal
Jerry Hansen, Senior Manager
Jennifer Baskin, Manager

Introduction

Fraud investigations have been in the news with greater frequency over the past decade and have involved some of the world's largest companies, such as Enron, WorldCom, and Siemens. It is estimated that U.S. organizations lose 7 percent of their annual revenues to fraud, amounting to potentially $994 billion in fraud losses when 7 percent is applied to the U.S. gross domestic product.[1] How can companies weather the storm of a fraud investigation? How should a company prepare to address a potential fraud? Although the timing and extent of a fraud are impossible to predict, each investigation requires procedures focused on the fraud, regardless of its size or scope. This introductory chapter of the book will provide an overview of investigations and the various considerations that an entity involved in a fraud investigation must consider.

The success or failure of an investigation can be due to many factors; however, the procedures used by the investigative team are most crucial in determining the investigation's outcome. Processes and procedures to be considered will be discussed throughout the various chapters of this book.

The overall goal of this chapter is to give an overview of fraud and fraud investigations, to set the tone for the rest of the book, and to answer those overarching questions listed at the beginning of this chapter.

The Current Context of Business Fraud Investigations

Dealing with complex issues of fraud, regulatory compliance, and business disputes can detract from efforts to achieve a company's potential. Better management of fraud risk and compliance exposure is a critical business priority, no matter the industry sector and geographical location.

The nature of business fraud is such that a formal investigation requires the services of many professionals across several different fields of practice, including accounting, law, forensics, auditing, regulators, and ownership. In the global world of doing business, fraud investigations often require that the right multidisciplinary and culturally aligned team is organized at the very start of an investigation. This team will work with the company's internal and external stakeholders and other professional advisors and regulators. Over the course of a full investigation, professionals in these various fields will all work with each other at various points and times, and this book covers those interactions in detail in later chapters. For the accounting professionals or owners involved in an investigation, it is important to not only understand the specific roles and responsibilities', duties, and expectations that he or she will encounter but also the general functions of the other groups of professionals, such as legal advisors, regulators, and other constituents involved in the investigation.

Historically, the number of fraud cases in the United States in the past two decades has ranged between 1,498 and 4,572[2] and is considered to be on the uptick in this current, weak economic environment. The following examples illustrate the frauds that have received the most visibility in the last several years. Box 1-1 includes a short overview of each high-profile fraud case to give insight to the issues dealt with in each investigation. When the general public reads about these high-profile cases, they often do not realize that business fraud occurs with much greater frequency every year in the United States. To the extent that cases make the news, the prevalence of fraud is quiet astounding.

If a business is on the cusp of a fraud investigation, it may seem like a daunting task to marshal the necessary resources and manage an investigation from the outset. However, it is important to understand that all areas have professionals who are professionally trained with extensive forensic, accounting, legal, and investigative experience and who are

---

1 Association of Certified Fraud Examiners *2008 Report to the Nation on Occupational Fraud & Abuse.*
2 Ibid.

Box 1-1: *Top 10 Frauds of the Decade*

1. *Stanford.* Allan Stanford has been charged in a Ponzi scheme fraud that began to unravel as a result of the economy and the uncovering of the Madoff scheme.

2. *Madoff.* Bernard L. Madoff operated a Ponzi scheme that has been called the largest investor fraud ever committed by a single person. On March 12, 2009, Madoff pled guilty to 11 counts of fraud. He admitted committing the fraud that affected thousands of investors, with losses potentially exceeding $65 billion during the time he perpetrated the fraud. A federal judge sentenced Bernard L. Madoff to 150 years in prison for running a huge Ponzi scheme that devastated thousands of investors, calling his crimes "extraordinarily evil."*

3. *Siemens.* Officials from Siemans traveled around the world with large sums of cash, paying in excess of $1 billion dollars in bribes to win large, lucrative contracts in various countries around the world. The German engineering company was ordered to pay $1.6 billion in fines to U.S. and German regulators for violating the Foreign Corrupt Practices Act (FCPA), which is the largest fine to date under this statute.

4. *Computer Associates.* According to a report issued by the Computer Associates' (CAs') board of directors, "Fraud pervaded the entire CA organization at every level, and was embedded in CA's culture, as instilled by Mr. Wang, almost from the company's inception." The report was authored by two directors at CA, with assistance from outside counsel, in response to a massive accounting fraud estimated at $2.2 billion. The report aimed to determine the board's position on recovering funds from Wang and other executives, as well as its position on shareholder lawsuits arising from the fraud. The board report recommended suing Wang in order to recover $500 million. Prior to the report, Wang had not been publicly accused, despite a Department of Justice (DOJ) investigation and prosecution that led to the indictment of 8 CA executives and a 12-year prison sentence for the former CEO.

5. *Parmalat.* Parmalat, the largest financial fraud in Europe to date, was able to achieve both its size and massive fraud through international expansion. By purchasing companies around the world and then reporting complex intercompany transactions in obtuse financial statements, the Italian-based company was able to operate under little scrutiny for years.

   However, once the Securities and Exchange Commission (SEC) equivalent in Italy began inquiries into the classification of current assets and debts in November 2003, the company's corporate malfeasance was quickly made apparent. Within weeks, the CEO, Calisto Tanzi, and the entire audit board of directors had resigned, and Parmalat's stock was trading at zero. Almost immediately, the board of the directors hired an outside accounting firm to conduct an investigation.

   The investigators were unable to review all the evidence because much of it had been destroyed, but they did determine in initial estimates that earnings before interest, taxes, depreciation, and amortization were overstated by 530 percent; liabilities understated by €1.8 billion; and net indebtedness understated by 800 percent. The Tanzi family owned 51 percent of the company and occupied executive positions within it. Yet a company the size of Parmalat interacted with external auditors, investment bankers, and credit-rating agencies throughout its 13 years life as a public company. Thus, with its downfall, came additional investigations into the responsibilities of the external professionals and their respective companies. Tanzi and the former CFO were ultimately sentenced to jail time in Italy, though Tanzi served his on house arrest due to his age.

(continued)

---

* *New York Times,* June 30, 2009.

Box 1-1: *Top 10 Frauds of the Decade (continued)*

6. *HealthSouth*. Through a series of fraudulent financial transactions, HealthSouth's executives overstated revenues and assets to hide the fact that the company wasn't meeting Wall Street projections.

7. *WorldCom*. Company executives created fraudulent financial accounting transactions by inflating company assets in excess of $12 billion, which ultimately led to the company filing bankruptcy in 2002.

8. *Waste Management*. Waste Management fraudulently manipulated the company's financial results to meet predetermined earnings targets by improperly deferring and eliminating current period expenses to inflate earnings.

9. *Enron*. Through a series of fraudulent financial accounting schemes, executives within Enron designed the fraud to make the one-time giant energy company appear more profitable and stronger than it actually was. This became one of the largest corporate scandals in American history and was primarily responsible for the desires of Congress to push through the implementation of the Sarbanes-Oxley Act of 2002.

10. *Sunbeam*. Albert Dunlap, CEO of Sunbeam, directed a fraudulent financial earnings management scheme to create the illusion of a successful restructuring of Sunbeam and to inflate the price of the company prior to the sale, which benefited him.

focused on performing the tasks needed to execute a fraud investigation. What is of critical importance is assembling the correct team of professionals on a timely basis depending on the nature and extent of wrongdoing.

Business Fraud Investigation Practice

The purpose of fraud investigations is to help manage risk, investigate alleged misconduct, review financial activity, measure the financial implications, and assess legal and regulatory ramifications of noncompliance. This often involves electronic evidence discovery. A fraud investigation helps determine what happened, how it happened, who was involved, how long it went on, and what evidence supports the findings.

Experienced fraud examiners, forensic accountants, auditors, electronic data analysts, and lawyers work together with a company's board of directors, executive management, audit committee, and employees to understand the facts in a fraud investigation. When an event occurs, such as a whistleblower allegation, a regulatory inquiry, or a business

dispute, a company must decide whether to conduct an internal investigation or hire outside counsel to conduct an independent investigation.

Investigations of corrupt business practices have been among the headlines in recent months. Companies have seen their reputations diminished as fines were imposed; profits disgorged; and, in some instances, executives were sent to prison. Companies, therefore, have to abide by anticorruption laws in their home countries and the foreign countries in which they have commercial interests. The FCPA has become the de facto international standard regarding the bribery of foreign officials.

Earnings management involving revenue recognition and other accounting fraud would result in restating the financial statements of a company. An investigation involving financial restatement requires the investigating team to assist management in identifying the full scope of issues, implementing controls to compensate for deficiencies in the financial systems, implementing a remedial measure program, and providing additional financial resource capacity.

The Calm Before the Storm—What Can a Company's Management Do to Be Prepared for an Investigation?

A fraud investigation can be a very expensive event for any company, not only in monetary cost but in reputation, time, regulator scrutiny, employee retention, shareholder reaction, and so on. The time commitment for a fraud investigation by company management and its board of directors can be significant and costly. No longer is management's focus on the large task of running a company; now management and the board must work through all aspects of an intrusive investigation. A company suddenly facing the financial and reputational risks associated with an allegation of wrongdoing may be tempted to keep investigations as low-key and narrow as possible. However, that approach carries its own risks because an investigation sends a strong signal about management's integrity and how management actually feels about wrongdoing. A timely, thorough, visible, and independent inquiry shows that senior management really wants to correct misconduct, not simply out of fear of penalties but because of a desire to run an honest and ethical company. Time invested in developing and implementing fraud prevention controls and a plan to respond to fraud events pays dividends when fraud occurs.

Because of the resource costs associated with conducting an investigation, it is critical that a company have appropriate fraud prevention and detection measures in place, as well as a detailed response plan to a suspected fraud occurrence. Perhaps the most important piece of a company's fraud prevention strategy is to establish and follow a framework to handle various types of fraudulent activity. The following section outlines a practical fraud framework based on how an investigation is conducted over time. By taking these preliminary prevention measures and following a fraud investigation framework, a company can aim to prevent fraud while potentially minimizing the overall cost of identifying, quantifying, and correcting any fraud discovered.

Additional internal control activities that company management should institute to help prevent fraud and minimize the cost of an investigation can be found in box 1-2.

In addition to the internal controls found in box 1-2, consultation with both internal and external counsel should be one of the first steps taken if an allegation or identification of fraud occurs. By taking these proactive steps, a company's management can lessen the likelihood of fraud occurring, but in the event a fraud is alleged or identified, management will be prepared to respond quickly. Regulators will expect a company to have a defined fraud detection and prevention plan, and companies could face larger penalties or fines if found to be deficient in this area.

A swift and organized response to a potential fraud event is never more important than when it is actually needed. For example, the CFO of a company could be performing his or her normal duties for any given day when he or she gets a call from the board of directors demanding an immediate response to one of the following:

- A whistle-blower sends an anonymous letter to the audit committee raising concerns about management.
- An internal audit report notes significant variances in reserve accounts for a foreign subsidiary.
- A letter from the SEC informing the company of an investigation into the company's accounting practices.
- The controller raises potential travel and entertainment report discrepancies during a random audit.

What is the CFO's response? If the company has a response plan in place, the response will be organized and quick; however, without a plan, critical mistakes could be made and valuable evidence may be lost.

Box 1-2: *Business Fraud Internal Control Measures*

- *Reviewing, implementing, or strengthening internal controls designed to prevent fraud.* This is probably the most important step company management can take to prevent fraudulent activity. Even an investment in an external company to help develop these controls will pay dividends over time.

- *Ensure that the tone at the top of key management at the parent and subsidiaries does not create an environment that would encourage fraud to avoid reporting bad news.* Every company wants to be successful, and, often, the pressure to report ever-increasing earnings and profits is a trigger to "cook the books." The fraud can occur for personal gain, such as a performance bonus for meeting targets or out of fear of losing a job. Driving employees to excel should not be communicated in such a way that "do whatever it takes or else" is the message.

- *Have a documented plan to preserve hard copy and electronic media in the event knowledge of a possible fraud comes to light.* The documentary evidence, whether hard copy or electronic, is key to the investigation. A plan should be in place to preserve all such documentation once a fraud is suspected.

- *Develop a whistle-blower program and a response plan to investigate any whistle-blower allegation.* Whistle-blowers should feel comfortable coming forward, but that is only part of the purpose of the whistle-blower program. There must be a documented investigation plan to follow up on the allegation; otherwise, the whistle-blower program has no real purpose.

- *Company management should consult with internal or external counsel to understand the difference between the criminal and civil laws regarding fraud.* This is an important distinction, and it should be considered at the onset of any fraud investigation and throughout the investigation as facts regarding the fraud are identified.

- *Employee training programs regarding fraud prevention and reporting should be developed and delivered on a regular basis.* Training programs that heighten the employees' awareness of fraud increase the incidence of detecting red flags and prevention of fraud.

The Fraud Investigation Framework

Combating business fraud crimes is not an optional exercise. One of the difficult but necessary aspects of business ownership involves planning for potentially fraudulent activities to occur within the business at some point and time. It is shocking to think that even in Fortune 500 businesses, fraud risk management plans can be in disarray. Too often, in both big and small business culture, policy and practicality do not intersect. The authors of this book have seen many high-profile cases in business mismanaged because a measured, practical, and consistent investigation framework was not implemented and followed by the affected business.

There is no one correct way of approaching a fraud investigation. It is the primary responsibility of management to take appropriate action when an event involving fraud or alleged fraud is brought to his or her attention. An inadequate response to fraud or an allegation of fraud can result in a protracted investigation that involves rework and wasted time and resources. In such instances, a fraud investigation framework comprises involvement of people who lack credibility or are perceived to lack objectivity relative to the issue, activities, or persons involved. Another investigation scenario could involve participants, investigators, and advisors who lack sufficient competence in critical areas. Investigators and decision makers stumble into preventable pitfalls. The potential downsides of certain decisions are not understood until after the fact. Poor decision making in the first few hours after an allegation or a fraudulent activity is brought to light can lead to disastrous consequences.

By contrast, a strong, credible, and competent response ensures that adequate, relevant, and complete information is assembled to support decision making; legal rights and responsibilities are respected; and any applicable legal privileges are preserved.

Unique considerations for each business are on the front end of fraud investigation planning, but the most critical consideration involved in implementing a fraud investigation framework for any business is practicality and timeliness. If you learn nothing else from this book, take this away: what is key for any fraud management architecture, regardless of how the framework is structured, is that the architecture is followed consistently over time. The best way to encourage the proliferation of fraudulent activity in a business is to either not follow an investigation framework or to do so inconsistently.

This book approaches a fraud investigation from the standpoint of looking at the different components of an investigation over time.[3] Approaching an understanding of fraud investigations in this manner allows for the reader to enter into a knowledge base at any point before, during, or after an investigation and locate where they are in an investigation timeline. Figure 1-1 depicts an overview of the investigation framework that this book follows in subsequent chapters in great detail. Following this framework will provide the foundation for a base understanding of fraud and the steps that must be addressed in sequence over the course of a fraud investigation.

This approach has been found to be a highly practical one, and the concepts discussed within this framework can be applied collectively or selectively to any size and type of business. The following sections outline how this framework has been constructed and should be approached at various points in time over the course of a fraud investigation.

Defining Fraud

The *American Heritage Dictionary* defines fraud as "a deception deliberately practiced in order to secure unfair or unlawful gain," and the *Collins Essential English Dictionary* defines an investigation as a "careful search or examination to discover facts." Although these two definitions provide guidance on what legally constitutes a fraud investigation, they do not address the practical nature of uncovering

and remediating a fraud scenario. What is more important is being able to encompass the entirety of not only what the crime is and who has perpetrated it but the effect(s) that the crime and an investigation may have on a company or organization.

In grade school, most of us were introduced to the five "Ws," which are generally understood to represent fundamental rhetorical questions to be used in scholarly, journalistic, and other evidence-based treatises. Although it seems reasonable that arriving at evidence-based conclusions in an investigation need not be mentioned in a field that deals with forensics, it should be. The framework presented in figure 1-1 and throughout this book is designed to arrive at those conclusions in a systematic fashion.

Types of Fraud

Fraudulent activities in businesses can fall into three main classes of activity: asset misappropriation, financial statement fraud, and corruption. Understand that the type of event is a significant factor in determining a proper response. Furthermore, in each class, unique activities (if understood) can help focus an investigation even further. Chapters 2-4 cover each of these three classes in great detail, but the following examples should help serve as real-world case studies for these three types of fraud.

Asset Misappropriation

- The former CFO, accounting manager, and accounts payable supervisor conspired to embezzle over $35 million dollars from PBSJ,[4] an employee-owned engineering and construction firm, in Miami, Florida. The FBI conducted the investigation and revealed that the employees were able to steal the funds by writing unauthorized checks to a private account and also by transferring funds from the medical benefits account into private checking accounts. The money was then shown to be spent on real estate, luxury cars, a yacht, jewelry, and gambling activities. The accounting manager, who had

---

3 This book does not look into the legal ramifications arising from fraudulent activity or misconduct. Legal responsibilities of the company's management, board of directors, audit committee, and legal advisor also are not the focus of this book. This publication is intended for general guidance only. It is not intended to be a substitute for detailed research or the exercise of professional judgment.

4 See Securities and Exchange Commission Litigation Release No. 20340 issued October 18, 2007.

Figure 1-1: *Business Fraud Investigation Framework*

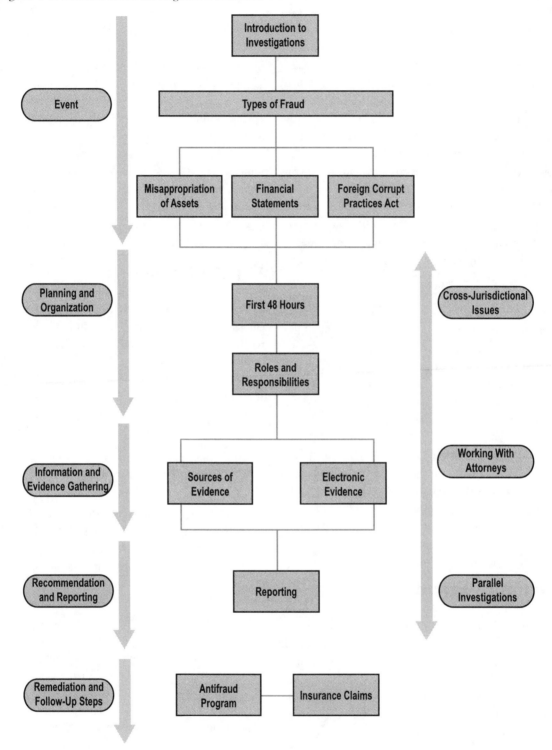

worked for the company for over 25 years, was sentenced to 63 months in prison and ordered to pay over $10 million in restitution. The CFO was sentenced to 97 months in prison on the embezzlement charges and 24 months on the campaign finance charge, to run concurrently.

- The president and CFO of Continental Express,[5] an Arkansas-based trucking company, worked closely together to transfer funds into personal accounts, only to have the CFO testify against his accomplice at trial. Together, the two men established an insurance company with the same name as that used by Continental Express, but it was incorporated in a different state. They then made payments to the fraudulent insurance company. In addition, they paid themselves multiple salaries. According to the prosecution, it was a sense of entitlement that motivated the former president to scam the money from his employer. The CFO received a reduced sentence for his cooperation in the prosecution.

Financial Statement Fraud

- In August 2007, Dell announced the completion of a year-long internal investigation, overseen by its audit committee, into the accounting practices that led to an overstatement of profits by $50 million. The audit committee investigation was in response to, but conducted separately from, a continuing SEC investigation. Employing outside professional services firms, the investigation required 375 professionals who conducted 233 interviews and reviewed over 5 million documents. As a result of the investigation, Dell restated financial statements for 4 years and reported management would continue to report to the audit committee on their actions to correct previous control deficiencies.

Corruption

- Pacific Northwest Financial Services (PNFS),[6] using a name quite similar to the publicly-traded and trusted Pacific Financial, sold fake surety bonds to 57 trucking companies. The trucking industry is required to purchase $10,000 bonds from licensed bonding companies. Licensing is obtained through the Federal Motor Carrier Safety Administration (FMCSA). The FMCSA discovered the documents filed with them by PNFS were falsified and notified the Department of Transportation's Office of the Inspector General. The owner of PNFS, Larry James Jackson, never intended to actually provide the bonding service and spent the money on himself. Jackson was sentenced to 70 months in prison and ordered to pay $236,347 in restitution.

- Kmart conducted an internal investigation into management practices amidst their 2002 bankruptcy and external investigations by both the SEC and FBI. The investigations were triggered by anonymous letters claiming to be from employees who accused Kmart of intentionally violating accounting standards. Kmart's CEO, who was overseeing the investigation, reported that they uncovered "credible and persuasive evidence demonstrating that certain former managers of Kmart violated their stewardship responsibilities to Kmart, its employees, and shareholders." The investigation included more than 570 interviews and the review of more than 1.5 million pages of documents. In addition, Kmart provided over 620,000 pages of documents for use in the external investigations.

Phases of the Investigation

Understand that each fraud case is different, and every investigation must be adjusted to the variables encountered by the investigation team. The timeline of the investigation either can be focused and short in duration (a few weeks to a couple months)

---

5 See *USA v. Wooldridge*—4:08cr137 and *USA v. Tiefel*—4:08cr42.
6 See *USA v. Jackson*—2:05cr49.

or wide ranging and last for several months or even years. Although the specific procedures employed to investigate an alleged fraud vary depending on the size of the fraud and its potential scope, each investigation will typically include all of the following steps:

- Occurrence of the event
- Planning and organization
- Information and evidence collecting
- Recommendation and reporting
- Remediation and follow-up steps

These steps align with the framework found in figure 1-1 and are generally sequential, and it is important to understand that all investigations, regardless of scope, should address all of these considerations across time. It is recommended that the reader reference figure 1-1 often throughout the course of studying this text to help him or her locate what aspect of the fraud investigation is being studied in relation to the framework.

Multiple components go with each of these steps, and a wealth of considerations must be taken into account. The following sections describe each of these steps in general terms, and chapters 5-14 address the most common approaches, considerations, techniques, and possible outcomes at each of these points across a fraud investigation timeline.

Occurrence of the Event

Ground zero for any fraud investigation is the actual fraudulent activity. Some examples include the following:

- An employee makes a report on the company's whistle-blower hotline alleging that his or her supervisor has been inflating his or her expense report to receive reimbursement in excess of the amounts actually incurred.
- A significant overseas customer calls to complain about the quality of the large volume of product they were recently shipped. They state that the country manager routinely pressured them to take the product in excess of their needs, especially at the end of the quarter.
- When the controller of a division follows up on vendor complaints of slow payments, the controller learns that the actual cash in the bank was almost zero. Upon scrutiny, the bank statements in the company's files look as if they may be inauthentic.

Planning and Organization

Depending on how the fraud was identified or why an alleged fraud was suspected, the scope and issues will be identified based on personnel involved and accounts and operational groups impacted. Instituting and following a fraud framework, such as the one presented here, will guide the investigation team concerning the extent of time and resources that will need to be dedicated to any given occurrence. Numerous factors should be considered when planning an investigation, including the following:

- What are the key issues involved in the suspected fraud?
- Who is potentially involved in the fraud, or who could have knowledge of the company operations involved in the fraud?
- How pervasive is the fraud, potentially?
- Should external counsel be engaged?
- Should external consultants be engaged, and, if so, in what capacity?
- What is the potential population of relevant documentation, both hard copy and electronic, that could provide information related to the suspected fraud?
- Who should be informed?

Once these questions are answered, the investigation can be planned to allow for the best chance of success in identifying the fraud and its impact. Several of these questions are discussed in detail in later chapters of this book, such as the types of evidence and working with external counsel.

Information and Evidence Gathering

Evidence consists of anything that can provide factual information about a particular matter, including the testimony of witnesses, records or hard copy and electronic documents, and communications. This is a wide-ranging definition that basically includes all company documents, electronic media, information gathered from interviews, and any other identified source. The process of gathering should be well planned, organized, and documented. By answering the questions in the planning phase, the investigation team will know who and what to target in a search for relevant evidence.

The evidence gathering process will include the following steps:

- *Preservation.* This includes activities designed to prevent the loss of relevant evidence, such as the company issuing a communication to its employees to not destroy any hard copy or electronic information and to cease rotating server backup tapes.
- *Collection of evidence.* This is the actual retrieval by the investigation team of the preserved documentation and other document collections, whether hard copy or electronic. The potential electronic evidence sources include backup tapes, network drives, hard drives, flash drives, and BlackBerry devices.
- *Processing.* This involves the organization of the relevant hard copy and electronic documentation and, in the case of electronic media, the processing of the electronic files to identify information directly related to the fraud investigation.

Once the evidence has been processed, it is ready to be reviewed and analyzed to answer the "who," "what," "when," "where," "why," and "how" questions. This is accomplished through both a review of the hard copy documents as well as a review of electronic media, including documents and e-mails. In addition, although interviews are a source of evidence, interviews of other personnel and second interviews also are conducted after the analysis of the evidence due to new information obtained or new questions raised.

The gathering and analyzing of evidence is repeated throughout an investigation to answer the investigation questions. The "why" question is typically the key to the investigation and can be answered in the following ways:

- *Interviews of key company personnel.* Once the potential scope has been identified, key personnel should be interviewed. This will include those company personnel suspected of the potential misconduct, as well as personnel with knowledge of the operations and accounts that are the focus of the fraudulent activity, who may or may not themselves be involved in the fraud.
- *Hard copy document collection, preservation, and potential processing.* This is a key step in any investigation, and it should be planned and executed

as early as possible to avoid the potential destruction of relevant evidence.
- *Electronic media collection, preservation, and potential processing.* Similar to the hard copy document collection, electronic media should be collected early to preserve it for further review.
- *Analysis of collected data.* The hard copy documents and electronic media will be reviewed to identify the extent of the fraud, the method employed to perpetrate the fraud, and the individuals involved.

Recommendation and Reporting

Once the investigation has been completed, the fraud has been identified, and the impact has been quantified, the results must be reported. Most investigations occurring at publicly traded companies will have reporting requirements to both internal and external constituencies. The reporting to the various constituencies could be verbal, written, or both.

The internal constituencies would typically include the following:

- The board of directors or subcommittees, such as the audit committee or a special investigation committee
- Management
- External constituencies, which could include the following:
  - Regulators, such as the SEC
  - Auditors
  - Other investigative bodies
  - Shareholders and the public

As noted earlier, the remaining chapters in this book will provide detailed discussions of many of the topics highlighted in this chapter, such as the following:

- *Determination of findings, results, and recommendations.* The results of the analysis of available evidence and interviews of key personnel will lead the investigation team in arriving at a determination regarding the impact of the fraud.
- *Communication of findings, results, and recommendations to appropriate parties.* The investigation team will document and communicate the results of the investigation in either a verbal or written report to the appropriate parties.

Remediation and Follow-Up Steps

Those performing an investigation are in a unique position to provide information to a company about potential weaknesses in internal controls or areas where fraud prevention could be enhanced. In many cases, suggestions to improve prevention or detection controls or procedures are part of the communication of findings to the company.

The Fraud Triangle

One commonly referenced schematic in a fraud investigation study is called the fraud triangle. Introduced to professional literature in Statement on Auditing Standards No. 99, *Consideration of Fraud in*

a *Financial Statement Audit* (AICP, *Professional Standards*, vol. 1, AU sec. 316), the fraud triangle concept is one way to determine the "why" of an incident. This concept provides the drivers that allow a fraudulent event to occur and, as the triangle name would imply, includes the following three items:

1. Incentive or pressure on the person(s) who will commit the fraud, such as debt problems
2. Opportunity to commit the fraud, such as an identified weakness in controls that does not provide for proper segregation of duties
3. Rationalization for the fraud, such as "this is what I have coming to me"

Figure 1-2 summarizes the interrelationship among these three elements.[7,8]

Figure 1-2: *The Fraud Triangle*

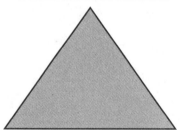

Pressure or Incentive
Pressure on employees to misappropriate cash or other organizational assets.

Opportunity
Circumstances that allow an employee to carry out the misappropriation of cash or other organizational assets.

Rationalization
A frame of mind or ethical character that allows employees to intentionally misappropriate cash or other organizational assets and justify their dishonest actions.

The following examples of fraud are focused on each of the triangle's component parts:

- *Small business suffers from lack of oversight (fraud triangle: opportunity and incentive)*. The opportunities to commit fraud may seem less numerous at a small company, but one rogue bookkeeper was able to embezzle material amounts by taking

advantage of the opportunity of lack of supervision. The bookkeeper had an alcohol and gambling addiction, resulting in large personal debt.

The owner only found out about the stolen funds after two years. According to the owner, "I trusted her. She was a full charge bookkeeper, and I didn't check her work. She took care of

7 Wells, Joseph T. *Occupational Fraud & Abuse*. Obsidian Publishing Co., 1997.

8 Albrecht, W. Steve and Chad O. Albrecht. *Fraud Examination and Prevention*. Thomson South-Western Publishing, 2003.

everything on the financial side so I didn't have to worry." The bookkeeper was able to siphon off funds through her paycheck, benefits, and expense reimbursements. Since uncovering the fraud, the owner has taken a greater role in overseeing the financial management and reporting and has changed the payroll responsibilities to include two people.

- *Small business suffers from lack of oversight (example 2) (fraud triangle: opportunity).* The bookkeeper of Aloha Termite and Pest Control in Hawaii began siphoning off funds in her first month of work. Over three and one-half years, she stole between $900,000 and $1.2 million in her fourth embezzlement scam. As the fraud was being perpetrated, the owner knew he was struggling financially and was even considering filing for bankruptcy. However, the bookkeeper had so much independence over the financial records that she was able to conceal the fraud from the owner and his accountant, despite their review of the financial statements. Upon indictment, the bookkeeper blamed a gambling problem. The owner will not likely see any of the funds returned due to the bookkeeper's gambling, and he struggles to keep his business afloat.

- *Revenge as rationalization for fraud officer's scam (fraud triangle: rationalization).* In 1999, a police officer on the Canadian telemarketing fraud task force was arrested after conducting a phone scam against senior citizens. During his presentencing hearing, the former fraud officer told the judge he was out to embarrass his bosses. He complained of unfair treatment by senior officers, including refusals for time off. The officer was caught within two months of the scam, but the department admitted the ordeal was nonetheless embarrassing.

- *Revenge as rationalization for controller's embezzlement (fraud triangle: rationalization).* The assistant financial controller of Chromalock, an electronics firm in England, embezzled company funds after deciding her compensation was too low and not receiving promised bonuses. According to her defense lawyer, "By way of partial revenge, this is the only way she thought she could get back at them." The mother of 3 had worked at the firm for 14 years before she began the scheme. She was ordered to pay back funds and serve 10 months in jail.

Constituency Considerations

Not all investigations are initiated by regulators or law enforcement agencies, such as the SEC and FBI, and highlighted on the evening news. Many frauds are identified internally, and the investigation is conducted internally, even though external counsel and consultants are typically involved. However, if a fraud investigation is commenced by a company's management or its board of directors, certain other internal and external constituencies must be included or at least informed of the facts of the investigation, as identified in the following chart. Each identified constituency will have some role and responsibility in the investigation. Table 1-1 outlines in general terms the level of involvement that core stakeholders own during the course of different kinds of fraud investigations. The specific roles and responsibilities of these key stakeholders along with those of peripheral stakeholders are covered in chapter 9.

Table 1-1: *Stakeholders' Level of Involvement in a Fraud Investigation*

Type of Fraud (Internal Discovery and Investigation)	Internal			Neutral		External		
	Party Identifying the Fraud	Direct Employee Supervisor	Management of the Subsidiary	Executive Management	Board of Directors	Auditors	SEC	DOJ
Asset Misappropriation (Immaterial)	Owner of the asset	X	X	X	X			
Asset Misappropriation (Material)	Owner of the asset	X	X	X	X	P	P	P
Financial Statement Fraud	Varies		X	X	X	P	P	P
Fraud	Varies		X	X	X	P	Civil	Criminal
Whistle-blower	Whistle-blower— either known or anonymous		X	X	X	P	P	P

"P"=Peripherally involved.

Conclusion

One of the keys to success in dealing with issues of fraud, bribery, and corruption is the system a company has for reporting and investigating allegations of misconduct. If the subsequent investigation is perceived by stakeholders to be biased or not competently managed, negative consequences could ensue. Trust in senior management to do the right thing will be eroded and disillusioned employees will think twice about future cooperation.

Investigations offer management the opportunity to demonstrate that, although everyone will be treated fairly, dishonest or unethical behavior will not be tolerated. Commitment from the top to do the right thing and act responsibly builds a culture in which employees with concerns will come forward, confident that they will be taken seriously and treated professionally.

A robust investigation helps safeguard the company's reputation. A key aspect is having an experienced and independent investigating team that has the ability to discover relevant facts and secure the relevant documentary and electronic evidence. Many companies, boards of directors, and independent auditors insist on a competent and thorough investigation performed by an independent investigative team. This often includes a law firm and a professional advisory firm with experience in forensic accounting and leading investigation practices.

In the subsequent chapters, this book will discuss in detail the various aspects and areas of a fraud investigation.

2

Misappropriation of Assets

Charles Owens, Executive Director
Vince Walden, Senior Manager

Introduction

Protecting a company's assets is one of the most important roles of management. Frauds against and thefts from companies can be perpetrated by company insiders acting alone or in collusion with others and outsiders sometimes acting with the cooperation of insiders. In its fraud research, the Association of Certified Fraud Examiners (ACFE) has labeled fraud perpetrated by insiders as *occupational fraud*. Occupational fraud is a pervasive problem for organizations, and, year after year, studies demonstrate that both the incidences of and the losses attributable to fraud are significant across all types of companies.

As defined by the ACFE, fraud takes three primary forms: asset misappropriation, financial statement fraud, and corruption. *Asset misappropriation* comprises any scheme that involves the theft or misuse of an organization's assets. *Financial statement fraud* is the deliberate misrepresentation of a company's financial statements in order to mislead users of the financial statements. *Corruption* entails a person using a position of influence to obtain an unauthorized benefit that is counter to his or her employer's interests. Figure 2-1 identifies the three forms of fraud and many of the schemes that comprise each one.[1]

The forensic accountant charged with investigating suspected fraud knows well that even though each fraudulent act is unique, common patterns are often present in asset misappropriation and the steps taken to cover up the act. This chapter will explore asset misappropriation fraud schemes in detail, and chapters 3 and 4 will address financial statement fraud and corruption, respectively.

Although not every asset misappropriation fraud scheme is addressed in this chapter, the more common schemes will be explored, which include frauds related to cash, procurement and accounts payable, payroll, inventory, and intangible assets. We also will discuss current best practices on deterrence, prevention, and detection, as well as some new fraud detection analytics that expand beyond the traditional, rules-based queries and matching functions.

A plethora of literature is available that addresses "red flags" regarding misappropriation of assets and internal controls that are designed to prevent misappropriation of assets. It is not our intention to include in this chapter the myriad of "red flags" and controls that exist because that would require much more than this one chapter. For additional resources on fraud prevention schemes, we recommend starting with the following:

- *The Corporate Fraud Handbook: Prevention and Detection* by Joseph Wells
- *Managing the Business Risk of Fraud: A Practical Guide*, a joint publication by the Institute of Internal Auditors, the AICPA, and the ACFE
- Resources and publications available on the ACFE's website at www.acfe.org, as well as the AICPA's antifraud resource center Web site at http://fvs.aicpa.org/Resources/Antifraud+Forensic+Accounting

Notwithstanding high-profile cases of financial statement fraud in the last decade, asset misappropriation, due to its high incidence, is the type of occupational fraud that is most likely to occur and is, therefore, of great concern to both large and small businesseses. The problems for businesses that handle cash, produce goods easily transported, or develop technologies critical to the success of the business are particularly acute; however, any asset is vulnerable to theft by employees or third parties acting alone or in collusion with others. Accordingly, it is vital for financial managers, internal auditors, and other executives to at least have a general understanding of the nature of these schemes and have controls in place to minimize exposure from these risks.

In the ACFE's *2008 Report to the Nation on Occupational Fraud & Abuse*,[2] a detailed review of fraud cases reported in its survey revealed approximately

---

1 Wells, Joseph T. *Occupational Fraud and Abuse*. Dexter, MI: Obsidian Publishing Company, Inc., 1997.
2 See www.acfe.com/documents/2008-rttn.pdf.

Figure 2-1: *Financial Fraud Schemes by Category*

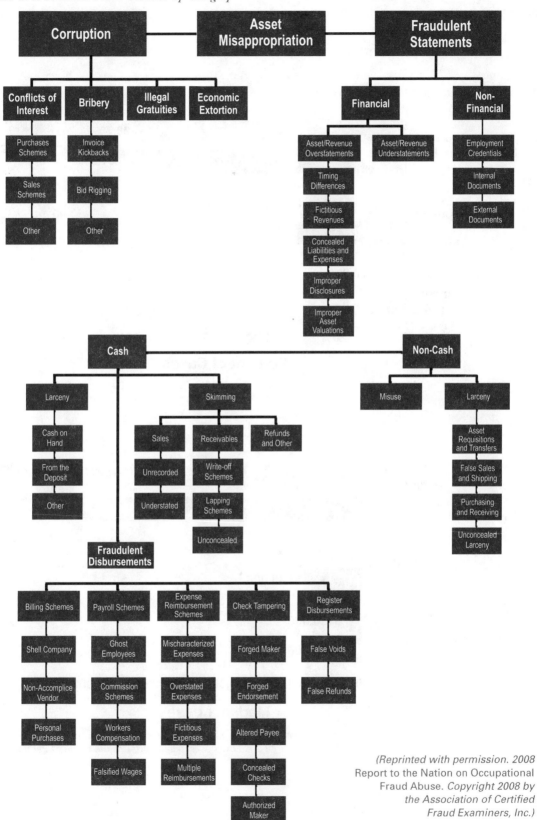

(Reprinted with permission. 2008 Report to the Nation on Occupational Fraud Abuse. Copyright 2008 by the Association of Certified Fraud Examiners, Inc.)

89 percent included asset misappropriation (figure 2-2). This number is only slightly lower than the 91 percent reflected in the 2006 report. In the 2008 survey, the median loss from asset misappropriation was $150,000 (figure 2-3), which was identical to the loss from asset misappropriation reported in the 2006 report.

Figure 2-2: *Percentage of Fraud Cases Reported in 2008*

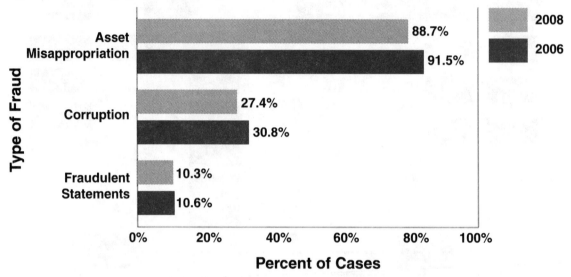

(Reprinted with permission. 2008 Report to the Nation on Occupational Fraud Abuse. Copyright 2008 by the Association of Certified Fraud Examiners, Inc.)

Figure 2-3: *Cost of Fraud Cases Reported in 2008*

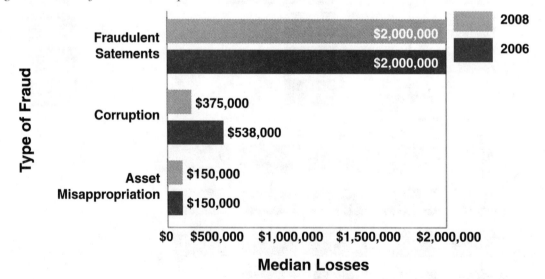

(Reprinted with permission. 2008 Report to the Nation on Occupational Fraud Abuse. Copyright 2008 by the Association of Certified Fraud Examiners, Inc.)

As is the case with any other fraud or business risk, the company's executives and its operational management have the ultimate responsibility for safeguarding the organization's assets; however, attending to fraud is not always a high priority. Frequently, executives and managers do not have the knowledge to appropriately address the risks of fraud faced by their organizations or, for other reasons, do not take steps to adequately address the risks. Consequently, fraud is usually addressed after the fact rather than proactively. Fraud prevention is an overhead expense, and although the cost of postincident investigation is high, oftentimes, companies are only willing to commit minimal funds to fraud prevention measures and proactive assessments that could result in early detection of fraud and potentially reduce losses from fraud. For lengthier discussions on business owner roles and responsibilities as well as fraud prevention strategy, see chapters 6 ("Roles and Responsibilities: How Different Stakeholders Work During Investigations") and 14 ("Antifraud Programs") respectively.

The following sections describe more common schemes of misappropriation of assets, such as cash fraudulent schemes that can occur in the asset categories or processes previously indicated in figure 2-1. These schemes represent what is typically encountered in misappropriation of assets frauds, and, therefore, this chapter does not describe each misappropriation of assets scheme. The area of noncash misappropriation of assets schemes, as depicted in figure 2-1, has not been described in this chapter due to the minimal significance of this information and these schemes related to misappropriation of assets in general.

Cash Frauds

Although any business asset can be stolen by employees or others acting alone or in collusion, cash, by its very nature, is the easiest to steal and one of the most frequent targets for theft. Cash includes cash on hand in petty cash or any other cash fund or reserve and cash in bank accounts. As with all company assets, cash should be properly accounted for in the company's books and records and is generally classified as cash on hand or cash in bank accounts.

The amount of cash on hand varies according to the needs of the business and its operational philosophy. From a global perspective, in certain countries where the banking system is not well developed or trusted, businesses conduct more and larger cash transactions. The increased amount of cash on hand in these countries presents an inviting target for persons inclined to misappropriate cash.

In conducting forensic accounting work, it is often an objective to determine if off-book cash is being maintained. Such cash is often referred to as *slush funds*, and it can be used for illicit purposes, such as corruption or the personal benefit of those company representatives generating and maintaining the funds. Slush funds are frequently built from the improper conversion of a company's cash. The forensic accountant should always be alert for indications of the maintenance of slush funds.

Misappropriation of cash can be categorized as follows: (1) larceny or theft of cash on hand, (2) skimming of cash, and (3) fraudulent disbursements of cash. Each category is addressed subsequently.

Larceny

Cash larceny is defined as the straightforward or actual theft of cash on hand or from daily receipts. Attempts to conceal cash larceny are typically undertaken in one of three ways: by making no record of cash received, by altering supporting documents to conceal theft of cash, or by falsifying journal entries to cover up the fraud.

Certain types of businesses, including retail stores, restaurants and bars, convenience stores, and gas stations, as well as religious and charitable organizations are more vulnerable to cash theft simply because large amounts of cash are collected in these businesses. Increased opportunities for cash larceny arise in these and other organizations that vest a high degree of trust in individuals handling the cash. Unfortunately, it is not uncommon to hear of cash theft in all of these organizations and efforts to mask the theft.

Petty Cash

Many businesses maintain one or more petty cash funds to have cash on hand to pay for generally small operational expenses or other small items in a convenient and expedited manner. Theft from petty cash is a common form of larceny. When a petty cash fund is established, appropriate controls should be instituted to prevent misuse or theft of funds, and the amount of the fund should only be the amount deemed necessary to meet the obligations for which the fund was established. The controls should include assigning responsibility of the fund to one person and performing periodic unannounced cash counts to account for the full amount of the fund.

Stealing from petty cash can occur in a number of ways. In most cases, petty cash thefts are small in amount, although if not uncovered timely the amounts can become substantial. Thefts from petty cash can be outright thefts (though the perpetrator will often justify the actions by thinking of the theft as a "loan" to be repaid); another theft is through submitting bogus, forged, or altered receipts, suggesting that the cash was used for the purchase of goods or services that were never in fact purchased. Providing bogus receipts and illicitly obtaining funds from a business is a common practice in some parts of the world, including Asia. Such bogus receipts have been known to be acquired at local markets in Asia and often include counterfeit tax or regulatory stamps to make them appear authentic.

Other forms of cash larceny have the potential to result in much greater loss and are described subsequently.

Cash Larceny From the Deposit

As businesses take in cash, it is prudent to deposit that cash in the bank as soon as possible. It is critical to have good internal controls from receipt of the cash until the deposit is verified. This includes having a method to document all incoming cash and different individuals responsible for recording incoming cash, making the deposit, and performing bank reconciliations. When these controls are not maintained or if there is collusion, thefts of cash intended to be deposited in the bank may well occur.

Concealing theft of cash from deposits may occur by altering original cash receipt documents, bank deposit slips, or deposit receipts after the deposit has been made. In such instances, detection is very likely as long as there are good internal controls. When there is collusion, detection is much more difficult.

Sales Process Voids and Returns

This type of cash larceny is most prevalent in businesses that rely heavily on cash sales. After a sale has been completed and payment has been received, the unscrupulous clerk can steal cash by voiding the sale in the system or entering a return while simultaneously removing cash. Businesses often give their clerical employees authority to void a transaction or process a return in order to provide a high level of customer service. With such authorization, a measure of internal control is removed. Requiring approval for voids or returns minimizes the risk of losses from this scheme but also can be perceived as reducing the level of customer service.

From Cash Register

Cash register thefts are generally small in amount but can grow quickly if remedial measures are not taken when shortages are reported or theft is suspected. Frequently closing out the registers, requiring that all customers receive copies of receipts, and requiring that each register operator is solely authorized to operate only a designated register are some controls that can minimize cash register thefts.

Counterfeit Checks, Check Theft, and Forgery

With the advent of more sophisticated payment systems and controls, these frauds are less common but are still prevalent. High quality word processing and graphics programs are available to assist fraudsters in creating counterfeit checks that can be negotiated and placed into the bank clearing system and potentially victimize companies. Law enforcement has indicated that many of these attempted frauds are being perpetrated by company outsiders who are affiliated with criminal rings or gangs but often have the assistance of company insiders. Companies should be ever vigilant in responding to evidence that their corporate checks are being counterfeited, in an effort to minimize any damage. Serious consideration should be given to bringing such matters to the attention of law enforcement to assist in combating these crimes and, hopefully, reduce the exposure to the company and others, as well.

Check theft and forgery, on the other hand, are generally perpetrated by company insiders taking advantage of any weaknesses in controls to gain access to company checks. The check theft schemes include those in which blank checks are obtained and fraudulently prepared or checks intended for a legitimate payee are pilfered and altered in some way for the benefit of the fraudster. The basic scheme is one in which a blank check is obtained and made payable to the perpetrator or an illegitimate payee, and the perpetrator negotiates the check with a forged signature of an authorized signer. Other schemes include intercepting a check made payable to a legitimate third party and either altering the payee of the check or affixing a fraudulent endorsement on the check and then negotiating the check or having a cooperator negotiate the check. Check fraud also can be carried out by preparing a check payable to an entity name controlled by the perpetrator and having it signed by an authorized signer. This scheme can be successful when the check signer is signing many checks and is not diligent about closely looking at each check and supporting documentation.

Skimming

One of the most common forms of asset misappropriation is skimming. *Skimming* is the theft of all or a portion of the cash receipts of a business at a particular point of sale or other point when cash or payments enter a business. Skimming schemes are off-book frauds, meaning that the money is stolen before it is recorded in the accounts of the victim organization. By its nature, a skimming scheme leaves no direct audit trail. Because the stolen funds are never recorded, the organization may not be aware that the cash was ever taken. Depending on the nature of the business, many persons may be in a position to receive cash or payments. Some skimming or cover-up methods include accounts receivable and sales fraud schemes; lapping of accounts receivable; manipulation of credits, discounts, and receivables write-offs; underrecorded sales; and overshipments, which are described subsequently.

Accounts Receivable and Sales Fraud Schemes

Accounts receivable and some sales schemes differ from the cash misappropriation schemes previously described because they occur after there has been a sales transaction recorded in the books, and they can take different forms. An unscrupulous employee who has access to payments on account may take steps to manipulate that activity for his or her benefit. Likewise, certain actions can be taken with regard to credits, discounts, and bad debt write-offs as a means of covering up misappropriation of assets.

Lapping of Accounts Receivable

In an accounts receivable lapping scheme, an unscrupulous employee diverts a customer's payment on account to realize a personal benefit and conceals the diversion by applying other customers' payments to cover the account from which the payment was originally diverted. Once started, such a scheme demands an ongoing juggling act of applying subsequent customer payments to cover the last account from which payments were diverted and can become a daunting task to conceal and keep going.

Manipulation of Credits, Discounts, and Receivables Write-offs

Another method for concealing diverted funds from customer payments involves fictitious credits or discounts or a write-off of a portion or all of the receivable balance as uncollectible. The unscrupulous employee can issue credits or discounts to cover a diversion of a customer payment or benefit a customer who has paid a bribe or kickback or with whom the employee has an undisclosed relationship or hidden interest. *Bribes* can be defined as something of value provided to an individual in a decision-making or other role of authority in an effort to encourage or reward the individual to violate his or her responsibility in such a way that the person paying the bribe is benefited. Similarly, *kickbacks* are something of value, usually money, generally paid to an individual in a decision-making or other role of authority after the individual has awarded a contract or payment to the person paying the kickback.

Underrecorded Sales and Overshipments

In these schemes, the value of a sale is underrecorded or excess product is shipped, resulting in a loss to the company. When a customer is the beneficiary of one of these schemes, the unscrupulous employee has likely been compromised with a bribe or kickback or is the beneficiary in some other way. A variance of the overshipment scheme is when the unscrupulous employee diverts the excess shipment to another party to realize a personal benefit. In this case, inventory is overstated unless some effort is made to manipulate the amount of the sale in the books and records.

Fraudulent Disbursement

The procurement of goods and services and accounts payable roles presents opportunities for unscrupulous employees to personally benefit to the detriment of the company. In this section, we address some of the schemes in which companies sustain losses as a result of the actions of its employees in performing these functions. Procurement and accounts payable disbursement frauds include paying vendors for goods and services never provided or procured at excessive amounts, usually due to bribes or kickbacks being paid by the vendor, and paying fictitious vendors who were set up with the intention of perpetrating a fraud. Losses also can be sustained when competitive bid policies are ignored and in construction contracts when insiders are not operating with the best interest of the company or contractors actively attempt to defraud the company.

When organizations are operating globally, cultural issues in some countries and regions of the world place a greater acceptance on bribery and corruption; therefore, the risk that a company's assets may be misappropriated is increased. Companies are well served by understanding the culture and experiences concerning corruption in the global markets in which they operate. Chapter 9, "Cross-Jurisdictional Issues in the Global Environment" discusses the various factors involved when considering issues in a fraud investigation that involve overlap of global markets.

Fictitious Vendors

One common procurement fraud is carried out when a fictitious vendor is successfully placed in the company's approved vendor list. If a company has weak internal controls or the controls concerning approving vendors are circumvented, the unscrupulous employee has taken a significant step toward successfully perpetrating a procurement fraud by getting approval for adding a fictitious vendor to a company's vendor list. Thereafter, the fraudster need only get an approved invoice into the system to have payment disbursed. Payments to fictitious vendors are often made to a post office box or an address under the control of the person perpetrating the scheme. These frauds are particularly insidious because they reflect advance planning and the clear intent to defraud the company. Depending on the level of controls existing at the company, this scheme can be carried out by a lone individual or may require collusion and can become very costly.

Overpurchasing

This scheme results in a company paying more than appropriate or necessary for goods or services that may have been totally unnecessary or may have been procured at a price above the best price. Usually, when this occurs, the employee with procurement responsibilities has been compromised through bribery or kickbacks. In such circumstances, the corrupt vendor can benefit greatly by successfully submitting excessive invoices for which payment will be made, in excess of or sufficient to cover the amount of the bribe or kickback paid to the corrupt employee. If the compromised employee is not too greedy, this scheme can be difficult to detect or prove and can go on for an extended period of time, thus increasing the loss to the company.

Contract and Construction Fraud

Large contracts or construction projects present inviting opportunities for fraud to be perpetrated against a company. For unscrupulous employees and vendors, the rewards for compromising the award or completion phase of the process can be great if they are willing to accept the risks. This type of fraud usually occurs when there are lax procedures for awarding such contracts or when there is bid-rigging.

Bid-rigging is a particularly pervasive and costly problem in certain industries. Generally, bid-rigging occurs in the procurement process when a member of the offering organization that has placed a request for proposal fraudulently assists a vendor or contractor in winning a sale or contract through some form of manipulation of the competitive bidding process. Several phases of the bidding process are susceptible to bid-rigging and are outlined in box 2-1.

Box 2-1: *Bid-Rigging Phases*

Prebid Technical Specification Phase

In the context of large contracts, the prebid phase is where technical specifications are developed as the basis of a request for quotation or solicitation. One of the most common schemes during this phase is to design bid specifications that completely match the qualifications and abilities of a targeted, sole source or favored vendor who then pays a bribe in exchange for the exclusivity of the contract requirements. These requirements may be either prequalification procedures that meet only the target vendor's products or services as they presently exist or are specifications prepared in a manner such that only the target vendor can understand the specifications or design its products to meet them.

Request for Quotation or Solicitation Phase

In the invitation phase to bid on a project or purchase contract, a common fraud is to provide advance notification and specifications only to the target vendor or create fake quotations from fictitious vendors to paper the file to make it appear that other bids were made when in fact only the target vendor submitted a bid.

Presubmission Award Phase

Common frauds during this phase of the process when the organization receives submissions from the various bidders include providing the competitors' bids or pricing to the favored vendor or providing additional details or privileged information to a favored vendor that other vendors did not receive, thus affording the favored vendor an unfair (and likely winning) advantage.

Pay-and-Return Schemes

So-called "pay-and-return" schemes are frequently carried out by using the invoices of legitimate third-party vendors who are not a part of the fraud scheme. In these cases, the perpetrator is an internal employee who intentionally mishandles payments owed to legitimate vendors. The following different versions of the scheme generally are used:

- *Double paying invoices.* In such cases, someone in the Accounts Payable department purposely double pays a legitimate vendor invoice. For example, a clerk might intentionally pay an invoice twice then call the vendor and request that one of the checks be returned. The clerk then receives or takes steps to intercept the returned check and converts it for his or her benefit.
- *Paying incorrect vendors.* In these cases, an accounts payable clerk or another company employee intentionally pays the wrong vendor (that is, sends a check written to vendor A to vendor B). After the check is mailed, the employee calls vendor B to explain the "mistake" and requests that vendor B return the check to his or her attention. When that check arrives, the employee converts it for his or her personal benefit. Of course, if vendor A is still due payment, that will have to be addressed by the fraudster.
- *Vendor overpayment.* In cases of overpayment, an employee in the accounts payable function intentionally overpays a legitimate vendor and then contacts the vendor to request that the excess funds be sent back to the employee's attention. The employee converts any funds returned for personal benefit.

Personal Purchases

Some pervasive frauds can be very simple. Many fraudsters simply purchase personal items using company accounts, corporate credit cards, or some other company-based mechanism. Such frauds usually begin on a small scale but can become costly if not detected early. Companies should require that employees be diligent in adhering to controls and react appropriately when there is an indication fraud has occurred, even if the amounts involved appear to be small. Often, these schemes can be detected by comparing an individual employee's purchases to his or her employee peer group.

Non-Cash Fraud

Payroll Fraud

Misappropriation of a company's assets can occur when actions are taken to cause disbursements through its payroll system that are not proper. The most common types of payroll schemes include falsification of wages that result in overpayment, placing so-called "ghost employees" on the payroll, fraudulent commission or bonus schemes, and false workers compensation claims.

Falsified Wages

The most common method of misappropriating funds from the payroll is overpayment of wages. For hourly employees, the size of a paycheck is based on two factors: the number of hours worked and the rate of pay. For an hourly employee to fraudulently increase the size of his or her paycheck, he or she must either falsify the number of hours worked or his or her wage rate must be changed. Because salaried employees do not receive compensation based on their time at work, excess payment to these employees generally is accomplished by arranging for the periodic pay rate in the payroll system to be changed.

Ghost Employees

Companies will sustain losses when names of individuals are entered in the payroll system, and the individuals are paid but do not perform any work. The individuals who do not work but are paid have come to be called "ghost employees." Sometimes the individual whose name is in the payroll system but does not work is the recipient of the payments, but on other occasions, bogus names are placed in the system and the proceeds are received by the person or persons who are perpetrating a fraud on the company. In another variation, although not common, entering "ghost employees" into the payroll system and receiving the proceeds can be a method of establishing a slush fund that can be used for off-book payments, which are frequently related to corruption. Entering a government official, either domestic or foreign, or a relative of the government official in the payroll system also can be a method of making an improper payment to that government official. For "ghost employees" to be successfully entered in the payroll system and paid, serious internal control weaknesses will have to exist.

Commission and Bonus Schemes

Schemes designed to improperly increase commission payments or pay bonuses to employees are other types of payroll frauds. Commission schemes are perpetrated by either falsely reporting sales or other activity for which a commission is to be paid or the rate at which the commission is to be paid. Bonus schemes are carried out when a bonus payment is improperly entered in the system and paid. For either of these schemes to be successful, internal controls must be weak or ignored or there must be collusion.

Workers Compensation

Payments for employees injured on the job are required to be made under the law. When the medical condition of the employee is falsely reported either by the employee acting alone or in collusion with a medical professional, companies are victimized.

Inventory Fraud

Misappropriation of inventory is a common scheme and represents a significant cost to many organizations. The schemes include the outright theft of inventory and more complex schemes designed to make it appear that inventory was not improperly removed.

A common inventory fraud scheme is to falsify records of incoming shipments of goods by marking the receiving documents as short of the quantity purchased in order to conceal theft. Another inventory misappropriation scheme is perpetrated by falsifying sales and shipping documents, shipping the goods to an alternate location out of the control of the company. Inventory also can be stolen by classifying it as scrap, which is then sold for pennies on the dollar. This scheme can be very costly for items such as precious metals and, in some cases, often includes collusion with third parties, customers, dealers, or distributors.

Theft of inventory can be concealed in a number of ways. One way is to charge a fake receivable, which will be written off through bad debts. The theft also could be concealed by writing off the missing inventory as part of the perpetual inventory system adjustment or, prior to the adjustment, classifying it as missing. Moreover, the inventory account may be used to conceal other types of fraud or theft of assets, such as when someone has stolen cash or written themselves a check and booked the amount to inventory. These types of schemes can be more easily disguised than other frauds because it is common to adjust the inventory account for the cost of goods sold or after a physical inventory.

Intangible Asset Fraud

Although there are complexities in valuing intangible assets for financial reporting purposes, it is clear that intangible assets, including intellectual property, such as copyrights, patents, trademarks, business methodologies, trade secrets, research and development, marketing strategies, and so on, can be of significant value to a business. If compromised, very negative consequences can occur, including substantial economic loss or loss of profit potential. Any such compromise of intangible assets in which closely held proprietary information is involved usually occurs by insiders of the company or with the cooperation of a company insider. Certain types of intangible assets are routinely targets of economic espionage schemes.

Much information about a company can be entirely obtained through legal methods, if one knows where to look. In order for a spy or corporate intelligence professional to harvest the real "plums" of information, however, it may be necessary to resort to illegal methods. Organizations that have intangible assets that would be valuable to competitors or foreign government entities must be cognizant that they are not immune from this form of attack.

Protecting intangible assets should be a priority of management. A clear policy should be designed to protect intangible assets, including proprietary information, and the policy should be effectively communicated to all employees. Protection should include clearly identifying all intangible assets as protected assets. Anyone who is in a position to have access to intangible assets that require a measure of confidentiality or secrecy should sign a confidentiality agreement, and management should make it clear that actions will be taken against anyone who improperly compromises these assets, including criminal prosecution.

Asset Misappropriation Detection, Prevention, and Deterrence

According to the ACFE's *2008 Report to the Nation on Occupational Fraud & Abuse*, the majority of fraud schemes were detected by tips or accident, not by internal audit, internal controls, or external audit (figure 2-4).

Figure 2-4: *Initial Detection of Occupational Frauds*

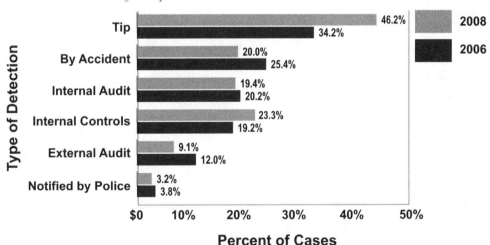

*The sum of percentages in this chart exceeds 100 percent because in some cases respondents identified more than one detection method.

(Reprinted with permission. 2008 Report to the Nation on Occupational Fraud Abuse. Copyright 2008 by the Association of Certified Fraud Examiners, Inc.)

Although all of the potential detection methods depicted in figure 2-4 are important and it is essential to follow the long-prescribed internal control mechanisms that are designed to minimize fraud, it is increasingly being recognized that it also is important to create an ethical culture within a company and effectively communicate policies, procedures, and expectations to employees. This fosters an attitude in which employees will respond appropriately and come forward when they observe something indicating possible fraud. Box 2-2 outlines some of the steps that should be taken in creating and maintaining that culture.

Box 2-2: *Creating and Maintaining an Ethical Culture*

- Establishing a code of conduct that clearly conveys the company's expectations that all employees will operate ethically and in compliance with the law and will report any information indicating possible misconduct

- Displaying a tone at the top by management that clearly conveys management fully supports the company's ethical standards and will enforce them

- Following up on any indication or allegation of misconduct that appears credible and taking remedial action when appropriate

- Punishing those persons found to have violated company ethical policies, including dismissal if deemed appropriate and referral to law enforcement for criminal prosecution when laws may have been potentially violated

- Conducting fraud awareness training for employees

- Requiring annual attestations from employees that they are not aware of any wrongdoing in the company, including any potential conflicts of interest

Additionally, companies are seeing the benefit of performing fraud risk assessments to identify areas where frauds are most likely to occur and those frauds that will have the greatest impact on the company if they do occur. After identifying the high-priority fraud risk areas, enhanced attention can be given to these areas to minimize the fraud risk and economic exposure, should fraud occur in these areas. This is when substantive testing and forensic analytics can be of high value to the organization, and specific tests are designed around the areas of most risk, as described in the next section. For a more comprehensive discussion on risk assessments and preventions, see chapter 14, "Antifraud Programs."

Beyond Traditional Fraud Detection Analytics

One potential reason why fraud is detected more by chance (that is, by tip or accident) rather than by proactive efforts, is that companies are still using traditional rules-based queries and analytics, which rely heavily on the individual to ask questions of the data based on what is currently known. Further, these analytics are sometimes done with minimal input from outside the Internal Audit department (for example, interviewing the business line leaders about where fraud risks might occur in their division) or by simply doing a repeat of last year's standard testing. Although traditional approaches are vital to ongoing efforts to monitor and detect errors in the data, they are limited (with respect to success in detecting fraud) due to the fact that they often require a significant amount of both time and luck to uncover potential anomalies in the accounting data. Also, they typically focus on structured, financial, and accounting data, such as ledgers and transactional database systems, which, according to Gartner Research, only make up about 20 percent of the data within an organization. The remaining 80 percent of an organization's data is made up of text-based, unstructured data (for example, documents, e-mails, presentations, Web sites, and so on).[3]

---

3 *Introducing the High Performance Workplace: Improving Competitive Advantage and Employee Impact.* Gartner Research, May 2005.

Albert Einstein is attributed with saying: "The definition of insanity is doing the same thing over and over again and expecting different results." Rather than pouring more resources into the same technologies and processes over and over, a more sophisticated approach to increasing fraud detection is to incorporate a proactive model-based approach, which, when coupled with leading visualization tools and unstructured data analytics, allows the data to define itself. When combined with traditional rules-based analytics, these technologies can be a powerful toolset to identify large and unusual transactions derived from the multidimensional attributes in the data. Model-based mining shifts the focus to high-risk areas in which controls may not necessar-

ily exist or, if they exist, may be bypassed. Integrating visual analytics also can increase detection rates, based on the identification of patterns or clusters.

A helpful framework for describing the types of available tests for asset misappropriation, as well as other leading fraud schemes, is set forth in figure 2-5. Note how detection rates increase while the number of false positives decrease as we move beyond traditional rules-based queries and analytics (structured data) and keyword searching (unstructured data). Moving up the spectrum into model-based visual analytics, latent semantic analytics, and natural language processing helps companies better analyze, categorize, and draw conclusions from large amounts of data in a more efficient manner.

Figure 2-5: *Asset Misappropriation Tests Framework*

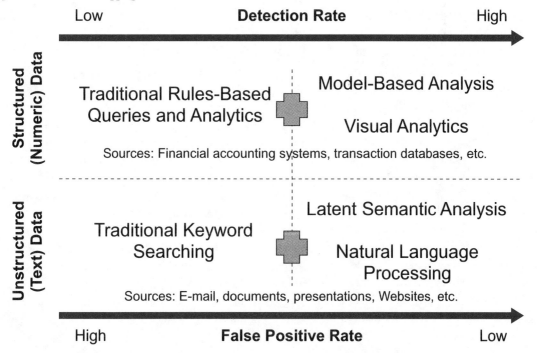

Structured Data

Query instructions like "sort," "match," "compare," and "filter" are typically used to describe tests that are rules based. For years, internal and external auditors have used these types of queries that match one discrete set of data, such as the vendor master table, to another discrete set of data, such as the employee master file, to look for employees or employee ad-

dresses that also appear on the vendor's list. Numerous tests of similar nature incorporate all the ledgers, subledgers, and master tables of a corporate accounting system and are readily available in a multitude of accounting, internal audit, and fraud-detection literature. Contrary to this approach, however, analytics that incorporate statistics and use more sophisticated analytics, such as cluster, anomaly detection, regression, predictive modeling, heat mapping, and data visualization, move into the model-based computing range in which higher levels of detection rates coupled with a lower number of false positives typically resonate. Today, software applications have become more affordable and sophisticated, and you don't have to have a PhD in statistics to run some simple, yet powerful, analyses.

Using model-based computing can be particularly helpful in detecting accounts receivable schemes in which clients who have high returns or defaulted on their accounts can be profiled to look for clusters of similar variables (for example, location, frequency, product type, and so on) so that a predictive model can be built to monitor for risks. On the procurement and accounts payable side, known erroneous or suspicious transactions can be analyzed to build a statistical model to spot future suspicious payments.

Unstructured Data

When it comes to unstructured text-based data, words like "Boolean syntax," document or e-mail "date range" filtering, or "file type" sorting are common under the traditional keyword searching model. Typically, accountants avoid doing these types of queries on a proactive basis, especially within e-mail communications, given the high number of false positives these searches generate, coupled with the extensive amount of time and perceptions of privacy surrounding such data sources. On the other hand, forensic accountants are well aware of the importance of unstructured data in a reactive investigation or litigation because e-mail is one of the first data sources requested by fraud investigators, government agencies, regulators, or opposing counsel. However, unstructured data can and should be considered on a proactive basis without undergoing the drudgery of sifting through countless documents or reviewing the personal communications of an employee's e-mail word-for-word.

Software applications that incorporate analytics, such as document concepts, name extraction and recognition, "fuzzy searching," social network analysis, sentiment (emotional) analysis, clustering, and fraud triangle e-mail analytics, also are becoming more affordable and, in some cases, integrate

with structured data applications in the form of a text analytics module or add-on.[4] When combined with traditional keyword searching, these analytics help forensic accountants understand the "who," "what," and "when" of key business events or risks that are particularly applicable to asset misappropriation fraud schemes. Chapter 8, "Electronic Evidence," covers unstructured data retrieval and analysis in greater detail.

Practical Applications for Model-Based Analytics in Structured Financial Data

As previously indicated, using model-based computing can be particularly helpful in detecting accounts receivable schemes in which clients who have high returns or have defaulted on their accounts can be profiled to look for anomalies (or unusual patterns) for risk analysis. Additionally, accounts receivable data could be analyzed to identify clusters of similar variables to spot trends, (for example, location, frequency, product type, and so on) so that a predictive model can be built to monitor for risks based on confidence intervals (for example, 95 percent confident that, based on previous fraudulent case data, this account matches the fraud risk profile). Many large companies may already be doing these types of analytics from a business risk-management perspective; however, few apply these analytics to look for fraudulent activities.

On the procurement and accounts payable side, known erroneous or suspicious transactions can be analyzed to build a statistical model to spot future suspicious payments. For example, in one engagement, the team sampled 2,000 transactions from a population of 400,000 vendor payments that were deemed "high risk" from the fraud risk assessment previously completed. Of the 2,000 transactions, the team identified approximately 400 suspicious payments, with the remaining 1,600 being labeled not suspicious. By analyzing the fields in the payment ledgers, including the date; location; vendor name and ID; amount; and, of note, the unstructured text in the comments field, the team created a statistical model to analyze the remaining 398,000

4 Torpey, Dan, Vince Walden, and Mike Sherrod "Exposing the Iceberg: E-mail Analytics and the Fraud Triangle," *Fraud Magazine* (May/June 2009).

transactions, based on the profile of a suspicious and not suspicious transaction. The team then applied a confidence interval of a 95 percent threshold of "is suspicious," which identified approximately 15,000 similar transactions totaling over $8 million in payments. The team started with the highest confidence interval at 99.9 percent (that is, lowest hanging fruit) and worked its way down in terms of remediation and identification of internal controls weaknesses.

Practical Applications for Unstructured Data Analytics Using the Fraud Triangle and Text Mining

In a hypothetical case, suppose internal audit was concerned about a group of employees collaborating in a suspected cash larceny scheme, although no direct evidence was provided to launch a full in-

vestigation. In this case, six months of live server e-mail would be copied from the IT department's servers for analysis (not necessarily e-mail review). Through collaboration, terms unique to the industry and company's culture would be developed to look for the frequency of words or phases in employees' e-mail communications related to the fraud triangle theory, which include "incentive," "pressure," "opportunity," and "rationalization."[5] The individuals who "scored" the highest, in terms of hit counts, on all three components would be the focus of additional inquiry, according to the fraud triangle theory. Figure 2-6 provides a diagram of the keyword frequency "hits" for the individuals from each component of the fraud triangle. As shown, those individuals with the highest frequency rose to the top, are easily spotted,[6] and will then be the focus of additional inquiry.

Figure 2-6: *Plotting an Individual's Fraud Score Relative to Their Peers*

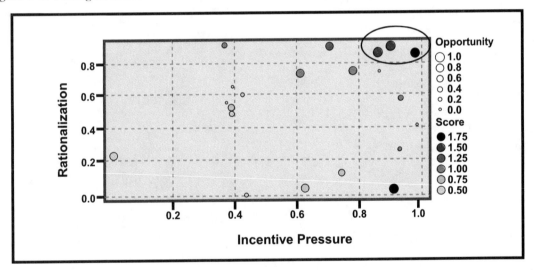

5 In many companies, corporate policy states that e-mail communications are the property of the company itself, not the individual. However, before analyzing e-mail communications, one should consult with management or in-house counsel to determine if such analytics are authorized from a corporate policy and, if multinational, from a data privacy perspective.

6 For more information on this type of analysis, please see "Fraud Triangle Analytics: Applying Cressey's Theory to E-Mail Communications," *Fraud Magazine* (July/August 2009).

Once identified, additional text mining techniques can be run on the high-risk individuals to uncover who is talking to whom (social network analysis), about what (latent semantic analysis), and over what time period (time series analysis).

Conclusion

This chapter has addressed a number of asset misappropriation schemes that can occur and result in losses for businesses, ranging from small amounts to very substantial amounts. Although the median loss for asset misappropriation, according to the occupational fraud survey conducted and reported in the ACFE's *2008 Report to the Nation on Occupational Fraud & Abuse*, was $150,000 per incident, asset misappropriation accounted for almost 89 percent of all occupational fraud cases reported in the survey. Given the relative high frequency of occurrences, individuals responsible for protecting assets of businesses will benefit from understanding the wide variety of schemes that exist; however, awareness of the fraud schemes is only a small fraction of the battle. Detection, prevention, and deterrence, implemented within the combines of a strong corporate culture; a zero tolerance fraud policy; adequate internal controls; and advanced, efficient analytical monitoring procedures are what will ultimately protect and preserve the assets of a business.

3

Financial Statement Restatements: Protocols and Process

James McCurry, Partner/Principal
Barb Lambert, Manager

"Based on recent events, our previously issued financial statements for the period ended December 31, 20XX, can no longer be relied upon."

Introduction

These words above, when included in Form 8-K filings and press releases, can result in drastic changes in share price, employee morale, and customer sentiment.

The corporate scandals earlier this decade, as well as the continuing market turmoil from the credit crisis, have heightened the public awareness of financial statement restatements resulting from business fraud, which is the focus of this chapter. The sections that follow provide additional background on the motivations driving financial statement fraud, the internal and third-party implications of large financial statement restatements, and the protocols and processes followed during a large-scale investigation of a financial restatement.

What are Financial Statement Restatements?

Financial statement restatements are required when a company (or their auditor) identifies an error in historical financial information. Financial statement errors may be the result of an unintentional mistake or the consequence of intentional and fraudulent actions intended to deceive the users of financial statements. The latter case, financial statement fraud, is typically evidenced by the falsification of accounting records and the misapplication of accounting principles to achieve a desired financial statement result. This is certainly the more well-publicized type of financial statement restatement. The primary focus of this chapter is intentional financial statement misstatements that are the result of business fraud and result in a financial statement restatement. Financial Accounting Standards Board (FASB) Statement No. 154, *Accounting Changes and Error Corrections—a replacement of APB Opinion No. 20 and FASB Statement No. 3*, (FASB ASC 250, *Accounting Changes and Error Corrections*) which replaced Accounting Principles Board (APB) Opinion No. 20, *Accounting Changes*,

May 2005, is the prevailing U.S. generally accepted accounting principles (U.S. GAAP) guidance relative to accounting changes and error corrections. FASB Statement No. 154 (FASB ASC 250) defines an error as follows:

> [A]n error in recognition, measurement, presentation, or disclosure in financial statements resulting from mathematical mistakes, mistakes in the application of GAAP, or oversight or misuse of facts that existed at the time the financial statements were prepared. A change from an accounting principle that is not generally accepted to one that is generally accepted is a correction of an error.

In recent years, there has been a global movement toward International Financial Report Standards (IFRS) to provide consistency in worldwide reporting standards. Although IFRS is not yet the financial reporting standard in the United States, it has been adopted in Europe and other countries around the world, and its guidance relative to errors and restatements offers a relevant comparison to U.S. GAAP. International Accounting Standards (IAS) No. 8, *Accounting Policies, Changes in Accounting Estimates and Errors*, offers the following, similar definition of an error under IFRS:

> Errors can arise in respect of the recognition, measurement, presentation or disclosure of elements of financial statements. Financial statements do not comply with IFRS if they contain either material errors or immaterial errors made intentionally to achieve a particular presentation of an entity's financial position, financial performance or cash flows.

IAS No. 8, as opposed to FASB Statement No. 154 (FASB ASC 250), notes that financial statements containing immaterial errors, not just material errors, may not comply with IFRS. In practice, however, errors made intentionally by management to achieve a particular financial result are typically material. After all, management would rarely have the incentive to manipulate financial statements in an immaterial way that would ultimately not influence the decisions of end users.

The overall importance of materiality cannot be understated because it often makes the difference between maintaining the status quo and undertaking a costly and time-consuming financial statement restatement. Both U.S. GAAP and IFRS do not require immaterial items to be restated. IAS No. 8 notes that "the accounting policies in International Financial Reporting Standards (IFRS) need not be applied when the effect of applying them is immaterial." Similarly, FASB Statement No. 154 (FASB ASC 250), consistent with other standards issued by FASB, concludes with the statement that "[t]he provisions of this Statement need not be applied to immaterial items."

How does a company determine if an error requires a financial statement restatement? In general, both U.S. GAAP and IFRS deem an error material if it influences the decision making of a financial statement user. Securities and Exchange Commission Staff Accounting Bulletin (SEC SAB) No. 99, *Materiality*, references FASB Concept No. 2, *Qualitative Characteristics of Accounting Information*, for a definition of the concept of materiality. FASB Concept No. 2 promulgates the following:

> The magnitude of an omission or misstatement of accounting information that, in light of the surrounding circumstances, makes it probable that the judgment of a reasonable person relying on the information would have been changed or influenced by the omission or misstatement.

This definition is similar to the explanation provided in IAS No. 1, *Presentation of Financial Statements*:

> [I]tems are material if they could, individually or collectively, influence the economic decisions that users make on the basis of the financial statements. Materiality depends on the size and nature of the omission or misstatement judged in the surrounding circumstances. The size or nature of the item, or a combination of both, could be the determining factor.

The Supreme Court interpretation of federal securities laws, as it pertains to materiality, generally concurs with this interpretation, as well. According to the Supreme Court's interpretation, a fact is material if there is "a substantial likelihood that the ... fact would have been viewed by the reasonable investor as having significantly altered the 'total' mix of information made available."

U.S. GAAP and IFRS do not offer any quantitative thresholds to be used by a company in judging materiality. However, in SAB No. 99, the SEC did acknowledge that companies and auditors typically use some sort of "rule of thumb" as a basis to determine the materiality of misstatements. The SEC staff noted the following in regard to using such a "rule of thumb" in assessing misstatements:

> The staff has no objection to such a 'rule of thumb' as an initial step in assessing materiality. But quantifying, in percentage terms, the magnitude of a misstatement is only the beginning of an analysis of materiality; it cannot appropriately be used as a substitute for a full analysis of all relevant considerations.

Therefore, SAB No. 99 states that it is important to consider both quantitative and qualitative factors when assessing materiality. Box 3-1 (quoted from SAB No. 99) outlines certain considerations that suggest a quantitatively small misstatement of a financial statement may be material.

In addition, SAB No. 99 goes on to state the following:

> This is not an exhaustive list of the circumstances that may affect the materiality of a quantitatively small misstatement. Among other factors, the demonstrated volatility of the price of a registrant's securities in response to certain types of disclosures may provide guidance as to whether investors regard quantitatively small misstatements as material. Consideration of potential market reaction to disclosure of a misstatement is by itself 'too blunt an instrument to be depended on' in considering whether a fact is material. When, however, management or the independent auditor expects (based, for example, on a pattern of market performance) that a known misstatement may result in a significant positive

or negative market reaction, that expected reaction should be taken into account when considering whether a misstatement is material.

Box 3-1: *Qualitative Factors That Could Affect Materiality*

- [W]hether the misstatement arises from an item capable of precise measurement or whether it arises from an estimate and, if so, the degree of imprecision inherent in the estimate

- [W]hether the misstatement masks a change in earnings or other trends

- [W]hether the misstatement hides a failure to meet analysts' consensus expectations for the enterprise

- [W]hether the misstatement changes a loss into income or vice versa

- [W]hether the misstatement concerns a segment or other portion of the registrant's business that has been identified as playing a significant role in the registrant's operations or profitability

- [W]hether the misstatement affects the registrant's compliance with regulatory requirements

- [W]hether the misstatement affects the registrant's compliance with loan covenants or other contractual requirements

- [W]hether the misstatement has the effect of increasing management's compensation—for example, by satisfying requirements for the award of bonuses or other forms of incentive compensation

- [W]hether the misstatement involves concealment of an unlawful transaction

It also is important for companies to consider that the failure to accurately record immaterial items may result in violations of federal securities laws. Federal regulations note that each registrant "must make and keep books, records, and accounts, which, in

reasonable detail, accurately and fairly reflect the transactions and dispositions of assets of the registrant and must maintain internal accounting controls that are sufficient to provide reasonable assurances that, among other things, transactions are recorded as necessary to permit the preparation of financial statements in conformity with GAAP."[1]

Why Do Intentional Misstatements and Fraud Occur?

Certainly, the specific drivers of intentional financial misstatements and fraud are unique to each individual company, but three common factors will provide the opportunity or cause for their occurrence: weak internal controls, the relationship of executive compensation to financial reporting, and the corporate culture and tone at the top.

Weak Internal Controls

One of the purposes of internal controls is to foster the preparation of accurate and reliable financial statements. Effective internal controls can help companies prevent accounting fraud or at least detect fraudulent practices earlier. Section 404 of the Sarbanes-Oxley Act of 2002 reemphasized the importance of effective internal controls and defined additional management responsibilities that pertain to internal controls over financial reporting.

The absence of effective internal controls creates the opportunity for officers and employees to perpetrate inappropriate accounting actions that may necessitate a later financial statement restatement. Certainly, a company may not have intentionally designed a poor system of internal controls. In a fast growing company, it is often the case that the internal controls are just not able to keep pace with the rapid growth of the company, particularly in new and enhanced risk areas.

It also is possible that a company has designed and developed a strong system of internal controls, but the company does not have the sufficient resources available to implement, monitor, and test the effectiveness of its internal controls. Essentially, the

---

1 SEC 17 CFR Part 211, Staff Accounting Bulletin: No. 99 *Materiality*.

internal audit department, audit committee, and other compliance functions may not have the stature, independence, and resources within the company to be effective.

A key component of an effective internal control system is providing employees the opportunity to report observations of possible misconduct. A 2006 report by the U.S. Government Accountability Office indicated that 58 percent of all financial statement restatements are prompted by notifications from internal parties.[2] If whistle-blower lines and other reporting systems are not implemented correctly or advertised effectively, there may be insufficient opportunities to take action on reports received.

Relationship of Executive Compensation to Financial Reporting

Executives are often rewarded based on the financial performance of the company. Bonuses, stock options, and granting of shares are particular forms of compensation that may create an improper or excessive alignment between executive compensation and certain subjective financial reporting measures. This can create tremendous pressure to book or record transactions in such a way that may increase performance-based remuneration.

Bonuses, in particular, can be linked to the profitability of the company or the performance of the share price, which can result in pressure to make or exceed the analysts' expectations so that bonuses are paid and the share price is boosted, thereby maximizing the return to the executive. In addition, corporate executives and management may find themselves pressured not only to meet analyst expectations but also to meet internally designated targets or established debt covenants.

Finally, in the case of a distressed company, officers or other employees may initiate accounting improprieties to ensure that they are not fired due to the poor performance of the company or to perhaps pass blame to a previous employee for the poor performance.

Corporate Culture and Tone at the Top

In all companies, leadership sets an example through its actions and communications, which is commonly referred to as the tone at the top. Ideally, leadership should foster an environment of integrity and compliance; however, if leadership continually overrides or ignores internal controls, the message may transfer down through the company. Additionally, a message from the corporate executives that emphasizes meeting financial targets, regardless of the consequences, may send the impression (or, in the worst case, a mandate) that proper accounting practices can be bypassed in order to meet the necessary earnings targets. Statements such as these create a culture that facilitates business fraud and the manipulation of financial statements.

What Parties are Involved in a Financial Statement Restatement?

Numerous parties representing varying interests are frequently involved in the financial statement restatement process. These parties and their roles are outlined in box 3-2. To place financial statement restatement roles and responsibilities in a larger context, see chapter 6, "Roles and Responsibilities: How Different Stakeholders Work During Investigations."

Common Types of Financial Statement Issues

Investigations into potential financial statement manipulation can be identified by a number of sources, including whistle-blowers, internal and external auditors, senior management, or regulators (SEC, Department of Justice [DOJ], and so on). Post Sarbanes-Oxley, changes in the regulatory and oversight environment have prompted an increased focus on corporate governance. This is causing corporations to focus more internal efforts on the identification and remediation of financial statement irregularities, and, as a result, a growing number of

---

2 July 2006 U.S. Government Accountability Office report titled *Financial Restatements: Update of Public Company Trends, Market Impacts, and Regulatory Enforcement Activities.*

Box 3-2: *Roles of Key Parties Involved in a Financial Statement Restatement*

Management—This could include both senior level executives of the company, such as the CEO and CFO, and midlevel management, such as the financial controller and the internal audit director. The greatest interaction is typically with those personnel in the finance and internal audit groups.

Audit Committee—For a publicly traded company in the United States, the audit committee comprises nonexecutive members of the board of directors, and the committee is charged with overseeing financial reporting, disclosure, and risk-management protocols for the company. As such, the audit committee would typically take the lead role in overseeing a fraud-related financial statement restatement for the company, including hiring any external law firm and forensic accountants.

External Auditor—External auditors are independent accountants who may be hired to conduct a financial statement audit for the company in accordance with generally accepted auditing standards (GAAS). The opinion of an auditing firm typically provides reasonable assurance to third parties that the financial statements of a company are free of material misstatements. To maintain their independence and comply with regulatory requirements, the external auditing firm would not be hired by a publicly traded company in the United States to assist in an investigation or restatement process. The external auditing firm, however, would ultimately audit the financial statements that reflect the results of the restatement process.

External and Internal Counsel—This includes both the company's internal general counsel's office as well as any external law firms engaged to provide legal advice to the company during the restatement process. Counsel also would have direct involvement in assisting the company in responding to any regulatory inquiries received during the restatement process. Certain company executives also may have individual representation in defending any civil or criminal charges resulting from the restatement.

Forensic Accountants and Consultants—Forensic accountants are often engaged either by the company or external counsel to provide the financial and accounting expertise necessary to assess and correct any financial statement issues. Due to independence considerations, forensic accountants are not the external auditors engaged to conduct the annual financial statement audit.

Regulators—The SEC and DOJ typically investigate and prosecute civil and criminal charges, respectively, resulting from financial misstatements. Both government agencies have an important role in protecting the rights of the shareholder, ensuring stability of the financial markets, and minimizing corruption in the system.

Shareholders—Shareholders are essentially the owners of a publicly traded corporation in the United States, and, therefore, they have a particular interest in the outcome of a financial restatement because it affects the value of their stock and their financial interest in the corporation. The board of directors, executive leadership of the company, and government agencies are all ultimately accountable to the shareholders and the public interest.

Plaintiff's Firms—Large plaintiff firms may have a role in cases in which the shareholder is facing financial losses due to fraud or misrepresented financial statements and the shareholders elect to initiate legal action against the company.

financial statement frauds are being identified by internal sources.

The first step in any investigation into potential improper financial statement manipulation is to identify the nature of the allegations and the available information. Each financial restatement case is unique, and the detailed issues to be considered will vary from company to company. In general, companies and industries with more complicated products or accounting guidance are more susceptible to irregularities.

A few of the common areas for financial statement fraud are as follows.

Revenue Recognition

Revenue recognition schemes seek to increase the amount of revenue recognized or accelerate the timing of the revenue recognition. For example, financial statement fraud may include recording sales in the current period that actually occurred after the quarter close or recognizing revenue in cases in which the key conditions of the sale have not yet been completed.

It also is possible that financial statement fraud may be the result of booking nonexistent revenue. For example, the SEC filed a civil action against GlobeTel Communications Inc.[3] and three of its former officers on May 1, 2008, related to revenue recognition. In this case, an employee initiated a deliberate act to overstate revenue by creating false records and intentionally misleading the external and internal auditors. According to the SEC complaint, the company recorded $119 million in revenue on the basis of fraudulent invoices created by two individuals in charge of its wholesale telecommunications business. To conceal the fraud, the officers booked entries in the general ledger that improperly offset the receivables associated with the revenues against the liabilities.

SAB No. 104, *Revenue Recognition*, issued in 2004, is the prevailing accounting guidance related to revenue recognition and specifies the following criteria for revenue recognition:

- Persuasive evidence of an arrangement exists
- Delivery has occurred or services have been rendered
- Seller's price to the buyer is fixed or determinable
- Collectability is reasonably assured

To accelerate revenue recognition, companies may try to bypass one or more of the preceding criteria, such as recognizing revenue of the sale of goods prior to the transfer of the associated title or risk of loss or in cases in which there is the right of return. As an example, on February 21, 2008, the SEC filed civil charges against one of the former executives of AXM Pharma, Inc.[4] The complaint alleged that the officer directed the company to overstate its revenues by over 700 percent for the quarter ended June 30, 2005, by inflating sales to distributors. The distributors had a right to return the goods and were not obligated to pay for them until they resold the goods; thus, the company had not met the SAB No. 104 criteria to recognize the revenue for these sales.

Two other common schemes used by companies to accelerate revenue recognition are bill and hold arrangements and channel stuffing.

Bill and Hold Arrangements

Bill and hold arrangements may arise when a company completes the manufacturing of a product, but the customer is not, in reality, ready to take delivery of the goods, due to lack of space, delays in customer production schedules, and so on. To accelerate the recognition of revenue, companies might try to segregate the inventory or ship it to a third-party warehouse and then recognize the revenue before the goods have been delivered to the customer.

In general, the SEC staff has stated that delivery is not considered to have occurred unless the customer has taken title and assumed the risks and rewards of ownership of the products specified in the customer's purchase order or sales agreement. This typically occurs when a product is delivered to the customer's delivery site (that is, free on board [FOB] destination) or shipped to the customer (that is, FOB shipment). However, the SEC has provided the following list of criteria[5] that constitute a general guideline for recognizing revenue in cases in which delivery has not occurred:

1. The risks of ownership must have passed to the buyer.

---

3 Securities and Exchange Commission (SEC) Accounting and Auditing Enforcement Release No. 2822 issued May 1, 2008.

4 SEC Accounting and Auditing Enforcement Release No. 2790 issued February 25, 2008.

5 SEC Staff Accounting Bulletin No. 104, *Revenue Recognition*, issued December 17, 2003.

2. The customer must have made a fixed commitment to purchase the goods, preferably in written documentation.

3. The buyer, not the seller, must request that the transaction be on a bill and hold basis. The buyer must have a substantial business purpose for ordering the goods on a bill and hold basis.

4. There must be a fixed schedule for delivery of the goods. The date for delivery must be reasonable and must be consistent with the buyer's business purpose (for example, storage periods are customary in the industry).

5. The seller must not have retained any specific performance obligations such that the earning process is not complete.

6. The ordered goods must have been segregated from the seller's inventory and not be subject to being used to fill other orders.

7. The equipment [product] must be complete and ready for shipment.

Channel Stuffing

Channel stuffing occurs when a company offers large discounts and other incentives to a distributor or retailer to take large orders late in the reporting period in order for the company to meet the designated sales or profit targets. The problem is that these sales may not have met the standard criteria for revenue recognition set forth in SAB No. 104. One reason for this may be because the distributor has a side agreement with the company that gives them the right to return any unsold merchandise. It is important to note that in cases in which the distributor or customer ultimately does want to purchase the goods, companies may have difficulty making future sales targets because channel stuffing is essentially advancing future sales into the current quarter.

Costs and Expenses

Although there are certainly many high-profile examples of financial statement restatements resulting from revenue recognition schemes, companies also may manipulate their costs and expenses in order to achieve bottom-line profit targets. Box 3-3 provides a list of expense schemes that may result in a financial statement restatement.

Box 3-3: *Types of Financial Statement Restatement Expense Schemes*

Delaying Expenses—Failing to accrue for goods and services at the period end or creating a prepayment for an expense for which the good or service has already been received by the end of the period.

Capitalizing Expenses—Capitalizing costs as an asset on the balance sheet that should be expensed in the income statement, such as research and development charges.

Long-Term Contracts—Underestimating the costs to completion on a contract or not adjusting costs for overruns on the budget.

Impairment Charges—Not writing off fixed assets or inventory that has become obsolete or otherwise declined in value.

Nonrecurring Expenses—Defining ongoing expenses as one-off, nonrecurring items. For example, companies might try to include routine expenses in restructuring charges because analysts and other users often focus on the operational results that exclude the nonrecurring expenses.

Big Bath Adjustments—Taking a large charge in a quarter in which the company knows that it will not make its earnings target. The idea is that a company will incur a "big bath" charge in a bad year in order to artificially inflate its earnings in future quarters.

Rebates—Receiving significant rebates from suppliers without maintaining sufficient paperwork or basing rebates upon verbal agreements.

Clothing retailers are one type of industry that has faced significant financial statement restatements due to understating expenses, particularly from rebate charges and inventory write-offs. As an example, the SEC filed a civil injunctive action against luxury department store owner Saks

Incorporated[6] on September 5, 2007. Saks has subsequently settled the case, but the original complaint alleged the Saks Fifth Avenue Enterprises division engaged in the following two deceptive practices to materially overstate income in order to achieve financial targets from the mid-1990s to 2003:

- Saks buyers allegedly understated to vendors the sales performance of the vendor's merchandise. Based on that information, Saks was able to collect from the vendors millions of dollars in "vendor allowance" payments to which the company was not entitled. This practice allegedly continued from 1996 to 2003, with net income being overstated by 32.3 percent for the fiscal year ended February 2, 2002, and 42.6 percent for the fiscal year ended February 1, 2003.
- Additionally, the SEC alleged that Saks improperly deferred (or "rolled") permanent markdowns or inventory impairment charges from one period to the next. Deferring permanent markdown charges to future periods would result in a lower cost of goods sold amount in the current period and higher net income on the income statement. Inventory balances on the balance sheet also would be overstated in the current period. The SEC's complaint alleged that the markdown rolling allowed Saks to overstate its net income by 86.5 percent in the second quarter of fiscal year 1999.

Reserve Manipulation

Recent scandals have heightened the awareness of financial statement fraud committed through the manipulation of reserves (or "cookie jars"). A reserve is a contingency or liability that is placed on the balance sheet in anticipation of a future expense or loss. FASB Statement No. 5, *Accounting for Contingencies* (FASB ASC 450, *Contingencies*), defines a contingency as

an existing condition, situation, or set of circumstances involving uncertainty as to possible gain

... or loss ... to an enterprise that will ultimately be resolved when one or more future events occur or fail to occur. Resolution of the uncertainty may confirm the acquisition of an asset or the reduction of a liability or the loss or impairment of an asset or the incurrence of a liability.

At the time that a company books a reserve for a liability, a corresponding expense is charged to income.

FASB Statement No. 5 (FASB ASC 450, *Contingencies*) defines the following criteria for accruing a loss contingency:

An estimated loss from a loss contingency (as defined in paragraph 1)[7] shall be accrued by a charge to income if both of the following conditions are met:

a. Information available prior to issuance of the financial statements indicates that it is probable that an asset had been impaired or a liability had been incurred at the date of the financial statements. It is implicit in this condition that it must be probable that one or more future events will occur confirming the fact of the loss.

b. The amount of loss can be reasonably estimated.

Reserves are particularly subjective and, therefore, are especially open to abuse. It is management's responsibility to determine a reasonable estimate of those losses that are probable and that require charges to income. The judgmental nature of reserves provides management with the opportunity to use them to smooth out the results of a company using transfers to and from reserves. For example, a company can overstate reserves (and the corresponding expense) in times when the company is exceeding expectations and can subsequently release the excess reserve into income in future quarters when additional income is needed to meet earnings targets.

6 SEC Accounting and Auditing Enforcement Release No. 2674 issued September 5, 2007.

7 Paragraph 1 of FASB Statement No. 5, *Accounting for Contingencies* (FASB ASC 450, *Contingencies*) states, "For the purpose of this Statement, a contingency is defined as an existing condition, situation, or set of circumstances involving uncertainty as to possible gain (hereinafter a "gain contingency") or loss (hereinafter a "loss contingency") to an enterprise that will ultimately be resolved when one or more future events occur or fail to occur. Resolution of the uncertainty may confirm the acquisition of an asset or the reduction of a liability or the loss or impairment of an asset or the incurrence of a liability."

By establishing reserves in periods when earnings targets are exceeded and by dipping into "cookie jar" reserves during more difficult times, management can report more consistent earnings from quarter to quarter.

As another example, Nortel Networks,[8] the large Canadian telecommunications manufacturer, faced particular scrutiny from both U.S. and Canadian regulatory authorities for its use of reserves to meet internal targets and Wall Street expectations from 2000 to 2003. The SEC complaint alleged that Nortel improperly established over $400 million in excess reserves by the time it announced its fiscal year 2002 financial results. SEC Auditing and Enforcement Release No. 2740 cited the following:

> [T]hese reserve manipulations erased Nortel's fourth quarter 2002 pro forma profit and allowed it to report a loss instead so that Nortel would not show a profit earlier than it had previously forecast to the market. The complaint alleges that in the first and second quarters of 2003, Nortel improperly released approximately $500 million in excess reserves to boost its earnings and fabricate a return to profitability. These efforts turned Nortel's first quarter 2003 loss into a reported profit under US GAAP, and largely erased its second quarter loss while generating a pro forma profit.

In April 2004, Nortel's management terminated its CEO, CFO, and controller. During 2004 and 2005, Nortel performed an extensive review of its financial records, ultimately restating over $2 billion of revenue.

Unrecorded Financial Statement Activities

Unrecorded financial statement activities as a form of fraud first came to the public's attention during the Enron restatement. Although certain special purpose entities are permissible under the accounting guidance, these vehicles also can be used to mislead investors about the true nature of the underlying transactions. As an example, off-balance sheet financing can be used as a way for companies to raise financing that is ultimately not reflected in the balance sheet. If not properly disclosed, investors may not understand the total substance of the liabilities incurred by the company.

More recently, Refco Group Ltd.[9] and its former chairman Phillip R. Bennett faced SEC action for allegedly orchestrating a scheme to conceal hundreds of millions of dollars from Refco through the use of a private entity (a so-called "special purpose entity") controlled by the former chairman. The complaint alleged that shareholders incurred hundreds of millions of dollars in losses after the scheme was revealed to the public in October 2005. From 1998 to October 2005, Refco allegedly concealed debt, resulting from trading losses and operating expenses, that was owed to it by Refco Group Holdings, Inc. The company used a series of short-term loans to temporarily transfer debt to third parties immediately before the end of the fiscal periods, and then the company would reverse the transactions shortly after the close ended. This ultimately had the impact of understating the amount of liabilities that were reported in the quarterly and annual financial statements.

The Financial Restatement Process

When allegations of potential financial statement fraud first surface, the board of directors typically forms a special committee (usually comprised of independent directors) to evaluate the veracity of the allegations and lead the related investigation. The special committee also would be responsible for engaging and managing any third parties that are involved, such as external counsel and forensic accountants.

The financial restatement process can be traumatic for a company and require the dedication of significant resources. To continue our discussion of the restatement process, we look at the following steps

---

8 See SEC Accounting and Auditing Enforcement Release No. 2740 issued October 15, 2007.

9 See SEC Accounting and Auditing Enforcement Release No. 2788 issued February 19, 2008.

typically involved in the financial statement restatement process:

- Defining the Project Scope
- Evidence Collection: Establish the Facts
- Analyze the Evidence
- Evidence Retrieval and Reporting: Quantifying the Amounts Involved
- Solving the Problem—Before, During, and After the Restatement

Defining the Project Scope

The most difficult and critical activity for the special committee tasked with evaluating the allegations is defining the scope of the investigation. Allegations are often very broad and yet potentially touch such a high level in the organization that they cannot be ignored. The special committee must work closely with its outside counsel and their advisors, including the forensic accountants and the company's external auditor, to ensure that the scope of the work is sufficient to completely address the allegations.

Once agreement is reached and the special committee has identified the areas of focus, the next step is to define the overall scope of the project. The following questions when analyzed in detail help to provide insight into the overall scope of the project.

What are the specific allegations?

The company, with the assistance of external counsel and the forensic accountants, must first consider the types of financial reporting issues that are evident in the allegations. As previously described, each financial restatement case is unique, and the detailed issues to be considered will vary from company to company. Some common issues include revenue recognition, cost and expense manipulation, reserve manipulation, and unrecorded financial statement activities.

How many of the company's operations, countries, divisions, and offices may be affected by the restatement?

It may be appropriate for the company to conduct some type of diagnostic review in its other locations to determine whether the financial reporting issues have a broader reach beyond those initially suspected.

What are the responsibilities of each of the parties involved in the restatement, including the external counsel forensic accountants, and consultants?

This may include responding to any regulatory inquiries, defending company personnel in any regulatory proceedings, and managing which documents may need to be turned over to regulators as a result of any requests or subpoenas.

Will there be any residual impacts of the financial statement restatement? For example, what are the tax implications of the restatement? Would restated financial statements affect historical debt covenants?

The company and its advisors should be aware of potential residual impacts on an ongoing basis, such as tax considerations and potential debt covenant violations.

What are the time constraints that need to be considered? Will the company face any SEC penalties by delaying the release of its financial statements or potentially breach any debt covenants?

The company may need to consider delaying the release of the quarterly financial statements until the issues have been appropriately addressed and there are no concerns over the adequacy of the internal controls over financial reporting.

It is also important to note that both management and the external auditors, in cases of financial statement fraud or other illegal acts, have specific responsibilities under the accounting guidance that are important to consider in the context of defining the project scope.

Management and Audit Committee Responsibilities

The Sarbanes-Oxley Act of 2002, passed by Congress in response to the Enron and other scandals, defines the responsibilities of management and the audit committee, relative to financial reporting. Under the Sarbanes-Oxley Act, the audit committee is responsible for addressing any accounting or internal control complaints received by the company. To respond to these concerns or in the context of addressing financial statement fraud, the audit committee also has the authority to engage independent counsel and other advisors as it determines necessary for carrying out its duties.

The Sarbanes-Oxley Act requires the principal executive officer or officers of the company to certify each annual or quarterly report filed or submitted under sections 13(a) or 15(d) of the Securities and Exchange Act of 1934. By certifying the financial statements, the officers are attesting that the report does not contain any material false statements (or does not omit any material information), and that the financial statements fairly represent in all material respects the financial condition of the company.

U.S. auditing and accounting standards, as well as the Sarbanes-Oxley Act, place the responsibility on management to establish and maintain effective internal controls. The burden is ultimately on management to disclose to the auditors and the audit committee all significant deficiencies in the internal controls that could adversely affect the company's ability to record, process, summarize, and report financial data. Management also must report any form of fraud, whether material or immaterial, that involves management or other employees who have a significant role in the company's internal controls. To place management and audit committee roles and responsibilities in a larger context, see chapter 6, "Roles and Responsibilities: How Different Stakeholders Work During Investigations."

External Auditor Responsibilities

Management, not the external auditors, has the primary responsibility for ensuring that the company's annual financial statements fairly represent the financial condition of the company in all material respects. External auditors have a more limited responsibility for considering and addressing illegal acts and fraud.

Statement on Auditing Standards (SAS) No. 54, *Illegal Acts by Clients* (AICPA, *Professional Standards*, vol. 1, AU sec. 317), describes auditor responsibilities that relate to considering the possibility of illegal acts when conducting a financial statement audit, as well as auditor responsibilities when a possible illegal act is detected. In the context of SAS No. 54, an *illegal act* is a violation of law or government regulations. Generally, an auditor's responsibility to detect and report misstatements resulting from illegal acts

is limited to those acts having a direct and material effect on the determination of financial statement amounts.

With regard to acts that have a material indirect effect on the financial statements, the auditor should be aware of the possibility that the acts may have occurred and apply necessary procedures to determine if the illegal acts have occurred. Due to the nature of illegal acts, however, an audit conducted in accordance with GAAS provides no assurance that illegal acts will be detected during the course of the audit.

SAS No. 54 provides the following guidance to external auditors when an illegal act is identified during the course of the financial statement audit:

> When the auditor becomes aware of information concerning a possible illegal act, the auditor should obtain an understanding of the nature of the act, the circumstances in which it occurred, and sufficient other information to evaluate the effect on the financial statements. In doing so, the auditor should inquire of management at a level above those involved, if possible. If management does not provide satisfactory information that there has been no illegal act, the auditor should
>
> *a.* [c]onsult with the client's legal counsel or other specialists about the application of relevant laws and regulations to the circumstances and the possible effects on the financial statements. Arrangements for such consultation with client's legal counsel should be made by the client.
>
> *b.* [a]pply additional procedures, if necessary, to obtain further understanding of the nature of the acts.

Unless the matter is clearly inconsequential, the auditor should ensure that the audit committee, or others with equivalent authority and responsibility, is adequately informed about the illegal acts that have come to the auditor's attention.

Specific to fraud, an external auditor's responsibilities are defined in SAS No. 99, *Consideration of Fraud in a Financial Statement Audit* (AICPA, *Professional Standards*, vol. 1, AU sec. 316). SAS No. 99 defines *fraud* as "an intentional act that results in a material misstatement in financial statements that are the subject of an audit." Consistent with SAS No. 1, *Codification of Accounting Standards and Procedures* (AICPA, *Professional Standards*, vol. 1), SAS No. 99 reiterates that it is management's responsibility "to design and implement programs and controls to prevent, deter, and detect fraud."

It is an external auditor's responsibility to plan and perform the audit to obtain reasonable assurance about whether the financial statements are free of material misstatements, whether caused by fraud or error. Due to the nature of fraud, however, it is not possible to obtain absolute assurance that an audit detected a material misstatement resulting from fraud. SAS No. 99 defines the following responsibilities for an auditor in detecting and addressing material misstatements of the financial statements resulting from fraud:

- Auditors should conduct a financial statement audit with an attitude of professional skepticism, recognizing the possibility that a material misstatement of the financial statements may exist.
- Audit engagement teams should conduct discussions as part of the planning stage of the audit to consider how the financial statements might be vulnerable to a material misstatement due to fraud.
- Auditors should accumulate the information necessary to determine the risks of fraud, including interviewing management, considering the results of analytical procedures, and assessing other risk factors.
- The audit team should identify the appropriate fraud risk factors, which may be based on the size, complexity, and ownership of the client or the incentives and pressures, opportunities, and attitudes and rationalizations to commit fraud.
- The auditor should consider the internal controls that the company has in place to address the identified risks of material misstatement due to fraud and determine whether these programs appropriately address the identified risks.
- As necessary, the auditor should adjust the nature, timing, and extent of the audit procedures to respond to the identified risks of material misstatement due to fraud.

- If a material misstatement due to fraud is identified, the auditor should communicate the issue to the appropriate level of management or report the issue to the audit committee.

To place external auditor roles and responsibilities in a larger context, see chapter 6, "Roles and Responsibilities: How Different Stakeholders Work During Investigations."

Evidence Collection: Establish the Facts

At the start of an investigation, once the project scope is defined, it is important to secure the transactional data to prevent the accidental (or intentional) modification or deletion. This may include suspending the routine recycling of backup tapes to ensure that all transactional data and electronic correspondence is maintained. In establishing the work plan, the special committee, external counsel, and accountants must work together to identify the sources of available documentation and client resources and initiate the collection of both hard copy and electronic evidence. The parties involved in an independent investigation should maintain frequent contact with the audit committee and special committee to ensure they are adequately informed and have the opportunity to provide assistance as appropriate and needed. Additional content on evidence collection can be found in Chapter 7, "Sources of Evidence."

An investigation might include the collection of the following documents:

- Internal audit working papers that discuss any prior reviews or investigations related to revenue recognition, depreciation estimates, the calculation of reserves or other pertinent issues.
- Accounting policy documentation used in the controllership organization, particularly those policies related to revenue recognition.
- Accounting policy documentation related to revenue recognition, depreciation, and reserve estimates. General accounting policy documentation related to the quarterly close process also may be helpful.
- Manual journal entries booked by the company at the end of the quarters at issue, particularly those that affected the allegedly manipulated accounts.

- An extract from the general ledger containing transactional level detail for the impacted accounts during the relevant time period.
- For relevant periods, the quarter-end calculations (and supporting documentation) of the reserve calculations.
- Based on the extract from the general ledger, it also may be useful to select a sample of transactions to determine if appropriate revenue recognition procedures were followed.

  Documentation for each of the sample selections may include the following:
  - Purchase orders
  - Invoices
  - Shipping documentation
  - Journal entries documenting revenue recognition
  - Accounts receivable ledgers
  - Proof of cash payment
- Correspondence with the external auditors, regulatory authorities, and accounting policy boards regarding any questions or concerns about the accounting issues that were raised
- Identify the custodians from whom to collect both hard-copy and electronic data. These custodians may be important to interview during the course of an investigation. Possible custodians may include:
  - CEO
  - CFO
  - Controller
  - Assistant controller
  - Director, Internal Audit
  - Senior accounting clerk
  - Accounting clerk(s)
  - Director, Sales & Marketing
  - Sales representative(s)

E-mail correspondence and attached files are an increasingly important source of information during an independent investigation. These records may be searched by "keyword" search terms and it is important to appropriately establish search terms at the onset of the investigation. This allows for a more focused investigation and review of the key issues. The following three categories of search terms are commonly used during an e-mail review process:

- Generic fraud and misconduct terms, such as kickback, manipulate, irregular, conceal, scandal, illegal, deception, and so on
- Terms specific to the issues in the investigation, for instance terms related to depreciation, revenue recognitions, sales and pressure, reserve and warranty, and so on
- Other accounting search terms related to the broader integrity of the financial statements, such as bad debt reserve, excess and reserve, earnings management, inventory reserve, unapplied cash, and so on

Based on the initial review of the search term results, it may be necessary to revise and refine the search terms, particularly those search terms that result in a large volume of e-mails.

For a broader discussion on data collection, see chapters 7 ("Sources of Evidence") and 8 ("Electronic Evidence").

Analyze the Evidence

Conducting interviews of individuals who may have information pertinent to the investigation is an important step in accumulating and analyzing the evidence in an independent investigation. Possible interviewees may include those previously identified as custodians during the electronic evidence gathering. Interviews may be led by the accountant or include both the accountant and the lawyers involved in the investigation. Some employees, particularly those potentially implicated in the investigation, may request the presence of their own counsel at the interviews. Topics to cover during the interviews may include the following:

- The employee's knowledge regarding the existence of irregular financial practices and unsupported journal entries, particularly those at issue in a whistle-blower letter
- Employee's perception of the financial reporting culture and tone at the top
- Information from the employee on the internal control structure and possible deficiencies

During the course of the investigation, key employees may leave the organization (either by choice or cause), which can make it difficult to obtain historical knowledge of the accounting practices and policies.

An independent investigation also may include an analysis of general ledgers and selected journal entries and transactions. The independent investigation team may want to identify potentially unusual entries and then conduct follow-up procedures, including additional interviews and document requests to assist management in determining the appropriateness of the entries. The selection of sample entries may be based on the following:

- A fixed dollar cutoff threshold to select those entries of a large magnitude
- Considering entries with debits and credits that do not appear to make sense (that is, debits to assets and credits to cost of good sales)
- Entries with large and rounded dollar amounts (that is, $100,000)
- Manual entries or those recorded late in the quarter-end process

The forensic accountants also may want to review and analyze particularly subjective accounts (that is, bad debt, inventory obsolescence, and so on.) as well as consider a critical review of the internal audit function and those internal audit issues previously raised. For additional discussion on analyzing evidence, see chapter 7, "Sources of Evidence."

Evidence Retrieval and Reporting: Quantifying the Amounts Involved

Errors in prior period financial statements are corrected by restating prior period financial statements. FASB Statement No. 154 (FASB ASC 250) specifies the following guidance to correct errors in prior period financial statements:

> Any error in the financial statements of a prior period discovered subsequent to their issuance shall be reported as a prior-period adjustment by restating the prior-period financial statements. Restatement requires that:
>
> a. The cumulative effect of the error on periods prior to those presented shall be reflected in the carrying amounts of assets and liabilities as of the beginning of the first period presented.

> b. An offsetting adjustment, if any, shall be made to the opening balance of retained earnings (or other appropriate components of equity or net assets in the statement of financial position) for that period.
>
> c. Financial statements for each individual prior period presented shall be adjusted to reflect correction of the period-specific effects of the error.

Consistent with FASB Statement No. 154 (FASB ASC 250), IAS No. 8 also requires retrospective treatment when correcting accounting errors, except to the extent that it is impracticable to determine either the period-specific effects or the cumulative effect of the error. IAS No. 8 provides the following guidance for restating financial statements:

> An entity shall correct material prior period errors retrospectively in the first set of financial statements authorised for issue after their discovery by:
>
> a. restating the comparative amounts for the prior period(s) presented in which the error occurred; or
>
> b. if the error occurred before the earliest prior period presented, restating the opening balances of assets, liabilities and equity for the earliest prior period presented.

For more information on evidence retrieval and reporting, see chapter 12, "Reporting on Fraud."

Quantifying Misstatements

SAB No. 108 describes the SEC's view on the process that should be followed to quantify financial statement misstatements. SAB No. 108 proscribes the following two approaches for quantifying financial statement misstatements: the rollover approach and the iron curtain approach.

Rollover Approach

The rollover approach quantifies a misstatement based on the amount of the error originating in the current year income statement. This approach ignores the effects of correcting the portion of the current year balance sheet misstatement that originated in prior years (that is, it ignores the carryover impact of prior year misstatements). In SAB No. 108, the SEC staff indicates that one of the limitations of the rollover approach is that it can result in the accumulation of significant misstatements on the balance sheet that are deemed immaterial, in part because the amount that originates in each year is quantitatively small.

Iron Curtain Approach

Alternatively, the iron curtain approach quantifies the misstatement based on the effects of correcting the misstatements existing in the balance sheet at the end of the current year, irrespective of the year of origination of the misstatement(s). The limitation of the iron curtain approach is that it does not consider the correction of prior year misstatements in the current year (that is, reversal of the carryover effects) to be errors. Correcting any immaterial errors that existed in those statements in the current period to reflect the "correct" accounting would not be considered errors in the current period.

SAB No. 108 proscribes that an entity should quantify a misstatement under both the rollover approach and the iron curtain approach and adjust the financial statements if either approach results in a material misstatement after considering all relevant quantitative and qualitative factors. Additionally, if a prior year correction is material to the current year, the prior year financial statements should be corrected even if the revision previously was (and continues to be) immaterial to the prior-year financial statements.

Disclosure Requirements

FASB Statement No. 154 (FASB ASC 250) specifies the following disclosure requirements when financial statements are restated to correct an error:

> When financial statements are restated to correct an error, the entity shall disclose that its previously issued financial statements have been restated, along with a description of the nature of the error. The entity also shall disclose the following:
> a. The effect of the correction on each financial statement line item and any per-share

amounts affected for each prior period presented
> b. The cumulative effect of the change on retained earnings or other appropriate components of equity or net assets in the statement of financial position, as of the beginning of the earliest period presented.

In addition, the entity shall make the disclosures of prior-period adjustments and restatements required by paragraph 26 of APB Opinion No. 9, *Reporting the Results of Operations.*

Solving the Problem— Before, During, and After the Restatement

One of the key challenges management faces in addressing allegations of financial statement fraud is the twofold challenge that accompanies the allegations: how do you ensure the current financial information being prepared by the company is accurate while at the same time fixing the historical financial statements. In our experience, management is best served by addressing these two questions simultaneously. As facts are determined from the investigation, immediate implementation of remedial actions are required and demonstrate management's commitment to getting to the right answer. These actions can include the following:

Personnel Actions

Terminations, warnings, and job changes can all play a part in reestablishing an appropriate control environment. One of the largest challenges a company can face is to prove that it has changed the tone at the top after allegations of a fraud are proven. However, wholesale changes at the most senior level of the organization can destroy a company's ability to function and are only warranted in the most extreme situations. Independent investigators often recommend a tiered series of actions (ranging from termination to compensation adjustments) based on the findings related to specific personnel.

New or Improved Internal Controls

In some cases, significant deficiencies are found around key accounts that require subjective estimates. These deficiencies may have enabled inappropriate adjustments to the estimates to be recorded to achieve a particular goal. Management can implement immediate control enhancements to ensure that unwanted adjustments or adjustments without appropriate approval are not recorded. The immediate implementation of these controls can provide a starting point for confidence in the level of controls over current financial information. Companies that wait too long to implement needed control improvements can find themselves reviewing massive amounts of historical information, further delaying the issuance of financial statements.

Increasing Technical Accounting Expertise

A key finding of independent investigators is often that there is a lack of awareness of accounting guidance and the correct application of that guidance. By increasing a company's technical resources, either through engaging outside advisors or hiring additional highly qualified individuals, management can again demonstrate its focus on addressing the root cause of the historical error. Creating a technical accounting function that reviews and approves significant subjective estimates or key accounting decisions provides a level of clarity and additional control that can provide further confidence in the preparation of financial information.

Employee Education

Highlighting the issues identified by an independent review to employees is a useful method to illustrate the tone at the top. Often, management will present to key employees (sales personnel, legal and compliance officers, accounting and finance personnel, and others) the findings of the independent review, including key documents that illustrate the nature of the issue and the unacceptable behaviors that resulted in the investigation and ensuing actions. Regulators often look to the robustness of this type of education as an illustration of the company's efforts to implement remedial actions to address the root causes of the restatement. Chapter 14, "Antifraud Programs," goes into greater detail on the types of employee

education policies that an organization can institute to help make employees aware of fraudulent activity and the potential consequences of a fraud event.

Document Holds and Preservation

Due to the significant amount of regulatory inquiry and litigation that can result from financial statement restatements, management must often oversee large scale document holds and preservations. Ensuring document hold notices are followed can be difficult, but the cost and harm that can befall an organization without significant focus on this area can be important. In addition, the time between the initiation of a document hold and the conclusion of regulatory inquiry can span more than five years, which is why ensuring a reliable and consistent process across that length of time is key.

Impact of Financial Statement Restatements

Financial statement restatements can have significant and lasting impacts on employees, shareholders, and other corporate stakeholders. The company may face financial penalties from regulatory authorities, not to mention the significant fees incurred for attorneys, accountants, and consultants to quantify and effect the restatement. Employees, creditors, and shareholders frequently face a financial impact through job cuts, reduction in market capitalization, and limited and increasingly expensive access to the capital markets. Operationally, the efforts required by the company to address the restatement may detract from the company's strategic initiatives and growth imperatives, resulting in a competitive disadvantage.

Financial Penalties and Related Costs

Fines and penalties that are imposed by government authorities related to financial statement restatements can be significant. As an example, the fines imposed on Fannie Mae[10] by the SEC and the

---

10 May 23, 2006, SEC press release titled *SEC and OFHEO Announce Resolution of Investigation and Special Examination of Fannie Mae.*

Office of Federal Housing Enterprise Oversight in May 2006 were $400 million. In addition to civil and criminal fines, a company may face significant administrative, legal, accounting, and staffing costs related to financial statement restatements.

As previously mentioned, when faced with a financial statement restatement, particularly one driven by accounting improprieties, a company will typically initiate a formal independent investigation at the direction of the audit committee or a smaller subset of the board of directors, which is often referred to as a special committee. These independent investigations frequently require the services of outside counsel and forensic accountants, at a significant cost to the company. Fees for the company's external auditors also will rise as the auditors work to understand the work of the independent investigation and audit the restated financial statements. In addition to external resources, restatements require considerable internal staffing from the company to prepare revised financial statements and respond to inquiries from the auditors, external counsel, forensic accountants, creditors, shareholders, and regulators.

In recent years, regulators have increased the use of deferred prosecution agreements. With deferred prosecution agreements, the government will file charges against the company but will agree to delay prosecution, pending the company's successful completion of certain remedial actions. Although deferred prosecution agreements may delay or otherwise limit the civil and criminal fines previously

mentioned, the remediation process inherent in deferred prosecution agreements is not without cost. Deferred prosecution agreements increase the company's costs of regulatory reporting, particularly if an independent monitor is appointed to track the company's compliance with the agreed remedial actions.

The company also will likely be required to designate certain internal resources within the company to meet the demands of the deferred prosecution agreement and other restatement issues. These regulatory demands (and additional costs) also may include the replacement of senior company staff if they are deemed involved in the intentional misstatement of the financial statements.

Reduction in Market Capitalization

One of the most obvious impacts of a financial statement restatement is the reduction in the company's market capitalization. Restatements can have a considerable impact on share prices in both the immediate and longer term and can result in significant financial losses to investors. A U.S. Treasury report[11] released in April 2008 and covering the period from 1997 to 2006 noted that the average market reaction to restatement announcements is negative. The study also found more severe market reactions in cases in which the restatement involved fraud or revenue accounting.

The U.S. Treasury study noted the following average, median, and most negative market returns (in percentages) that resulted from fraud restatements:

	1997	1998	1999	2000	2001	2002	2003	2004	2005	2006	Over
Number	20	27	28	42	29	39	21	12	25	21	264
Average	−15%	−27%	−16%	−17%	− 6%	−13%	−10%	− 6%	− 5%	− 8%	− 13%
Median	−13%	−19%	− 3%	− 8%	− 2%	− 9%	− 5%	− 3%	− 4%	− 4%	− 6%
Most Negative	−59%	−92%	−76%	−79%	−70%	−93%	−75%	−53%	−64%	−28%	− 93%

A weakened market capitalization may have broader impacts beyond just the loss in stock value to investors. In some cases, a depressed stock price may leave the company vulnerable as a takeover target, and, in extreme cases, the company's ability

to continue as a going concern may be threatened. The company may be forced to declare Chapter 11 and in some cases Chapter 7 bankruptcy. The U.S. Treasury report also noted that average debt ratings tended to decline significantly around the time of a

---

11 April 2008 U.S. Treasury report titled *The Changing Nature and Consequences of Public Company Financial Restatements: 1997–2006.*

restatement announcement. Specifically, the study found that the average rating decreased 0.59 from the preannouncement to the announcement year, or slightly more than half a rating category.

Commercial and Operational Impacts

Restatements have negative effects on the commercial and operational activities of the company. In addition to the financial hardship imposed by the financial penalties and the distraction to corporate staff, companies facing financial restatements are typically wrought with considerable negative publicity.

The brand name and reputation of the company may suffer as a result of the publicity, and the company may be forced to expend additional costs to offset the negative effects of the restatement. Customers become more reluctant to enter into transactions and demand better concessions, bankers are more reluctant to extend lines of credit, and general confidence in the company is shaken.

Operationally, restatements also can result in the breach of loan covenants of current loan agreements, which could lead to a large loan facility coming due immediately, in certain circumstances. Obtaining waivers of the loan covenants so operations can be continued is extremely expensive and places high demands on the time of senior management. Restrictions in funding uses limit a company's ability to expand business operations and meet prior commitments. Ultimately, the renegotiation of loan facilities may lead to increased rates of interest and difficulty in identifying suitable sources of financing.

Personal Effect on Employees

Individual employees and executives of the restating company can be faced with large personal financial exposure through fines, penalties, legal fees, and disgorgement of their compensation for the period of the restatement. Many executives' wealth is tied to the value of the company and can be significantly diminished as a result of the falling share price.

Employees, officers, and directors may face criminal and civil actions, in addition to the disciplinary actions that may be imposed by the company. The SEC and DOJ may commence investigations that have the possible result of either enforcement actions or criminal charges. Employees also may face civil litigation from investors. Consequently, an individual officer may be left with the considerable financial burden of defending civil and criminal charges using his or her own resources, in addition to any penalties, fines, and disgorgement of bonuses.

It should be noted that the Sarbanes-Oxley Act increased the number of criminal offenses faced by employees as a result of corporate accounting frauds. Examples include the whistle-blower retaliation laws, increased jail time for certain offenses, and increased criminal sentences of up to 20 years for the offenses of mail fraud and wire fraud.

For employees not implicated by the wrongdoing, the impacts of the restatement may be demoralizing and also may affect the employees financially if the company initiates job layoffs or the employees' compensation is tied to the stock price of the company.

A rather well-known example is the Computer Associates financial restatement case,[12] which demonstrates the impact of a company's restatement. The company had been running a company-wide scheme to meet market expectations by backdating contracts and extending the quarterly close to record revenue from contracts executed after the end of the quarter. In total, the company prematurely recognized over $3.4 billion in revenue from January 1, 1998, to September 30, 2000. Three of the company's former top executives also were charged: the CEO and chairman, the head of Sales, and the general counsel. The outcome for each of the former top executives looked like this:

- The Company agreed to pay $225 million in restitution to shareholders to settle a civil case brought by the SEC and to defer criminal charges by the U.S. Department of Justice.
- The CEO and the head of sales were forced to resign.

---

12 SEC Accounting and Auditing Enforcement Release No. 2106 issued September 22, 2004.

- The General Counsel pleaded guilty to securities fraud conspiracy and obstruction of justice and agreed to be barred from working as an officer or director of a public corporation.

Conclusion

As previously described, financial statement restatements due to fraud are incredibly damaging to companies, shareholders, board members, and employees. Since the implementation of the Sarbanes-Oxley Act, SEC-registered companies have significantly improved their fraud-detection capabilities. However, continued vigilance is necessary because incentives to commit fraud for personal benefit continue to exist. Many companies have adopted a best practice of annual fraud risk assessments throughout their businesses, which are designed to identify those areas that could be subject to manipulation. These assessments, when shared with the internal and external audit function, create awareness around financial statement fraud risk that can act as both a strong deterrent and detection mechanism. Through continued vigilance and evolution of their internal control structures, corporations will continue to stay ahead of potential problems.

4

Foreign Corrupt Practices Act Investigations

SanDee I. Priser, Partner/Principal
Jennifer Baskin, Manager

Introduction

The Foreign Corrupt Practices Act (FCPA) has attracted renewed attention in recent years with an increasing number of enforcement actions taken against companies and significantly higher penalties imposed on them. When FCPA-related allegations are raised, investigations and corresponding forensic accounting engagements ensue.

Potential FCPA pitfalls can be encountered in the day-to-day activities of most companies. Problem areas for companies include the following:

- Paying intermediaries with a vague business purpose or no tangible work performed
- Obtaining and retaining detailed documentation describing the substance, purpose, and approval of transactions
- Determining whether facilitation payments can or should be made
- Giving gifts and paying for or reimbursing lavish travel or entertainment expenses
- Making large payments made in cash
- Mischaracterizing payments in the accounting records

In this chapter, we will discuss the history and provisions of the FCPA, considerations for FCPA investigations, examples of FCPA investigations, and effective antibribery and corruption compliance programs.

History[1]

The FCPA is not a new law. It was enacted in 1977 following investigations in the mid-1970s that uncovered over $300 million of bribes or other questionable payments to foreign government officials. The law was designed to help restore confidence in the integrity of U.S. companies and generally prohibited payments to foreign officials for the purpose of obtaining or retaining business.

American companies soon complained that the law created an uneven playing field when competing abroad for business. First, their foreign competitors were not subject to the same restrictions. Second, the practice of providing money or other benefits to government officials was widely accepted in many other countries. Finally, some jurisdictions even allowed payments to government officials to qualify as tax-deductible expenses. The U.S. government encouraged other countries to adopt similar legislation, but it wasn't until the late 1990s that the Organization of Economic Cooperation and Development (OECD) issued its *Convention on Combating Bribery of Foreign Public Officials in International Business Transactions*.[2] Since that time, 37 countries have ratified the convention and have begun enacting legislation in their countries to implement the convention.[3]

Passage of the OECD convention has helped create a relatively consistent set of rules regarding antibribery payments in most industrialized countries, but many developing countries are not parties to the convention and do not have similar laws. Additionally, even among the OECD signatories, enforcement efforts vary significantly. The practical result for U.S. companies is that they are still held to a high standard globally but may be subject to local investigations and prosecution efforts in countries that have enacted legislation in response to the OECD convention.

FCPA Overview

The FCPA has two primary provisions—the antibribery provisions and the books and records provisions. Although the provisions regarding books and records may be more closely related to accounting, an understanding of the antibribery provisions is important in determining how to structure and conduct an investigation related to FCPA allegations. Separately discussed is the provision for facilitating

---

1 Helpful background and information is available in the U.S. Department of Justice's (DOJ's) *Lay-Person's Guide to FCPA*, available at www.usdoj.gov/criminal/fraud/docs/dojdocb.html.

2 See generally www.usdoj.gov/criminal/fraud/fcpa/intlagree/ for the DOJ Web site that contains information and links relating to the Organization of Economic Cooperation and Development and other international agreements.

3 See www.oecd.org/pages/0,3417,en_36734052_36761800_1_1_1_1_1,00.html.

payments exceptions. Background information considerations in planning an investigation are included when appropriate.

Antibribery Provision

At its most simple level, the FCPA makes it unlawful to corruptly take action in furtherance of directly or indirectly providing anything of value to a foreign government official with the intention of obtaining or retaining business or an improper advantage. In practice, this requires an understanding of each of the following specific elements:[4]

Applicability of the FCPA

The original FCPA applied to issuers of registered securities businesses based in or organized within the United States; "any officer, director, employee, or agent" of those businesses; and U.S. citizens or residents.[5] As noted previously, U.S. businesses complained that the FCPA did not apply to foreign businesses, which created an unfair advantage for them. The application of the FCPA was broadened in 1998 to also include foreign companies and foreign nationals.[6]

Issuers, U.S. companies, and foreign nationals are liable for actions that use U.S. commerce vehicles, including written, verbal, and electronic communications or even international travel. Beyond those activities with a domestic nexus, U.S. parent companies also are liable for the activities of their foreign subsidiaries. Nonissuer foreign companies or individuals are liable for furtherance of payment–related activities that take place within the United States.

⚑ Investigative background considerations

- What is the organizational structure of the legal or operational entity(ies) to which the FCPA allegations apply?

- Are third parties used to effect transactions? Is a background check of third parties completed to understand their structure and business activities?

- Are the entities involved controlled by an issuer or U.S.-based entity?

- Are transactions ordered or authorized by a U.S-based entity or issuer?

- Are key individuals citizens or residents of the United States?

- Do transactions with the local country make use of U.S. commerce vehicles?

- Do transactions take place in the United States?

Corrupt Intent

A corrupt intent in acting in furtherance to a payment to a foreign official is required by the FCPA, however, actual payment is not necessary to establish a violation because a promise of a benefit may be sufficient.[7] The Senate and House committees that created the FCPA in 1977 defined the word *corruptly* as "having an evil motive or purpose, an intent to wrongly influence the recipient."[8] Additionally, the act must be for the purpose of (1) influencing the government official or political party to sway an official act or decision or (2) inducing an official to perform or refrain from performing an act

---

4 Detailed coverage of applicability of the Foreign Corrupt Practices Act (FCPA) is beyond the scope of this chapter. A careful reading of the statute and consultation with legal counsel are recommended before commencing any FCPA-related investigation or antifraud compliance program. References to key portions of the statute are included in footnotes throughout this discussion.

5 15 U.S.C. §§ 78dd-1(a), 77dd-2(a) and (h)(1).

6 *Id.* §§ 77dd-3(a) and (f)(1).

7 *Id.* §§ 78dd-1(a), 78dd-2(a), 78dd-3(a).

8 S. Rep. No. 95-114, at 10 (1977).

in order to obtain or retain business.[9] Corrupt intent may be inferred by secretive or surreptitious actions in pursuit of a quid pro quo arrangement. Corrupt intent is often assumed by enforcement officials if other elements are present. The FCPA does include an exception for "routine governmental action,"[10] which is discussed in more detail later.

In a recent case, a naturalized U.S. citizen was charged with violations of the FCPA by bribing, offering a bribe, and attempting to bribe a foreign government official. While working for a French company, the individual attempted to influence Chinese government officials to award a substantial contract to the individual's company and also illegally provided technical information and assistance about the development of systems at a major facility. Although this case has not been tried, it should be noted that the charges center around not just payment of a bribe but also the promise or offer of a bribe.[11]

⚑ Investigative background considerations

- How are government contracts or other government business arrangements awarded in the local country?

- Business permits

  - What business permits are required to operate in the local country?

  - How are they obtained?

  - Are set fee schedules for the permits available?

  - Which general ledger accounts are used to track expenses related to government permits?

- Government or state-owned customers

  - How does the company pursue contracts or business with government entities?

  - How many customers does the local company have that are government customers?

  - How many contracts does the company have with the local government or its agencies?

    - Who manages those contracts and relationships?

    - Is there a special process for setting up a government customer in the financial or other systems?

    - Does the company maintain a list of all government or state-owned customers and does that list undergo periodic review?

    - Are contracts centrally maintained to allow for efficient management and oversight of the government relationships?

- Government or state-owned vendors

  - How many vendors does the local company have that are government vendors?

  - Are the government vendors, if any, related to utilities or other municipal services?

  - Are payments to utilities made on a regularly scheduled basis (monthly, quarterly, or annually) or on an irregular schedule?

  - Are payments to government vendors periodically reviewed?

  - How is business awarded to nonutility government vendors? Are bids solicited? Is there competition for the bids?

  - Does the company maintain a list of all government or state-owned vendors and does that list undergo periodic review?

  - Are contracts centrally maintained?

---

9 Ibid.

10 *Id.* §§ 78dd-1(b), 78dd-2(b), 78dd-3(b).

11 DOJ Release No. 08-851 issued September 24, 2008.

Prohibited Actions

The FCPA also prohibits not only actual payments but also acts in furtherance of an "offer, ... promise to pay, or authorization of the payment."[12] An actual payment need not be made by the entity or individual for a violation of the FCPA to have occurred. Potentially violative actions could include approving a payment, relaying e-mail instructions to make the payment, discussing payments via telephone, acquiescing in payment, knowingly cooperating in payment, covering up the payment, or creating or accepting false documentation.

Discussed later are the intricacies of the related books and records provisions of the FCPA that cover how payments are recorded in the accounting system.

by a foreign official, scholarships or travel for family members of the recipient, overpayment for services or underpricing of assets, or excessively "facilitating payment." Red flags and other travel and entertainment considerations are discussed in more detail later.

In a recent case, the subsidiary of Delta & Pine Land Company required business permits in order to operate within Turkey. To secure the business permits, Turk Deltapine, Inc., paid officials of the Turkish Ministry of Agricultural and Rural Affairs over $43,000 in bribes of cash and other forms, including travel expenses, hotel expenses, computers, office furniture, refrigerators, and air conditioners.[14]

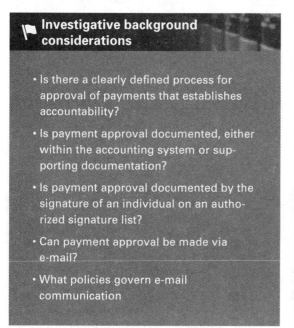

Investigative background considerations

- Is there a clearly defined process for approval of payments that establishes accountability?

- Is payment approval documented, either within the accounting system or supporting documentation?

- Is payment approval documented by the signature of an individual on an authorized signature list?

- Can payment approval be made via e-mail?

- What policies govern e-mail communication

Investigative background considerations

- Does the company have policies regarding gift giving or donations? Is training provided for those policies? Are compliance audits conducted?

- What types of gift giving are considered reasonable and customary in the local country?

- Based on the economic and political environment of the local country, what might the threshold be to consider a gift or payment of sufficient value to influence a business decision?

- What types of gifts does the company or its agents in the local country typically give to customers or others? For example, company-branded items or gifts for specific occasions (birthdays, name days, anniversaries, births, deaths, weddings, promotions, and so on). What forms do those gifts take?

- Is authorization required to give gifts generally or is it based on the size of the gift?

(continued)

A Bribe or Anything of Value

The FCPA further specifies that a payment includes not only monetary transfers but also an "offer, gift, promise to give, or authorization of the giving of anything of value."[13] This covers a wide variety of items beyond cash, such as lavish gifts or entertainment, lavish travel expenses, improper campaign contributions, contributions to charities endorsed

---

12 *Id.* §§ 78dd-1(a), 78dd-2(a), 78dd-3(a).

13 Ibid.

14 Securities and Exchange Commission (SEC) Administrative Proceeding Release No. 34-56138 issued July 26, 2007.

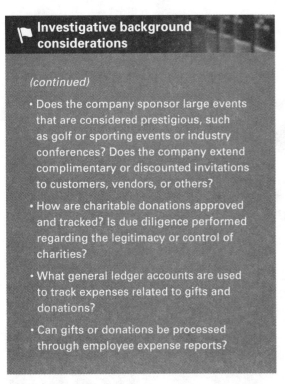

Investigative background considerations

(continued)

- Does the company sponsor large events that are considered prestigious, such as golf or sporting events or industry conferences? Does the company extend complimentary or discounted invitations to customers, vendors, or others?

- How are charitable donations approved and tracked? Is due diligence performed regarding the legitimacy or control of charities?

- What general ledger accounts are used to track expenses related to gifts and donations?

- Can gifts or donations be processed through employee expense reports?

To a Foreign Official

The FCPA prohibits payments or other benefits to "any foreign official,"[15] which includes not only high-level officials but also traditional government employees, persons acting on behalf of a government, private advisors to the government, relatives of government officials, and political party officials or candidates, to name a few.[16] Examples of individuals who have been considered foreign officials include ministry or agency employees; judges; legislators; local officials; employees of government-controlled companies; employees of state-owned universities; private persons acting in an official capacity; officials of public international organizations; candidates for office; political parties or their officials; and spouses, dependents, or siblings of an official.

The inclusion of political party officials can become complex in countries where state-owned entities are common. Additionally, when state-owned entities are privatized, members of management may still have affiliations with political parties that may qualify them as foreign officials. Existence of royal

family members and the extent of their involvement in the government or political parties also may warrant consideration.

Investigative background considerations

- What are the structures of the government, political parties, and government agencies in the local country?

- Does the company have a policy regarding government interactions?

- Is there a contact in the local country who coordinates government relations or regulatory affairs?

- Do employees or agents interact with government employees on a regular basis? If so, in what capacities?

- Are donations given to local or municipal organizations (for example, schools and hospitals)? If so, how are they solicited, approved, and tracked?

- Is an effort made to determine whether customers or vendors are state-owned entities or led by individuals who have political party affiliations? If so, how is that information tracked and maintained? Which department is responsible for collecting and maintaining that information?

Directly or Indirectly

In addition to prohibiting corrupt payments to foreign officials that are made directly by entities or individuals, the FCPA also prohibits making those payments through "any person" knowing that all or part of the payment "will be offered, given, or promised" to a foreign official with corrupt intent, as previously described.[17] The term *knowing* has been interpreted to include both conscious disregard as well as deliberate ignorance.

In a recent case, the owners of the U.S. company Film Festival Management, Inc., were charged with

---

15 *Id.* §§ 78dd-1(a)(1), 78dd-2(a)(1), 78dd-3(a)(1).

16 *Id.* §§ 78dd-1(f)(1), 78dd-2(h)(2).

17 78dd-1(a)(3), 78dd-2(a)(3), 78dd-3(a)(3).

paying bribes both directly and indirectly to foreign officials while seeking contracts to run the Bangkok International Film Festival (BKKIFF). The BKKIFF receives funds from the Tourism Authority of Thailand (TAT), a government agency. To secure their position in the BKKIFF, the U.S. company paid over $900,000 in bribes to the BKKIFF "president" who was also a senior government official of the TAT. In addition to making cash payments directly to the foreign official, the US company made indirect payments to the bank accounts of the daughter and a friend of the government official.[18] Additionally, the individuals were charged with paying kickbacks to a former governor of the TAT in order to secure additional contracts with the TAT.[19]

Use of agents, distributors, joint ventures, or other third parties who may make corrupt payments to foreign officials may thus create vicarious liability for the entity that allows the third party to act on its behalf.

For example, the CEO of Kellogg, Brown, & Root, Inc., entered into sham contracts with two "agents" to funnel money to Nigerian officials through "consulting" or "services" agreements. The CEO pled guilty to FCPA and mail and wire fraud violations related to the sham contracts. He faces seven years in prison and payment of $10.8 million in restitution.[20] Outside parties involved in agency agreements, consultant agreements, service agreements, and third-party agreements are all subject to review and background investigation.

Contracting third parties requires careful screening and due diligence procedures to ensure the partner is reputable and to avoid potential liability. Recent Department of Justice Opinion Procedure releases stress the need for in-depth preacquisition due diligence and expansive postacquisition training and investigations into potential FCPA violations, especially in cases in which preacquisition due diligence is limited in scope or timing.[21] Although the recent opinions do not give a free pass to companies purchasing foreign operations that have FCPA violations, the opinions do provide companies with

a clear reminder of the importance of due diligence in all activities with third parties and acquisitions.

Examples of due diligence procedures are discussed later in this chapter.

Investigative background considerations

- What types of third parties are used to transact business in a particular country?
  - Distributors?
  - Joint venture partners?
  - Independent contractors?
  - Others?
- Is the decision to engage third parties made locally or is regional or headquarter approval required?
- Are due diligence procedures performed prior to engaging the third party?
  - What types of procedures?
  - Is there standard documentation or checklists of procedures to perform?
  - Who performs the due diligence procedures?
  - Who reviews the due diligence results?
- Are there limits to the duration of contracts with third parties?
- Is due diligence performed periodically after the third party is engaged? How often? Only at contract renewal?
- Is the third party contractually required to follow the FCPA and other local country antibribery or anticorruption laws?
- Is training on company policies and procedures (for example, FCPA and corporate code of conduct) provided to management or employees of the third parties?

---

18 DOJ Release No. 08-032 issued January 17, 2008.

19 DOJ Release No. 08-134 issued October 2, 2008.

20 SEC Litigation Release No. 20700 issued September 3, 2008.

21 DOJ Opinion Procedure Release Nos. 2008-01 and 2008-02 issued January 15, 2008, and June 13, 2008, respectively.

To Obtain Business or Improper Advantage

The purpose of the provision of a bribe or anything of value to an official must be to obtain or retain business or an improper advantage. As discussed subsequently, there is an affirmative defense for bona fide business expenses and an exception for payments to expedite nondiscretionary government action. It is when payments cross the line to being exchanges in return for something to which the company is not entitled that the expense and related advantage may become improper.

Examples of improper advantage may include the following:

- Efforts to increase profits on transactions with a particular entity
- Prevent adverse government action
- Obtain regulatory approvals
- Obtain or renew a contract
- Have access to bids of competitors
- Attempt to reduce or avoid taxes

⚑ **Investigative background considerations**

- What is the general process for making sales within each business unit or for each product line?
- How are decision makers identified for sales?
- Is training provided to sales or marketing employees describing what is appropriate or inappropriate in expenditures that may influence decision makers?
- What sales techniques are taught or otherwise encouraged during sales training?
- What types of expenditures are explicitly allowed for sales and marketing purposes?
- Are budgets set for those categories?

- Are expenditures and comparison to budgets monitored?
- To which general ledger accounts are each of these types of expenditures booked?
- Which of those types of expenditures may benefit an individual or group of individuals rather than the general business (for example, entertainment expenditures versus printing of product brochures)?
- Do the company's policies prohibit certain types of expenditures that are considered inappropriate for sales and marketing?
- For which types of expenditures are third parties involved?

Books and Records Provision

In addition to the antibribery provisions previously described, the FCPA imposes additional requirements on Securities and Exchange Commission (SEC) registrants related to books and records and internal controls. These provisions are designed to complement the antibribery portions of the FCPA so that it is more difficult for issuers to make or hide corrupt payments.

The FCPA requires that books and records be kept to, "in reasonable detail, accurately and fairly reflect the transactions and dispositions of the assets of the issuer."[22] Further, an internal control system must be maintained to provide "reasonable assurance" that transactions are executed and recorded in a way to permit preparation of financial statements in accordance with generally accepted accounting principles and that access to assets is permitted only in accordance with management authorization.[23]

The net results of the books and records and internal control provisions are that bribes must be

---

22 78m(b)(2)(A).
23 78m(b)(2)(B).

recorded as bribes, not obscured or described as something else. The issuer's management is responsible for ensuring correct classification and accounting for all operations of the company, regardless of the country in which the books are maintained or a transaction occurs. No direct knowledge is required of officers of the issuer to hold the issuer accountable, which essentially establishes strict liability for inaccurate books and records. Finally, the FCPA conspicuously does not define a materiality threshold for a violation so any size payment or object of value can be violative.

Although the SEC and Department of Justice (DOJ) have not provided direct guidance on how bribes or facilitating payments should be recorded, many of the charges brought against companies have included a violation of the books and records and internal control provisions. Because violations under this portion of the FCPA can bring criminal fines of up to $25 million against the company and individual fines of up to $5 million with up to 20 years of imprisonment, companies and their executives should maintain an awareness of company internal controls and develop an accounting policy that specifically defines how these transactions should be recorded.

Recently, Willbros Group, Inc., and several executives entered into a judgment agreement with the SEC and DOJ for violations of the FCPA, including a criminal prosecution of the books and records provision. The company was ordered to disgorge $8.9 million of profits in addition to prejudgment interest of $1.4 million. Jason Steph, a former supervisory employee in the Nigerian operations, may pay a civil penalty (the amount to be determined in the future by the court). Gerald Jansen, a former administrative supervisor in the Nigerian operations, will pay a civil penalty of $30,000, and Carlos Galvez, a former accounting employee in Bolivia, will pay a civil penalty of $35,000.[24] One additional defendant, Jim Bob Brown, settled criminal and civil charges; however, he is awaiting sentencing.

Investigative background considerations

- Do company policies clearly state how expenses should be described in the accounting system and documented with support?

- Is training provided to the accounting department on classification of expenses for charitable contributions, marketing expenses, and other miscellaneous expenses?

- Is training provided to the accounting department on the key aspects of the FCPA books and records provisions?

- Is training provided to the sales and marketing departments on the key aspects of the FCPA books and records provisions? Are sales and marketing department executives familiar with company policies governing how expenses are recorded and required support for recorded expenses?

Facilitating Payments Exception and Affirmative Defenses

The FCPA provides an exception for payments known as *facilitating payments* to expedite or obtain a routine government action. The FCPA mentions specific examples, such as obtaining business permits or licenses; processing paperwork, such as visas; providing general government services related to transit of goods within the country; or basic services, such as utilities.[25] It does not, however, extend to the award of new or the extension of existing business with the government.[26] Further, the official action that is being expedited must not be discretionary.

In the Turk Deltapine, Inc., case discussed previously, payments were made to government officials to obtain certifications and approvals that officials

---

24 SEC Litigation Release No. 20571 issued May 14, 2008.

25 *Id.* §§ 78dd-1(f)(3)(A), 78dd-2(h)(4)(A), 78dd-3(f)(4)(A).

26 *Id.* §§ 78dd-1(f)(3)(B), 78dd-2(h)(4)(B), 78dd-3(f)(4)(B).

prepared during their standard course of business. Issues arise when payments made to an official influence the official to do something he or she should not do beyond the timing of the performance of his or her duty. Inspectors who received payments from Turk Deltapine, Inc., sometimes failed to conduct inspections or failed to conduct them properly; however, the officials provided paperwork certifying that the inspections had been completed.[27]

Westinghouse Air Brake Technologies Corporation, owner of Indian subsidiary Pioneer Friction Limited, entered into a nonprosecution agreement with the DOJ for improper payments made and facilitated to several railway regulatory boards. The payments were made in order to schedule preshipping product inspections and obtain the issuance of compliance certificates. Payments also were made to the Central Board of Excise and Customs to stop what the company thought were excessive audits. The payments were as small as $67 per product inspection and $31.50 per month to decrease the audits, but they totaled $40,000 during one year. This case highlights one of the main difficulties for companies with multinational operations—how the corporate office monitors payments, whether illegal or potentially legal facilitating payments, made by subsidiaries.[28]

Many companies ban facilitating payments because, although they are not FCPA violations, they are hard to monitor and may violate local laws.

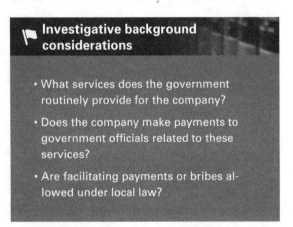

Investigative background considerations

- What services does the government routinely provide for the company?
- Does the company make payments to government officials related to these services?
- Are facilitating payments or bribes allowed under local law?

Local Law

Exempted payments must be permitted under the written laws and regulations of the host country. General practice in the country is not sufficient. Where bribery is not prohibited, local law opinion can help defeat allegations of corrupt intent; however, the local law defense has never been applied in court.

Promotional Expenditures

Exempted payments must be bona fide, reasonable, and directly related to the (*a*) promotion, demonstration, or explanation of products or services or (*b*) execution or performance of a contract with a foreign government or an agency of the foreign government. A frequent example used is the provision of a trip to the United States for an official government customer to visit the plant where a product is manufactured or learn more about how to use the product. This may be a bona fide expense in certain circumstances. However, if the company also pays for a family member of the foreign official to visit the United States or provides a side trip to Las Vegas, the expenses would not appear to be defensible as bona fide promotional expenditures.

A recent settled case against Lucent Technologies Inc. brought to light a common business practice of providing presale and postsale trips, also known as *factory inspection trips* or *training trips*, to foreign officials. Although legitimate trips for customers to visit the factories of businesses are common, the FCPA prohibits trips with the primary purpose of visiting a tourist destination. Lucent Technologies Inc. provided over 315 trips to locations such as Hawaii, Las Vegas, the Grand Canyon, Niagara Falls, Disney World, Universal Studios, and New York City, with very little time spent visiting the Lucent Technologies Inc. factory sites.[29] Lucent Technologies Inc. also was found to have paid for educational opportunities, including tuition and living expenses

---

27 SEC Administrative Proceeding Release No. 34-56138 issued July 26, 2007.

28 DOJ Release No. 08-116 issued February 14, 2008; SEC Administrative Proceeding Release No. 34-57333 issued February 14, 2008; and Westinghouse Air Brake Technologies Corporation agreement with the DOJ issued February 8, 2008.

29 SEC Litigation Release No. 20414 issued December 21, 2007.

of an official attending graduate school and paying educational expenses for the child of an official.[30]

TRACE International, Inc., recently submitted an FCPA Opinion Procedure Request regarding plans to pay certain expenses for 20 journalists employed by media outlets in China to attend a press conference held by TRACE International, Inc., in Shanghai. The media outlets are mostly owned by the Chinese government. The Opinion Release stated that the planned expenses are "reasonable under the circumstances and directly relate to 'the promotion, demonstration, or explanation of [TRACE's] products or services.'" The DOJ did note that during the determination of its opinion, it gave no weight to the common practice of "companies in the PRC to provide such benefits to journalists attending a press conference."[31]

Penalties and Enforcement

The FCPA has both criminal and civil penalties. The DOJ is the primary enforcer and handles all criminal penalties. Enforcement of civil penalties is generally performed by the SEC, with some enforcement by the DOJ in certain instances.

The penalties can be severe, ranging from fines to jail time. Antibribery provision violations can result in fines of up to $2 million per occurrence for entities and fines of up to $100,000 or five years in prison, or both, for individuals. The penalties for violation of the books and records and internal control provisions can be even harsher—fines of up to $25 million for entities and fines of up to $5 million or 20 years in prison, or both, for individuals. In addition, civil penalties also may apply, and companies are prohibited from indemnifying convicted officers, employees, or other individuals for payment of fines.[32]

Enforcement of the FCPA has dramatically increased in recent years. Enforcement actions increased from only 15 in 2006 to more than 30 in both years 2007 and 2008. Recent years have shown an increase in the number of voluntary disclosures, cooperation among multinational prosecutors, increasing fines and disgorgement payments, and higher penalties for companies without effective compliance programs. The government also has been seeking more intrusive remedies, such as government-imposed monitors who may be given access to corporate records, real-time access to calendars of top officers, and the ability to impose changes to FCPA-related compliance processes. The costs of these monitors must be borne by the entity and can often be quite costly such as the well-publicized fee between $28 and 52 million charged by the independent monitor for Zimmer, Inc. under its deferred prosecution agreement that ended March 2009.[33]

A few recent examples may serve to illustrate the current state of FCPA enforcement:

- Baker Hughes Incorporated agreed to pay a total of $44 million in penalties that comprised an $11 million civil penalty and disgorgement of approximately $33 million. In Kazakhstan, a Baker Hughes Incorporated subsidiary paid approximately $4.1 million in commission payments to a consulting firm for a services contract that generated $205 million in business for Baker Hughes Incorporated. An additional $1.4 million of commission payments were made to another agent for the purpose of influencing government decision making.[34]

- The Titan Corporation paid $3.5 million over 3 years to its agent in Africa in an effort to secure a telecom contract. The agent was a business advisor to the country's president, and the payments were recorded as consulting services. In 2005, The Titan Corporation pled guilty to 3 felonies,

---

30 DOJ Release No. 07-1028 issued December 21, 2007, and DOJ Non-Prosecution Agreement issued November 14, 2007.

31 DOJ Opinion Procedure Release No. 08-03 issued July 11, 2008.

32 78dd-2(g)(2), 78dd-3(e)(2), 78ff(c)(2).

33 See Zimmer Holdings Inc. Press Release at http://investor.zimmer.com/secfiling.cfm?filingID=950137-07-16322 which states a monthly monitorship fee of between $1,550,000 and $2,900,000 for a period of 18 months.

34 SEC Litigation Release No. 20094 issued April 26, 2007, and SEC filing against Baker Hughes Incorporated issued April 26, 2007.

paid a $13 million fine, entered into an SEC consent degree, paid $15.5 million in disgorgement of ill-gotten gains, and was required to retain an independent monitor.[35]

- Four of Vetco International Ltd.'s subsidiaries authorized an agent to make multiple payments totaling $2.1 million to Nigerian Customs Services to procure preferential customs treatment for deepwater oil drilling equipment. In 2007, 3 of the subsidiaries pled guilty to antibribery violations and conspiracy, resulting in a $26 million total fine, which was the largest fine to date in a DOJ prosecution.[36] A deferred prosecution agreement was created for one subsidiary, which consented to DOJ preapproval of appointments of executive chairpersons, majority members of the compliance committee, and compliance counsel.[37]

- Baker Hughes Incorporated; Schnitzer Steel Industries, Inc.; Ingersoll-Rand Company Limited; York International Corporation; Paradigm B.V.; Vetco International Inc.; Statoill Iydro; ABB; Diagnostic Products Corporation; DPC (Tianjin) Ltd.; InVision; Micrus Corporation; Monsanto Company; and Titan Corporation all have monitors or consultants to ensure FCPA compliance as part of their settlement agreement with the SEC and DOJ. In some cases, the monitor can be appointed for a period of up to three years.

- Siemens AG and certain of its subsidiaries agreed to pay a combined total of $1.6 billion in fines, penalties, and disgorgement of profits following investigations led by the DOJ, SEC, and the Munich Public Prosecutor's office. It was the largest monetary sanction imposed related to FCPA violations. Close cooperation and international mutual legal assistance were cited as keys to the successful prosecution. Over $800 million of the fines related to SEC and DOJ charges relating to violations of the books and records and internal control provisions, including criminal charges. The global investigation revealed corrupt payments of more than $1.4 billion were to government officials in Asia, Africa, America, the Middle East, and Europe. Siemens agreed to retain an independent compliance monitor for 4 years. The SEC noted the "pattern of bribery by Simens was unprecedented in scale and geographic reach."[38]

Conducting the Investigation

FCPA investigations are in many ways similar to other types of forensic accounting investigations. However, as previously described, specific legal requirements and cultural considerations often differentiate an FCPA investigation; the manner in which it is conducted; the types of procedures that may be performed; the types of information gathered and analyzed; and the form of a report to the client, if any. The sections that follow provide additional details and considerations when planning and performing forensic accounting investigations for an FCPA matter and help companies proactively develop FCPA policies, procedures, and monitoring programs.

When conducting an investigation, the investigation team should keep the questions outlined in box 4-1 in mind because they may be asked to provide a report to the investigating government.

Box 4-1: *Report Submission Due Diligence Considerations*

- What happened?
- How did it happen (for example, failure of controls or collusion)?
- Who was involved?
- What documentation or electronic media has been preserved and is available?
- What subsidiaries and jurisdictions are involved?

---

35 SEC Litigation Release No. 19107 issued March 1, 2005.
36 DOJ Release No. 07-075 issued February 6, 2007.
37 DOJ Deferred Prosecution Agreement with Aibel Group (Vetco).
38 DOJ Release No. 08-1105 issued December 15, 2008.

- What disciplinary actions, if any, have been taken against involved individuals?

- What is the approximate value of corrupt payments?

- What procedures did you perform to determine what happened?

- How do you know this behavior is limited to specific countries or divisions?

- How will the company ensure that this will not happen again?

The general steps in the investigation will be similar to those described in chapter 1, "Introduction to Investigations," but can be summarized as follows:

1. Engagement planning and scope setting
   a. Company, counsel, and forensic accountants discuss and determine scope
   b. Forensic accountants organize country team(s) and issue-specific industry experts
   c. Outline workplan
   d. Discuss budget
   e. Identify company, counsel, and forensic accountant points of contact
2. Predeployment team meeting
   a. Review current situation
   b. Review project management expectations
   c. Set expectations and protocols
   d. Discuss language needs across countries and locations
   e. Discuss global issues
3. Site visits and data collection
   a. Teams visit site locations
   b. Gather hard-copy and electronic documentation
   c. Constant discussion and communication between points of contact on issues and difficulties
   d. Establish data review environment
4. Document review and analysis and interviews
   a. Document review—hard copy or electronic

   b. Analysis of documentation and accounting system detail, including time and expense reports, general ledger activity, and so on
   c. Interviews of key company personnel
   d. Constant discussion and communication between teams and identified points of contact on issues and difficulties
5. Discussion of investigative findings and reports
   a. Combination of analysis from individual country teams
   b. Discussion of findings among company, counsel, and forensic accountants
   c. Communication of findings
6. Wrap up and follow up
   a. Follow up on any open issues or points recognized through discussion of findings
   b. Wrap up of all remaining items

Industry Considerations

Most companies have some interaction with government officials, whether as customers, providers of utilities, obtaining business permits, importing goods, or other activities. Certain industries, by their very nature, tend to have more regular contact with government officials and potential incentives to develop relationships with government officials in order to receive business or preferential treatment. Additionally, industry issues may arise based on the industries in which customers and vendors operate.

Defense and Construction

In the defense and industrial construction industries, companies often are selling large projects to a foreign government, such as through defense contracts with the military or construction of large power plants that may belong to or be run by the local government. A contract win often represents a significant amount of revenue to the proposing companies, creating incentives to influence government officials who may influence the purchasing decision. The sales pursuit cycle is often very long and may involve multiple parties. This can create a large amount of expenses related to the pursuit, making it potentially difficult to identify specific payments that may be made with corrupt intent. Subcontractors also may be involved for certain portions of the project, creating the potential for indirect payments. Finally, because government approval of the contracts is required, there are likely numerous legitimate contacts and business-related expenses, making it difficult to determine which expenses are made with an intent to improperly influence the decision-making government official.

The case against Albert Stanley, the CEO of Kellogg, Brown, & Root, Inc., highlights not only the difficulties of operations in Nigeria but also the challenges faced by construction companies. Stanley pled guilty to paying bribes to Nigerian government officials to obtain contracts to build natural gas facilities and faces a seven-year sentence.[39] Construction companies face not only strenuous bidding competitions to win a contract but must then obtain numerous permits.

Oil and Gas

Oil and gas companies often find themselves interacting with government officials to negotiate for the extraction of oil or natural gas from property located within and often owned by the country. Negotiations may take place for extraction rights, construction of oil rigs or other structures, customs on inbound equipment or transport of the gas or oil, and general business permits. As with defense and industrial construction, these arrangements are often the result of months or years of negotiations, represent a significant source of revenue both for the local country and for the company extracting the resources, and may involve the use of agents or subcontractors. Additionally, the natural resources are often located in underdeveloped countries; it is not uncommon for the negotiations and permission received to include provisions of capital improvements or infrastructure to the local country, such as schools, hospitals, water treatment plants, and so on.

The case against Willbros Group, Inc., discussed earlier displays some of the complexities of operating in the oil and gas industry. This industry is heavily scrutinized by the SEC and DOJ due to the prevalence of operations by oil and gas companies in countries with a high corruption risk.

Logistics

Logistics companies regularly transport goods in and out of countries that may be subject to customs, duties, or other charges. Because a logistics company operating in a large number of countries will be subject to a complex combination of charges and processes that may be difficult to coordinate, it may employ freight forwarders and local agents in different countries to handle the processing of the shipments.

The customs and duties are often assessed and collected by low-level government employees. Although certainly the legal customs and duties must be paid, in some cases additional "grease payments" may be made to these low-paid employees to receive expedited processing. Those payments may be legal in the local country and under the FCPA, depending on the specific nature of the payments. However, the customs official may offer the company or the agent (or accept the offer of the company or the agent) the ability to process goods at a lower tariff rate in exchange for a bribe to the government employee, which does not qualify as a facilitation payment.

Without careful agreement in advance, there may be little visibility to the logistics company on the amount and nature of fees that the agent is paying on its behalf. For example, an agent may offer a per-shipment charge and provide the logistics company with documentation supporting the number of shipments processed. However, if the per-shipment charge includes corrupt payments and the logistics company booked the entire per-shipment charge as a transportation expense, it could be violating the books and records provision of the FCPA because it did not properly classify the portion of the payment related to corrupt payments.

The Panalpina Group, under investigation by the DOJ for violations of the FCPA, completed the withdrawal of operations from the Nigerian market. Monika Ribar, the Panalpina Group CEO,

---

39 SEC Litigation Release No. 20700 issued September 3, 2008.

stated, "Admittedly foreign companies operate in an ongoing uncertain and hard to assess legal environment in Nigeria. This makes it difficult for Panalpina to offer both a comprehensive service portfolio and at the same time meet the high ethical standards as outlined in Panalpina's Code of Business Conduct."[40] Many other logistics companies face similar challenges operating in countries with a high risk of corruption.

Pharmaceutical and Medical Devices

In many countries, health care providers work for government health programs or institutions and qualify as government officials. Sales representatives of pharmaceutical, biotechnology, and medical device companies meet with health care providers on a regular basis to explain the benefits of their products and encourage the health care providers to use or prescribe their products. The companies also may pay doctors to perform research for clinical trials or speak at medical conferences, make donations to the hospitals where physicians work, or pay for health care providers to attend training sessions. Because each of these interactions may be with a government official, they may raise the specter of improper payments based on the type of payment or benefit provided to the health care provider (for example, the company may receive valuable services in return for the provided payment or the payment may be related to genuine exchanges of scientific information or to improve patient care).

Some countries or regions have developed health care compliance codes that address some of these exchanges and indicate what may be appropriate or inappropriate in a certain situation, which may be helpful in understanding general practice. In addition, most companies have similar internal health care compliance policies and procedures and may have periodic audits by compliance personnel; however, these compliance audits are not always designed to identify potential FCPA violations.

As noted in the Schering-Plough Corporation case, payments do not have to be made directly to a foreign official or their family. A charitable donation by the pharmaceutical company to an established charity caused a $500,000 fine because the charitable organization was found to be heavily supported by a senior Polish official. The charitable donation of approximately $76,000 was made to encourage the Polish official to influence the purchase of Schering-Plough Corporation's pharmaceutical products. The payments were recorded as charitable contributions, but the true purpose was concealed in accounting records by both false medical justifications and through limiting the payments to a dollar limit that was able to be paid without additional review or approval. The Schering-Plough Corporation's policies and procedures were found to be "inadequate in that they did not require employees to conduct any due diligence prior to making promotional or charitable donations to determine whether any government officials were affiliated with proposed recipients."[41]

Local Business Practices and Laws

Understanding the culture of the local country and its business practices is critical in conducting an effective FCPA investigation and identifying potential issues that must be investigated. Bribes are not prohibited by law in some countries and may be a part of generally accepted business practices. Employees in the local countries may not understand, without specific FCPA training, that payment of bribes creates liabilities for the parent company. To get a high-level understanding of the prevalence of bribes in a particular country prior to being in the field, it may be helpful to consult resources such as Transparency International's Corruption Perception Index.[42] The index is widely used and provides an overview of how the perceived level of corruption in a particular country compares with other countries.

Local laws and practices can create additional complexities for an FCPA investigation. For example, privacy laws in many countries may prevent the investigation team from taking documents (electronic or hard copy) out of the local country if they

---

40 Panalpina Group press release titled "Panalpina reports dynamic growth in the first half year" and issued July 30, 2008.

41 SEC Administrative Proceeding Release No. 34-49838 issued June 9, 2004, and SEC Litigation Release No. 18740 issued June 9, 2004.

42 Information about the index can be obtained at www.transparency.org/policy_research/surveys_indices/cpi.

contain personal or private information. This may result in the need to perform all procedures within the country and redact names and personal information from reports that are distributed outside of the local country.

In some countries, employees can consent to the sharing of their data, such as the information contained in their business files and business computer, but knowledge of this consent varies. However, if certain employees are not available to provide consent or, in fact, refuse to consent, this may still result in at least some documents and procedures needing to be performed within the country.

Additionally, some companies are signatories to the safe harbor provision of the European Union privacy directive, which allows them to share otherwise private or protected information within the company. However, even if that allowed the company to transfer data to the United States, it could still not share that data in the United States with other entities that are not signatories to the safe harbor provision, once again causing the majority of procedures and analysis to be performed in the local country.

This situation may be further complicated if the investigation also is being prosecuted by the local government. In that instance, the police may perform raids and remove documents from the company's premises before they can be reviewed. Individuals can be arrested or held for questioning, which may limit their ability to consent to the review of their documents by the company. Additionally, the concept of attorney-client privilege and the attorney work product doctrine that are ever-present in U.S. investigations and legal proceedings may not apply to the same extent, if at all, in the local country.

No Materiality Threshold

The FCPA does not establish a materiality threshold for the value of payments or other objects of value that are potentially violative. As a result, a $5 payment to a low-level customs official may be just as illegal as a $100,000 payment to a minister of health. An expense for a $30 dinner with a customer may not seem extravagant to an auditor from one country but may represent a significant amount to a low-level government official in an undeveloped country.

Paradigm B.V., a Dutch company headquartered in Houston, Texas, provides software to the oil and gas exploration and production industry. Among other violations of the FCPA, during the sale of their software to the Zhonghai Petroleum (China) Co., Ltd., a subsidiary of the China National Offshore Oil Corporation, Paradigm B.V. employed an agent to make payments of $100–$200 per official. Paradigm B.V. voluntarily disclosed the FCPA violations and completed an internal investigation. Paradigm B.V. has been fined $1 million and is required to implement rigorous internal controls, retain outside compliance counsel, and fully cooperate with the DOJ.[43]

As a practical matter, this makes identifying potentially corrupt payments difficult during an investigation. Relationships and patterns of payments may be more relevant in investigating an FCPA allegation than the value or number of payments. For example, are there vendors with the same addresses as employees or customers of the company who might lead to identification of ways of getting funds out of the company for illicit purposes? Are certain individuals mentioned frequently in expense reports of employees? Are certain employees responsible for interactions with government officials and do their expense reports reflect meetings, travel, entertainment, gifts, and meals with or for foreign officials?

Cash and Treasury Functions

When many people think of bribes, they may think of a suitcase full of cash. As financial institutions and services have matured, this scenario is less frequent, though instances remain. This results in investigators needing to understand a company's cash management and treasury functions in order to identify how money could enter or leave the country.

---

43 DOJ Release No. 07-751 issued September 24, 2007.

Travel and Entertainment Expenses

Travel and entertainment expenses are generally bona fide business expenses but can easily become illegitimate benefits when numerous or lavish expenditures are incurred with or on behalf of government officials. An FCPA investigation should generally review employee expense reports or any reimbursements to customers or others for expenses that they incurred that are ostensibly related to company business. In many companies and countries, receipts may not be required for reimbursement of small transactions, which can be a way of indirectly obtaining funds from the company that can be used for corrupt purposes.

⚑ Background considerations

- How many bank accounts do the local country operations have?

- How often are the accounts reconciled? Who performs the reconciliation?

- What is the primary means of payment in the country and for the company's operations (for example, wire transfers, checks, or cash)?

- Is there a petty cash fund at the local operation? Who is responsible for disbursements from petty cash? What documentation is required for petty cash disbursements? How often is the petty cash fund balanced or refunded?

- Are cash advances made to employees for international travel or other purposes? How is repayment tracked?

- Are cash management or other treasury functions performed at a regional or corporate basis? If so, how are the local accounts funded?

- Do local country banking regulations require flagging of disbursements over a particular amount? If so, how many payments were made in the past year or other period that exceeded that amount?

- Are varying levels of approval required depending on the type of disbursement authorized, amount to be disbursed, and destination of disbursement (for example, Isle of Man, Cyprus, or numbered account)?

- Were disbursements paid out of an account that is not on the bank accounts included in the general ledger?

- Does the company review transactions for payments to employees outside of standard payroll and expense reimbursement? Are companies listed as vendors for the company?

⚑ Background considerations

- Business purpose is, or seem to be, incidental to entertainment purpose

- Official is strategically located to grant business or improper business advantage to the company

- Expenses are lavish or out of line with company guidelines and local customs

- Spouse or children are invited to meals or included in travel

- Expenses are personally paid to the official

- Official is unwilling or unable to get written approval for the trip from the employing agency

- Altered receipts or lack of original receipts

- Numerous expenses incurred relating to the same government official

- Payments of large expenses in cash in countries where cash is not the primary means of payment for such expenses

Gifts

Gifts are another form of value that may be provided to officials and may not be as easily tracked as payments made directly to the official. In many countries, gift giving is an expected part of the business culture, though certain countries limit the value of gifts that can be given to officials. However, to be in compliance with the FCPA, gifts must never be given in connection with obtaining or retaining business. They should be modest in amount and never be cash.

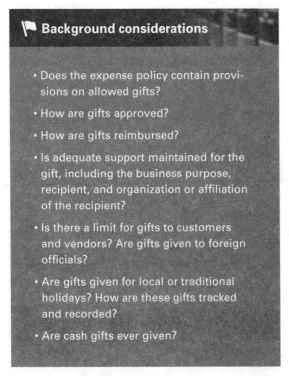

⚑ Background considerations

- Does the expense policy contain provisions on allowed gifts?

- How are gifts approved?

- How are gifts reimbursed?

- Is adequate support maintained for the gift, including the business purpose, recipient, and organization or affiliation of the recipient?

- Is there a limit for gifts to customers and vendors? Are gifts given to foreign officials?

- Are gifts given for local or traditional holidays? How are these gifts tracked and recorded?

- Are cash gifts ever given?

Charitable and Social Contributions

Donations can be considered "anything of value" even though the donation is not provided directly to a government official. If other elements of an FCPA violation are established, it is not a defense that the charity is legitimate. As noted in the proceeding against Schering-Plough Corporation, a complete understanding of both the reason for the donation and the controlling members of the charity is required.

⚑ Background considerations

- Do company policies contain provisions on allowed charitable contributions?

- Are employees allowed to make charitable contributions through expense reports?

- Is appropriate support provided for the reimbursement of charitable contributions, including the recipient and purpose of the expense?

- How are charitable and social contributions approved?

Substantiation and Valuation of Services Provided

Documentation or other evidence of performance of services or other value provided in exchange for a payment is very important when attempting to prove whether a particular transaction was a bona fide business expense, as previously outlined regarding affirmative defenses. Valuation of services also can be troublesome.

A common trouble area in these respects is payments classified as consulting fees. Often, there is no documentation of what consultation was provided and there may be claims that the consultation was oral. In other cases, a report may be provided but the content may not appear relevant to the company's business or to have been used.

The following questions should be asked from a valuation perspective:

- Does the amount of the consulting payments to a particular vendor appear proportional to the value received?
- Do the payments appear to represent a large proportion of the government official's income?
- If the fees are based on an hourly rate, is the hourly rate consistent with fair market value for similar services?
- Does the number of hours charged over a particular period of time appear excessive for the work performed or when compared to the number of hours available in a day, considering the number of hours the government official should be engaged in performing official duties?

Although these circumstances do not necessarily indicate that the payments were not bona fide expenses, they may be difficult to defend during the course of an investigation. To attempt to prevent issues in this area, the company should have formal contracts in place for each consultant or consulting entity. The contract should specify the precise nature of services to be provided, how the fees will be calculated, the time frame over which the services will be provided, and the report or other work product that must be delivered at the end of the consulting engagement. The contract should be executed in advance of the commencement of the services and have appropriate approval based on the types of services to be provided and the potential aggregate amount of payments.

Use of Third Parties

Although the most common agents may be sales representatives, distributors, or consultants, law firms, customs agents, and freight forwarders; accounting firms, tax consultants, and advisors; and other professional services firms also may serve as agents in certain circumstances. Because actions of agents can create vicarious liability for the company, as previously described, it is important to perform due diligence prior to entering into the relationship to identify potential unreported relationships, financial problems, lawsuits or claims against the entity, or other red flags. Due diligence procedures may include some or all of the items outlined in box 4-2.

Box 4-2: *Third-Party Due Diligence Procedure Considerations*

- Internal approval process with elevated vetting for high-risk agents and consultants
- Questionnaires for basic information
- Verification of information provided
- Review of ownership structure

- Reference checks with external entities (for example, Dun and Bradstreet, banks, U.S. Department of Commerce, U.S. State Department, U.S. Treasury Department restricted parties lists, and U.S. embassy check)
- Search for government affiliations, political party affiliations, and any other relationships with government officials or government-affiliated agencies
- Press and public information searches
- Local law check
- Documenting benchmarking of compensation
- Investigation of specific red flags
- Interviews and awareness training
- Review of the entity's FCPA compliance program and controls

Red flags, such as the following, should be considered during due diligence and monitored throughout the relationship with the agent:

⚑ Background considerations

- Country has historical bribery problem or current political unrest
- Excessive commissions awarded or requested
- Government customer recommends or requires use of an agent
- Partner or agent related to foreign official
- Suggestions that money is needed to "get the business"
- Partner or agent refuses to agree not to violate FCPA or other antibribery and anticorruption laws
- Requests for false invoices or other documents

(continued)

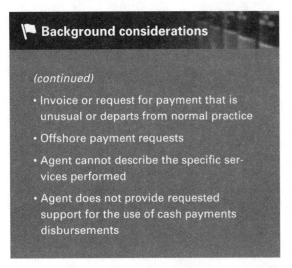

Background considerations

(continued)

- Invoice or request for payment that is unusual or departs from normal practice
- Offshore payment requests
- Agent cannot describe the specific services performed
- Agent does not provide requested support for the use of cash payments disbursements

A contract with the agent should be executed only after the performance of due diligence. The contract should clearly specify work to be performed, payment terms, invoice requirements, and so on. It also should include FCPA language and certification, as well as audit rights for potential improper payments.

Payments to Third Parties or Different Countries

Payments are not always made directly to foreign officials. In order to conceal the payment, they may be made to third parties, such as a relative of the official or a shell company, which then forwards the payment to the foreign official.

In order to identify payments to a particular foreign official, it may be helpful to perform a public records search related to the official in order to identify the names and addresses of family members, companies in which the official may have an interest, or other entities of interest. Searches of the vendor files can then be made to identify payments to vendors with names or addresses in common with those individuals or entities identified through the public records search.

It also may be helpful to perform a public records search for vendors that appear suspicious. Such a search may reveal owners who may be of interest or suggest the company is a pass-through entity that may serve as a tax haven for an entity in another country.

Accounting Requirement Violations

As previously discussed, the books and records component of the FCPA has received renewed attention because more companies are being prosecuted for records that fail to record improper transactions, are falsified to disguise aspects of improper transactions that were otherwise recorded correctly, and correctly set forth the quantitative aspects of the transaction but fail to record the qualitative aspects that would have revealed their illegality or impropriety.

Transactions that are often improperly recorded include the following:

- Bribes to foreign government officials
- Payments to agents
- Commercial bribes or kickbacks
- Expediting payments on imports or exports
- Facilitating payments
- Gifts
- Excessive entertainment

The following examples of improperly recorded transactions, including payment descriptions for some of the cases already mentioned, show the ease of recording improper payments as routine transactions, the difficulty in detecting violations through the review of transaction descriptions, and the need for internal controls:

- In the case of Kellogg, Brown, & Root, Inc., funds were funneled through agents and recorded as payments for "consulting" or "services" agreements.
- A corporation controlled by Baker Hughes Incorporated had their outside auditor make a payment to a foreign official. The outside auditor then billed and collected an invoice for the amount of the services provided and the payment to the foreign official as "professional services rendered."
- A subsidiary of a corporation owned by Baker Hughes Incorporated contracted with an agent that was supposed to obtain shipping certificates for the company. The agent was provided with money, and the transaction was recorded as a "shipping permit."
- During a reorganization of Baker Hughes Incorporated's subsidiaries in Brazil, an agent was hired to obtain the approval of a Brazilian government entity. The agent was provided

with money, and the transaction was recorded as "advance payment for expenses related to the commercial registry board of Rio de Janeiro."

- An employee of Faro Technologies Inc. made payments to foreign officials that were recorded as "referral fees." A higher-level employee directed the accounting department to record the transactions as "customer referral fees" instead of "referral fees" because the employee said in an e-mail that he did not want to "'end up in jail' as a result of 'this bribery.'" Payments were recorded under the "selling expenses" category.
- In return for a contract to modify a pipeline, Willbros Group, Inc., agreed to pay foreign officials and recorded the payments as "consulting expenses," "platform expenses," or "prepaid expenses."

The preceding examples of FCPA accounting violations highlight situations in which the company knowingly paid bribes, improperly recorded or booked the bribes, and falsified documentation. Other examples of FCPA accounting violations include the following:

- Knowingly paying false invoices and keeping the invoices in company's files
- Knowingly providing a false description of improper payment on executives' Travel and Entertainment report
- Booking a bribe as a facilitating payment
- Booking a freight forwarder's bribe payment to a customs official as "freight expense"
- Making an improper payment from subsidiary A on behalf of subsidiary B and then recording it on the books of subsidiary A

Sarbanes–Oxley Related Disclosures

The existence of an investigation or potential liability from the investigation may need to be disclosed in notes to the financial statements of a publicly traded company. This is generally handled by the company's disclosure committee or similar body. The disclosure committee also can be a source of information for the investigation team. The committee often gathers information on a periodic ba-

sis to determine whether disclosures are necessary. Matters previously considered for disclosure but not actually disclosed could be relevant to investigations or previously known risks.

Similarly, matters reported through the company's internal certification process also may be useful. Sections 302 and 906 of the Sarbanes–Oxley Act require that the CEO and CFO certify to the SEC that they are "responsible for establishing and maintaining internal controls" and "have designed such internal controls to ensure that material information relating to the company and its consolidated subsidiaries is made known to such officers by others within those entities, particularly during the period in which the periodic reports are being prepared."[44] Most companies have an internal certification process in which financial and other individuals throughout the company are asked to provide a similar certification to the CEO and CFO in order to provide them with some comfort of the accounting and financial information and controls system at the lower levels. The certifications generally have a section where individuals can write in concerns or items noted during the year that could help the investigation team identify potential risks that have previously been identified or other concerns employees have raised.

In addition to the fine levied against Schering-Plough Corporation, the company was required to retain an independent consultant to "review and evaluate Schering-Plough's internal controls, record-keeping, and financial reporting policies and procedures as they relate to Schering-Plough's compliance with the FCPA." This penalty was enforced against Schering-Plough Corporation due to the finding that it violated the internal control provisions of the FCPA.[45]

The SEC and DOJ have increased enforcement against individuals. David M. Pillor, former Senior Vice President for Sales and Marketing and member of the board of directors of InVision Technologies, Inc., was charged with violations of the FCPA and agreed to pay a penalty of $65,000 without admitting or denying the allegations against him. Pillor was found to have "aided and abetted InVision's

---

44 15 U.S.C. § 7241(a)(4).

45 SEC Administrative Proceeding Release No. 34-49838 issued June 9, 2004.

failure to establish adequate internal controls." The company was found to provide "only informal training about the FCPA to its employees and foreign agents" and "failed to monitor its employees and foreign agents to ensure that they did not violate the requirements of the FCPA."[46]

Voluntary Disclosure

Another related disclosure issue is whether the company should self-report to the government when an FCPA issue is identified. Voluntary disclosure should be discussed with legal counsel. The FCPA itself does not mandate disclosure, though other laws, including foreign laws, may require disclosure, and self-disclosure is encouraged by the DOJ and SEC.

From a positive perspective, self-disclosure avoids the risk of involuntary disclosure by third parties, such as government investigations or whistle-blowers. If the government discovers that the company knew about the issue and did not raise it with the government, the punishment meted out by the government could be more severe. If the company identifies the issue, there is a general belief that the government may be more lenient in punishing the company because it shows the company's willingness to cooperate and that it has an internal control structure that was able to identify the behavior so the matter could be investigated and corrective action taken. Neither the DOJ nor the SEC has quantified the degree of credit or leniency a company may receive if it chooses to self-report. However, in the case of BJ Services Company, the company voluntarily disclosed improper payments discovered during a routine audit and received a cease and desist order but no fines. The SEC noted that the company's remedial actions and cooperation were reasons why fines were not imposed. Further, the McNulty memorandum, "Principles of Federal Prosecution of Business Organizations," includes "the corporation's timely and voluntary disclosure of wrongdoing and its willingness to cooperate in the investigation of

its agents" in its factors to consider when charging corporations.[47]

Voluntary disclosure has potential detriments, however. First, the risk of the government opening a formal investigation often results in significant costs to the company in resolving the investigation. It also may involve pressure to waive rights and privileges to show cooperation with the government, although the McNulty memorandum places restrictions on the government's right to request a waiver of privilege. Under the McNulty memorandum, the government may only request a waiver of privilege when there is a "legitimate need for the privileged information to fulfill their law enforcement obligations." A "legitimate need" depends upon the likelihood and degree to which the privileged information will benefit the government's investigation, whether the information may be obtained in a timely manner through means other than a waiver, the completeness of prior voluntary disclosures, and the collateral consequences of a waiver to the company.[48] As noted by Alice Fisher, former Assistant Attorney General, Criminal Division, United States DOJ, "[A]lthough nothing is off the table when you voluntarily disclose, I can tell you in unequivocal terms that you will get a real benefit."[49]

If the FCPA issue is identified during preacquisition due diligence, it could result in a delay of the transaction. Also, the hoped-for benefits of reduced penalties do not always materialize. For example, in the Vetco International Ltd. and Baker Hughes Incorporated cases described earlier, both companies engaged in a large degree of cooperation yet still received record fines, in addition to their expenditures on the investigation. For more information on how voluntary disclosure fits in with a fraud investigation see Chapter 11, "Working with Regulators and Parallel Investigations."

Whistle-blowers

Following the passage of the Sarbanes-Oxley Act, publicly traded companies now have whistle-blower

46 SEC Litigation Release No. 19803 issued August 15, 2006.

47 Memo titled "Principles of Federal Prosecution of Business Organizations" by Paul J. McNulty, Deputy Attorney General.

48 Page 9 of the McNulty memorandum.

49 "Prepared Remarks of Alice S. Fisher, Assistant Attorney General, United States Department of Justice, at the American Bar Association National Institute on the Foreign Corrupt Practices Act, Omni Shoreham Hotel, Washington, D.C., October 16, 2006."

hotlines or other means available for individuals to anonymously report issues. The audit committee is tasked with monitoring and addressing issues raised through these means but may delegate day-to-day tasks to others. The creation of the whistle-blower hotlines has resulted in an increase of reported complaints, though few result in specific allegations with enough support to warrant a full-scale investigation. Nevertheless, logs maintained of whistle-blower complaints and their resolution can be an important source of information to the investigation team. They can indicate whether a particular issue has been reported before, what steps were taken to address the complaint, whether control deficiencies were noted, and any corrective or remedial actions taken as a result.

From an FCPA perspective in which most related actions occur outside the United States, it is important that the whistle-blower hotline be available 24/7, rather than during business hours of the United States. If the number is not toll-free (and particularly if it is an international phone call), that may be a deterrent to individuals. The number should be posted so that all employees are aware of the hotline and its confidentiality and that making calls will not result in retaliation to the employee if they were made in good faith. Finally, the hotline should have operators available who can speak with the whistle-blower in his or her local language, rather than only taking complaints in English. It also is helpful if the hotline provides a call-in ID so that messages can be left for the whistle-blower indicating whether the matter has been resolved or whether additional information would be helpful.

Acquisition Considerations

Acquisitions of other entities create potential FCPA issues in three areas: acquisition by a foreign official of a government-owned entity or an entity with government ownership interest, the need for government approval of the acquisition, and the

successor liability for past FCPA violations. Thus, FCPA-specific procedures should be part of both preacquisition and postacquisition due diligence.

Two recent examples underscore the need for due diligence. The Titan Corporation issue, described earlier, resulted in the collapse of Lockheed Martin Corporation's proposed $1.6 billion acquisition of Titan Corporation. In the case of Syncor International Corporation, it was discovered during preacquisition due diligence that Syncor International Corporation had made more than $600,000 in corrupt payments, which resulted in a hefty civil penalty, a cease and desist order, and the hiring of an independent consultant to audit and recommend corrective compliance programs for the seller.

Due diligence procedures are somewhat similar to the due diligence procedures described earlier for the engagement of agents and are outlined in box 4-3.

Because time is often limited when performing preacquisition due diligence procedures, some additional follow-up procedures may be required after the acquisition. The DOJ provides substantial guidance regarding pre- and postacquisition due diligence procedures when preacquisition procedures are limited.[50] DOJ Opinion Procedure Release No. 08-02 stated that Halliburton Company, a U.S. issuer, could complete the acquisition of a foreign target with potential FCPA violations without exposing itself to FCPA liability immediately upon the close of the deal. Per Opinion Procedure Release No. 08-02, the deal would be subject to a 180-day due diligence period and postclosing plan requiring, among other things, immediate disclosure to the DOJ of potential FCPA violations of which Halliburton Company became aware. The DOJ stated that the fact pattern presented by Halliburton Company was unique because the country of the target company has a bidding process that does not allow for proper FCPA due diligence prior to acquisition. In countries where such restrictions are not present, the DOJ stated the expectation is for a thorough preacquisition FCPA due diligence to be completed by the acquiring company.

---

50 DOJ Opinion Procedure Release No. 08-02 issued June 13, 2008.

Box 4-3: *Acquisition Due Diligence Procedure Considerations*

- Assess corruption levels of the countries in which the target entity does business, either directly or through agents

- Investigate the identity of the target entity and key individuals

- Review the target entity's existing FCPA compliance program and controls

- Test adequacy of the target entity's books and records and internal controls

- Evaluate the target entity's risk profile (for example, use of agents and frequent interactions with government officials)

- Identify prior instances of FCPA issues or violations

Internal Control and Compliance

Before a problem is found or an investigation occurs, companies can review their internal controls and compliance programs to verify that the FCPA is being considered by the company, perform training for company employees and agents, and prevent future problems by strengthening existing processes. Internal control provisions to be aware of include the following:

- Typical FCPA internal control issues
- Unauthorized payments and off-books accounts
- Payments contrary to company policies
- Payments without prior due diligence
- Payments just under authority limits
- Payments without adequate documentation

In addition to a strong internal control environment, it is critical to create a culture of compliance through education of all employees, agents, and outside consultants on FCPA and antibribery or anticorruption laws. The lack of corporate compliance on FCPA and FCPA training has been sited as reasons for stiffer penalties in recent actions. Box 4-4 outlines the areas where companies should seek to institute internal control policies and procedures.

Box 4-4: *Internal Control Best Practice Compliance Areas*

- Train employees to recognize and report red flags with special training for finance professionals, senior executives, marketing executives, and others in high-risk FCPA positions

- Create policies, procedures, and financial controls around high risk areas (for example, dealings with governments and government-owned entities; dealings with customs; and dealings with licensing authorities, tax authorities, and regulators)

- Perform due diligence and financial controls over agents, consultants, and other high-risk vendors, including counteracting controls and payment review processes

- Enforce strict accounting and financial controls surrounding cash, petty cash, expense authorization, and reimbursement

- Enforce strict controls around gift giving, travel and entertainment of government officials, and charitable contributions, including a preapproval process and transparency for transactions

- Create a robust FCPA compliance program, including clear company policies, communication of polices, training and education, investigative functions, discipline, and zero tolerance for violations

- Create an extensive FCPA auditing process for compliance

- Create documentation of FCPA internal control processes

Conclusion

There are myriad ways for companies and their employees and agents to run afoul of the FCPA. The risk of investigations and potential costly deferred prosecution agreements may continue to increase as companies increase their global reach, additional countries adopt their own antibribery and corruption laws, U.S. enforcement agencies increase their focus and resources devoted to FCPA enforcement, and cooperation increases among enforcement agencies around the world. As discussed in this chapter, although the FCPA has not changed significantly since its inception, the penalties and enforcement have increased significantly. Understanding the elements of the FCPA and issues specific to industries and business processes will assist the forensic accountant in planning and executing engagements, as well as help companies develop effective FCPA compliance programs.

5

The First 48 Hours of an Investigation

Lynda Schwartz, Partner/Principal

Introduction

The first 48 hours of an investigation are critical. Most forensic and investigation professionals have heard of an investigation, one that became protracted or involved rework, wasted time and resources. Others can tell of investigations that failed in their objective of uncovering and assembling the full, reliable and objective understanding of the facts needed for decision making by business executives, directors, external auditors, regulators and investors. Still others can point to pitfalls, such as those related to engagement structure and evidence handling, that increased the investigation-related time and cost over and above what might have been necessary in the circumstances.

Consider the following scenario:

> *The Grand Forge Company Company CEO Bill Peterson, sits in his office, exhausted. Grand Forge Company's Form 10-K has been delayed and cannot be filed until the financial statements are finalized and the audit completed. The external auditors keep raising questions about what started as a small internal investigation. When the issues initially arose they seemed to be simple problems, but the investigation now seems to be much more complicated. In an effort to resolve the issues quickly, Bill had directed the company's internal people look into all the issues. As more information became known, it was decided that they needed an independent investigation conducted by lawyers and forensic specialists. These investigators seemed to cover all the same ground again, and more.*[1]

The root causes of such deficient investigations usually can be traced to decisions made in the first 48 hours after the allegations emerged. In those early hours, companies and their executives often face a crossroads relating to the nature and extent of their responses to allegations of impropriety or similar issues.

Poor decision making in these first few hours can lead to disastrous consequences. If the level and intensity of the response are not appropriate, a company can miss important issues, delay or frustrate the resolution of problems or waste resources. If steps are not taken to appropriately preserve and collect the evidence that may be needed, it could be irrevocably lost or might be retrievable only at great cost. Actions that might tamper with the evidence or taint the recollections of witnesses can do great harm. If the persons executing the work lack the competence and objectivity to investigate properly, their efforts could waste time and resources and even spoil the evidence.

Further, when external auditors and regulators perceive a company's investigation was incomplete, inadequate, biased, advocacy-oriented, or poorly executed; they may find its conclusions and findings to be unreliable for their purposes. This, in turn, can affect the nature and extent of the inquiries, testing and investigative procedures performed by both auditors and regulators, and the time it takes to complete the audit or resolve any regulatory inquiries. Finally, if a company is not perceived to be doing the right thing in response to an allegation, investors and other stakeholders may lose confidence in the company, possibly undermining a potential resolution of the issue and the company's own reputation and brand.

By contrast, a strong, credible, and competent response ensures that adequate, relevant and complete information is assembled to support decision making, that legal rights and responsibilities are respected, and that any applicable legal privileges are preserved. A competent and independent investigation also may assist the company by reducing the need for external auditors and regulators to conduct their own inquiries of certain allegations. Finally, a well-organized and coordinated response will allow the company to not only address any issues with the proper intensity, but also to remain focused on its core business activities throughout the process.

---

1 The reader is invited to read the detailed case study of Grand Forge Company found in the Introduction to this book.

Box 5-1 further illustrates potential differences in outcomes flowing from these decisions, many of which are faced in the first 48 hours.

Box 5-1: *Potential Impacts Associated with Decisions in the First 48 Hours*

Positive	Negative
Critical evidence is secured and made accessible. Less critical evidence is preserved for later use, if needed.	Evidence is lost, destroyed, or its integrity or authenticity is compromised
Investigation is conducted by objective and respected persons whose work will be acceptable to directors, managers, regulators, external auditors, and other stakeholders.	Investigation is compromised by involvement of people who lack credibility or are perceived to lack objectivity relative to the issues, activities, or persons potentially involved.
Investigators have the necessary industry, business process, accounting, legal, regulatory compliance, technology, operations, language, or cultural backgrounds that are relevant to the particular issue. Their expertise is shared proactively to allow stakeholders to make good decisions.	Participants, investigators, and advisors lack sufficient competence in critical areas. Investigators and decision makers stumble into preventable pitfalls. The potential downsides of certain decisions are not understood until after the fact.
Activities are timely, reasonably predictable, and understandable, evolving as necessary to adapt to changes in facts and circumstances.	Insufficient planning and coordination lead to delays, conflicting objectives, or rework. Activities seem to be out of control or unpredictable.
The level of resource commitment is understood and the overall effort has adequate sponsorship by those in authority.	The resources devoted to the process seem inappropriately high or low, relative to the issues at hand.
Roles and responsibilities are understood by all participants. Accountability is taken for assigned responsibilities. Decisions are made by those with the appropriate authority.	It is unclear who is responsible for various activities. Poor authority and accountability are reflected by poor decision making, inadequate or inappropriate responses, or wasted resources.
Factual information gathered in the investigation is handed off to those who need it in a timely and appropriate manner.	Poor communication among the various users of the investigation outputs leads to incomplete understanding of the results of the investigation or rework.

(continued)

Box 5-1: *Potential Impacts Associated with Decisions in the First 48 Hours (continued)*

Positive	Negative
The transition from crisis response to more routine business activities occurs as rapidly as possible.	Attention remains focused on investigation activities and side issues for a prolonged time, as opposed to being focused on the underlying business.
A company is seen by investors, regulators, and other third parties to have done the right thing in the circumstances and to have responded appropriately.	Unresolved uncertainties or perceived deficiencies in a company's handling of the issue have a negative impact on the company's reputation or brand.

This chapter is intended to prevent unnecessary missteps in investigations, especially in the first 48 hours. It also focuses on helping business professionals and the forensic professionals who advise them to anticipate the decisions they will face in the very earliest hours of their response to the allegations. Although this chapter is not intended as a substitute for competent legal advice, it also will identify some of the legal issues that may need to be addressed. These suggestions and observations will help companies achieve the goal of assembling clear, reliable and useful information in a way that uses resources efficiently and supports a company's long-term needs and objectives.

Anticipating the Decisions to Be Made After an Allegation Arises

The path from the initial identification of an allegation of impropriety to a more complete understanding of the facts and an understanding of the evidence related to fraud is, and always will be, dependent upon the facts and circumstances. The path is often unfamiliar to business managers and executives and frequently requires course changes. Because of financial reporting deadlines and the exigencies of business, time pressures usually force people to travel this unfamiliar path at a sprint. Anticipating what is coming next is a key to successful navigation in the first 48 hours.

Returning to our case study of Grand Forge Company, let us set aside the picture of a messy, protracted investigation outlined at the beginning of this chapter. Instead, let us put ourselves back in the very first moments when the allegations have just arisen. During this chapter, we will assume that Grand Forge Company has recently become aware of four separate allegations and issues, including the following:

(1) The controller of one of Grand Forge Company's foreign subsidiaries called corporate headquarters. The subsidiary held about $2 million in cash balances at local banks. When the controller had recently followed up on vendor complaints of slow payments, the controller learned that the actual cash in the bank was almost zero. Upon scrutiny, the bank statements in the company's files look as if they may be inauthentic. One of the subsidiary's cash clerks admitted to the controller that he had taken the cash. The controller also said that the clerk sounded suicidal over their discovery.

(2) A Grand Forge Company employee made a report on the company's whistle-blower hotline, alleging that her supervisor had been inflating his expense reporting to receive reimbursement in excess of the amounts actually incurred.

(3) Grand Forge Company recently received a seemingly routine inquiry from the Securities and Exchange Commission (SEC) which suggests some regulatory inquiry or scrutiny of the company's executives trading in stock and stock options.

(4) A significant overseas customer called to complain about the quality of a large volume of product they were recently shipped. They stated that the country manager, Mr. Smith, routinely pressured them to take product in excess of their needs, especially at the end of the quarter. Now they allege that the product they received is substandard, unusable, and outside their contract specifications. They allege damages to their company related to the substandard product.

Because there are such a large number of tasks and considerations in the first 48 hours of an investigation, various decision makers can easily overlook critical decisions or become overwhelmed. To streamline the decision process, it is helpful to think of the various decision points as being part of several stages in the decision making process. Although they are presented in discrete stages in this chapter, in practice, the issues may be addressed in a different sequence, or they may be intertwined. Using our case study as an example, each of these stages can be considered:

- *Identifying and surfacing the allegations.* In our case study, we will assume that Grand Forge Company's allegations and issues came to light relatively quickly. For a variety of organizational, process-related and behavioral reasons, this is not always the case. We will discuss these reasons and some of the strategies to ensure that allegations are identified, surfaced and raised to the attention of the right person or function in the organization.

- *Initial triage.* When allegations or issues do emerge, they should not go without a response. To determine the right response with the right resources and the right urgency there must be some process to evaluate the matter with whatever information may be available.

- *Responding to threats to the business, its employees, or other people.* Sometimes, the nature of the allegation or issue is such that it raises concerns about the safety and security of people, whether they are employees, customers, or other third parties, or the person who is suspected of wrongdoing. Other times, an immediate need exists to stabilize or safeguard some aspect of the business. These situations require immediate action.

- *Consideration of obligations to report the situation to third-parties, such as regulatory authorities or the investing public.* Sometimes, specific external and internal reporting obligations emerge within the first 48 hours. Companies should consult with counsel about whether reportable events have occurred, whether public disclosures are required and what types of disclosures are appropriate. In some situations, it also may be appropriate to report specific issues to the external auditors or insurance carriers. Additionally, after initial triage, there should be an assessment about whether all the appropriate internal reporting has occurred, such as whether reporting obligations under the Sarbanes-Oxley Act of 2002 have been considered. Finally, depending on the situation, it may be appropriate to make some communication to employees or to halt any insider trading in company stock.

- *Organizing an investigation.* Once it is clear that an investigation is warranted, decisions about the structure, scope, and execution of the investigation are very important. Routine matters are typically handled by internal resources in the ordinary course of business and benefit from strong practices and procedures. By contrast, the more significant nonroutine investigations often need to be structured to fit the unique facts and circumstances that the business faces. Among the considerations to be addressed in the first 48 hours is whether the investigation should be led by counsel to preserve any legal privileges that may be available. Other critical questions that may affect the independence and objectivity of the investigation include who will oversee and be responsible for the investigation and who will conduct the various investigation activities, considering the skills and resources that will be necessary.

- *Securing evidence.* Lawyers sometimes counsel companies to preserve documents and other evidence as soon as there is reason to believe they might be relevant to an investigation or litigation. In the United States, federal law may require the retention of records relevant to a likely government investigation. Legal requirements aside, any investigation is only as good as the evidence. Because records are destroyed or altered in the ordinary course of business, evidence can be lost through inaction. Further, those under investigation sometimes delete or destroy evidence out of the fear of what might be found, regardless of whether they themselves did anything wrong. Companies and investigators must preserve and secure evidence as early as possible in an investigation or risk losing it. The first 48 hours may be the best, and sometimes the only, chance to secure evidence.

- *Transitioning to conclusion or a longer term project, if necessary.* After the first flurry of activity, most investigation engagements are either found to be without merit or are found to need a more comprehensive assessment. When a full-fledged investigation is warranted, the activities in the first 48 hours should have set the stage for a well-organized, well-managed, and appropriate investigation. By then, the scope of the work to be performed and a work plan to accomplish that scope should be established. After the first 48 hours, the success of the investigation will rely on both legal and forensic skills and strong project management.

In our case study, Grand Forge Company's executives may attempt to shortcut these stages or rush to judgment. In our experience, however, a rigorous and thoughtful approach to the early stages of an investigation tends to avoid the missteps that can be very costly. Avoiding knee-jerk reactions and working carefully though the early-stage issues pays off in the end because allegations are identified, addressed, and triaged quickly, without festering into larger problems. If a full investigation is warranted, the decisions made in the early stages will help ensure that the investigation is reliable: that rework by the company or third parties is minimized; and that the investigation itself does not become a source of additional scrutiny, uncertainty, or litigation.

Using our Grand Forge Company case study as an illustration, the following sections of this chapter will dissect each of these stages and discuss the various considerations for those facing a potential investigation.

Identifying Allegations

Making decisions in the first 48 hours would be simpler if allegations of financial impropriety were quickly raised in a timely fashion to the general counsel, managers, or other persons in authority. In practice, many obstacles can inhibit employees from recognizing the importance of a claim or allegation and reacting appropriately. Three challenges that commonly arise are the following:

1. Identifying the allegation or issue and recognizing it as a problem
2. Elevating the matter appropriately within the organization
3. Ensuring that those in authority appropriately respond to the issue

Employees and outsiders may not recognize particular events or situations as problematic issues. In some situations, employees lack sufficient understanding of the issues to identify which transactions or issues are problematic. For example, workers who have been routinely operating in an improper or illegal manner may not recognize their practice as improper, especially if that was the way they were trained to perform their duties or if the practice is long-standing. In another example, employees of a non-U.S. company or subsidiary may be subject to the Foreign Corrupt Practices Act, yet be unaware of the particular requirements of the law or that common local practices are violations of U.S. law. Even when employees have received training or are aware of rules and requirements, they may fail to recognize fact patterns that are indicative of potential problems.

The second of these challenges is appropriately elevating the issue within the organization. Smaller issues that might indicate larger problems are sometimes dismissed as unimportant or immaterial and are not shared with those in authority. Sometimes issues are raised but not shared with people in the organization who can or will respond appropriately. Other times, employees may fear retribution on their own behalf or on behalf of similarly situated business colleagues. For these reasons and others, employees may keep questions or concerns to themselves. Differences of language, business practices,

Is Your Whistle-blower Hotline Working?

Mechanisms for anonymous reporting of suspected wrongdoing, including whistle-blower hotlines, are a critical antifraud control for many companies. Such mechanisms are required by the Sarbanes-Oxley Act of 2002 and are identified as an element of a comprehensive ethics and compliance program by the U.S. Federal Sentencing Guidelines for Organizations. Further, the Association of Certified Fraud Examiners has found that organizations with hotlines significantly decrease their fraud losses. Since the passage of the Sarbanes-Oxley Act of 2002, many companies have implemented new hotlines.

Some executives may take comfort if their hotlines produce few or no incidents; however, an unused hotline should be a cause for concern. Anecdotal evidence from tests of whistle-blowers suggests that such reporting mechanisms can fail in a number of ways. Finding the logjams and implementing best practices can yield the best results from such hotlines. Several important considerations to take into account when designing a hotline include:

- **Is it known?** *Surveys or inquiries of employees sometimes uncover that employees are unaware of the hotline or cannot recall how to access it. Regular messaging in the local language helps ensure that employees know about the hotline and helps reinforce the perception that the company wants to know about suspected wrongdoing.*
- **Does it work as designed?** *Audit testing has sometimes identified mechanical difficulties with the hotlines, such as phone numbers that fail to connect or messages that are not routed appropriately. Periodic testing of the system helps identify and correct such difficulties.*
- **Is it localized?** *Global corporations must find ways to implement hotlines that comply with local legal requirements and are usable in the various geographies where business is conducted. In some areas, such as Europe, strict guidelines exist regarding anonymous reporting mechanisms and the transfer of electronic data. Specific consideration should be given about whether the hotline-related communications should be provided in local languages. Companies also must be aware of and sensitive to differences in local customs, particularly those related to loyalties between managers and subordinates and among countrymen.*
- **Are hotline reports properly disseminated?** *Each hotline should be designed with a specific reporting of hotline calls to appropriate persons within the organization. Disseminating to multiple people, such as the general counsel and audit committee, can help ensure that reports are not lost or that allegations of suspected wrongdoing are not sent to only one individual.*
- **Is the hotline process monitored?** *Successful hotlines are managed with the same rigor as any other business process: good design, case management processes, testing, analysis, and managerial oversight. A reliable reporting tool helps provide the summary data that can identify issues and potential improvements to the anonymous reporting process.*

and communication across cultures and time zones can exacerbate these challenges. In our preceding case study example, if the customer complaints about shipping volumes or product specifications are seen by employees as merely operational snafus that, if reported, would reflect poorly upon the work team, then they might not be surfaced to management. Even if they are reported, they might not be shared outside the sales and operations groups within the affected business unit.

When allegations arise, it is important that the information is shared with those who have both the responsibility and skill to fully address the issues. Many businesses operate across a variety of business units, functional, and geographic boundaries. An initial claim or event can emerge from anywhere in the organization. Sometimes, those who first learn of such a matter may try to handle it themselves and avoid reporting it to others in the organization. It is human nature to try to address an issue within

Developing Procedures to Report Allegations

One organization has developed a policy it calls the 60 Minute Rule. This policy stipulates a process for dealing with issues by breaking them down into two main decision paths: one for Red Alerts and another for Yellow Alerts. Red Alerts include events that could potentially involve significant injury or harm to any person and also legal matters requiring prompt attention, such as service of process or nonroutine visits by government authorities. The 60 Minute Rule requires that a Red Alert be reported by telephone within 60 minutes of its occurrence live to a member of the senior management team. Yellow Alerts are defined as matters of high importance that are not emergencies. Yellow Alerts must be reported by e-mail within 24 hours to various designated contact people in the home office and followed up to ensure receipt of the e-mail. The organization acknowledges that no policy can contemplate or effectively communicate every possible scenario, so employees are frequently reminded, "When in doubt, report it!"

(Reprinted with permission courtesy of Block, Janice L., "Rules of Responsibility," Inside Counsel Magazine, August 2008.)

the work group because that approach may limit potential embarrassment or managerial displeasure. Further, many organizations encourage employees to take responsibility for driving solutions to business problems and incentivize them to do so. An appropriate response needs to balance these business drivers with the need for transparency and oversight, especially with potential emerging issues or allegations. For these reasons, organizations benefit by having clear policies and procedures for elevating potentially problematic events and issues to the right level within the organization. Such policies and procedures should be specific regarding the "what," "who," and "when" of reporting potential allegations of financial impropriety or other matters that may significantly affect the company.

A third challenge is whether the issue, when raised, receives an adequate and appropriate response. Even matters that are reported to whistle-blower hotlines can sometimes fall through the cracks or be dismissed as unworthy of follow-up. For example, in the first of the allegations in our Grand Forge Company case study, the local controller may have been aware for weeks that there was some sort of snafu in the cash disbursements system but might not have recognized there was a risk that the cash had been misappropriated.

Generally speaking, matters or allegations that would affect the safety of employees, customers, or the community; would require action to safeguard the company's brand or assets; or would affect the company's regulatory or civil liability should be handled fully, competently, and robustly. Other matters that do not necessarily have immediate or broad-reaching impacts may require a lesser response, based on the facts and circumstances. At the other end of the spectrum, overblown, incompetent, or excessive responses to allegations or fact patterns that are clearly insignificant and pose little real risk exposure waste resources and time and may actually create problems for the company.

To address this challenge, businesses should design policies, procedures, and processes that allow for supervision and oversight of claims, events, allegations, and the company's response to increase the visibility of the decision making process and ensure that it is appropriate. Individual employees, even if they are based outside the company's home office, should feel that they are adequately supported by a network of resources that can be responsive to important business matters, no matter where he or she is located. Similarly, the organization, and specifically those with corporate governance responsibility, should feel that they have adequate oversight and control over emerging risks and issues.

Initial Triage

Initial triage is the process of making a rapid assessment of the currently available information and critical initial decisions on the nature and extent of the response. Almost always, initial triage is conducted

Chapter 5: The First 48 Hours of an Investigation

before all or even most of the facts are known. The risks of triage comprise two sides of the same coin: the risk of over response to an incident and the risk of inadequate response.

The starting point for initial triage is to assemble the facts that are known, trying to separate fact from assumption. Although information is almost always fragmentary, a bullet-point summary or short memorandum may be prepared to articulate what is known, such as the following:

- The nature of the issue or allegation and how it came to light
- Whether the matter relates to a single event or transaction or might apply to multiple events, transactions, or practices
- Whether the situation is current or relates to past events
- The number or extent of people that may be involved or affected
- The likely dollar impact, if it can be determined
- The geographies, business units, or organizational groups that may be affected
- Whether the issue is highly confidential or likely to be sensitive
- Whether there is a previous history of similar allegations or issues related to this topic or the people who are potentially involved
- The dates of any upcoming financial reporting deadlines
- Whether there are any potential regulatory violations, either related to financial reporting, data privacy, or industry-specific regulation.

The goal of the initial triage is to form a preliminary assessment about whether the allegations raise significant concerns, such as the possibility of the following:

- Material impacts to current or previously-issued financial statements or disclosures
- Indications of significant deficiencies in either the design or operation of internal controls
- Indications of lack of personal integrity of any of a company's officers or senior executives or managers responsible for financial reporting functions
- Material violations of laws, regulations, or contractual requirements
- An operation- or product-related concern that may affect public or employee safety or have a significant impact on the business

"Just a Disgruntled Employee"

In our experience, a common initial reaction to a whistle-blower allegation is to describe the whistle-blower as "just a disgruntled employee." The implication of this epithet is that the whistle-blower has an ax to grind, may not be credible, or may merely be seeking protection under one of several legal protections for whistle-blowers without an underlying meritorious claim.

Focus on the motives of the whistle-blower should not, however, be the first question during triage. That might distract from the more critical question of whether the allegation itself has substance.

In some senses, all whistle-blowers are "disgruntled employees." If the whistle-blower believed that a concern could have been resolved in the ordinary course by openly reporting that concern to a member of management, the whistle-blower probably would have done so. The very reason for whistle-blower hotlines is to encourage reporting when employees may not be able to resolve such concerns in their normal work channels. Whistle-blowers tend to use anonymous hotlines when other avenues of reporting have failed or are perceived as risky to the individual.

In triaging allegations, it may be helpful to set aside questions related to the motivations of the whistle-blower. These questions can be much better assessed later when more information is known. Rather, ask whether the allegation is specific; whether evidence is available that can support or refute the alleged facts; and whether the existence and nature of the report requires further follow-up, based on its substance.

The purpose of initial triage is not to reach a final conclusion but to form a basis for decisions about how the company should respond and the speed and intensity of that response.

A common reaction is to rush to a preliminary judgment about the merits and importance of a particular incident. When that preliminary judgment serves to discount the evidence or question the credibility of the allegation at the early stages, the risk of inadequate response is high. For example, it is all too common to describe a whistle-blower call to a hotline as a crank and dismiss the report as unworthy of follow-up. Similarly, concerns raised by a person seen as a "complainer" or not a "team player" are sometimes not given credence.

Other times, the merits of a particular allegation or concern are not addressed because the person did not raise the issue in a way that was considered appropriate. Although some whistle-blowers make clear, unambiguous assertions, others may only vaguely identify the problem, may make generalized or non-specific assertions, or might seem overly-emotional or biased. Other times, the issue is raised in a way that only obliquely asserts a problem. For example, a subordinate could ask a manager to "Take a look at these documents and see what you think," without clearly saying, "They look like a problem to me." The focus must be on the substance of the issue or allegation, not on the perceived attributes of the person raising the issue or the form of the report.

Ideally, initial triage and the related decisions should be made by a person who is independent of the underlying issues or affected business processes. An independent person is more likely to see the broader issues more clearly than a person who might be personally involved in the activities or might have a preconceived opinion regarding the situation or the people involved. Similarly, those upon whom the administrative or resource burden of an inquiry might fall may find it more difficult to call for an investigation. Having an independent decision maker reduces the chance of a poor decision and minimizes the ability of others to second-guess that judgment.

Companies and those with responsibility for initial triage can prepare for these judgments by developing company-specific risk criteria to assess incoming reports of matters potentially requiring investigation. Objective criteria help in at least two ways. First, developing criteria for the initial triage of allegations allows for input from various people within the organization well in advance of an event. It may be impossible to gather such input on a timely basis after a particular allegation arises. Second, having such criteria clearly articulated enhances the quality of decision making during triage. The fragmentary nature of some allegations or the "color" around the specific facts may make decision making difficult. Having a predetermined set of criteria helps decision makers sort through the available information in a more objective way. Finally, a set of predeveloped criteria greatly enhances the consistency and speed of the triage process. Box 5-2 indicates a sample set of company-specific playbook attributes to assist in driving an appropriate response.

Box 5-2: *Company Playbook Response Attribute Drivers*

Greater Response	Lesser Response
Immediate concerns of safety or security of employees, customers, or third parties.	No safety or security threats to persons.
Potential financial impact is quantitatively or qualitatively material.	Financial impact is of nominal amount.
Issue may impugn the company reputation or brand.	Matter has only internal impact or does not create reputational risk.
Potentially criminal conduct or government enforcement scrutiny.	Relates to individual employees, private conduct, or violation of internal policies.
Indications that internal controls and process controls may lack integrity or not function as expected.	Issue was properly detected by internal controls and processes.

(continued)

Box 5-2: *Company Playbook Response Attribute Drivers (continued)*

Greater Response	Lesser Response
Indications that internal controls and process controls may lack integrity or not function as expected.	Issue was properly detected by internal controls and processes.
Involves high-level employees, officers, directors, or persons with fiduciary duties.	Matter involves only low-level employees or persons isolated from the financial reporting process.
Involves misstatements to auditors or regulators or inaccurate financial reports.	Misstatements, if any, are internal and have no affect on external reporting or communication.

In conducting initial triage, it also is important to think beyond the specific allegation to its broader context and potential implications for other processes, people, or transactions. One consideration in triage might be What if this allegation is true? Considerations might include the following:

- What else could be wrong?
- Are there indications that other transactions or situations could have similar issues, either currently or in the past?
- Would this indicate a failure of controls, and, if so, what other problems might not have been detected?
- Could there be similar claims by others?
- Could this be indicative of a regulatory compliance issue or governmental inquiry?
- Is there reason to doubt the integrity or competence of employees?

During the initial triage, a company should take steps to preserve the confidentiality of the process. This will include limiting the number of people who are privy to the allegations and the facts that are currently known. Although information leaks are common, a confidential process can help minimize rumors and even external publicity. Importantly, taking early steps to limit the dissemination of information about the issue helps make sure that any follow-up investigation interviews are not compromised. Sometimes, while an investigation is being organized, potential subjects of the investigation will destroy or alter evidence, cover their tracks, or collaborate on a story. Investigations can be tainted

unintentionally, when "who knew what and when" is confused by leaks during triage or later in the investigation.

Similarly, a company also must take care to protect the reputations of accused employees. If the allegations are found to be without merit, the employees should be able to continue in their roles and careers without the stigma of having been accused of wrongdoing.

Leadership in the initial triage stage involves more than the right process and decision making. It also is about promoting a response that is thoughtful and balanced. Reflexive responses are common but do little to advance the interests of the organization. Because the information available during initial triage is usually incomplete and things may not turn out to be as they initially appear, knee-jerk reactions often miss the mark. In our experience, when decision makers work to separate fact from supposition, consult with others, reflect on the steps to be taken, and come to a reasoned business judgment, the organization benefits.

Safeguarding People and Business Operations

Recall that in our case study, the controller of one of Grand Forge Company's foreign subsidiaries called corporate headquarters to report an apparent defalcation of $2 million held in non-U.S. banks. Although there will be keen interest in what happened, how it happened, whether anyone was guilty of wrongdoing, and whether any recovery is possible, the situation calls for urgent action to safeguard the business and its people. The controller has indicated that the alleged perpetrator is suicidal, suggesting a possible threat to himself and others. Further, the company must consider whether any immediate steps can be taken to prevent further loss.

Safety of Employees and Other People

When an immediate concern is identified (per the policy on identifying allegations) regarding the potential safety or security of employees, customers, or third parties, immediate action is imperative.

Examples of workplace violence are well documented. Such violence may sometimes be spurred after an allegation of impropriety is made or a fraud is discovered. For example, a suspected individual might threaten to hurt him or herself or others. Depending on the facts and circumstances, it may be appropriate to notify law enforcement, restrict access of suspected individuals from business locations or workplaces, strengthen workplace security, seek specialized assistance, or take other actions to protect others.

Securing Business Operations and Assets

A suspected person also may take action to damage a business or impede its normal operations. Sometimes, these actions are provoked by anger and reflect an attempt to retaliate after an accusation. Other times, attempts by the suspected person to frustrate the investigation will include actions that result in broader collateral damage. For example, attempts to delete or destroy documents relevant to an investigation are relatively common. Other times, a suspected person may attempt to modify computer programs or systems, damage or destroy operating assets, or otherwise impede business activities, either to make the investigation more difficult or retaliate against the organization.

Depending on the facts and circumstances, it may be appropriate to restrict certain employees' access to the workplace, electronic systems, business locations, resources, and assets. Determining the nature of the restrictions and on whom they should be im-

posed is a matter of considerable judgment. On the one hand, it may be reasonable to restrict the access of any suspected person or other person who might be relevant to an investigation. On the other hand, businesses usually need their business operations to continue without disruption. The nature of the restrictions may vary, but it is reasonable to consider all types of access to operations and financial and other assets, including both physical and electronic access. In considering access, do not overlook remote access to the company's computer systems. Remote access technologies may be especially prevalent if the company uses technology to support its employees who work from home or travel extensively.

It also may be necessary to transition or limit an employee's job authority or responsibilities pending an investigation. For example, treasury employees under investigation might have their wire transfer authority suspended while the investigation is underway. Similarly, an employee might be placed on temporary administrative leave until the facts and circumstances surrounding an allegation are better understood.

Managing Corporate Crises

Some allegations can be readily identified as corporate crises, such as product liability that threatens the public safety, a significant allegation against the company or its senior officers, an issue that may cause immediate public outcry, or notice that a government authority is launching an investigation of corporate conduct.

Companies facing a corporate crisis will need to respond almost immediately. To be effective, the company, its executives, and board need to be prepared with a plan of action. Crisis management preparedness helps ensure that key players are coordinated and understand their roles. Company executives and board members should have a multidisciplinary team of advisors available to provide the necessary legal, regulatory, public relations, and financial skills that may be needed. Although many of the tools and approaches described in this chapter help to support the management of the crisis, specific planning for crisis-level events is important. For additional information about assembling a multidisciplinary team, see chapter 6, "Roles and Responsibilities: How Different Stakeholders Work During Investigations."

Special considerations are necessary in the event that the company learns that a government regulator or police authority is executing a search warrant, including whether to consent to a search, how to advise employees, and how to approach the myriad of issues associated with searches and seizures of company documents. Legal counsel with specific experience should be consulted immediately to assist with an appropriate response that will help stabilize and secure business operations and determine an appropriate course of action.[2]

Reporting Obligations

Suppose that initial triage has been completed and the issues that have been identified are potentially significant. Even after safety and security issues are addressed, there may be other reasons why internal or external reporting of the issue might be warranted. The company's evaluation of its obligations should begin early on and sometimes will continue throughout the investigation process. Specific requirements will greatly depend on the facts and circumstances, but companies should seek advice and counsel about the considerations found in box 5-3

Box 5-3: *Fraud Reporting Considerations*

- *Disclosures to the board of directors.* If there are any serious allegations related to a senior executive or any matters of corporate significance, it may be appropriate to schedule a meeting of the board or the relevant committee to advise the board members of the issue.

- *Regulatory reporting obligations.* Certain regulations require reporting almost immediately. For example, disclosures are required regarding a company's inappropriate public release of customer credit card data. In another example, certain events or situations might warrant a Form 8-K disclosure. After the first 48 hours, there may be other regulatory reporting obligations, such as compliance with the requirements of the Sarbanes-Oxley Act of 2002.

- *Suspension of insider trading of the company's stock.* The company should consider whether it is necessary to take action to prevent trading by persons who may be in possession of nonpublic information.

- *Consideration of impacts on public financial reports and filings.* Although the information may not be fully known, the company should consider (1) the impact of any known facts and information on the accuracy of any imminent public financial statements or regulatory filings and (2) whether there is reason to believe that prior public financial statements or regulatory filings should either be amended or should not be relied upon. If the company has a disclosure committee, its members should be advised of relevant issues and allegations.

- *Reports to external auditors.* Companies generally must disclose any allegations of financial impropriety to their external auditors. If the allegations involve a possible accounting impropriety, matters relating to internal controls, or the integrity of persons with whom the external auditors interact, the auditors will need to understand and evaluate both the allegations and the company's response as part of their audit planning and to determine the impact on the nature and extent of their audit procedures. They also will consider whether the information suggests that any prior opinion should be withdrawn.

- *Reports to insurance carriers.* Applicable insurance policies may require notice of claims or circumstances that are likely to result in a claim

---

2 Finnegan, Sheila, "The First 72 Hours of a Government Investigation: A Guide to Identifying Issues and Avoiding Mistakes," *Briefly...Perspectives on legislation, regulation and litigation* 11, no. 2 (February 2007).

Whether a company has a legal duty to make a public disclosure regarding the investigation or underlying issues and the nature and extent of such disclosure is a judgment to be made with advice and legal counsel, depending on the facts and circumstances. Generally speaking, to the extent possible, it is often desirable to keep the investigation confidential and limit the number of people who are privy to investigation information.

Many companies respond proactively when faced with a significant allegation. For example, they may disclose the allegation to enforcement authorities, together with their planned investigative response and, later, the factual findings because self-disclosure and self-policing may reduce the exposure to regulatory and legal liability.

Similarly, when allegations are public or widely known, there may be reasons that favor some type of proactive communication to individual employees, groups of employees, or the public. Companies may be able to communicate about the current situation, the actions the company is taking, and the size of the previously reported transactions at issue, even if they cannot quantify the outcome of the investigation itself. However, public statements early in an investigation can be dangerous, especially if the company yields to the temptation to downplay the issue or overstate the known facts. These types of disclosures are almost certainly problematic, especially if a later investigation exposes them as incomplete, inaccurate, or misleading.

Organizing Investigations

Routine Investigations

At any given time, companies may have an ongoing number of individually minor investigation matters ongoing. Often these are handled internally. Some are handled by internal counsel, internal audit, compliance officers, or internal security departments.

Consider, for example, the second allegation in our Grand Forge Company case study. In this example, a report from the whistle-blower hotline was from a Grand Forge Company employee who alleged that her supervisor had been misstating his expense reporting to receive reimbursements in excess of the amounts actually incurred. For the purposes of the case study, let us further assume that the supervisor in question did not have a financial reporting role. If initial triage found no other reason to suspect a broader issue, this might reasonably be handled as a routine internal investigation. Other examples of routine investigations might include the following:

- Nonexecutive employment-related matters
- Vendor fraud that is not likely to be material to the financial statements
- Allegations of embezzlement of amounts that are clearly immaterial to the financial reports by persons who are neither executives nor in a financial reporting role
- Matters identified through the operation of internal controls (as opposed to those suggesting control deficiencies)
- Violations of internal policies that are not indicative of illegal conduct
- Allegations without indication of a material violation of contract
- Allegations that are unrelated to matters of interest to regulators or outsiders
- Human resources-related reports, such as concerns over drug use, harassment, breaches of policies or procedures, and unfair or unsafe working conditions

Clear and appropriate policies and procedures should be established to ensure that each allegation receives an appropriate response and that whistle-blower allegations are tracked and monitored. Both human resources and legal counsel should be involved in the design and oversight of internal investigation processes to ensure that internal investigations respect the rights of individuals, comply with any legal requirements in the jurisdiction, and help to identify issues that may require a more significant response. For further information on response planning Chapter 14, "Antifraud Programs," also touches on the subject.

Indeed, with respect to accounting and auditing matters, the Sarbanes-Oxley Act of 2002 requires the audit committee of the board of directors to "establish procedures for the receipt, retention and treatment of complaints received by the Company regarding accounting, internal accounting controls, or auditing matters; and confidential, anonymous submissions by employees of the Company of concerns regarding questionable accounting or auditing matters." Such policies and procedures may be more broadly implemented to cover other types of ethical or business-related allegations.

It is clear that not every allegation will require the highest levels of attention and resources. Nonetheless, those who are overseeing the routine investigations of a company would do well to at least raise and evaluate the same considerations as with the major investigations, tailoring their responses and their investigation to the specific facts and circumstances.

Major Investigations

No clear boundary exists between a routine and major investigation. Nonetheless, when the underlying allegations may have a significant effect on the company or a material effect on its financial reporting or when the allegations implicate a senior executive, it becomes more critical to explicitly address some of the major considerations in organizing an investigation, including the following:

- Who will sponsor the investigation and take responsibility for it?
- Will the investigation be conducted under the auspices of attorneys to reduce the likelihood that the investigation work product will be disclosed to third parties?
- Who will conduct the investigation?
- What will be the scope of the investigation?
- What will be the initial work plan?

Chapter 1, "Basics of Investigations," goes into greater detail about the framework that covers these considerations.

Identifying the Investigation Sponsor

The investigation sponsor is the person or persons who will take responsibility for the investigation. Although many people may provide recommendations, counsel, and advice, the investigation sponsor takes the oversight and decision making role, with respect to the investigation. Although the role of investigation sponsors may vary from situation to situation, their responsibilities generally include the following:

- Making or concurring with the decision that an investigation is warranted
- Determining the scope of the investigation
- Deciding who will conduct the investigation
- Retaining outside professionals, including legal counsel and forensic specialists, as needed
- Monitoring the status of the investigation
- Considering the factual findings of the investigation
- Recommending or deciding upon remedial actions
- Taking responsibility for conducting the investigation and for its adequacy

The credibility, objectivity and reliability of the investigation are important for sound decision making and may be important to external auditors, governmental authorities, and others. Therefore, it is important to consider the independence and objectivity of the investigation sponsor. Sponsors should be independent of the activities, transactions, and people who could potentially be subjects of the investigation. Of course, it is difficult at the outset to determine who may potentially become subjects of an investigation. When making decisions regarding the structure of an investigation, it is wise to consider a wider circle of potential subjects at the outset and narrow that circle after more information is known. In short, the board and audit committee have responsibility but several other parties may have a role in making decisions (see also chapter 6, "Roles and Responsibilities: How Different Stakeholders Work During Investigations").

Investigation structures that include sponsorship by audit committees or special committees of the board are routinely employed for significant financial investigations that might result in a material or significant finding related to financial reporting or internal control matters. Similarly, they also are used for investigations that involve senior executives because of the perception that it will be difficult for any subordinate to be objective regarding those who have influence over his or her career.

Using the third of the allegations in our case study as an example, Grand Forge Company recently received a seemingly routine inquiry from the SEC suggesting scrutiny of the company's executives' trading in stock and stock options. Assuming an investigation was warranted, it might not be appropriate to have a member of Grand Forge Company's executive team sponsor an investigation of the stock trading of fellow executives. In that instance, it might be appropriate for the audit committee or special committee of the board of directors to take responsibility for the investigation. In such a case, the board committee would typically engage outside professionals to manage the investigation, subject to its oversight and direction. In such a case, the Board committee would typically engage outside professionals to manage the investigation, subject to its oversight and direction. By contrast, in more routine investigations, if Grand Forge Company were to investigate non-executive employee expense reporting, a member of management, such as the general counsel or internal audit leader, might sponsor the investigation.

Ideally, the investigation sponsor will be positioned with sufficient authority to make all necessary decisions. This is especially true of decisions regarding the retention of professionals, the scope of work, and the initial work plan. During the first 48 hours, there will be little time for debate regarding these decisions. Furthermore, sponsors need to have the organizational clout to commit necessary resources and ensure that critical decisions are implemented.

Considering Legal Privileges

Almost every company undertaking an investigation hopes for a quick resolution without litigation or regulatory scrutiny. In many instances, however, the investigation uncovers facts or situations that prompt some sort of civil or criminal investigation by a government or regulatory authority or some sort of legal action by shareholders and outsiders. These legal issues sometimes relate directly to the initial predicate for the investigation. Other times, a business practice or individual employee conduct that is tangential or unrelated to the initial allegation is uncovered during the course of the investigation, some of which may expose a potential legal liability.

A company's ability to favorably resolve such legal matters may depend on it being able to resist disclosing its investigation work product to third parties. In the United States, communications and work products that are legally privileged may generally be shielded from disclosure to third parties. There following two well-recognized privileges are commonly asserted:

- The *attorney-client-privilege* protects certain private communications between attorneys and their clients when given in the context of actual or threatened litigation. By contrast, in the United States, except for certain tax questions, no corresponding accountant-client privilege can be reliably asserted to restrict the discovery or disclosure of a forensic accountant's investigative work product.
- *The attorney work product doctrine* protects an attorney's internal documentation of the work or analyses created in support of the attorney's representation of the client. If accountants or other specialists work at the attorney's direction to assist the attorney in providing legal advice, their work may be similarly privileged.[3]

It is important to consider legal privileges at the very outset of an investigation, simply because they arise due to the structure and objective of the investigation engagement. If the engagement is structured in the context of an attorney's legal counsel, privileges may be available. If the attorney's role is an empty formality or if the attorney is not consulted until the end of the investigation, the investigation work and all communications may potentially be discoverable by third parties. Actions taken to properly structure the investigation and keep certain information confidential will help ensure that any legal privileges are available, and a company's ability to resist discovery of an investigation's work product is not compromised.

When there is a major investigation in the United States, because of the existence of these legal privileges, an attorney is usually retained by the investigation sponsor as the lead investigator. Then, the

---

3 The question of whether and to what degree various legal privileges attach to specific engagements, documents, or communications is, in itself, a legal judgment that is dependent on the facts and circumstances.

attorney may retain other forensic specialists, such as legal technology professionals or forensic accountants. With this structure, the investigation sponsor may shield the work products of the investigation and can choose whether to disclose them. The investigation sponsor and investigation team generally cannot be compelled to disclose privileged work products.

Even when an attorney is retained as the lead investigator, the actual work of the investigation can be apportioned among the company, attorneys, accountants, and other specialists in any way that is appropriate, as long as the attorney directs the work and the work is conducted in the context of assisting the attorney in rendering legal advice. Chapter 10, "Working with Attorneys: The Relationship With Counsel," explores the relationship between counsel and other members of an investigation in greater depth.

Determining Who Will Execute the Investigation

Identifying the people who will conduct the investigation is an important decision because the judgment and counsel of the investigators will influence the course of the investigation. Their skill will directly impact the quality and speed of execution. Finally, their experience will help the company avoid pitfalls and missteps. Chapter 6, "Roles and Responsibilities: How Different Stakeholders Work During Investigations," covers all of the interactions among stakeholders, but this section focuses on the investigation sponsor.

Usually, the investigation sponsor makes the decisions regarding which attorneys and accountants will work on an investigation and whether internal resources will be devoted to the investigation. Although the selection and retention of attorneys, accountants, and specialists can be revisited, mid-course changes are rare due to the costs associated with bringing a new team up to speed. In any event, any professionals who become involved at later dates will be affected by the decisions made by the investigators working in the first 48 hours.

There are a variety of considerations that may be relevant in selecting an investigation team, and some of the most important are outlined in box 5-4.

In addition to these skills, the company also may need to consult with other advisors, some of whom may be needed after the first 48 hours. These might include counsel with particular regulatory expertise, litigation counsel, settlement counsel,

Box 5-4: *Selecting an Investigation Team*

- *Independence and objectivity.* Just as the investigation sponsor should be independent and objective regarding the matter being investigated, so should the investigators. Regulators, external auditors, and other stakeholders generally find independent investigation by external specialists to be more credible than those performed by internal persons because of perceptions regarding independence and objectivity. They also may consider the reputation of the law and professional services firms, attorneys, and other professionals involved. For example, the SEC has stated that its enforcement considerations include factors such as whether the investigation was sponsored by company employees or outside directors, whether employees or outsiders conducted the review, or whether any outside counsel or professionals had previously worked for the company.[4] External auditors also will consider independence and objectivity in evaluating the reliability of the investigation work for their purposes, sometimes conducting more testing when necessary to address any unresolved risks or conducting more limited testing if a reliable, objective investigation has been conducted. By contrast, a biased, advocacy-oriented investigation may be worse than useless because it may undermine the company's credibility and impede the company's ability to resolve any outstanding matters.

(continued)

4 Securities and Exchange Commission Release No. 44969, *Report of Investigation Pursuant to Section 21(a) of the Securities Exchange Act of 1934 and Commission Statement of the Relationship of Cooperation to Agency Enforcement Decisions*, issued October 23, 2001, and available at www.sec.gov/litigation/investreport/34-44969.htm.

Box 5-4: *Selecting an Investigation Team (continued)*

- *Understanding of the legal requirements in relevant jurisdictions.* Sponsors and investigators should be advised by legal counsel who have appropriate expertise about each of the localities and jurisdictions that are relevant to the investigation. Ideally, any accountants and specialists also will have a working familiarity with those legal requirements. The entire investigative team needs to work within the legal requirements for conducting an investigation, must be respectful of the rights of those with whom they will interface, and must anticipate the ways the investigation outputs may be used.

- *Competence.* Investigators may need a variety of industry, business process, accounting, legal, regulatory compliance, technology, and operations expertise. Because it is rare that one individual professional possesses all the relevant skills and experience, the overall competence of the team and the team leaders is the most appropriate measure. Further, it takes more than an understanding of underlying issues to properly conduct an investigation. The investigators also need an understanding of the investigation process itself. They should understand the commonly performed and generally accepted procedures for gathering and analyzing investigative evidence and the strengths and weaknesses to various approaches for addressing the company's investigation needs. They should be able to anticipate preventable pitfalls and be willing and able to provide sound advice and counsel to other stakeholders of the potential upside and downside of decisions that will need to be made throughout the process. Competent investigators help prevent surprises during the work and help ensure that it will be usable for all the different stakeholders who might have need of the investigation outputs. In short, this is no time to educate a professional who has never previously participated in an investigation.

- *Electronic evidence expertise.* Few investigations do not need to consider whether and to what extent electronic evidence should be preserved, collected, and analyzed. Therefore, someone on the engagement needs this expertise. Because they are involved in security and collecting evidence at the very start of engagements, forensic technology specialists are frequently among the first professionals retained. Forensic technology specialists may or may not be employed by the same company or professional firm as other members of the investigative team. In any event, they should be capable and willing to work cooperatively with others on the investigative team.

- *Subject matter expertise.* Although some investigations address general or commonly understood issues, specialized knowledge may be helpful or even essential to the investigation. For example, the matter under investigation may be affected by industry practice; the unique aspects of a particular company's business process; or some technical or specialized accounting, tax, or regulatory compliance issue. Deep expertise can always be added to the team after the early hours, but it is often helpful to have subject matter experts who can help recognize unusual or suspicious fact patterns quickly.

- *Language and geographic reach.* Geographic reach affects both the quality and speed of an investigation. Even smaller businesses have global business transactions, and some investigations involve interviews of people in areas around the world. Other investigations will need to consider documents and evidence in languages other than English. Although there are many appropriate ways to gather and analyze information from around the world, investigators with deep familiarity with local languages, local business customs, and culture are a great asset. For example, interviews in the local language can convey rich detail and nuance, whereas interviews conducted through a translator may be stilted and slow. Similarly, investigators who are aware of the local laws or business practices can ensure that the investigation complies with such requirements. Finally, working with an investigative firm or team that has adequate geographic reach can be a significant timesaver. If skilled resources are readily available where they are needed, the time associated with travel and logistics in the early hours of an investigation can be significantly reduced.

advisors regarding business process improvement and internal controls design and implementation, tax advisors, and media and public relations specialists. Consultation with these experts in these areas is a consideration, but may or may not be necessary in light of the facts and circumstances.

Scope of the Investigation

The investigation sponsor should articulate the scope of the investigation, often with the advice of counsel and investigative specialists. Articulating a specific scope will focus the work of the investigators and avoid unnecessary and costly distractions. Ideally, the scope of the investigation should be sufficiently broad to answer the likely questions of the various stakeholders For example, if there is an allegation of a particular type of potentially fraudulent transaction, the scope of the investigation might focus on the specific transaction in the allegation but also might include the question of whether there were any other potential frauds of this type in a relevant time frame. Generally, it is preferable that the scope be slightly broader than the known allegations to provide confidence that the investigation has caught all the related issues. Although the scope should be broad enough to ensure that the investigation is adequate, it also must be sufficiently narrow to permit the work to be targeted and timely.

Both the sponsor and team should have a clear understanding of the scope of the investigation at the outset. Therefore, decisions regarding the scope of the investigation are important and should be addressed in the first 48 hours, even if they are revisited later. As the team and sponsor learn more, the scope of the investigation may need to be revised. For example, the investigation could be cut short if issues are put to bed based on the evidence. Alternatively, it is common that the scope of the investigation is expanded if the facts lead to new questions or concerns.

Although they frequently receive advice and counsel, investigative sponsors have the overall responsibility for setting the scope of the investigation and ensuring that the scope is adequate. Because the scope guides the team in determining the nature and extent of procedures, third parties who may wish to consider or rely on the investigation outputs often ask for a clear articulation of the investigation scope. The SEC, for example, considers the breadth and adequacy of an internal investigation's scope among its enforcement considerations. Similarly, the external auditors may ask the investigation sponsor to affirm responsibility for the investigation scope and its adequacy and explain any rationale behind decisions about the scope.

Organizing the Team and Developing a Work Plan

Time spent addressing the details of team organization and logistics usually pays off handsomely by speeding the execution of the work and ensuring that all team members understand their roles, responsibilities, and expectations. Examples of such steps include the following:

- Identifying the team members and developing contact lists.
- Identifying the key decision makers within the team.
- Ensuring that all team members understand the investigation scope, any other project objectives, and on whose behalf the investigation is being conducted.
- Clarifying whether there is an intent to conduct the investigation within any available legal privileges and providing guidance to nonattorneys regarding work processes, work paper labeling, and communication protocols to avoid inadvertent waivers of legal privileges or disclosure of confidential information.
- Identifying any relevant laws, investigative practices, or regulatory requirements that may affect the conduct of the investigation. For example, in the United States, it may be appropriate to provide so-called Upjohn warnings to people being interviewed to ensure that there is no confusion regarding whether legal counsel is representing those people.

In the same way that the scope of an investigation may change as more information is learned, work plans tend to evolve during the execution of an investigation. Although few plans survive contact with the evidence, they remain essential to coordinating the effort of the team.

Ideally, a preliminary work plan will set the over-arching objective and divide the tasks into manageable work streams. Engagement planning also requires consideration of any matters on the critical path. For example, it may make sense to have brief information-gathering interviews to identify the sources of evidence and the people most likely to have knowledge of the matters at issue. Similarly, it may make sense to postpone any analysis of evidential matter until documents are secured and collection is underway.

In a major investigation, it is generally desirable to have an opportunity to review e-mails, paper-based documents, and other evidence prior to conducting critical interviews. Rarely is there time to do so in the first 48 hours. A preliminary work plan allows for planning of the order and objectives of any interviews and for beginning the process of considering any evidence that should be analyzed prior to the interviews.

Project planning, at least in a tentative way, should consider the nature of the desired output of the investigation. For example, the team should ascertain whether the investigation sponsor desires a written or oral report or specific analyses. In some instances, decisions about outputs will be influenced by external auditors and regulators. Nonetheless, even a preliminary understanding of the expected outputs can help investigators begin to orient their procedures toward the desired result.

Because of their oversight role, investigative sponsors should approve the preliminary work plan. Often, if external auditors and regulators are aware of the investigation, they may be willing and able to provide input to the work plan. These stakeholders will usually not assume the responsibility for the adequacy of the work plan, and their inputs are sometimes characterized as suggestions. Nonetheless, early input regarding the work plan can help increase the likelihood that the external auditors, regulators, and other third parties will look favorably on the investigation. This, in turn, may mitigate or reduce the likelihood of duplicative audit procedures or investigation proceedings.

Securing and Gathering Evidence

Securing and gathering evidence are among the most important tasks in the first 48 hours of an investigation. Arguably, many other tasks could be accomplished or revisited later. By contrast, some evidence may be lost or destroyed, if not preserved immediately.

Once an allegation is made, there may be little time to lose. If a person who has committed wrongdoing is aware that information is coming to light or that the possibility of an investigation looms, that person may be powerfully motivated to alter or destroy evidence or make it much more difficult to find. Further, if proactive steps are not taken, even normal business processes may result in the destruction of evidence.

Although the process of securing and gathering evidence typically swings into full gear when the investigation team is assembled, companies can and should begin securing and gathering evidence as soon as it is clear it will be needed.

The goal in the first 48 hours should be to maintain the integrity and completeness of any available records, in order to ensure that a complete investigation can be conducted sometime in the future. In addition, companies should consider and address any legal or regulatory requirements to preserve or gather evidence.

Often, there is a rush to investigate and analyze the evidence immediately. In most cases, however, it makes sense to secure relevant records first and begin the analysis either in a parallel process or after the tasks related to securing the evidence are complete. For more information regarding collecting and analyzing evidence, see chapters 7 ("Sources of Evidence") and 8 ("Electronic Evidence").

Early Interviews of Employees and Other People

Understandably, obtaining information from knowledgeable people is often among the first steps in an investigation. Many good reasons exist to make investigation inquiries in the first 48 hours, including the following:

- *Inquiries of the whistle-blower or first person with knowledge of the issue.* Often, these inquiries are made in the context of initial triage, and have the purpose of developing an understanding of the nature and details of the allegation.
- *Inquiries to gather evidence.* If the issues are discrete and straightforward, inquiries of other knowledgeable people can sometimes uncover information directly and efficiently. Even when the issues are complex and unlikely to be resolved in the first 48 hours, initial inquiries can help determine whether the initial allegation has merit and can help direct the investigation's next steps.
- *Interviews to establish a working knowledge of relevant business processes, sources of information, and likely custodians.* Many of the interviews in the early stages of the investigation lay the foundation for evidence gathering and provide the context for additional, more comprehensive investigation inquiries. Investigators typically must develop a baseline understanding of the normal business process that will be investigated; how it may have evolved over time; the role of individual people within that process; which people are likely to have relevant paper or electronic evidence; and the nature, extent, format, and location of the evidence.

Notwithstanding the value and need for early interviews, a number of risks and considerations are associated with investigation-related interviews. Because early interviews are sometimes conducted prior to the retention of counsel and before the investigation team and processes are fully in place, these risks are worthy of mention.

The company or its investigators should seek counsel related to the legalities associated with the interviews. First, the company should consider whether it should conduct the interviews under the purview of an attorney. The company and its counsel may wish to rely on legal privileges to limit the ways in which the information developed during such interviews may be legally shielded from external disclosure to permit the company to better defend itself against any follow-on litigation related to the issues under investigation. Good legal counsel can help address questions about whether legal privileges are desirable and how to structure the inquiries to best preserve any available privileges.

In addition, a competent attorney can advise regarding proper ways to

- obtain the cooperation of employees.
- limit exposure to wrongful termination, defamation, or other claims by employees associated with an investigation.
- avoid confusion about whom any attorneys actually represent.
- advise employees about seeking their own counsel, if appropriate.
- avoid witness tampering or even the appearance of it.
- respect unique legal requirements in different countries or legal jurisdictions.

During investigation inquiries, it is important to keep the process confidential, to the extent possible. When making inquiries, investigators may ask the people with whom they speak to keep the inquiry and information gathered confidential. Although such requests are not always respected, making this expectation explicit may help reduce gossip and alarm among employees.

Investigators also should take care to avoid divulging unnecessary information related to the allegation. They should take care to avoid disclosing the identity of any confidential whistle-blowers. It may be appropriate to put procedures in place to prevent employees from being updated or informed about emerging investigation outputs. Executives who are subjects of the investigation should not be permitted to interfere with the investigation or substantively discuss the investigation with others who are being interviewed. Investigators themselves also should be careful not to taint the recollections of those they are interviewing by unnecessarily disclosing what others have said in interviews or sharing documents and other information that are not necessary to the interview.

Although time pressures are common during the early stages of an investigation, it is important to clearly document any interviews. It is generally a good practice to memorialize the interview in clear notes or a memorandum that documents the statements or assertions made by each person.

Document Preservation Orders and Similar Instructions to Employees

Depending on the issue and relevant legal jurisdiction, companies may be required to preserve documents and evidence related to the matter. Whether and to what extent document preservation is required is a legal judgment. Lawyers sometimes advise companies to preserve documentation as soon as there is reason to believe that such evidence may be relevant to an investigation or litigation matter. U.S. federal law generally requires the retention of records relevant to a likely government investigation.

Working with internal or external counsel, companies typically use a variety of approaches to ensure compliance with whatever level of document preservation is required, including the following:

- Direct communication of requirements to individual custodians
- Written document preservation and collection orders to individual custodians
- Actions to secure, collect or copy existing electronic or paper-based evidence
- Actions to secure existing archives or repositories

Importantly, one aspect of document preservation is to halt any regular, ongoing or scheduled destruction of documents. These can include, among other things, the scheduled destruction of records in archival storage, everyday deletions and discarding of documents by employees, or overwriting electronically stored information.

Commonly, the company's internal counsel will issue a written document preservation or collection order to people who are believed to have custody of relevant information. Such written orders are usually drafted broadly to include a very wide range of possible documentation, including both paper-based and electronically stored information. Once the need for document preservation becomes apparent, a company should develop a plan for ongoing compliance with those requirements. This may include identifying a person to communicate to the appropriate employees and disseminate any specific instructions regarding the order. Once such orders are in place, that person or persons should take responsibility for the ongoing management of such orders, including updating and monitoring compliance document preservation and collection orders, identifying and communicating to employees when such orders have been lifted, maintaining whatever collections of documents have been gathered, and addressing documents retention questions that will arise during the pendency of the order.

Another early decision concerns which of the following approaches to document preservation and collection will be employed:

(1) *Instruct the custodians to preserve such evidence but leave the evidence in their care and custody.* This is generally the least costly and disruptive of these approaches. Nevertheless, it relies entirely on the compliance of individual custodians, some of whom may have little appreciation for the importance of the activity. Also, some custodians may misunderstand or fail to heed the instructions. Even these preservation activities can be somewhat disruptive because individual custodians must change their business practices to avoid destruction in the ordinary course. In one example of this approach, back-up tapes containing electronically stored information might merely be secured and preserved. Decisions about whether to collect and analyze such evidence can be postponed until more information is known.

(2) *Instruct the custodians to preserve and produce the evidence (self-collection).* This middle-ground approach asks employees to produce copies of the evidence to a designated person who will take responsibility for the documents and addressing any litigation- or investigation-related document requests. This approach can be costly because the employees will necessarily bear the time burden and inconvenience associated with collecting and transmitting the evidence. It also can be cumbersome, incomplete, and unreliable, to the extent that employees are unable or unwilling to comply with the requirements. For certain types of electronically stored information, this collection responsibility may be delegated to IT personnel who may copy and set aside information that is accessible on servers or other centralized storage media. This approach also carries with it the cost associated with maintaining a repository of documentation for as long as needed for the investigative or litigation purpose. Once collected, however, the chain of custody and the risk that evidence will be altered or corrupted is greatly mitigated. This approach might be used, for example, if investigators want to secure, as of a particular date, certain records that are amended frequently in the course of day-to-day operations. In that instance, it might be easier and more cost-effective to have the custodians copy and produce the relevant documents. Then they might be able to continue to use the documents in the ordinary course.

(3) *Collection by investigators or forensic specialists.* When performed by competent forensic professionals, this approach provides the highest degree of comfort that the evidential matter as of a given time is preserved with integrity and that a chain of custody can be established. It is used most commonly when the matters at issue may be litigated or scrutinized by regulators or third parties; when the risk of loss due to tampering, destruction, or inadvertent deletion is high; or when there is a technical challenge to the collection. Sometimes investigators perform the collection of evidence out of the sheer need for speed and the desire to avoid burdening the company's regular staff. For example, this approach is frequently used for the preservation of evidence on employee laptops and server-based e-mail. Outside specialists frequently collect forensic images of laptops to ensure that the collection is of high quality and could later be used in court. A forensic copy, if properly taken, is as useful as the original. By contrast, a copy made by the internal IT staff who are not familiar with forensic requirements may lack metadata or other attributes that can be useful to investigators. Once a forensic copy is taken, regular business processes can continue unchanged, with employees using their laptops and e-mail in the same way as before.

Chain of Custody

Chain of custody refers to the chronology of who has had possession of physical evidence and where that evidence was stored. Providing a clear account of the chain of custody can be important when litigation matters go to trial. Then, investigators may need to show that there has been no tampering of the evidence.

When transferring, moving, or securing evidence, it may be appropriate to document the chain of custody. For example, work papers can document the capture and handling of forensic images of electronically stored information to provide support for an assertion that the evidence is unaltered from the version that was initially collected. Similarly, documentation regarding the chain of custody of physical evidence could include contemporaneous cover letters, transmittal documentation, or memorandums.

In any investigation, multiple approaches can be used. Indeed, the approaches may change during the course of the investigation as more information becomes known.

Decisions about the need, nature, extent, and approach to document preservation and collection are always based on the unique facts and circumstances of each situation. A key consideration in determining which approach to take for each kind of evidence available is the current assessment of whether the custodian is likely to be implicated in the matters to be investigated, whether suspected people might have access to the evidence, and whether the records may be altered or changed as a result of normal business processes. Other considerations include the cost, the potential for burden on the company and its employees, the relative importance of the issue at hand, and whether third-party litigation or regulatory scrutiny is likely. As discussed in chapter 7, "Sources of Evidence," the form and format of the evidence, whether it is easily changed or altered, and whether the documents or data are needed in everyday operations also can weigh heavily in this decision.

Preparing in advance for document preservation and collection

An effective records management program not only reduces costs in the long run but also supports more effective preservation and collection of electronic and paper-based information when such litigation and investigation needs arise. Advance preparation helps ensure that information is present and readily obtainable when needed. To prepare, companies should consider the following:

(1) Developing policies and creating time-tables for the disposal of records, including electronic and paper records, once they have reached the end of the applicable business, legal, and regulatory retention period. Special consideration must be given to areas of the company that are highly regulated or more susceptible to litigation.

(2) Creating formalized plans for responding to discovery requests. Such plans may include appointing the person(s) responsible, establishing processes to identify relevant information, and developing templates for preservation orders and instructions to employees.

(3) Monitoring compliance with records retention policies and procedures. Controls could include testing a sample of documents against a department's records retention policy or evaluating the activities and documentation related to outstanding preservation orders. Monitoring activities will support an assessment of whether retention policies and procedures are functioning as designed, where practices are strong, and where there is need for improvement.

What to Preserve or Collect

In the first 48 hours, investigators develop and begin to document an understanding of the type of evidence that is available, where it is, who is responsible for it, and whether any steps must be taken to preserve or secure it. Oftentimes, early interviews will provide this information.

An investigation team's understanding of the nature and extent of evidence can evolve considerably during the course of an investigation. Documentation of the initial assessment of the nature and extent of the evidence and the initial steps taken to preserve and gather that information are very helpful in the long run because they assist those who use the outputs of the investigation in understanding the decisions made at the outset when knowledge was incomplete.

Custodians From Whom to Collect

Often, as suggested earlier, initial inquiries help identify which custodians should receive a document preservation order and which might be the most fruitful sources of needed information. Investigators often think first of current employees, including any suspects; any persons who are involved in the specific business process under scrutiny; administrative assistants; direct managers; and direct subordinates. It helps to think broadly about others who also might have custody of relevant information, such as former employees, officers and directors, vendors, professional services firms, and customers, if appropriate.

Although it might be reasonable to ask all custodians to preserve or produce the same types of evidence, situations may exist when such requests can be tailored so that some custodians are only asked to provide specific information. For example, certain IT professionals might be asked to provide system-wide data but those responsible for a particular business process might be asked for procedural documentation.

Securing Paper-Based Books, Records, and Documents

Although the overall philosophy and goal of document preservation are generally the same, regardless of the form or format of the information, different practical considerations exist depending on whether the information is paper based or electronic.

One way to approach the process of securing and gathering paper-based records and documents is to think through the issue in terms of which custodians have the records and the relative security of the location where the documents are stored.

As with the decision about whether to preserve or collect evidence, the key considerations in securing paper-based evidence revolve around a current assessment of whether the custodian is likely to be implicated in the matters to be investigated, whether suspected people might have access to the evidence, and whether the records may be altered or changed as a result of normal business processes. Using the third allegation in our Grand Forge Company case study as an example, suppose the investigation was focused on the seemingly routine SEC inquiry related to executives' trading in company stock and stock options. If records related to these trades were maintained by the corporate secretary and if there was no reason to believe that the corporate secretary's conduct or responsibilities were related to the inquiry, it might be reasonable to ask that person to preserve the relevant documents and take no further action to secure or collect them.

By contrast, a different response might be appropriate for the fourth allegation in the Grand Forge Company case study, arising from complaints by overseas customers that the country manager had pressured them to take product in excess of their needs and below contract specifications. For the investigation of that fourth allegation, it might be reasonable to evaluate whether the country manager's paper-based records could reasonably be considered secure in his own custody or the custody of his subordinates while an investigation was pending. In that case, Grand Forge Company might conclude that additional steps to physically secure or copy the relevant documents are necessary to maintain the integrity of the paper-based evidence.

Additional considerations, based on the custodian and location of the evidence, may include the following:

- *Documentation in the suspected persons' offices or work spaces.* Depending on the nature of the allegation and the facts and circumstances, materials under the control of suspected persons are sometimes secured by changing locks on the office door, copying and moving the copies of the relevant documentation to a secure location, or moving the original records to a secure location. Initially, the goal may be to secure the documents and maintain the integrity and chain of custody of the data set. Later, it is helpful to inventory the collected evidence, evaluate the nature of it, determine whether continued preservation of the documentation is warranted or necessary for ongoing operations, and make a plan to balance any litigation or regulatory preservation requirements with the needs of the investigation and the ongoing needs of the business.

- *Documentation maintained by other employees at the work site.* In the first 48 hours, it is helpful to develop at least a rough inventory of the relevant books, records, and documentary evidence that are available at the company's work sites and the people who are responsible for the custody of that evidence. A rough inventory can be helpful to ensure that all the relevant evidence is preserved and, if necessary, secured. Often, the rough inventory is an evolving working document because the types, nature, and extent of evidence may need to be updated, revised, or expanded as the investigation team learns more and clarifies its understanding.

- *Documentation retained in long-term storage areas or in off-site storage.* In the first 48 hours, consideration should be given to securing and preserving any records in long-term storage. For example, it may be appropriate to suspend regular document destruction if potentially relevant documents may be lost. Some companies have routine off-site and on-site document destruction processes, such as standing orders with off-site storage

The following are possible sources of paper-based evidence:

- *General ledgers, subsidiary ledgers, and other financial reports*
- *Personnel files*
- *Nonfinancial corporate records, such as operational statistics, production records, and customer relationship management records*
- *Payroll reports and subsidiary documentation*
- *Employee desk files*
- *Records in off-site archives and long-term storage locations*
- *Customer files*
- *Publicly-available documents*
- *Documents at employees' homes*

Securing Electronic Evidence

Electronic data on live computers are extremely volatile and are readily susceptible to updates, modifications, and deletion. To preserve the data, electronic information must be in the control of people who understand its volatility and are committed to protecting the data. Often, in the context of an investigation, that commitment means that the investigation team makes a forensic copy of the evidence and retains the copy, taking care to preserve the chain of custody. In certain situations, it also may be reasonable to have individual employees preserve their own electronic information.

Any decisions regarding electronic evidence will be informed by an understanding of the nature, breadth, and depth of the information that has been stored electronically. Often times, companies are surprised to find that their knowledge of their formal systems for storing electronic information is incomplete or outdated. There may be both formal data systems and informal data processes. Companies may have multiple work sites and external locations with electronically stored information. In addition, employees and work groups may have retained a wide variety of electronic information in web-based repositories, informal storage arrangements, personal electronic devices, portable media, home computers or other places, some of which may not be within a company's control. Companies can be prepared well in advance of an actual allegation by developing an understanding of the electronic data environment, key systems and sources of electronic evidence. A broad discussion of litigation technology and electronic evidence preservation, collection, and processing is found in chapter 8, "Electronic Evidence."

A key objective in the first 48 hours is to identify the systems and data that may be relevant to the allegation, including a broad array of the potential sources and types of data. During this phase, it is helpful to think expansively, even if the investigation scope is later narrowed. Typically, the risk of

providers to destroy documents over a certain age or arrangements for on-site shredding with a third-party document-shredding vendor. In those instances, it may be necessary to take affirmative steps to prevent the destruction of documents. Similarly, it may be appropriate to change the locks or otherwise secure storage areas that might have valuable but vulnerable archival records or other documents.

- *Documentation related to the initial allegation or early interviews.* Some whistle-blowers provide a sheaf of supporting documents for their allegations. Other times, even very early interviews can result in a collection of documents. For example, employees responding to an inquiry about a problematic business transaction may provide the relevant documents as part of their responses.
- *Documents maintained by non-employees and third parties.* Sometimes, documentation from public sources or in the private hands of nonemployees and third parties can be highly relevant. Usually, investigators must obtain this information through voluntary compliance with a document request.

The following are possible sources of electronically stored evidence:

- *Archived e-mail.*
- *Server e-mail.*
- *Employees' hard drives (including both laptop and desktop and both present and past employees, if available).*
- *Employees' laptops, desktops, and personal computers, if used for work purposes. (This may be particularly relevant when remote connection is possible.)*
- *Private network file shares, including departmental shares and home drives.*
- *Public network file shares.*
- *Network devices and records, such as VPN logs; firewall logs; and desktop, laptop, and server system logs.*
- *Knowledge bases, such as eRoom, Lotus Notes repositories, virtual work and collaboration rooms, and chat rooms provided by the company.*
- *Financial systems.*
- *Back-up tapes.*
- *Instant messaging.*
- *Voicemail.*
- *Fax machines and copiers with resident electronic memory.*
- *Disks and other media, including CDs and DVDs.*
- *Electronic document retention and archival systems.*
- *Portable hard drives, including USB devices, data sticks, and flash or thumb drives.*
- *Personal mobile devices, including cell phones, personal digital assistants, BlackBerrys, iPhones, and other smart phones.*
- *Digitized voicemail.*
- *Electronic data hosted by third parties.*
- *Transactional systems, such as general ledger, human resources, payroll, financial reporting, accounting, customer relationship management, enterprise resource planning, accounts payable, and accounts receivable systems and subsystems.*
- *Backups of any of these sources.*

identifying too much data is low becausethe cost or impact can be mitigated at any time by narrowing the investigation. By contrast, the risk of failing to identify relevant data can be high because data can be lost forever if it is not properly secured. Data loss may, in turn, irrevocably jeopardize the quality and results of the investigation.

Typically, the work will start with an interview of the IT points of contact for the relevant information systems. This interview, and any follow-up inquiries, could focus on the following:

- An overview of the current IT systems and data
- The history of any past changes or pending updates to hardware, software, or processes
- How particular IT systems relate to company processes
- The physical and logical locations for hardware and data, including any systems or software used
- Backup protocols and schedules and tools for relevant systems
- Any inventories of relevant IT hardware
- Available data repositories, including both online and off-line data

Even when a company has a well-established baseline understanding of its systems, interviews in the first 48 hours can assist in updating and confirming current understandings by identifying any additional elements of electronic evidence that should be considered and helping understand any unique aspects relevant to the particular systems in question or time frame of the allegation.

In addition to understanding the overall electronic environment, the preservation of electronically stored information also should address the following:

- *Backup tapes.* Almost every IT environment has a backup protocol, which usually includes some method of backing up live electronic data and software onto tapes or other media. These tapes are primarily used for restoring data and systems that may be inadvertently lost due to disaster or some disruption in the IT environment. For this reason, they are often kept only as long as needed, and older backup tapes are frequently deleted or overwritten on an established rotation schedule. Considered in the context of litigation or investigation, these tapes are a valuable source of evidence because the backups may include e-mails or other data as it existed at historical dates. When restored, backup tapes provide historical evidence and help fill in gaps, especially with respect to deleted information. Because they are so important, one of the first steps in electronic evidence preservation is the suspension of any normal destruction of backup tapes. Theoretically, this preservation order could be sent to the IT professionals almost at the very first indication that preservation will be needed, and it could be lifted or modified as needed after more information becomes known.

- *Prior litigation repositories.* Because litigation and investigation are now more common, it is increasingly likely that companies may have previously preserved electronically stored information related to some prior matter, even if that matter is entirely unrelated. During the process of preserving and collecting information, the team should consider an inventory of any previously preserved document and electronic data repositories to determine whether the collection contains copies of potentially relevant data sources.

- *Differences in privacy and electronic evidence laws in other jurisdictions.* In the United States, investigators may usually gain access to employees' e-mails and other electronically stored information on company computers. In other jurisdictions, there may be restrictions on the collection and analysis of this information, such as those imposed by the European Union's Directive 95/46/EC on data protection. Investigators should seek competent counsel to understand the requirements of all the localities in which they are working.

- *Employees' personal computers and stored data.* Employees may have stored relevant company records on their own personal computers or on web-based storage, either for personal convenience or to preserve a collection of evidence regarding some matter about which they had some concern. During investigative interviews, it is helpful to ask whether individuals have any relevant information in their personal custody and to ask for it to be produced to the team. Although the company or team may not be able to compel someone to produce evidence,

individuals sometimes do so voluntarily. Even if they do not, asking the question may be good investigative diligence.

The goal of securing electronic evidence is to preserve and make accessible authentic copies of the electronic evidence. Electronic data is fragile and can be manipulated or spoiled, even unintentionally. *Metadata*, the embedded electronic data about the data, are even more fragile. All of this information can be highly relevant in certain investigations. Investigative specialists take care to make forensic copies, which can be demonstrated to be exact copies of the evidence, not mere logical copies. It is incredibly easy to make unintentional modifications to the data and metadata of electronic files. Many stories exist of the eager investigator or IT professional who scanned or reviewed the electronic data prior to forensic preservation and unintentionally destroyed metadata or corrupted the integrity of the files. In one example, simply using Microsoft's Windows Explorer to look at the properties of a Microsoft Word document changed the metadata about that document. It is a best practice to secure and preserve the relevant data before any analysis or work is performed on it.

Notwithstanding this, forensic specialists can use a variety of techniques to analyze large populations of electronic evidence. Although it is rare that any investigator will have a full grasp of the electronic evidence in the first few days of an investigation, a number of tools and techniques give a proper early view of the issues by using electronic evidence.

As with the paper-based evidence and information gathered from interviews, an understanding of the nature and extent of the evidence may evolve over time. Although the collection and analysis of electronically stored information will continue well after the first 48 hours, the team should begin its documentation of its electronic evidence preservation steps immediately. The investigation also should consider preserving electronic data that serve as a record of the document preservation and collection efforts. For instance, the team could preserve reports from the company's asset tracking system to demonstrate that all the computers for each custodian were preserved and collected. Preservation of the reports from the technology help desk or "trouble ticket" system related to the custodians' computers may help demonstrate whether custodians had a recent hard drive replacement and whether the team searched for any old computers. For more information regarding collecting and analyzing evidence, see chapters 7 ("Sources of Evidence") and 8 ("Electronic Evidence").

After the First 48 Hours

When the Allegation Is Found to Be Without Merit

Thankfully, many instances are found in which the issues and allegations have little merit. In some cases, an allegation may be found to be unworthy of follow-up after an assessment during initial triage. In others, the allegation is investigated, and an assessment to close the investigation is made after some evidence gathering and analysis. In both cases, the critical element is a thoughtful assessment based on the information available.

The company can reasonably anticipate that it will be asked to defend its conclusion. For example, an external auditor could ask about the resolution of any matters reported on the whistle-blower hotline. In another example, a whistle-blower could go to a regulator and cause an inquiry to be opened. The company can anticipate and mitigate this by articulating and documenting its resolutions. Documentation of the assessment and basis for the conclusions will vary, based on the facts and circumstances.

Among the elements of such an assessment is the consideration of the evidence and a determination of whether that evidence is an adequate basis for the conclusion. When evidence is found, assessing its adequacy is relatively straightforward. It is much more difficult to reach that conclusion when little or no evidence is found. The critical question is whether there truly is no evidence or whether relevant evidence exists but was not found.

The corollary to this question is whether the investigators have done enough work to find and consider all the relevant evidence. The logic of this type of assessment flows deductively from the adequacy of the procedures to the gaps or absence of evidence despite adequate procedures, the nature of what is known, and the conclusion itself.

Consider, for example, the fourth allegation in our Grand Forge Company case study related to the overseas customer who complained of being pressured to take goods in excess of their needs and receiving poor quality goods. Assume that Grand Forge Company conducted an initial investigation that was perfunctory, consisting only of a limited inquiry of the country manager and his subordinates and a scan of recent invoices gathered in the corporate headquarters. Assume further that these procedures identified no evidence that would support the allegation. In this example, it might not be reasonable for Grand Forge Company to conclude that the allegations lacked merit because the investigation failed to gather and consider critical information.

Now, assume an alternate scenario in which Grand Forge Company conducted adequate investigation procedures. Assume that Grand Forge Company secured and gathered paper and electronic evidence; interviewed the customer, the country manager, and others with knowledge of the customer relationship; and considered the information in the company's possession, including the records in the subsidiary's local office. If these types of procedures were determined to be adequate in light of the facts and circumstances and Grand Forge Company found nothing that would reasonably support the allegation, the conclusion to close the investigation is much better supported and reasonable.

In addition, before closing a matter, it is reasonable to ask whether the company has identified the underlying reason for the allegation or issue. Whistle-blowers rarely come forward without any reason, although their motivations can be varied. Oftentimes, employees have a genuine concern or workplace grievance that should be addressed. Other times, the employee's concern is real, but the report is based on a misunderstanding or partial understanding of the facts. In a number of situations, whistle-blowers may be acting based on a personal grudge, may seek to gain personally from their reports, or may be seeking employment protections through a variety of laws and rules that protect whistle-blowers. Regardless of the motivation, understanding the reason for the allegation, if it can be determined, can help give comfort that the right disposition has been made.

When the First 48 Hours are Just the Beginning

For investigations with more significant issues, the first 48 hours may be just the beginning. Even though the steps outlined in this chapter may seem onerous and shortcuts may be tempting, in our experience, a rigorous and thoughtful approach in the early hours of the investigation pays off in the end. Processes that quickly identify and raise allegations help ensure that underlying issues do not fester to larger, harder-to-manage problems. Sound and thoughtful initial triage helps channel allegations to the appropriate response, neither ignoring issues nor overreacting.

When issues require an investigation, the decisions in the first 48 hours regarding how to structure the investigation, who will investigate, and what they will do form a basis to move forward. Further, the actions taken to preserve and collect evidence lay the foundation for the analytical and investigative work to follow. A well-organized and thoughtfully structured investigation can be executed more swiftly, is much less likely to waste resources on unnecessary digressions and rework, and will serve as a basis for sound decision making. A sound, independent investigation also tends to reduce the time and expense of expanded external audit procedures and costly responses to regulatory inquiries.

If litigation follows, a properly-structured investigation may put the company in the best position to determine whether any legal remedies may mitigate any damages experienced. Furthermore, prompt legal advice and attention to the preservation of any legal privileges that may attach to the work of the investigators may minimize unnecessary disclosures to third parties who may seek to sue the company.

Conclusion

Allegations of fraud, issues regarding regulatory compliance and other possible improprieties can and do occur in almost all types of businesses. Given human nature, it is inevitable that every business will experience some sort of financial or workplace impropriety. Although business executives can remain hopeful that allegations and investigations will be nonroutine in nature, such challenges should take no executive or company by surprise.

Because such challenges are almost unavoidable, companies need to have business processes in place to identify, raise, and triage allegations and reports of possible wrongdoing. Companies should be prepared to respond to a range of potential issues. To the degree possible, they should try to anticipate the challenging sprint that is the first 48 hours of an investigation.

At the outset of this chapter, we described a CEO in the throes of a prolonged and expensive investigation that seemed out of control. This chapter has highlighted the ways to prevent this outcome by focusing their processes on the steps outlined in this chapter: quickly identifying allegations and issues, objectively triaging them, responding to threats, appropriately reporting the situation and mobilizing resources to properly investigate. No process can fully anticipate all the different issues and allegations they will face, but advance planning can reduce the uncertainties associated with these stressful situations. These steps will promote thoughtful responses and will, ultimately, help a company to respond appropriately to allegations, while maintaining its focus on the long-term success of the underlying business.

Bibliography

1. ——, *Anonymous Submission of Suspected Wrongdoing (Whistleblowers)—Issues for Audit Committees to Consider*, AICPA Antifraud Programs and Controls Task Force, 2005.

2. ——, "Best Practices in Global Ethics Hotlines: A Guide to Navigating Hotline Compliance Guidelines Worldwide," Association of Certified Fraud Examiners Web site.

3. ——, "Eighteen Safeguards To Corporate Self-Investigation," *The Metropolitan Corporate Counsel* (December 2004).

4. Bennett, Robert S., Alan Kriegel, Carl S. Rauh, and Charles F. Walker, "Internal Investigations and the Defense of Corporations in the Sarbanes-Oxley Era," *The Business Lawyer* 62, no. 1 (November 2006): 55–88.

5. Block, Janice L., "Rules of Responsibility," *Inside Counsel Magazine* (August 2008).

6. Dougherty, Thomas J., *The Directors' Handbook, 2008 edition.* Corporation Service Company, 2008.

7. Exall, Marian and Joh D. "Jack" Capers, "Audit Committees under the Sarbanes-Oxley Act: Establishing the New Complaint Procedures," *ACCA Docket* (July/August 2003): 102–110.

8. Finegan, Sheila, "The First 72 Hours of a Government Investigation: A Guide to Identifying Issues and Avoiding Mistakes," *Briefly...Perspectives on legislation, regulation and litigation* 11, no. 2 (February 2007).

9. Johnson, Mary Jo, Peter J. Kolovos, Lynda Schwartz, and Carol Palmer Wining, "Responding to a Corporate Crisis: Ten Initial Steps to Consider When a Corporate Crisis Emerges," January 15, 2009.

10. Malone, Tony and Ralph Childs, "Best Practices in Ethics Hotlines: A framework for creating an effective anonymous reporting program," Association of Certified Fraud Examiners Web site.

11. Slovin, David, "Blowing the Whistle," *Internal Auditor* (June 2006): 45–49.

12. Young, Michael R., *Accounting Irregularities and Financial Fraud, A Corporate Governance Guide*, 3rd ed. CCH Company, 2001.

6

Roles and Responsibilities: How Different Stakeholders Work During Investigations

Ruby Sharma, Partner/Principal

Introduction

During every fraud investigation, different internal and external stakeholders and advisors take on important roles and responsibilities; for the investigation to succeed, all must clearly understand those responsibilities. Necessarily, the roles vary greatly due to the interests of various stakeholders and the fiduciary duties they must perform. Each group often will make important contributions to assist the investigation in achieving thorough, complete, and accurate results while maintaining their integrity.

Internal stakeholders who typically play an important role during an investigation include the board of directors, the audit committee, executive management of the company, the general counsel, and internal auditors. External stakeholders and advisors include legal counsel, forensic accountants, external auditors, and regulators.

Although the roles and responsibilities of different stakeholders can be fairly constant throughout investigations, each investigation is unique, and the various roles can change substantively depending on the uniqueness of each case. Variables include the size of the company being investigated, the relative complexity of its business structure, and the character of the allegation of misconduct, the scope of the investigation, and the specific technical accounting or legal aspects of the issues being investigated.

The recent criticisms of the Securities and Exchange Commission (SEC) over the handling of the Bernard Madoff matter have increased the pressure on financial regulators and law enforcement to deliver results. Therefore, management, audit committees, and special committees of the boards of directors of public and privately held entities could potentially be faced with intensified scrutiny of issues involving complex financial transactions, corporate misconduct, fiduciary and officer responsibilities, and related matters.

Accordingly, companies will need all stakeholders to work together effectively to develop and implement effective investigations.

This chapter takes a close look at the various stakeholders and advisors during an investigation and explores their unique roles and responsibilities. For each of the internal stakeholders previously introduced, their typical role within the company is summarized and then how that role may change during an investigation is examined. After reviewing the respective roles and responsibilities of internal stakeholders, we address those of external stakeholders and advisors.

Figure 6-1 illustrates, as is discussed throughout this chapter, how the roles of the various stakeholders and advisors inter-relate, during an independent external investigation and/or during an internal investigation conducted by management.

Internal Stakeholders

How we govern our corporations plays a central role in the health of our global economy. Risk management, especially in times of crisis arising from wrongdoing or impropriety, requires that an effective process be in place to investigate fraud and take corrective action.

The board of directors and its special committees, audit committees, and management of public and privately held entities will need assistance in developing and implementing effective investigations to address certain regulatory and voluntary demands brought about by alleged improper actions.

At an introductory meeting, Grand Forge's[1] senior executives explain the circumstances around the allegations of abusive accounting practices from employees in its operations in the Shanghai office. They identify their pressing objectives: to investigate the allegations of wrongdoing, examine accounting procedures in the Shanghai office, and assess the risk that similar activities could be occurring elsewhere in the organization. Management asks Perusi & Bilanz LLP how the accounting firm can help.

First, says the accounting firm, senior management at Grand Forge should advise the board of directors, audit committee, and the company's counsel of the circumstances, if they haven't done so already. They should also apprise both of their meeting with Perusi & Bilanz LLP.

---

1 The reader is invited to read the detailed case study of Grand Forge Company found in the Introduction to this book.

Figure 6-1: *Internal and External Stakeholders and Advisors*

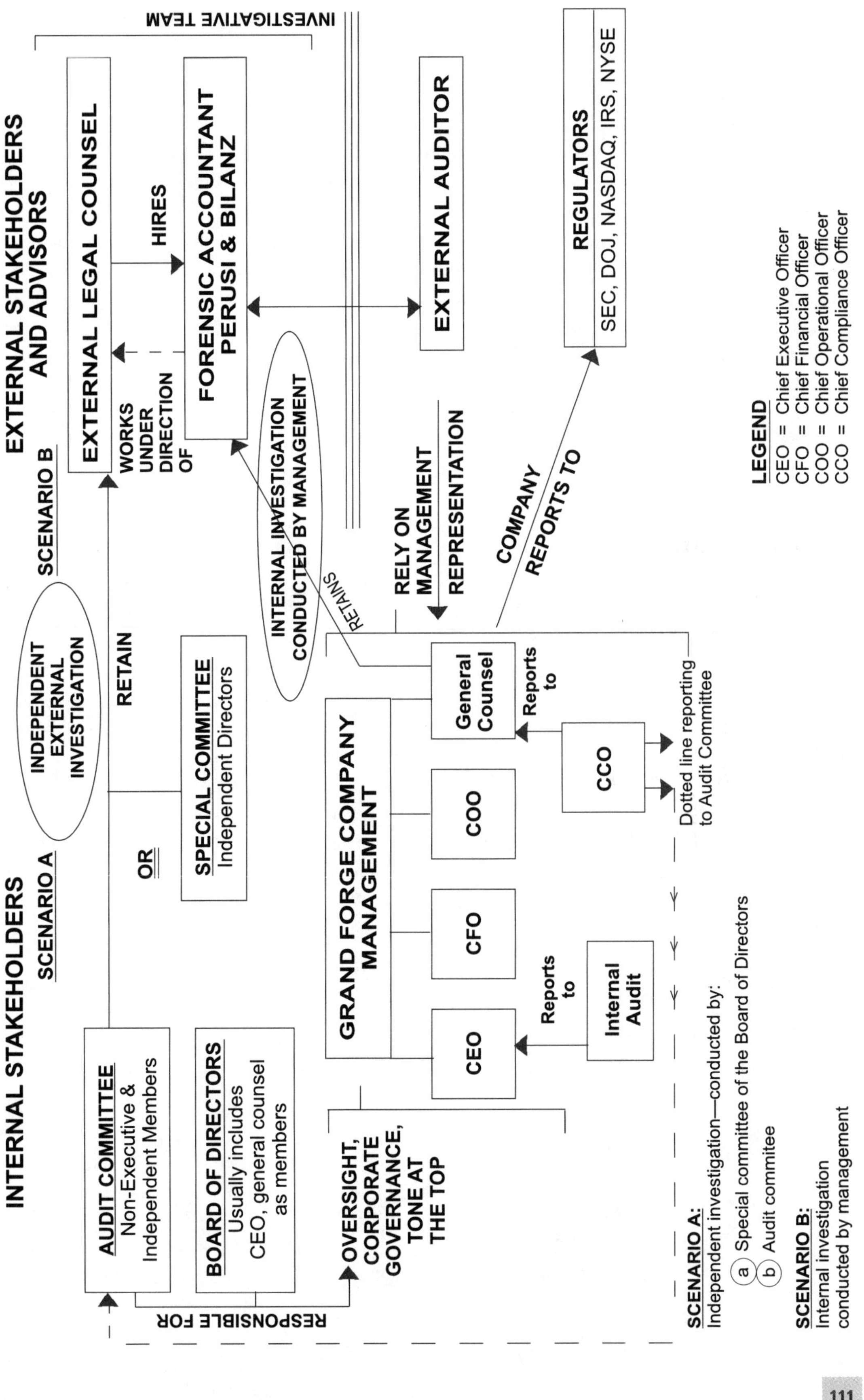
INTERNAL STAKEHOLDERS
SCENARIO A
INDEPENDENT EXTERNAL INVESTIGATION
SCENARIO B
EXTERNAL STAKEHOLDERS AND ADVISORS
AUDIT COMMITTEE
Non-Executive & Independent Members
RETAIN
OR
SPECIAL COMMITTEE
Independent Directors
BOARD OF DIRECTORS
Usually includes CEO, general counsel as members
RESPONSIBLE FOR
OVERSIGHT, CORPORATE GOVERNANCE, TONE AT THE TOP
GRAND FORGE COMPANY MANAGEMENT
CEO
CFO
COO
General Counsel
Reports to
Internal Audit
Reports to
CCO
Dotted line reporting to Audit Committee
EXTERNAL LEGAL COUNSEL
WORKS UNDER DIRECTION OF
HIRES
FORENSIC ACCOUNTANT PERUSI & BILANZ
INVESTIGATIVE TEAM
INTERNAL INVESTIGATION CONDUCTED BY MANAGEMENT
RETAINS
EXTERNAL AUDITOR
RELY ON MANAGEMENT REPRESENTATION
COMPANY REPORTS TO
REGULATORS
SEC, DOJ, NASDAQ, IRS, NYSE
SCENARIO A:
Independent investigation—conducted by:
a Special commitee of the Board of Directors
b Audit commitee
SCENARIO B:
Internal investigation conducted by management
LEGEND
CEO = Chief Executive Officer
CFO = Chief Financial Officer
COO = Chief Operational Officer
CCO = Chief Compliance Officer

Second, mindful that few facts are yet known about the alleged activity, Perusi & Bilanz suggest that they perform an investigation of the allegations and provide a confidential report directly to board of directors, management and the audit committee. Emphasizing that it is premature to determine if their work will uncover actual fraud and with management's understanding that no assurance is immediately required, Perusi & Bilanz explain that their work will be conducted as a consulting engagement, not as attest services. Perusi & Bilanz LLP will work under the direction of external counsel retained by the special committee of the board of directors or the audit committee. They suggest that their work will result in recommendations and advice on the accounting issues to Grand Forge's management.

Now let's consider the various roles and responsibilities taking this scenario.

Board of Directors

A company's board of directors is obligated, as fiduciaries, to act in good faith to promote the best interests of the company; its key function is to protect the investment of shareholders. The board does this by overseeing management, operations, and financial reporting of the company to ensure that management is working in the best interest of the company and its shareholders by enhancing company value. Correspondingly, the board must ensure that management has the qualifications and competence to perform their specific roles and also must review the company's operational performance and compare it against set financial objectives, budgets, and other key measures. All significant business decisions must be presented to and reviewed by the board for approval.

Equally important, the board works with management to uphold corporate, legal, and ethical compliance by enforcing sound accounting policies and ensuring that internal controls exist that are sufficient to "deter fraud, anticipate financial risks, and promote accurate, high quality and timely disclosure of financial and other material information to the board, to the public markets, and to shareholders."[2] The tone set by the board usually influences the behavior of others within the company (for an expanded discussion of tone, see chapter 14, "Antifraud Programs").

When confronted with allegations of fraud or misconduct, board members must act to investigate the facts surrounding the allegations and agree to a course of action that is in the best interest of the company. During an investigation into any such allegations, directors must consider all of the relevant facts, and once the facts are known, they must act to end the misconduct and prevent its recurrence.[3]

The senior executive of our hypothetical Grand Forge Company should inform the board of directors of the allegations and consult with them prior to meeting with the independent accounting firm, or at least as soon as practical. The board will consider, in consultation with management, whether an internal or external independent investigation is in the best interest of the company. Additionally, Grand Forge's board will consider the timing, scope of the investigation, and resources required.

As a result, Grand Forge's board should ensure the organization develops a system of prompt, competent, and confidential review, investigation, and resolution of the allegations of abusive accounting practices. The board also should define its own role in the investigation process. Grand Forge can improve its chances of loss recovery, minimize exposure to litigation, and protect its reputation by establishing and adequately planning an investigation and corrective action processes.

Typically, boards comprise independent directors; however, some also include select internal executives, which may present the appearance of or create an actual conflict of interest.

Maintaining credibility is the key to success in these situations. For example, the allegations in the Grand Forge scenario are serious. Having complete and total transparency with all members of the board is key to maintaining credibility, both with the ultimate decision makers within the company as well as with any government officials. Therefore, the

---

2 John C. Whitehead and Ira M. Millstein, Co-Chairs, *Report and Recommendations of the Blue Ribbon Report on Improving the Effectiveness of Corporate Audit Committees.* A publication of the New York Stock Exchange and the National Association of Securities Dealers 1999, 20.

3 *Graham v. Allis-Chalmers Manufacturing Co.* 188 A.2d 125. 130 (Del 1963).

composition of the board becomes especially important during an investigation because the company will want to protect itself against any allegations of bias or, worse, a "whitewash" investigation, due to the presence of company executives on the board. Grand Forge must conduct a thorough and independent investigation of the allegations to determine if they have merit. If the allegations have merit, what needs to be determined is who was responsible and what consequences will result from internal remedial measures to external reporting disclosures, including a possible restatement. A board can be rendered ineffective when management overrides the board's monitoring responsibility, influences the selection of outside directors, controls meetings and agendas, and delivers inside information to certain members.

For this reason, a board facing the need to initiate an investigation often creates a special committee comprised entirely of independent directors (with no management influence) to lead the investigation or instead allows the audit committee, also comprised of independent directors, to do so.

Absent subpoenas from government regulators, the board also needs to decide on how it will report the corporate misconduct, if it reports it at all. In accordance with policies approved by the board, Grand Forge's investigation team should report its findings to the appropriate party, such as directors, legal counsel, and oversight bodies. Public disclosure may need to be made to law enforcement, regulatory bodies, investors, shareholders, the media, and others. Although the board generally does not have a duty to report corporate misconduct to government regulators, self-reporting to regulators may be in the company's best interests. Additionally, the board must consider the strict SEC reporting rules mandating the disclosure of any facts that are material to the company, such as reportable transactions and material weaknesses that require disclosure.

The Audit Committee

Alongside the board of directors, the audit committee (which usually comprises nonexecutive and independent board members) plays an important part in upholding the oversight and integrity of a company's external audit, as well as its management, operations, and financial reporting. The audit committee and the board are integrally linked, as they are responsible for corporate governance and have vital oversight responsibilities. This vital role includes overseeing the financial reporting system with attention to any weakness or vulnerabilities and the need for identifying "red flags" should the risk of financial misreporting take place. The success of the audit committee depends on its working relationships with other corporate participants.

The audit committee must ensure that the parties responsible for internal controls and the financial reporting process, including the company's management, internal auditors, and external auditors, understand their roles in the process and are held accountable.

Surprisingly enough, historical records indicate that most major frauds are perpetrated by senior management in collusion with other employees. Vigilant handling of fraud cases within an organization sends clear signals to the public, stakeholders, and regulators about the attitude of those at the top (management and the board) toward fraud risks.

Insofar as the audit committee must hold company's management accountable, independence from the company is an important aspect of audit committee membership. Regulations require that the audit committee solely comprises independent directors. No member may be an employee of the company, nor may any member receive any type of advisory or consulting fees. The audit committee also must have at least one financial expert, defined as a person knowledgeable in U.S. generally accepted accounting principles, financial statements, internal controls, and overall audit committee functions. Its independence from the company allows the audit committee and its individual members the objectivity to oversee an investigation.

Section 301 of the Sarbanes-Oxley Act of 2002 (SOX) amended Section 10A of the Securities and Exchange Act of 1934 by adding additional requirements for the audit committee. Specifically relating to any complaints or so-called "whistleblower" allegations, the committee needs to have established procedures for "the receipt, retention, and treatments of complaints received by the issuer regarding accounting, internal accounting controls, or auditing matters; and the confidential, anonymous submission by employees of the issuer of concerns regarding questionable accounting or auditing matters."[4] The act also gives the audit committee the authority to engage and fund the payment of independent counsel or advisors if they deem necessary.[5]

Precisely because of its independence from the company, the audit committee should be responsible for handling any anonymous allegations of impropriety received by the company, including allegations of fraud or of a lack of integrity on the part of company management. It also is responsible for ensuring an investigation takes place if fraud is revealed. "If fraud or improprieties are asserted or discovered, the audit committee—through the external auditors, internal auditors, or forensic accounting consultants, as appropriate—should investigate, and, if necessary, retain legal counsel to assert claims on the organization's behalf. Forensic accounting consultants, in particular, may be needed to provide the depth of skills necessary to conduct a fraud investigation, and if it is desirable to get an independent assessment."[6]

As discussed earlier, the only way to assess risk is to have a thorough independent investigation. In some situations, the audit committee will insist on having its own counsel conduct the investigation.

In most investigations, the audit committee retains external legal counsel to investigate allegations of fraud or impropriety. Sometimes the audit committee will allow in-house counsel to hire outside counsel to conduct the investigation. In most situations, external counsel also retains forensic accountants to act as fact gatherers on behalf of counsel and the audit committee. Periodically during the investigation, external counsel and often the forensic accountants report to the audit committee on the investigation's progress. External counsel often assists the audit committee in its communications with regulators, as well as the company's external auditors. At the conclusion of the investigation, external counsel report to the audit committee their final observations and conclusions and provide advice regarding necessary steps, including remedial actions.

Whatever the scenario, it is imperative that the investigation is conducted in an efficient and effective manner and is not criticized later. This is a difficult balance to achieve, but total transparency between the board of directors and its special committee and the audit committee is critical. Often, the independent investigation is conducted in a very short time frame because the company has to meet its reporting requirements; therefore, open and regular communication is key.

Company Management

Although management's roles and daily tasks may vary during an investigation, their fundamental obligations and responsibilities do not. During an internal investigation, management maintains and controls information and coordinates the resources needed; therefore, it plays a critical role in the investigation's development and success. Management's attitude toward the investigation also largely determines how outside stakeholders and advisors plan and perform their own respective tasks and roles in order to achieve the investigation's objective.

The board of directors and the audit committee play an oversight role, and management is responsible not only for the company's operations but also for maintaining its internal controls, recordkeeping, and financial reporting processes. Management's responsibility also includes preparing the company's financial statements.

Generally accepted auditing standards (GAAS) specifically state that "[m]anagement is responsible for adopting sound accounting policies and for establishing and maintaining internal controls that will, among other things, record, process, summarize, and report transactions (as well as events and conditions) consistent with management's assertions embodied in the financial statements."[7]

The company's transactions and related assets, liabilities, and equity are within the direct knowledge and control of management.[8]

---

4 The Sarbanes-Oxley Act of 2002 (SOX), Pub L. 107-204, 116 Stat. 745. Section 301.

5 Ibid.

6 *The AICPA Audit Committee Toolkit.* A publication of the American Institute of Certified Public Accountants, Inc. New York, 2004.

7 Au Section 110.03 Responsibilities and Functions of Independent Auditor.

8 Au Section 110.03 Responsibilities and Functions of Independent Auditor.

Management has the paramount responsibility for all of the financial and operational activities of the company and is rightly required to be extremely familiar with those activities. In particular, a key player of the management is the Chief Financial Officer (CFO). The CFO's primary responsibility is to run a good financial reporting system. Although management's roles within different departments, such as accounting, finance, sales, and operations, can vary greatly, they also are interconnected; for example, accounting personnel must understand the operational and sales aspects of a transaction in order to determine the proper accounting to reflect the nature of the transaction. Although the fundamentals of the entire business must be understood by all of the different departments of management, it is extremely important for the investigative team to have access to people in these different functional roles during an investigation because each person knows their own roles and responsibilities in great detail.

The investigative team, which generally comprises independent forensic accountants working under the direction of outside counsel, relies on management, especially the CFO for the speedy and effective conduct of its investigative processes.

In our hypothetical Grand Forge scenario, the independent forensic accountant Perusi & Bilanz LLP will depend on management to provide the following:

1. The type of accounting system used by the company in Shanghai and at corporate headquarters
2. The document retention policy
3. The location of electronic files on servers
4. The location of selected hardcopy files
5. The e-mail servers' backup protocols
6. A list of key people in the accounting, finance, internal audit, and IT groups who can provide immediate, needed assistance in these types of investigations

Given the tight timeline, the success of the investigation will depend on the level of cooperation from the company's senior management and local management in Shanghai. Access to relevant documentation and personnel also will be crucial to the speedy and efficient completion of the investigation.

Everyone in senior management will have a pretty good understanding, in short order, that something is going on in Shanghai. Document preservation orders, computer imaging, and general "water cooler talk" will lead to information and misinformation being disseminated. To ward off the spread of misinformation and control the dissemination of information that could undermine the objectives of the investigation that is taking place, it is important for senior management to communicate certain key points to management and other employees as soon as possible. These key points include, but are not limited to, the following:

1. The existence of an investigation and the general nature of the allegations being investigated
2. The authority of the entity (for example, the audit committee or special committee of the board) conducting the investigation
3. The rationale for having the investigation conducted under the auspices of an independent body
4. The absolute necessity for relevant document preservation and collection
5. The absolute need for total confidentiality

As previously stated, the financial statements of a company are the responsibility of management, and it is the audit firm who is attesting to the information stated in the financial statements. The final report of an audit firm is issued after its audit of the company's financial statements. The knowledge obtained through the audit and used to issue the report is limited to that acquired through inquiry of management and the testing of accounting records provided by management. "Thus, the fair presentation of financial statements in conformity with generally accepted accounting principles is an implicit and integral part of management's responsibility.... [Conversely], the auditor's responsibility for the financial statements he or she has audited is confined to the expression of his or her opinion on them."[9]

---

9 Au Section 110.03 Responsibilities and Functions of Independent Auditor.

As the success of an audit depends on the reliability and credibility of management and the quality of the documentation provided, an effective investigation also relies on the same.

Commonly, a point person, usually the general counsel who is a member of management, facilitates the requests of all stakeholders during an investigation. Due to his or her intimate knowledge of the company's business, the general counsel typically assists external legal counsel, the forensic accountants, internal auditors, the board of directors, the audit committee, and management.

This point person's cooperation is vital because he or she determines to whom the investigative team has access and what information is provided. An open and trustworthy point person helps create an environment in which the investigation can proceed efficiently and effectively; one who is difficult and creates a barrier around critical employees can severely limit an investigation's scope and hinder the investigative team's ability to achieve their objectives.

Based on the type of investigation being performed, management may play either a supporting role or a more substantial role. When management initiates the investigation and retains both counsel and a forensic team to perform it, then management will be presumed not only to support and facilitate the investigators' work but also will evaluate the findings that result. Because management is ultimately accountable for financial data, it also must determine whether those findings are material or consequential to the reliability of the financial statements as a whole.

Adequate communication between all stakeholders during an investigation is key to the investigation running smoothly and, thus, is very important. In many circumstances, it is management's role to foster such communication. Because management is a nexus for all the information crucial to the investigation, it should ensure that all parties know the background of its business, performance, and operations. In addition, properly communicating to the investigative team any concerns not being addressed within the company is extremely important in bringing to light issues outside of the investigation's focus. It is not uncommon for new issues, unrelated to the initial scope, to emerge during an investigation; these issues ultimately can lead to separate investigations of their own.

General Counsel

Responsible for the day-to-day legal affairs of a company, the general counsel provides management with guidance on the regulatory and legal issues that affect business operations. He or she also ensures that the company's activities are in compliance with all applicable laws and that corporate compliance programs reinforce appropriate legal conduct.

Allegations of misconduct often are reported directly to the general counsel's office. When allegations of fraud arise or questions surface related to management's integrity, the general counsel's office usually is involved immediately. Faced with any of these situations, the general counsel needs to quickly determine if the potential issues can be investigated internally or instead need to be raised to the audit committee and possibly investigated by external counsel. An investigation carried out in house generally incurs a lower cost to the company (by saving fees that would otherwise be paid to external counsel or forensic accountants) and offers the important additional benefit of the investigative team having a better understanding of the company, including its corporate structure, operations, and culture. If the issue is to be handled internally, the general counsel's office usually investigates, with the assistance of internal auditors.

For many reasons, however, an internal investigation may not be the best course because of:

- an insufficient understanding of the technical legal or accounting issues at stake.
- management's and the general counsel's concern about the perception of the investigation not being completely independent and objective.
- a lack of significant investigative experience on the part of the internal auditors or general counsel.
- a lack of adequate resources for a full-scale investigation, in terms of personnel or available time.

When making this determination, the general counsel should keep in mind that regulators often scrutinize the company's response to allegations of improper conduct and typically insist on objectivity and independence from the company. In many cases, if material improprieties are alleged, retaining external legal counsel and forensic accountants who are independent of the company is critical.

If the general counsel elects to notify the audit committee, which leads to the commencement of an investigation, the general counsel most likely will assist in the investigation's execution, monitor its progress, and assist in communications with regulators. Even if not leading the investigation, in certain instances, the general counsel takes responsibility for specific tasks.

Internal Auditors

The purpose of the internal audit function, according to the Institute of Internal Auditors, is to conduct "an independent, objective assurance and consulting activity designed to add value and improve an organization's operations." Further, internal audit "... helps an organization accomplish its objectives by bringing a systematic, disciplined approach to evaluate and improve the effectiveness of risk management, control and governance processes."[10]

Internal auditors can play an integral role in deterring fraud by examining and evaluating the adequacy and effectiveness of the company's internal control structure and establishing control measures to reduce the company's risk. Effective internal controls and processes help mitigate the risk that a misstatement is not prevented or detected by the internal control system and that such misstatement is not corrected in an acceptable way and on a timely basis. However, internal auditors are not under the same requirements as external auditors to detect material fraud because, typically, they are not experts in fraud detection and investigation.

Despite their important duties surrounding a company's internal control environment, internal auditors should not assume the responsibility of management. Instead, they must remain objective in their assessment of evidence in order to provide an opinion or conclusion regarding a process, system, or other subject matter. Internal auditors' independence

from the company's management is structurally reinforced by a direct reporting line to the audit committee or the company's internal counsel, allowing them to express any concerns about management's attention to internal controls or report suspicions of fraud involving management.

It is critical that the internal audit activity be positioned well within the organization so that the internal auditors are not limited in what they can review and that both they and their proposed recommendations are respected by line management. However, the accountability for and ownership of good internal controls is the responsibility of management, not the internal auditors.

The internal auditors play a unique and vital role in the organization. The internal audit activity is motivated by a sense of mission, due to (1) its commitment to the organization and management and (2) its commitment to independence in allegiance to the board and the organization's stakeholders.

If an internal auditor detects a suspicious event or an indication of a possible fraud, he or she is ethically bound by the rules of the profession to respond. The first step is to investigate further until he or she can reasonably ascertain if a fraudulent or illegal act occurred. If so, the internal auditor is obligated to report the occurrence on a timely basis, either to senior management or the audit committee, depending on the nature and significance of the event. If the internal auditor notifies senior management of suspected fraud and senior management does not take the proper corrective actions, the internal auditor should report the matter to the audit committee. Any fraudulent behavior involving senior management should be reported directly to the audit committee or, if the company does not have an audit committee, the board of directors. In many cases, the company establishes in its code of conduct[11] or other policies the party to which the audit committee must disclose reportable events. In the case of evidence of fraudulent financial reporting by a company with publicly traded securities registered with the SEC, the audit committee or board

---

10 From the introduction to the *Code of Ethics* of the Institute of Internal Auditors. Available for viewing at www.theiia.org.

11 Code of conduct is an organization's clear statement of management philosophy, which includes concise compliance standards. The standards are consistent with management's ethics policy relevant to business operations.

of directors must be immediately informed, even if senior management is aware of the misstatement and in agreement with the internal auditors on the necessary actions.

As previously mentioned, if the board of directors or general counsel determine the cause and effect of the suspected act to be de minimis, internal auditors may conduct the investigation themselves without engaging outside experts. However, this alternative should be carefully considered because internal auditors do not have the specialized knowledge equivalent to someone whose primary responsibility is detecting and investigating fraud. Also, regulators may later determine that the company's internal audit function not only lacked appropriate expertise but was not objective in the testing it performed or in investigating deficiencies in a control environment that it had helped create.

If charged with a primary role in an investigation, internal auditors should, at the investigation's conclusion, assess the facts and circumstances uncovered to improve the company's internal control and antifraud measures. Specifically, internal auditors may assess what controls need to be implemented or enhanced to reduce control weaknesses; they also may design procedures or tests to help detect similar frauds. If specific remedial actions are recommended by the investigative team, management may delegate to internal auditors the responsibility for implementing and monitoring such new measures.

In sum, the board of directors or other stakeholders overseeing the internal investigation should determine how much involvement internal audit-ors should have in the investigation. Even if charged with a secondary role, internal auditors can greatly aid forensic accountants in an investigation because of the former's extensive knowledge of the organization's routine processes and controls. Internal auditors also may liaise between management and the investigative team, performing functions such as scheduling meetings and interviews and obtaining documents and financial records. Using internal auditors may be an efficient means of reducing the costs incurred by hiring forensic accountants, but their use must be kept at an appropriate level to ensure the integrity and competency of the investigation.

External Stakeholders and Advisors

Having reviewed the roles and responsibilities that can accrue to some of the more common internal stakeholders during an investigation, we now shift our focus onto the typical roles and responsibilities of external stakeholders and professional advisors.

External Legal Counsel

As previously noted, external legal counsel is typically retained by the special committee of the board of directors or audit committee to investigate allegations of fraud or the lack of management integrity. Depending on the circumstances, a company's external legal counsel can be charged with a number of responsibilities. In most investigations, external counsel plays a pivotal role.

When an audit committee decides to hire external counsel, they need to carefully consider which law firm to hire. A number of factors are important, including the following:

1. Whether the firm has a reputation that will stand up to the scrutiny of all parties involved in an investigation, including the bench in a possible civil proceeding
2. Whether the law firm has significant business and industry experience and, in particular, whether it has significant prior investigative experience and expertise
3. Independence from the company being investigated and the ability of the firm to be flexible in the face of changing demands throughout the lifecycle of the investigation
4. The company's specific investigative needs and the external counsel's ability to not only conduct the internal investigation but also represent the company in front of regulators

Once retained, external counsel takes a leading role, managing the various facets of the investigation as well as the many parties involved. Initially, external counsel often works with the general counsel's office as well as the audit committee to define the scope of the investigation. Prior to the investigation commencing, external counsel needs to develop and implement an execution strategy, which often is done in concert with the company. In some investigations, this strategy needs to be updated based on new facts, which can often significantly expand the scope of the investigation.

Once the investigation starts, the company is responsible for collecting and retaining all relevant documents, which should be secured immediately. External counsel is likely to manage this critical process to ensure it is thorough and complete and then, in conjunction with forensic accountants, is responsible for piecing together the factual record of events surrounding the misconduct. This usually entails a detailed review of all relevant documents as well as interviews with employees. This review can be daunting because certain large-scale investigations occur in companies with multiple business units around the world.

During the review, external counsel and the other members of the investigative team should be able to identify the parties responsible for the misconduct as well as its duration, nature, extent, and financial impact. As the investigation is being executed, external counsel periodically updates the audit committee about the investigation's status. Throughout this process, external counsel must be cognizant of their objectivity in handling the facts and must often rely on the forensic accountants they retained for the investigation. Upon having completed their investigation, external counsel then reports its findings to the audit committee in writing or verbally and will most likely share these findings with regulators as well, at the request of the company. External legal counsel also typically reports on remedial and preventive measures the company has previously undertaken or will take to ensure the same issues do not recur.

Forensic Accountants

In most investigations, external counsel retains forensic accountants to act as fact gatherers and investigate allegations of fraud or the lack of management integrity. Trained specifically in fraud prevention, deterrence, data collection and analysis, interviewing, investigation, and detection, forensic accountants provide significantly important expertise; many of the same considerations that apply to

external legal counsel's hiring of such investigative specialists apply to the audit committee's hiring of the law firm itself. In particular, it is important to establish whether the accountants have a respected reputation, are known for high-quality work, have significant prior investigative experience, and have the necessary business and industry experience and expertise. As with external legal counsel, independence from the company is extremely important; the forensic accountants should not have any existing working relationships with the company that could cause a conflict of interest.

During the investigation, forensic accountants work with counsel, in-house or external, to create and implement the strategy to execute all phases of the investigation, including retaining and collecting documents, reviewing and analyzing all relevant documents, analyzing evidence, interviewing employees, and helping report to the audit committee and regulators.

The forensic accountant provides services that involve "the application of special skills in accounting, auditing, finance, quantitative methods, certain areas of the law, research, and investigative skills to collect, analyze, and evaluate evidential matter and to interpret and communicate findings, and may involve either an attest or consulting engagement. Forensic accounting services consist of two major subcategories: (1) Litigation services; providing assistance for actual, pending, or potential legal or regulatory proceedings before a trier of fact in connection with the resolution of disputes between parties and (2) Investigative services or nonlitigation services; including all forensic services not involving actual or threatened litigation, such as performing analyses or investigations, that may require the same skills as used in litigation services, but do not involve the litigation process."[12]

A forensic accountant provides a number of advantages. First, he or she can take an objective look at the records of the company with the goal of answering the following very straightforward questions: What happened? Who was responsible? Why did this happen?

---

12 AICPA, Special Report 08-1, *Independence and Integrity and Objectivity in Performing Forensic and Valuation Services.*

Second, as highlighted in the hypothetical Grand Forge scenario, a number of allegations concerning financial improprieties exist. The forensic accounting firm Perusi & Bilanz LLP can help assess the scope of work to be done and also provide an early assessment of the time necessary to complete the task. That assessment will inform what counsel, in-house or external, reports to the board of directors or a special committee thereof when this situation is reported.

Finally, hiring a forensic accountant early also can help establish the credibility of the investigation, which is a critical factor in situations like this one in which there are allegations of improper conduct by senior level management who are members of the board of directors. To the extent that the audit committee has its own counsel, the forensic accountant should be included at this initial meeting and he or she should be acceptable to the audit committee council because this investigation will need complete independence, given the level of people targeted by the allegations.

For the investigation conducted at Grand Forge, the initial scope should be jointly determined by the company's general counsel, outside counsel, and the forensic accountants, with input from the company's director of internal audit. These parties also should obtain the external auditors' thoughts to ensure that the scope and procedures of the investigation will provide sufficient comfort for the external audit firm to sign off on the financial statements.

It is important for the forensic accounting firm to assist the investigation team in answering the following questions during the initial meeting(s):

- What is the nature of the alleged fraud and how far back does it go?
- Which locations to visit?
- What are the necessary resources required, including knowledge of local language and applicable laws?
- What types of computer forensics will be used, and what types of data protection will be considered?

In addition, a list of general questions for the initial meeting should be prepared in order to obtain relevant information, such as the type of accounting system used by the company, the document retention policy, the location of electronic files on servers, the location of selected hardcopy files, and the e-mail servers' backup protocols. Chapters 7 ("Sources of Evidence") and 8 ("Electronic Evidence") discuss in detail the considerations that a forensic accounting firm should address for evidence collection.

Forensic accountants need to formulate and communicate a work plan and budget as soon as reasonably practicable. They also will need to notify in-house and external counsel if they determine that they will need more time or go over budget. Communication is key, but they also should have extremely good explanations and justifications for any variances from the original plan. On that same note, forensic accountants need to provide in- house or external counsel with a list of their requirements in order to do their jobs effectively.

This list should include, at a minimum, a point of contact (likely general counsel), an organizational chart, a request for access to the general ledger, and an introduction from a trusted person within the organization to those whose help is required for the forensic examiners to do their jobs effectively. Forensic accountants also would do well to insist on a regularly scheduled call with in-house or external counsel to discuss progress, obstacles, and projections so that there are no surprises that could have been avoided.

Because most high-profile fraud investigations involve financial reporting or accounting issues, the technical accounting expertise of the forensic accountant is often crucial. The role of the forensic accountant differs greatly from that of the external auditors, and a fraud examination involves significantly different goals and execution than a financial statement audit.

A financial statement audit is performed specifically on behalf of the client, but the auditor's opinion is examined by a much larger audience, including investors, shareholders, and the regulatory community. It also is typically performed on a regularly recurring basis throughout the fiscal year. Additionally, by design, a financial audit utilizes sampling to test various accounts in the company's financial systems and focuses on the underlying accounting data supporting management's proposed financial statements. Whereas a financial statement audit begins with the premise that books and records need to corroborate what appears in the financial statements, the purpose of a fraud investigation almost always involves a suspicion that something may be amiss, and the forensic accountant is seeking to confirm whether fraudulent accounting, reporting, or the misappropriation of assets has occurred. Generally, too, the forensic accountant also seeks to assign accountability for the fraud by determining which party is responsible for the wrongdoing. Therefore, fraud examinations are performed irregularly and only when there is sufficient basis for supposing that a fraud may have occurred. Importantly, too, rather than simply sampling to test various accounts, forensic accountants look at every single piece of relevant evidence available to them.

In his book *Accounting Irregularities and Financial Fraud: A Corporate Governance Guide*, Michael Young summarizes the main difference between the role of an auditor providing a financial statement audit and that of a forensic accountant engaged in an investigation:

> In a normal GAAS audit, the predicate is that, absent evidence to the contrary, everyone is generally trying to tell the truth. This is not to say that an auditor is entitled to accept everything at face value. That is certainly not the case. However, a normal auditor under GAAS—again, absent evidence to the contrary—is entitled in the first instance to believe that documents have not been forged, that books and records have not been deliberately manipulated, and that management's representations to the auditors are true.... In a forensic investigation, that predicate changes to the complete opposite. Once it has been established that the bookkeeping has been infected by defrauders, the issue for the forensic accountant is: How deep and widespread does it go?[13]

As previously mentioned, forensic accountants attempt to identify the parties responsible for misconduct, as well as the duration, nature, extent, and financial impact of such misconduct. A significant portion of this work typically contains e-mail and document review. At the onset of the investigation, all company employees who potentially participated in the alleged misconduct will have their desk files copied and computer files scanned and copied. Forensic investigators then typically load these electronic documents into a software review platform and filter documents by key words applicable to the issues at hand. As more documents relevant to the investigation are identified, the forensic accountants review them in an attempt to further establish the fact pattern. Depending on the investigation's scope and the size of the company, this electronic review can vary from including only a few hundred documents to including hundreds of thousands of documents, and in some cases, the review scope includes millions of documents.

Although the primary focus of many investigations is to understand the potentially fraudulent transactions and their financial impact, it is equally important to establish facts around who, what, when, where, how, and why. It is not uncommon to find that many potentially fraudulent practices or transactions were approved by the fraudsters' superiors or senior executives but only because the fraudsters omitted critically important facts about which those superiors never knew. As such, they had no reason to believe the practices or transactions were anything but completely legitimate.

Armed with information from the document review, forensic accountants and external counsel often interview select employees to further amplify the fact pattern established from the document review process. Frequently, this increases the investigation's scope because answers to questions often lead to additional questions, identify new custodians of information or additional documents needing review, or highlight other previously unidentified issues. Forensic accountants also typically perform high-level analysis of the underlying detailed accounting records, supporting information, or financial statement balances to identify other areas requiring further investigation. Throughout this process, the forensic accountant continues to act as a fact gatherer

---

13 Michael R. Young and Jack H. Nusbaum, eds. *Accounting Irregularities and Financial Fraud: A Corporate Governance Guide,* 2nd ed. (Chicago, IL: CCH, Inc., 2001), 103.

and provide accounting advice and expertise to the external legal counsel and other stakeholders.

As the investigation is executed, forensic accountants also team with external counsel to periodically update the audit committee about its status. Once the execution phase of the investigation is complete, they work with external counsel to report findings to the committee, either through a written or oral report. At times, the forensic accountant's team will, with external counsel, share findings with regulators.

External Auditors

Users of audited financial statements typically expect external auditors to detect fraud and irregularities, but external auditors don't certify a clean bill of health for the audited company.

The responsibility of the external audit firm during the normal course of its work is to plan and perform an audit that provides company management and shareholders with reasonable assurance about whether the financial statements are free of material misstatement, whether caused by error, fraud, or illegal act. Although preparing the financial statements is management's responsibility, it is the responsibility of the auditor to express an opinion on them. To obtain reasonable assurance in order to express that opinion, the audit team has many responsibilities it must fulfill. In every audit, it is important for the auditor to remain completely independent of the client so that he or she can attest to the reliability of the financial statements, absent any conflicts of interest.

External auditors play a very important role in the lifecycle of a fraud investigation for a number of reasons. If and when fraud is detected, the auditor is required to report it to company management and its audit committee, as well as determine whether any illegal act actually occurred and its possible effect on the financial statements. Statement on Auditing Standards (SAS) No. 99, *Consideration of Fraud in a Financial Statement Audit*, speaks to the auditor's responsibility for fraud detection. It enjoins auditors to

develop an increased professional skepticism when conducting the audit: "The auditor should conduct the engagement with a mindset that recognizes the possibility that a material misstatement due to fraud could be present, regardless of any past experience with the entity and regardless of the auditor's belief about management's honesty and integrity."[14]

The auditor also is required to perform preliminary procedures to identify all the risks of material misstatement due to fraud. These procedures include, but are not limited to, inquiries of management, analytical procedures, and the consideration of whether the three fraud risk factors—incentive, opportunity, and rationalization—are present at the company.

All publicly traded companies also are subject to the Securities Exchange Act of 1934 and must conform to the rules of Section 404 of SOX, which describes management's required assessment of internal controls. Specifically, Section 404 states that a company's annual report must contain an internal control report stating (1) that it is management's responsibility to establish and maintain an adequate internal control structure and (2) the company's procedures for financial reporting. That internal control report also should include an assessment of the effectiveness of the internal control structure and the issuer's procedures for financial reporting as of the most recent year-end.[15] Section 404 also requires that any "registered public accounting firm that prepares or issues the audit report for the issuer shall attest to, and report on, the assessment made by management of the issuer."

If during the course of an audit, the external auditor discovers or suspects an illegal or fraudulent act, he or she should investigate to determine its nature and extent. The external auditor should consider its potential materiality, the possible effect on the financial statements, and whether any possible fines, penalties, or damages could result.[16] If the illegal act is clearly inconsequential to the financial statements, no communication is necessary. On the other hand,

---

14 AICPA Statement on Auditing Standards No. 99, *Consideration of Fraud in a Financial Statement Audit* (AICPA, *Professional Standards*, vol. 1, AU sec. 316 par. 13).

15 SOX, Pub L. 107-204, 116 Stat. 745. Section 404.

16 The Securities Exchange Act of 1934, Section 10A: Audit Requirements.

findings of material acts should be communicated to management or the audit committee, whichever is a more suitable option. In the compressed time frame of reporting in the current accounting environment, speedy communication of any findings is the key to resolving the issue.

The auditor also must pay close attention to how the issue is dealt with by management. If the latter does not quickly and adequately respond to the auditor's concerns and does not seek to remediate the issue, and if the issue would cause a departure from a standard audit opinion or precipitate the resignation of the audit firm, then the audit firm must report its conclusions to the board of directors. If a report has to be furnished to the board, the company must inform the SEC no later than one day after receiving the report and also must furnish the audit firm with a copy of the notice furnished to the SEC. If the audit firm fails to receive this notice, they need to either resign from the engagement or furnish the SEC with a copy of its report no later than one business day following such failure to receive the notice.[17]

When fraud is uncovered and an investigation does ensue, the external auditor plays a peripheral role. Because the burden most often shifts to the company to investigate, auditors are not typically involved in the day-to-day operations of the investigation. However, because the audit firm is still responsible for issuing an opinion on the financial statements of the company, it has a vested interest to maintain involvement in the investigation.

Keeping external auditors involved also helps investigators because the auditors have key information about the company obtained through their financial statement audits and SOX Section 404 compliance testing. It also is important for the company to keep the auditor informed of the scope, progress, findings, and recommendations of the investigation on a timely basis because, in order for the audit firm to issue an unqualified opinion, it must accept that the company has thoroughly investigated and remediated the issues. In the Grand Forge example , therefore, the external auditors Handel & Smith LLP would communicate regularly with in-house and external counsel and the forensic accountants Perusi & Bilanz LLP. Handel & Smith would be interested in understanding the scope of the investigation and its progress and findings. For this reason, the forensic accountant and external auditor have regular communications during an investigation. Many audit firms also find it useful to conduct a "shadow investigation" to independently assess whether the audit committee's findings, actions, and recommendations are appropriate. Once the investigation concludes, if the external auditor does not feel that senior management took appropriate and timely remedial actions related to the fraud or misconduct, the auditor could depart from a standard unqualified opinion or resign from the engagement altogether. Either action would undoubtedly have severe negative implications for the company.

As mentioned in earlier paragraphs, obtaining input from the external auditor at the onset of the investigation, especially as the scope of the investigation is being determined, is of critical importance. The external auditor needs to have comfort in management and its integrity and assurance it can rely on the representations made by management.

The forensic team determines the scope of the investigation without guidance from the external auditor. However, if they were not going to investigate an area or issue that the external auditor would like to be investigated, the external auditor would suggest that, based upon the facts and circumstances in this case, the concerned issue should be investigated because it may be an area of risk that deserves further in-depth investigation, regardless of what the auditor did or did not do during his or her audit.

Typically, the auditors do not make their working papers available unless they are subpoenaed; however, this does not mean that the outside auditor does not share pertinent information that might be helpful to the investigating team in conducting their investigation. For instance, providing information about the structure and management of the operations involved is oftentimes provided.

Cooperation and ongoing communication among all the parties will facilitate an effective and efficient process.

---

17 Ibid.

Regulators

Regulators typically involved in internal investigations include the SEC; the Department of Justice (DOJ); the IRS; the stock exchanges, including the New York Stock Exchange and NASDAQ; and the Public Company Accounting Oversight Board (PCAOB). The SEC and DOJ are the most often dealt with regulators. The SEC's mission is to protect investors, and the DOJ plays an important role in fighting economic crimes and investigating possible frauds.

As previously noted, absent subpoenas from government regulators, the board of directors needs to decide how it will report the corporate misconduct, if at all. The board generally does not have a duty to report corporate misconduct to government regulators, although self-reporting to regulators may be in the company's best interests. Strict SEC reporting rules insist upon disclosing any facts that are material to the company's financial statements.

Once a company has reported misconduct, either through self-reporting or disclosure in regulatory filings, regulators want to ensure that the ongoing investigation is thorough, complete, and adequately scoped. They will typically monitor the investigation by maintaining periodic contact with the company's audit committee, external counsel, or even forensic accountants. Status reports are provided by the company to the regulators. Moreover, it is not uncommon for regulators to request the auditor's working papers and, at times, to inquire about other potential issues not specific to the current investigation. Regulators often look for prompt reporting on potential exposures to fraud, from the initial discovery of the issue to its elevation to the board of directors. Regulators also expect the company to hire external legal counsel and forensic accountants to conduct the investigation. When necessary, they also may inquire about the removal from office of responsible employees, including those with an oversight role.

Conclusion

The answers to the tough questions conveyed in this chapter boil down to two issues:

- First, a company needs to be proactive and prepared. A company's audit committee or the board of directors should consider prescreening external law firms and forensic accounting firms it is considering so that they will be ready to hit the ground running (for example, knowing information about a company in advance and being ready to assign personnel as best they can). This is similar to a disaster recovery plan for information technology that asks the question: What are you going to do when the crisis occurs?
- Second, the spirit of "teamwork" is required throughout the process. Someone has to be in charge, but all of the players have to be flexible and allow each of the stakeholders to do their job in a credible way.

In the high-stakes world of company investigations and prosecutions, it is critically important to have successful investigations that are properly performed and that are thorough and complete. For an investigation to succeed, all stakeholders must clearly understand their responsibilities and perform their fiduciary responsibilities to the fullest. The interrelationships among internal, external, and independent counsel and outside auditors, forensic accountants, and other consultants can often mean the difference between a satisfactory conclusion of a matter and one that is not properly performed. The monetary and reputational costs of an unsuccessful investigation can be significant and detrimental. For a successful investigation, each stakeholder has to understand what the issues are, what must be done, and how their own efforts and work product fit into the grand anthology that is the investigation. It is therefore vital to understand the different roles and responsibilities of the various stakeholders who are accountable for how an investigation is ultimately conducted.

7

Sources of Evidence

Ruby Sharma, Partner/Principal
Virginia Adams, Senior Manager

"Whoever corruptly alters, destroys, mutilates, or conceals a record ... with the intent to impair the object's integrity ... shall be imprisoned for not more than 20 years."

Section 1102 of the Sarbanes-Oxley Act of 2002

Introduction

Numerous sources of evidence must be considered by a forensic accountant when conducting a fraud investigation. The primary source typically considered is the financial and accounting records of a company. Until relatively recently, reviewing financial and accounting records meant diligently perusing stacks and boxes of paper documents, along with ledgers and reports on computers. Although relevant to an investigation, the days of poring over paper ledgers and processing reams of physical documents are gone. In today's business environment, a major portion of a fraud investigation can be conducted through analyzing a company's electronic data, in addition to the review of hard copy documents. The process of preserving, collecting, processing, and analyzing the electronic data is of significant importance in an investigation and involves many complex processes that must be carefully undertaken. These processes, along with a discussion of standards for electronic evidence management, will be covered in chapter 8, "Electronic Evidence."

This chapter, however, focuses on the uses of a company's internal electronic evidence as a source of evidence in a fraud investigation once it has been processed and made ready for analysis by the forensic accountant. In addition to electronic evidence, this chapter addresses the importance of reviewing hard copy evidence in an investigation, including the various types of internal company hard copy documentation that should be considered. Finally, this chapter explores several other important types of evidence beyond internal company documentation, including oral evidence, publicly available evidence, and evidence from other third parties.

Electronic Evidence

When initially retained to assist in an investigation, typically one of the first steps undertaken by the forensic accountants is to identify and gather certain key pieces of electronic evidence relative to the case. Depending on the particular circumstances of an investigation, two types of electronic evidence commonly analyzed include e-mail correspondence of key individuals and financial records of the company. Because this data can be obtained in electronic format, the review can begin prior to commencing any fieldwork or site visits to client locations. For a discussion of methods for identifying, preserving, and collecting electronic evidence see "The Electronic Evidence Review Process" section in chapter 8, "Electronic Evidence."

E-mail Correspondence

Based upon initial information known or obtained from counsel or the client, key individuals should be identified who could have knowledge relevant to the investigation.

Once these individuals are identified, electronic data can be collected. Sources of this data could include the following:

- Individual company e-mail accounts, including attachments
- Company server data
- Individual company hard drives
- Personal e-mail accounts, especially when accessed from a company computer
- Instant messaging conversations
- Handheld personal devices

For a discussion of various categories of electronic evidence see the "Sources of Electronic Evidence" section in chapter 8, "Electronic Evidence."

Once the data is obtained and has been uploaded into a review tool, a team of forensic accountants will typically establish a review protocol to identify key e-mails and associated documents of interest in the investigation. Creating a robust review protocol ensures that the review team is reviewing e-mails consistently and that they are familiar with key issues in the investigation. Chapter 8, "Electronic Evidence," includes a discussion of review team training in the "Review" section.

One of the first steps in this process will be establishing keywords that are relevant to the investigation and based upon known information. For example, in the context of a revenue recognition review, keywords could include accelerate, big bath, cookie jar, stretch, gap, pull-in, close the gap, and so on. When the keywords have been identified, keyword searches can be run on the data to identify e-mails and other documents containing these words or phrases.

The next step in the process is to educate the team conducting the e-mail review on the topics relevant to the investigation. Typically, a memo detailing information known about a particular business or subject relevant to the e-mail review will be drafted and shared with the review team. Alternatively, and potentially in addition to the written memo, this information can be shared with the review team in a live discussion to give the reviewers the opportunity to ask questions.

The e-mail review protocol also should include establishing annotation codes to be included in the e-mail review tool so that the e-mail review team can code the documents as they review them. Annotation codes will typically be established for two reasons: first, to indicate the level of relevancy of a particular e-mail and, second, to put e-mails into meaningful categories. The forensic accountants should consider creating themes or categories for the e-mails to be grouped into, based upon information relevant to the investigation. These categories can be updated based upon new information obtained as the e-mail review is carried out, but establishing these categories from the outset will benefit the team in the long run. In addition, levels of relevancy could include "Hot," "Relevant," or "Not Relevant."

During the review process, the e-mail review team can use the annotations included in the tool to indicate the level of relevancy of the document as well as the preestablished category, when applicable. These categories will be useful to the forensic accountants when creating a summary of findings for the e-mail review portion of the investigation. It is important to note that because e-mail review is often one of the most crucial steps in the investigation, proper levels of quality review of the results and findings of e-mails identified is essential and should be considered part of the e-mail review protocol.

Creating a robust review protocol, as previously discussed, ensures that the team is reviewing e-mails consistently and that they are familiar with key issues of the investigation. Oftentimes, information highly relevant to the investigation is obtained from e-mails and documents identified during the review. This information can allow the forensic accounting team to identify key transactions, general ledger accounts, or payments to relevant parties that unveil schemes, which begin to tell a story. In addition, key individuals, perhaps not initially considered as important in the investigation, could be identified as potential targets as schemes are uncovered. Chapter 8, "Electronic Evidence," includes a section on forensic analysis and structured and unstructured data analysis for further information.

Also note that information relevant to the investigation can be obtained from other electronic sources, including personal e-mail accounts, especially when accessed on a company computer; instant messaging conversations; and blackberries and other handheld personal devices. It is important to identify all potential sources of key data for collection purposes.

Electronic Financial and Accounting Records

The second key type of electronic evidence typically analyzed in a fraud investigation is the financial and accounting records of a company. As an investigation begins, the forensic accountants submit a "request list" to the client asking for certain types of information and documentation believed to be relevant to the investigation, based upon information known at that time. Often, the majority of this information can be provided to the accountants electronically. Depending on the type of investigation, the request list would include different items, as described subsequently.

When conducting an investigation, obtaining the client's chart of accounts for the general ledger and the general ledger itself (depending on the size) are the two foundational pieces of evidence. The chart of accounts allows the accountants the ability to identify relevant general ledger accounts requiring further analysis, based upon account name, account number, and a description of items recorded in the account. When accounts are identified that appear to be relevant, details of transactions recorded in these accounts can be obtained from the general ledger itself. Performing an analysis of general ledger accounts allows the accountants to identify key transactions or patterns that will potentially require further analysis. These patterns, for example, could include transactions with repeating amounts, large amounts in comparison to other amounts, round amounts, or transactions made at regular intervals. In many ways, electronic general ledger data forms the cornerstone and serves a key starting point when conducting a fraud investigation.

In addition, other types of electronic reports containing financial and accounting data can be requested and obtained from the client. Examples include the following:

- Customer master file
- Vendor master file
- Employee authorization and approval levels
- Expense report databases
- Contract databases (typically maintained by in-house legal department)

These documents supplement the general ledger by allowing the forensic accountants to identify transactions with key vendors and customers or transactions approved by individuals of interest, all of which can be critical to the next steps in an investigation.

Hard Copy Evidence

Although obtaining and reviewing data in an electronic format has simplified the job of a forensic accountant in certain ways, the review of hard copy documentation is equally as significant when conducting an investigation. Typically, to gain access to hard copy and all relevant documents, the forensic accountants must conduct a site visit to certain locations of a company's operations. Being on-site at a client location affords numerous advantages to the forensic accountants. Among other reasons, such as being able to see that the location exists and to hold conversations with key individuals, reviewing documents in hard copy format is very advantageous. Seeing the documents in person allows the accountants to clarify information that is unclear by asking questions and gain useful information in person that would not be obtained if the accountants were not on-site.

The forensic accountant would typically request access to several categories of hard copy evidence, including (1) financial and accounting records; (2) contracts and other operational records; and (3) other documentation, including desk files and handwritten notes.

Hard Copy Financial and Accounting Records

For fraud investigators, the ability to see documents in person often affords the accountants the ability to identify key items that would not have been observable otherwise.

In addition to the general ledger, which can be obtained in electronic format, many other types of financial records of a company are critical to include for review in a fraud investigation. This documentation could include the following:

- Invoices for specific transactions to identify potentially fake invoices or vendors
- Company bank statements to review detailed cash inflows and outflows
- Copies of cancelled checks that identify the location where check was deposited or who endorsed the check
- Support for accrual journal entries to identify explanations for manual journal entries and authorizations

Contracts and Other Operational Records

In addition to financial and accounting hard copy documents, reviewing actual copies of contracts and other operational records is a key source of evidence to be considered. In particular, review of actual contracts affords the forensic accountants the ability to identify key pieces of information that might not otherwise have been identified. For example, reviewing draft versions of the contracts in comparison to final versions could lead to the identification of relevant information. Handwritten notes on the documents could also be relevant, in addition to written or oral side agreements and amendments to the contracts, which could potentially be identified.

For example, a contract could be amended to reflect changes in the timing of title transfer or risk of loss transfer. Depending on the revenue recognition accounting guidance a particular business has adopted, changes in the timing of title transfer and risk of loss could allow for revenue to be recognized earlier for a particular contract. Forensic accountants must therefore be aware of all amendments and addendums, in the context of this example, to understand if revenue is being recognized appropriately. In addition, a side agreement to an existing contract could provide an opportunity for an entity to receive bribes or kickbacks from a third party. Having knowledge of these side agreements, therefore, would be necessary for the forensic accountants, in the context of investigating fraud or alleged wrongdoing.

Operational records, including shipping documents, such as packing slips, bills of lading, and other key signatory documents, are typically maintained at a client location in hard copy form. Other types of operational records that could be obtained are outlined in box 7-1.

Box 7-1: *Types of Operational Records*

- Compliance materials, which detail company compliance policies and procedures. Examples of policies include T&E policies, FCPA policies, accounting policies, and policies related to regulatory bodies.

- Employee training materials.

- Ethics materials, including the code of conduct and whistle-blower or ethics violations reports. These reports could help the forensic accountants understand areas of past violations and others issues reported internally.

- Organizational charts, including both historic and current, which detail segregation of duties, titles, and reporting structure.

Example: FCPA Investigation

When conducting a Foreign Corrupt Practices Act (FCPA) investigation (see chapter 4, "Foreign Corrupt Practices Act Investigations"), a trip to certain client locations is typically required by the forensic accountants to review key hard copy documentation maintained only at those locations.

In particular, receipts and invoices supporting payments made to certain parties could be reviewed. In many countries, a large number of transactions take place in cash. To review support for outgoing cash payments, typically these receipts or supporting documentation would be kept on-site at the company's local office. On certain occasions, key information for cash payments can be determined by looking at actual receipts or invoices that would not be identified solely based upon analysis of a company's general ledger system. For example, in reviewing invoices maintained in a company's accounts payable files, a similar invoice template could be used numerous times to support payments made from petty cash to different parties. Reviewing copies of these invoices could lead the forensic accountant to the identification of fake vendors or falsified payments. In addition, information could be recorded on a receipt that is not recorded in the general ledger.

Also, documents that support travel and entertainment (T&E) reports could be an area of focus in this type of investigation. Of particular interest would be reviewing details of T&E reports and supporting receipts. For example, if a company officer took a government official to dinner, the general ledger would typically only capture that the expenditure was for dinner. It is possible that the company employee could have handwritten on the receipt that the meal was for him or herself and the name of the government official. This information would be uncovered only if the actual receipt itself was reviewed by the forensic accountants.

Other Hard Copy Documents

Although collecting and reviewing financial and operational records of an entity being investigated is customary, other types of evidence to consider includes personal desk files of key individuals as well as handwritten notes. As with e-mail and electronic evidence review, the investigating team should develop protocols for hard copy documents. The review protocol assists the team with an understanding of the issues important to the investigation and gives guidance to the review team about what to look for, how to record the findings of its review, and how to clear any queries that arise for the review. Again, proper protocol must be followed in obtaining these documents, but they can often contain information highly relevant to the case.

Working papers of the internal audit group of a company could also be relevant to a fraud investigation. Many large organizations have robust internal audit functions. Depending on the company, the role of this group could include documenting key processes and conducting analysis related to high-risk areas of a company.

Depending on the type of investigation, documentation and analysis performed by the internal auditors could be relevant to the investigation. Often, this documentation could reduce the work required in the investigation because it already exists. Internal audit findings and reports could include issues relevant to the investigation at hand, particularly accounting issues, such as revenue recognition. Furthermore, these reports could allow the forensic accountants to determine patterns of activity within business units or regions in which the company operates. The investigation can then be focused on those areas.

Other Sources of Evidence

In addition to electronic and hard copy evidence, several other key types of evidence need to be considered in a fraud investigation, including oral evidence, publically available information, and information from other third parties.

Oral Evidence

Because fraudulent activity involves deception, documents may be altered or falsified to cover the wrongdoing. Therefore, it is often difficult to identify which documents are fraudulent without gathering information through interviews of individuals possibly having knowledge about the fraud.

Therefore, an important step in conducting a fraud investigation is obtaining information in an oral form, including formal interviews as well as informal meetings of key parties. In many investigations, formal interviews are conducted in conjunction with in-house or external counsel and involve significant preparation. These interviews are conducted with individuals believed to be key to the investigation because they may have knowledge of the fraudulent activities or its perpetrators. Two or more interviewers are typically present during a formal interview and detailed notes are taken.

By comparison, informal meetings are often held with individuals not believed to be as central to the investigation at hand and take the form of common inquiries, such as discussing the controls and processes involved in a financial statement cycle, the reasons for unexpected fluctuations noted when performing analytical review procedures, management philosophies, or the understanding of the organization's accounting structure. These meetings could be one-on-one meetings between a forensic accountant and the individual and detailed notes may or may not be taken.

Formal Interviews

Interviews seek to (1) obtain information regarding various areas, including an individual's current and past roles at the company and his or her knowledge of certain business practices (particularly those at issue in the investigation), and (2) identify other areas for consideration in the investigation. Formal interviews of employees significant to an investigation should be conducted at the outset of the investigation to gather information and relevant facts. Follow-up interviews of these individuals can be conducted as needed, based upon new information obtained further into the investigation. Counsel typically prepares a formal interview memorandum, which could become part of the written record in an investigation.

Information obtained from formal interviews can be vital to the investigation and, therefore, preparation is critical. Forensic accountants and counsel want to gain as much relevant information as possible from the interview subject, and depending on the circumstances and timing of a particular investigation, a single interview might be the only chance to speak with this person.

In addition to conducting formal interviews of current and former employees of a company, interviews can be conducted of parties closely affiliated with the company, including board members and officers of the organization. As discussed previously, interviews are typically conducted in conjunction with in-house or external counsel assisting in the investigation. Forensic accountants are typically asked to assist counsel in preparing interview questions. Specific questions regarding documents or e-mails obtained at a certain point in an investigation can be posed to the interview subject. Identifying specific documents for questioning often allows for key information to be obtained from the interviewee. Typically, forensic accountants will be asked to attend interviews involving accounting or finance personnel and counsel will often give the forensic accountants the opportunity to ask questions during the interviews to ensure all relevant information is obtained. Chapter 10, "Working with Attorneys: The Relationship With Counsel," covers aspects of working with counsel in greater depth.

Informal Meetings with Employees

In addition to formal interviews, key information can be obtained by forensic accountants from individuals at a company in informal meetings. Similar to more formal interviews, the purpose of informal meetings is information gathering. Counsel may or may not be present for these meetings and meeting notes might be recorded but are not required. Informal meetings are typically held between forensic accountants and employees for a particular purpose, potentially to gain information regarding a certain document or transaction at hand. Relevant information obtained from these meetings would be captured in the forensic accountants' working papers, as deemed necessary.

Oral Evidence from Other Parties

In addition to conducting interviews and holding informal meetings with current and former employees of a company, information can be obtained from conversations with other key stakeholders affiliated with a company. These parties could include board members, officers of an organization, vendors, customers, consultants, brokers, agents, or external or internal auditors. Depending on the circumstances of a specific investigation, all relevant parties should be considered for collecting oral evidence.

For example, obtaining information from consultants, brokers, and agents could be highly relevant to an FCPA investigation. Understanding these parties' roles in business activities could be useful in understanding certain processes. For example, understanding the role of a customs broker and his or her interactions with customs officials could have an impact on the investigation. Understanding the sales process from the perspective of the sales agents could also be important to identify suspicious transactions or related parties.

Furthermore, conversations with both internal and external auditors could be important in conducting a financial fraud investigation. Typically, the external auditors would have knowledge regarding management's compliance culture or tone at the top. For example, external auditors could provide insight on management's willingness to make changes to the financial statements based upon audit findings.

The internal auditors, alternatively, would have knowledge regarding key internal processes of the business. In numerous fraud investigations, the forensic accountants work alongside the internal audit group to assist in the workload and also to ensure that information and resources are available to the forensic accountants, as needed. Often, if conducting site visits to client locations, the internal auditors accompany the forensic accountants to assist in the investigation.

Publicly Available Information

In conducting a fraud investigation, forensic accountants also can rely on another source for evidence and information that is complementary to the various internal records of an entity: public records.

A governmental unit is required by law to keep numerous records and make them available to the public. Although the Internet has made some public records more readily available, the application of such records' use in fraud investigations requires an in-depth understanding of a myriad of all available information.

Using Public Record Information in Fraud Investigations

Public records can provide forensic accountants and their clients with a broader overview of the entities and subjects under investigation. They provide evidence not typically available in the internal books and records of a company. Often, such supplemental information can improve, enhance, and give clarity to other aspects of the investigation. By researching, compiling, and analyzing such records, the accountant can establish a more comprehensive picture of the scenario in which a particular act or set of acts occurred. Particularly of value in a fraud investigation is that most public record retrieval leaves no "trail." The subject of the investigation and research has no knowledge that the online research is being conducted because he or she is not notified about the search.[1] Inquiries remain largely confidential, discreet, and nonintrusive. As such, they can provide strategically important information. Although such research can be as comprehensive as circumstances dictate, the investigative scope can be customized to target information specific to the case.[2]

Public information builds a more complete picture of its subject and allows for better profiles of what has occurred and what could have occurred. If retained to investigate one or more individuals, the investigator can begin to appreciate important aspects of an individual's life, including where he or she has lived and worked, what he or she has chosen to purchase, with what activities and organizations the subject is or has been involved in their communities, and legal actions (either as the subject defendant or claimant). Searches will help establish whether the subject has faced difficult personal is-sues in his or her life, especially those like divorce or alcohol abuse (for example, through DUI convictions), which can create financial stress and could have precipitated fraudulent activity; who their relatives are; what home and property he or she owns or has owned; what kind of cars he or she owns and has owned; what companies have employed him or her as officers; and more.

In some cases, assets identified in these investigations reveal indications of financial worth or a standard of living out-of-line with expectations. This information may provide indication of misappropriation of funds or other financial misconduct. When a known amount of funds are missing, asset tracing can be a key tool for tabulating specific assets in relation to the monetary loss. Other information, such as financial stressors, may indicate a motive for misconduct for fraud. A history of financial troubles, such as liens, judgments, bankruptcies, divorce, or litigation, would be typical indicators of financial stress.

Public record sources and investigations can provide useful information to prepare strategically for interviews of company officers or other individuals who may be suspected of committing fraudulent acts; such interviews are often part of a forensic accounting investigation. Background research provides historical insight and supplementary information that can sharpen the interview approach by not only saving time or helping clarify information but also by testing the veracity of the interviewee.

Similarly, publicly available information is applicable for investigating companies. It can substantiate the existence of vendors or demonstrate certain vendors to be a fraudulent (that is, a "ghost company"). Research can include information about officers, establish company sales and revenues, and identify assets like land, warehouses, aircraft, and vehicles. For companies publicly traded in the United States, all Securities and Exchange Commission (SEC) public filings are available, including not only quarterly, annual, and other required filings but enforcement actions and any other comments from the SEC.

---

1 The exceptions to this are when a person is asked for written consent for a credit report request and when a Dun & Bradstreet business report is requested for a company that has no existing report or is requested for an update on an existing report, in which case Dun & Bradstreet requests information from the company and can inform them that a request for information has been made.

2 See also appendix B for a more comprehensive listing.

Department of Justice (DOJ) enforcement actions and civil criminal court filings also can be identified, from the U.S. District Court level down to the state or county court level.

What Are Public Records?

Traditionally defined, public records include any document that has been filed or recorded by a public agency in a public office that the general public has a right to examine. Historically stored in hard copy, public record information now is widely available on searchable computer databases. Numerous governmental sources can provide information relevant to investigations, including federal, state, or local government records and disclosures made to the general public as required by federal, state, or local law.

What records qualify as public varies depending on state and federal law. Examples include government contracts with businesses; birth, marriage, and death records; court dockets and litigation filings; arrest records; property ownership and tax assessment information; regulatory filings; driver's license information; occupational licenses; and SEC enforcement actions and filings, including annual and quarterly audited financial statements of publicly traded entities.[3] Counties and states vary in their filing requirements, and federal regulatory agencies are required by law to provide some records publicly but others are not subject to disclosure. What information is rightfully public varies between jurisdictions and regulatory bodies, and care should be taken to understand the coverage, in particular when retrieving online public records whose jurisdictional coverage can be far more variable depending on the type of record.

Physical records are readily available and inexpensive; for U.S. entities and persons, such records are comprehensive and available nationwide. U.S. privacy laws are relatively limited in their purview, meaning a vast amount of information is readily available. Access to information about persons or entities outside the United States is more limited, but with the expansion of Internet sites and widely available electronic and online media, the sources and searchable information are rapidly expanding.

Many local, state, and federal agencies are upgrading their records systems to electronic format, establishing and maintaining searchable Web sites. For example, many U.S. counties maintain searchable Web pages that allow searches for property ownership by name, address, or other information, such as the parcel number of the property. When the property is identified, the researcher may find information about sales and purchases; improvements to the property; property descriptions; tax assessment records; land plots; and, in some cases, aerial or street view photographs of the property, or both. If the agency does not maintain records online, they usually provide information about who to contact to obtain the information offline, which is generally a clerk of the agency or office.

Open access to public record information provided by governmental sites, such as those for the SEC and DOJ, allows searches of enforcement actions and other documentation. In the rush to transparency, regulatory bodies, government agencies, and corporations and businesses worldwide have developed sophisticated Web sites with publicly available information.

Other Publicly Available Information

The breadth of publicly available information is not limited to the formal and legally kept public records held by federal, state, and local authorities. The world of publicly available information also now includes the enormous and growing repository of online data, including search engines, Web logs (blogs), and Web sites. Although this form of information may be useful in providing intelligence, such information requires utmost discretion in its use and application in a fraud investigation. Professional skepticism should be applied in determining how this open-sourced information fits in with the other facts and circumstances relevant to the investigation. Collaboration with other professionals should be considered, especially in light of the fact that the information uncovered may not be admissible as evidence and its integrity can be laid open to questions by interested parties. Furthermore, the decision to discuss information obtained through these

---

3 See also appendix A: Examples of Sources of Public Information.

sources with the client and attorneys or to include the information in client reports should be carefully weighed.

How to Get the Data

Forensic accountants generally work with investigative public record researchers who are familiar with all aspects of public records, including knowledge of sources and proper protocol in obtaining the information. These individuals can assist forensic accountants in managing all aspects of identifying the various sources of information, the jurisdictions in which they reside, and the process of record retrieval. When more detailed information is required and the investigator cannot easily reach the location where the records are being kept, paid researchers and investigators can conduct the research on your behalf and forward you the findings. Investigators also can call or write to many libraries, courts, and records offices to request specific searches and records; however, there can be wait times for the information because the clerk or librarian will have to identify the records, make copies, and either fax or mail them to you. These searches generally involve a modest fee. Be aware that in many smaller jurisdictions, an inquiry into any public record by an outside party can arouse suspicion or prompt gossip or discussion that may compromise an investigation.

In some investigations, hand searches (often called field searches) of public records may be required, involving the examination of original, hard copy, or source records. Various factors can trigger this requirement, such as a jurisdiction may not have records available online, the online information may be incomplete, more detail or absolute verification of the original document is required, or older records or information may not be archived. Often, such information can be located in reference libraries of governmental agencies. Most governmental reference library information is far more expansive than online information, and many libraries are located in the headquarter locations of the agencies in Washington, D.C. In-depth hand searching of public records is now rare and is usually secondary

to online research in the follow-up identification of relevant source and jurisdictional information.

Types of Information That Are Not Publicly Available

The following types of information could potentially be mistaken as being publicly available, but they are not:

- Banking records and other privately held accounts, such as 401(k), mutual funds, money market accounts, stock in privately held companies, and stock holdings of less than five percent majority ownership in public companies.
- Salary or income information, except for corporate officer salary disclosures in annual reports of publicly traded companies.
- Family trust and other trust records.
- Telephone call information, such as date, time, and origin of calls.
- Passenger lists and flight logs.
- Visa information.
- Privately held corporate records.
- Sealed court records.
- Credit reports. (*Note:* Can be obtained if the individual gives formal written consent.)
- Credit card information. (*Note:* Payment history on credit cards would be contained in a credit report.)

International Public Record Resources

It is important to note that privacy laws differ greatly outside the United States. The European Commission's Directive on Data Protection (Directive 95/46/EC)[4] applies to all businesses that collect personal data on European Union (EU) residents and includes all employee data in phone directories or accounting systems, as well as customer and patient data. Any record containing personal information also is protected under the same privacy law in Canada and in many other areas of the world. Even when in an overseas location, public record aspects of an investigation can be curtailed not only because privacy laws limit the availability of public record information but also because they regulate the

---

4 See http://ec.europa.eu/justice_home/doc_centre/privacy/law/index_en.htm.

transfer of this information outside the EU. Many U.S. companies operating within the EU therefore abide by Directive 95/46/EC.

Some online record information is available from U.S. sources. Companies House records, a United Kingdom equivalent of corporate filings, can be found in LexisNexis. Dun & Bradstreet provides reports on many companies. Industry and peer analysis sources, such as OneSource and Primark Corp., also provide summary information about companies, including financial and officer information and general information about the business itself. Many companies have Internet sites that provide information about the company and its operations, and they sometimes also offer annual reports, sales contacts, office locations, lists of subcontractors, and other information. The Internet also can identify information about individuals. As always, media and trade publications can provide information about a company or individuals who have a presence outside the United States.

Other Third Parties

In addition to providing oral evidence, third parties affiliated with a company can provide information essential to a fraud investigation. Oftentimes, these third parties hold information vital to putting together all the pieces of the puzzle when trying to redesign a fraud scheme.

For example, confirmations can be sent to vendors and customers. Contracts with customers could also be obtained. Information from third parties can be obtained only after the company gives consent to approach a third party. Once consent is obtained, appropriate personnel at the third party may be interviewed. This would enable clarity on any side agreements, verbal arrangements, and other noncontractual obligations. This additional information is often critical in understanding the complete picture in an investigation of alleged wrongdoing, kickback schemes, and the like.

In addition, external auditors' working papers could be considered in the investigation. Examples of sections of the audit working papers that could be of relevance include the following:

- *Control testing.* Identification of control weaknesses documented during previous years. Also, a documented understanding of controls in place related to certain processes and areas of the entity.
- *Summary of audit adjustments.* Identification of areas of the financial statements requiring the company to adjust the balances during previous periods.
- *Contingent liabilities.* If contingent liabilities are disclosed in the financial statements, the working papers would include documentation on how the auditors determined that the liabilities were probable or measurable.

For more information about third parties see Chapter 6, "Roles and Responsibilities: How Different Stakeholders Work During Investigations."

Access to Documents

What records are accessed and how they are accessed is determined in large part by the purpose of the investigation (whether it is internal or external) and who requests it. As discussed in chapter 6, "Roles and Responsibilities," a number of different entities may hire the accounting firm to investigate a company, including the audit committee, the board of directors or a special committee of the board, or the company itself, which may include its CEO, COO, or CFO. Occasionally, an outside party, which is usually a law firm representing persons or other companies with an interest in the company or alleged issue, may hire the forensic accountant for an internal investigation.

Although a complete review of all books and records would likely be unnecessary and, in most cases, would in practice be impossible, the best-case scenario for an investigation of any type would be to have ready access to all available books and records. The accessibility of records can vary from case to case, however, and can depend upon who hired the forensic accountant, the specific scope and requirements that the hiring party places on the investigation, and the situation and type of case.

In some instances, at the discretion of the attorneys involved in the matter and very likely with the input and recommendations of a forensic accountant or other investigative professional, a legal hold or preservation notice (in effect, a "do not destroy" order) is issued. Such an order of course seeks to ensure the preservation of any and all documents presumed to be pertinent to any given investigation. The order is issued to all employees of the company whose records are being reviewed and employees are bound to adhere to it. (See the "Preservation and Collection" section in Chapter 8: Electronic Evidence for a discussion on legal holds.) Typically, it is the investigating party's attorneys who issue formal requests for access to the documents presumed to fall within the scope of the investigation, in some combination with their own required documents. Accountants provide guidance to the attorneys in developing the scope and substance of such a request, but document request and retrieval is not a formal discovery process.

If the forensic investigator is hired directly by a company, it is expected to have more access and better direct communication in making determinations about document access. In reality, such access can vary: the owner of a midsize company, for example, may prove hesitant to reveal possible mismanagement and may not want to grant open access to a team of accountants for fear of undermining morale. In another case, however, an owner may give an accounting team carte blanche to access all documents in order to aggressively ferret out a perpetrator. Once document requests are issued, the forensic accountant may travel to the client site or some other site where the documents are stored, depending on the logistics of the fraud investigation; alternatively, the client may send boxes of documents to the accountant's office.

Legal Considerations

A forensic accountant can request documents and offer recommendations on what should fall within an investigation's scope. However, it is important to note that accountants have no legal standing in this regard, cannot represent themselves as legal experts, and cannot provide legal advice to their client for issues relating to documents. If approached by a client or a client's attorney for advice on the purview of a legal hold, a "do not destroy" order, or some other matter relating to the scope of a document request, the accountant's advice and recommendations should be issued strictly in accordance with that request and perhaps in consultation with their own attorneys.

In important legal matters, the client should have recourse to legal counsel to assist in making decisions regarding discovery issues (that is, when documents are discoverable by opposing counsel or an investigating or regulatory body) and to advise about what falls within or outside attorney-client privilege and strategic legal issues in criminal and civil litigation. However, the accountant can and should work with both the client and the law firm in decision-making and strategy regarding requests for documents. If the client is an external party, the accountant should emphasize to the client that the production of documents is usually an ongoing process. The accountant can further point out that if a law firm is involved, requests for hard copy and paper records differ from the traditional discovery process in being a cooperative exchange of information, rather than a response to a more formal legal document production request.

Any investigator should keep in mind that the findings of an investigation may be subject in the future to a subpoena or regulatory inquiries and requests prompted by litigation.

Correspondingly, the investigator's drafts, memos, notes, interview memoranda, reports, team communications, e-mails, and other information produced in the course of the investigation may be subject to a future request and review. Clearly, this suggests strongly that the investigator use discretion and forethought during the course of his or her work. Documents that may or will be used as part of the ongoing investigation as supporting information for a report, supporting evidence for testimony, or any other form of evidence should be carefully documented so they may be properly referenced (see chapter 8, "Electronic Evidence"). Original documents should be properly identified and retained for future reference. This also serves to maintain supporting evidence for any further inquiries.

Conclusion

The identification, gathering, and analysis of all sources of evidence form the foundation for conducting a fraud investigation. Despite the growing preponderance of electronically stored data, hard copy documents (the so-called "paper trail") remain an important factor and source of information in fraud investigations. In addition, evidence obtained orally through public sources and parties outside the entity under investigation are important information sources. Gaining access to relevant data and the various legal issues surrounding the use and application of that data also must be considered in an investigation. Ultimately, the success of any investigation relies on the various sources of evidence identified and the analysis performed thereof. Ensuring that all relevant sources of evidence have been considered and analyzed is crucial in determining the business and compliance risks the entity of interest may face.

Appendix A
Examples of Sources of Public Information

- *U.S. District Court civil and criminal filings, as well as bankruptcy court, tax court, and most state civil and criminal litigation proceedings.** Online databases, such as CourtLink, CourtExpress, and Pacer, are the leading providers of these filings, providing complete coverage of District Court filings and fairly comprehensive filings on dockets at the state and county levels. In some cases, specific case filings are available, but in many cases, filings should be ordered online or by phone. All searches are transactional.

- *Uniform Commercial Code filings.** Best obtained online because different jurisdictions have different filing requirements and locations. Can be searched on transactional public record databases.

- *Lien and judgment filings for many jurisdictions.** Best obtained through a transactional public record or a specific online court record database.

- *Secretary of state corporation and other business filings.** Most readily available through online transactional databases, although many departments are upgrading systems to make these records available. At present, many remain rudimentary and information on the Internet is limited.

- *Nongovernmental, governmental, and regulatory agency investigation reports or information (that is, United Nations, U.S. DOJ, offices of different U.S. states' attorneys general, Senatorial investigative committees, and so on).* Many readily available online and most directly through the entity or agency Web site; all have internal search engines that make them relatively easy to navigate. For a specific report or piece of information, Google may be easier.

- *Business and professional licenses.** Most readily available through online transactional accounts but also available on state and county Internet sites.

- *Property, tax assessment, and limited mortgage records.** Available through transactional online databases, on some county Web sites, and at county records repositories.

- *Vehicle ownership records.** If available online, may require a fee. Not available for all states.

- *Worldwide media and trade publications.* Available from numerous sources. Search engines (for example, Google) will identify publications and information from articles, research papers, and Web sites but narrowing the search can be difficult. Yahoo News and similar sites provide AP coverage and other newswire services but tend to expire quickly. Sites of companies like CNN, Fox, and the *New York Times* provide current information but are difficult to search for historical information. Vendor media and trade publication sources like Factiva and LexisNexis carry worldwide coverage and their searches are readily modifiable, but they charge a fee for searches and downloads of articles.

- *Address history information.** Can be a lodestone for learning more about a person, such as where they live and for how long, comparing their addresses to their property ownership (own or rent), and identifying where to look for more information about where they have lived or worked. All can enhance the investigation, allowing associations, improving fact-finding, and knowing which jurisdictions you should focus on for more public record information about the person.

- *Telephone information from reverse lookup telephone directories and Internet sites.** Can be more difficult to identify, particularly when cell phones are the rule rather than the exception. Cell phones are not included in reverse directory sources.

- *International tax haven corporate filings.* Usually contain limited information. Generally filed in the country

---

* Not available internationally.

providing the tax haven, although the company is usually located elsewhere. Can provide information about the officers and dates of incorporation.

- *Global business registrations and reports.* Contained in a variety of sources. These provide information about the location, officers, financial information (in some instances), and other information about companies.

- *SEC corporate and business filings.* Include annual and quarterly reports and enforcement filings for publicly traded companies, along with financial information, company activities and holdings, information about corporate officers and directors and their compensation, litigation activity, and corporate projections. Enforcement filings contain reviews conducted by the SEC of alleged or actual violations of regulatory law and SEC findings or decisions in the same.

- *International regulatory filings and enforcement news for companies traded on many foreign or international exchanges.* Available primarily through Internet sites for the exchanges. Challenges include language and understanding the regulatory rules and structure of other countries. Information can be outdated or incomplete, or both. Can include a surprising amount of information available about companies that are listed on foreign exchanges, and more exchanges now offer English translation.

- *Marriage and divorce filings for some states.** Online access limited to a handful of states, and information limited to the jurisdiction of filing, date of filing, date of final order, and parties involved. However, investigators can visit the jurisdiction and retrieve, for instance, a divorce filing to learn if there was a property settlement, but often this information is not disclosed in the final order. In larger settlements, this information is sometimes sealed.

- *Aviation ownership, pilot licenses, and water vessel registries.** Found in transactional databases and Federal Aviation Administration databases. These show who owns the aircraft or water vessel, the type of craft, and registration dates.

- *Educational credential verification.** Limited to verification of degree earned and date of matriculation when information is provided to college or university. Infrequently used in fraud investigations. Sometimes useful when a person is found to be misrepresenting their qualifications.

* Not available internationally.

Appendix B
Examples of Public Records Relevant to Investigations

The following information is readily available to the persistent and thorough investigator and can be helpful in investigations:

- Current and historical asset information
- Corporate and executive affiliations and associates for private and publicly held companies
- Civil and criminal litigation history
- Debt, lien, judgment, or bankruptcy history
- Company existence or nonexistence
- Enforcement proceedings or actions taken by governmental agencies
- Lifestyle or general background information
- Government contracts and awards issued to companies and individuals
- Information that can be used in preparation for interviews
- Information that may develop leads or supplement information identified from forensic accounting findings
- Financial or tax liabilities
- Related events, transactions, involved individual or business information, or other targeting information during time periods in which fraud may have occurred
- Current and historical address information allowing the investigator to assess locales that may be inclusive in the investigation
- General intelligence regarding the activities of a business or individual
- Organizational relationships
    - Individuals related to subsidiaries or affiliates
    - Affiliated and related companies
    - Complex business structures or unusual or numerous subsidiary or affiliated companies

- Lifestyle symptoms or conspicuous consumption of suspected perpetrators
    - Ownership of assets
        - Value of home or multiple property ownership
        - Vehicle ownership information
        - Water vessel ownership and registration
        - Aircraft ownership
    - Financial pressures that might prompt or foster fraud
        - Divorce
        - Failed or failing business ventures
        - Bankruptcy
        - Liens or judgments
        - Loans of lines of credit outweighing value of property
- Financial profiles of suspects
    - Personal assets
        - Real estate holdings
        - Vehicles, watercraft, aircraft
        - Significant shareholder ownership

8

Electronic Evidence

Ben Hawksworth, Senior Manager
Jennifer Hadsell, Senior Manager

Introduction

Many sources of evidence relevant to a fraud investigation may be stored in electronic form. This electronically stored information (ESI) is everywhere in today's corporate environment, and, frequently, the course of an investigation will turn on an understanding gained from the review and analysis of electronic evidence identified within a body of ESI. That evidence may take the form of information stored on backup tapes, in e-mail messages, and in trace remnants of deleted electronic files on a laptop. Investigators will often rely on technology professionals to assist in the collection and management of ESI during a fraud investigation. These professionals will employ tools and techniques designed to collect and manage ESI in a manner that supports the submission of relevant ESI as electronic evidence in a court of law or hearing. The corporate computing environment is ever-changing, and fraud investigators must be prepared to employ emerging advanced approaches to gain insights from this important source of evidence.

Sources of Electronic Evidence

An accountant investigating a fraud allegation will frequently review financial records, such as income statements, balance sheets, general ledgers, and cash flows. Until relatively recently, a large proportion of this information was maintained in paper form. Today, approximately 93 percent of new data is created electronically, of which 70 percent will never be printed. Seventy percent of companies' digital assets are now contained in e-mail form. Currently, 2.2 billion instant messages are sent each day, and the average user may send and receive 15.8 megabytes of e-mail each day.[1]

ESI can be stored on a range of computing devices, from laptops and desktop computers to powerful network computer servers and handheld personal digital assistants. Sources of electronic evidence in investigations can include the general ledger, accounts payable, and payroll, as well as documents, such as Microsoft Word, Excel, and PowerPoint files; Adobe Acrobat PDF files; internal corporate and personal e-mails; instant messaging logs; voicemail; and proprietary systems and software.

Categories

Many potential sources of electronic evidence are contained within the modern corporate computing environment. An investigator should consider each type of ESI that is available, the systems and repositories in which ESI may reside, and the location and storage of the data. In order to simplify and organize the process of preserving and collecting ESI, sources of ESI are typically broken down into categories. Figure 8-1 represents an approach to the categorization of ESI sources.

Categories of ESI may include the following:

- *Category 1: Corporate e-mail servers and archive and journaling systems.* The servers that process e-mail for individuals, business units, or geographies should be identified. Most e-mail systems, including Microsoft Exchange and Lotus Notes, keep both a server and local copy of e-mail. Most e-mail systems also have multiple e-mail servers to serve specific geographies or business units or to serve as redundant sites. The e-mail server hosting each custodian's e-mail needs to be identified, and the overall e-mail architecture should be discussed, so those responsible for collecting electronic evidence can determine if custodians' e-mail may exist on multiple servers.

  E-mail archiving systems enable companies to archive e-mail to a central repository separate from their active e-mail servers. The custodian may have the ability to selectively add and remove e-mail from the archive. E-mail archiving systems are frequently used to alleviate space issues on the active e-mail servers.

  Journaling systems capture all incoming and outgoing e-mail for particular custodians to a central repository, and the custodian has no control over the journaling system. Journaling systems tend to be used in highly regulated industries and may only capture the e-mail of senior employees, such as officers. Although

---

1 Seward, Brian E. "Email Discovery: Tape Is Not Enough" *Infonomics*, September/October 2005.

Figure 8-1: *Electronically Stored Information Sources*

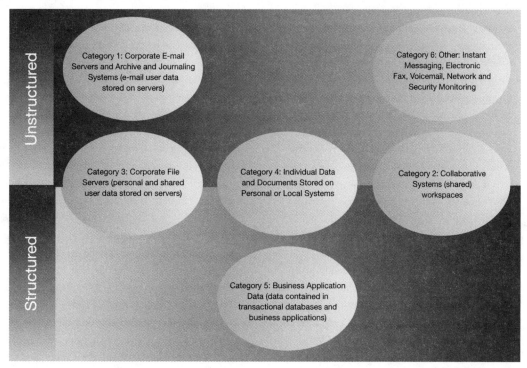

the developers of these systems do sometimes provide companion tools to search and retrieve discoverable e-mail from the archive or journal, their functionality is frequently limited. For example, these tools may not permit searching of the message body using Boolean operators (and, or, not), thereby limiting accurate and targeted retrieval. It may not be possible to search or export e-mail from the journal by custodian because e-mail from multiple custodians may be intermingled.

- *Category 2: Collaborative systems.* These systems allow users to collectively share and search a body of information typically related to a single project. They may include Lotus Notes databases, EMC Documentum eRooms, Lotus Notes QuickPlace, Microsoft SharePoint, or Microsoft Groove, as well as other formats. The storage location of the data is dependent on the individual program; therefore, the investigator should gain an understanding of the architecture to determine how to collect electronic evidence from these systems.

- *Category 3: Corporate file servers.* Companies often make extensive use of personal and departmental shares on file servers as repositories for user-created documents. A share is a portion of the file server's disk storage that has been allocated for file storage. A personal share or "home directory" is used by a specific custodian, and a departmental share may be used by multiple custodians. File server shares may contain ad-hoc databases (for example, Microsoft Access) that can contain key transactional information, and it also is fairly common for shares on corporate file servers to contain archives of employee e-mail databases.

- *Category 4: Individual data and documents stored on personal and local systems.* This includes any desktops, laptops, personal data assistants (for example, BlackBerry or Palm), cell phones, flash or thumb drives, CDs, DVDs, or other storage devices assigned to, or in the possession of, individuals employed by the company. These devices typically will contain user-created documents, as well as corporate and personal e-mail.

These assets often are leased from two to three years; therefore, it is possible that an employee may have been assigned multiple systems during the relevant time period. Each of these systems should be identified and preserved.

- *Category 5: Business applications and data.* Business and transactional systems contain the online financial and operational transaction records for a company. These systems may be multitiered with a presentation layer running on one computer system, a database layer on another system, and a business logic layer on yet another system. The key to collecting the business data is to discuss the architecture of the business system with the system owner to determine which layers contain business data and how best to collect the data.
- *Category 6: Other Sources of ESI.* In addition to the preceding categories, other sources of ESI may be relevant to the fraud investigator. The following sources should be considered carefully when setting the scope of the hold:
  - *Electronic fax.* These systems may contain a record of faxes sent and received by individuals or departments. The fax data may be centralized (stored on a server) or decentralized (stored on individual workstations or file shares). Both stored images of the actual faxes and logs of fax activity may exist.
  - *Voicemail and PBX.* Private branch exchange (PBX) phone systems and voicemail may contain call logs, recordings of voicemail, and other activity. Voice systems may not be homogeneous, due to growth or acquisitions. In addition, management of voicemail and PBX systems may be decentralized to multiple geographic locations.
  - *Instant messaging.* This may include corporate instant messaging systems, such as Lotus Notes Sametime, as well as personal-use programs, such as AOL Instant Messenger and Yahoo! Messenger. Storage of data may be centralized, local, or both. Those responsible for the collection of electronic evidence should inquire into and consider any additional logging or archiving capabilities the company may have established. To the extent that an organization supports an enterprise instant messaging

program that has centralized logging and storage capability, consideration should be given to collection of this ESI. Regulators may expect this data to be preserved in the normal course of business.
  - *Network and security monitoring.* Various types of physical or network security device logs also may be collected if the investigation seeks to determine whether the actions of individuals were logged. These may include card swipe logs, closed-circuit video, Internet logs, remote access logs, and intrusion detection server logs. The configuration of these systems and the availability of log information vary widely, and a discussion is best held up-front to determine whether these items should be collected.
  - *Residual data.* Whole files that have been deleted may be recoverable intact. Even if a deleted file has been partially overwritten, some parts or "fragments" of the file may be recoverable. Residual data may be identified in unexpected locations. For example, documents may be recovered from a hard drive stored in a networked office printer.

Location and Storage

Potential electronic evidence may be stored on a range of media during its lifecycle. For example, the evidence may be considered to be active and online when it is created and stored on a hard drive. It may be archived to backup tape periodically. When it is deleted, fragments of the deleted file may remain on the hard drive. The investigator should consider where the electronic evidence may be stored based on where it is in its lifecycle. The data may exist in any of these states during its lifespan:

- *Active online.* Stored on magnetic disks, such as hard drives, attached to a computer or server.
- *Near-line.* Stored on removable media, such as optical discs, that can be made available by a device, such as an optical "jukebox."
- *Offline storage.* Used for disaster recovery or archiving that must be made available through human intervention. Backup tapes are typically used for offline storage.
- *Erased, fragmented, or damaged data.* Retrievable only by using sophisticated forensic tools.

The IT Function

Most modern organizations have a dedicated Information Technology (IT) department. Larger companies may have a corporate IT department and IT departments within each business unit. In smaller companies, IT may only consist of one or two individuals. Regardless, key personnel will have operational knowledge of systems maintained by IT. The investigator will identify and contact personnel from these departments in order to better assess and understand the IT organization and the systems it operates or for which it is responsible.

The investigator must understand the organization and flow of information across a company's IT systems. Depending on the type of investigation, electronic evidence may be obtained from a variety of sources. The investigator needs to understand what data is available and must be obtained in order to support the requirements of the investigation. Typically, a company maintains specifications and other documentation describing internal systems and may maintain data flow diagrams that describe information flow, providing a better understanding of how the systems interact.

Identifying potentially relevant sources of electronic evidence may require an understanding of how IT governance is implemented in the organization. The IT Governance Institute (ITGI) describes IT governance as "the leadership and organizational structures and processes that ensure that the organization's IT sustains and extends the organization's strategies and objectives."[2] IT governance supports a focus on performance and risk management and has increased in importance since the passage of the Sarbanes-Oxley Act of 2002 (SOX). IT governance supports the documentation of strategies, policies, and organizational structures that can provide useful information to fraud investigators who must identify systems and data that may contain electronic evidence.

A number of frameworks have been developed that support the implementation of IT governance, as well as control and mitigate the risks associated with IT. The two most prominent are the Committee of Sponsoring Organizations of the Treadway Commission (COSO) and the Control Objectives for Information and Related Technology (COBIT). The COSO framework provides guidance to assess and improve internal control systems. Moreover, this framework can be used to describe and analyze the internal control structure implemented within an organization. The COSO framework has been specifically identified by the Securities and Exchange Commission as a methodology for achieving compliance with SOX regulations. COBIT is an open standard published by the ITGI and the Information Systems Audit and Control Association that specifically focuses on IT processes and controls.

Depending on the type of investigation and the maturity of the IT governance of the organization, the business may have documented risk assessments and risk mitigation plans available for review. These plans may contain information about the systems, as well as their constraints and controls, that is useful to the investigator. Furthermore, if the organization must comply with SOX, additional documentation may be available for financial reporting systems. At the very least, the IT organization should be able to describe the control policies and procedures surrounding relevant systems. This information can help the investigator determine what electronic evidence to collect for analysis.

Privacy and Confidentiality

Many companies based in the United States will have international subsidiaries, operations, or important third-party relationships with suppliers, contractors, or other key intermediaries. As a result, non-U.S. laws and regulations may come into play during an investigation when data must be retrieved from a location outside the United States, and it is important to consider the possible implications for privacy and confidentiality. Readers are advised to seek guidance from counsel prior to collecting employee data. The following information is intended as an overview of global privacy regulations and should not be a substitute for advice of counsel. For a broader discussion of global privacy regulations, see chapter 9, "Cross-Jurisdictional Issues in the Global Environment."

---

2 IT Governance Institute. Board Briefing on IT Governance, 2nd Edition, 2003.

The United States uses an approach to the protection of personal data based on legislation, regulation, and organizational self-regulation. In response to restrictions imposed by the European Union (EU) on the transfer of data from the EU to countries with weaker data privacy laws, the U.S. Department of Commerce developed a safe harbor framework. This framework allows U.S. organizations to evaluate their policies and procedures related to the use of personal data and then self-certify that the organization provides adequate privacy protection, as defined by the EU.

The United States and Switzerland also have established a safe harbor framework that "will simplify the transfer of personal data by Swiss firms to American companies certified by the U.S. Department of Commerce."[3] Organizations that wish to self-certify to the U.S.-Swiss Safe Harbor Framework will follow an identical process to that of self-certifying to the U.S.-European Union Safe Harbor Framework.

U.S. organizations that wish to self-certify must either become a member of a self-regulatory privacy program or form their own self-regulatory privacy policy, both of which must follow safe harbor requirements. Organizations also must comply with the principles found in box 8-1.[4]

Box 8-1: *Privacy Regulatory Policy Principles*

Notice	Organizations must notify individuals about the purposes for which they collect and use information about them. They must provide information about how individuals can contact the organization with any inquiries or complaints, the types of third parties to which it discloses the information, and the choices and means the organization offers for limiting the information's use and disclosure.
Choice	Organizations must give individuals the opportunity to choose (opt out) whether their personal information will be disclosed to a third party or used for a purpose incompatible with the purpose for which it was originally collected or subsequently authorized by the individual. For sensitive information, an affirmative or explicit (opt in) choice must be given if the information is to be disclosed to a third party or used for a purpose other than its original purpose or the purpose authorized subsequently by the individual.
Onward Transfer (Transfers to Third Parties)	To disclose information to a third party, organizations must apply the notice and choice principles. When an organization wishes to transfer information to a third party that is acting as an agent, it may do so if it makes sure that the third party subscribes to the safe harbor principles or is subject to Directive 95/46/EC or another adequacy finding. As an alternative, the organization can enter into a written agreement with such third party requiring that the third party provide at least the same level of privacy protection that is required by the relevant principles.

(continued)

---

3 See http://www.export.gov/safeharbor/eg_main_018244.asp.

4 See www.export.gov/safeharbor/eg_main_018236.asp.

Box 8-1: *Privacy Regulatory Policy Principles (continued)*

Access	Individuals must have access to personal information about them that an organization holds and be able to correct, amend, or delete that information when it is inaccurate, except when the burden or expense of providing access would be disproportionate to the risks to the individual's privacy in the case in question or when the rights of persons other than the individual would be violated.
Security	Organizations must take reasonable precautions to protect personal information from loss; misuse; and unauthorized access, disclosure, alteration, and destruction.
Data Integrity	Personal information must be relevant to the purposes for which it is to be used. An organization should take reasonable steps to ensure that data is accurate, complete, current, and reliable for its intended use.
Enforcement	In order to ensure compliance with the safe harbor principles, there must be (*a*) readily available and affordable independent recourse mechanisms, so that each individual's complaints and disputes can be investigated and resolved and damages awarded when the applicable law or private sector initiatives so provide; (*b*) procedures for verifying that the commitments companies make to adhere to the safe harbor principles have been implemented; and (*c*) obligations to remedy problems arising out of a failure to comply with the principles. Sanctions must be sufficiently rigorous to ensure compliance by the organization. Organizations that fail to provide annual self-certification letters will no longer appear in the list of participants, and safe harbor benefits will no longer be assured.

The EU relies on a body of comprehensive and highly restrictive legislation that "requires creation of government data protection agencies, registration of databases with those agencies, and in some instances prior approval before personal data processing may begin."[5] The European Commission's Directive on Data Protection (Directive 95/46/EC) became effective in 1998 and prohibits "the transfer of personal data to non-European Union nations that do not meet the European 'adequacy' standard for privacy protection."[6]

The Organization for Economic Co-operation and Development has developed widely accepted guidelines related to privacy protection and the transborder flow of personal data. These guidelines set forth fair information practice principles that form the basis of many privacy regulations and laws in the United States, Canada, Europe, and other countries that have enacted specific privacy protection regimens.

Other regulations and local country laws may affect the collection of data outside the United States. Investigators should consult with counsel who have expertise in data privacy prior to proceeding with such collections.

---

5 Ibid.
6 Ibid.

Professional Standards

Investigators and their clients are under increasing pressure to manage the preservation and collection of electronic evidence in an effective and defensible manner, consistent with professional standards, federal and state rules of evidence, and applicable national and international regulations. Because many investigators do not possess expertise in the technical skills and concepts necessary to manage electronic evidence effectively, they must rely on technical advisors who have this experience and expertise.

This reliance can be worrisome for the investigator. Given that the investigator may not fully understand how the corporate systems managing the evidence operate or where various sources of electronic evidence are located within the system, how can an investigator feel confident that the evidence the technical advisors are collecting reflects the scope identified by counsel and the investigators and that the advisors are conducting collection activities in a rigorous, sound, and defensible manner, according to applicable professional standards?

It is the responsibility of the client's in-house and outside legal counsel to identify the sources of evidence that are potentially relevant to the investigation (see chapter 6, "Roles and Responsibilities: How Different Stakeholders Work During Investigations"). Counsel and investigators should work closely with their technical advisors to define the universe of potentially relevant evidence that should be collected and processed for review and analysis. All potentially relevant sources of electronic evidence should be considered, but it is not necessarily the case that the same types of evidence will be collected for every investigation. The scope of the investigation, the nature of the alleged fraud, and the custodians involved will be important considerations in determining what electronic evidence should be collected.

Investigators and their technical advisors should document the processes used to collect and manage electronic evidence in an investigation. Interviews that seek information about the corporate technology infrastructure, data sources to which custodians have access, data destruction processes, and processes and procedures related to the management of data should be documented and reviewed. Understanding the capabilities and limitations of systems, processes, and procedures allows counsel and the investigator to tailor the review strategy to the key risks that are likely to affect the project, understand the nature and potential impact of the risks, and minimize the likelihood of unpleasant surprises.

Today's emerging technologies and global business market have tremendously affected the role of the accountant. Because accounting firms now provide a variety of consulting services, including advisory, implementation, transaction, and product services, they must continue to adhere to the guidelines set forth by the AICPA. Rule 201, *General Standards* (AICPA, *Professional Standards*, vol. 2, ET sec. 200), of the AICPA Code of Professional Conduct states the following general standards of the profession:

- Professional competence
- Due professional care
- Planning and supervision
- Sufficient relevant data

Forensic accountants and investigators must "provide valuable services in the highest professional manner to benefit the public as well as employers and clients."[7] The AICPA Code of Professional Conduct, as it relates to the collection and management of electronic evidence, is described in more detail subsequently.

Professional Competence

Undertake only those professional services that the member or the member's firm can reasonably expect to be completed with professional competence.[8]

When working with electronic evidence, investigators should consider retaining qualified and experienced technical advisors to assist with the collection and management of electronic evidence. Investigators should consider relevant experience, industry and subject matter publications demonstrating thought leadership, as well as professional certifications when choosing a technical advisor to assist

---

7 See the AICPA Mission at www.aicpa.org/About+the+AICPA/AICPA+Mission/.

8 See www.aicpa.org/about/code/et_200.html.

with the management of electronic evidence during an investigation. Box 8-2 provides some sample professional certifications that may demonstrate that the advisor has relevant skills.

Box 8-2: *Professional Certifications*

Professional Certifications	
CCE	Certified Computer Examiner
CFCE	Certified Forensic Computer Examiner
CFE	Certified Fraud Examiner
CISA	Certified Information Systems Auditor
CISM	Certified Information Security Manager
CISSP	Certified Information Systems Security Professional
CITP	Certified Information Technology Professional
CPP	Certified Protection Professional
CRM	Certified Records Manager
EnCE	EnCase Certified Examiner
PMP	Project Management Professional
SCERS	Seized Computer Evidence Recovery Specialist

It may be prudent to consider the credibility, reputation, experience, and relevance of the technical advisor. These factors are significant, particularly if the technical advisor must testify regarding the quality of the data acquisition and processing. Additionally, technical advisors often have to respond to the inquiries of regulators, law enforcement officials, or the client's auditors regarding the accuracy and completeness of their work.

Due Professional Care

Exercise due professional care in the performance of professional services.[9]

Technical advisors who have helped manage electronic evidence for a large litigation or investigation understand the importance of documenting the processes used to manage evidence. When data collection occurs in multiple locations around the world, when the list of key custodians changes frequently over the course of the investigation, or when the client's systems and technologies have inherent associated risks, due professional care can be difficult to demonstrate if the proper documentation is not maintained throughout the life cycle of the investigation.

Demonstrating the accuracy and completeness of the process used to collect and manage electronic data is critical to any investigation. Regulators, law enforcement officials, courts, and auditors have an increasingly sophisticated understanding and expectation of the technologies and systems used to collect and store electronic evidence, and investigators and technical advisors must demonstrate the professional care necessary to meet those expectations. Parties must be able to account adequately for all the data collected as it is prepared for review and analysis. All decisions related to deduplicating, filtering, rendering, displaying, and exporting the data should be documented. Further, investigators must be prepared to defend against challenges related to the procedures and technologies described in their reports.

Planning and Supervision

Adequately plan and supervise the performance of professional services.[10]

Adequate planning and supervision is necessary to demonstrate due professional care. During the planning process, investigators and their technical advisors should establish goals and objectives and the activities necessary to achieve them. Successful

9 Ibid.
10 Ibid.

planning includes regular communication among counsel, the investigators, and technical advisors in order to keep all parties well informed of current activities, observations, and potential changes in scope.

Project planning encompasses a range of planning activities related to scope, schedule, cost, quality, staffing, communication, risk, and procurement that are used to develop a project management plan and manage the project. The plans generated by these planning activities will together constitute the overall project plan that the project management team will execute to achieve the objectives of the project. According to the Project Management Institute, "[t]he project management plan, developed as an output of the Planning Process Group, will have an emphasis on exploring all aspects of the scope, technology, risks, and costs."[11] Effective planning will take into account all phases of evidence management for a fraud investigation. The planning phase also is iterative, so plans will tend to be revised as new information is learned.

It is very important that the project team involve all appropriate stakeholders in the planning processes, in order to benefit from their skills and knowledge. The collection and review of electronic evidence may involve a number of stakeholders. Technical advisors, investigators, the company's in-house counsel, the company's internal computer forensics team, IT, outside counsel, and outside counsel's litigation support team, among others, could all be involved. In practice, some of these stakeholders may be excluded from some or all of the planning process because they are not involved in the investigation for reasons of privilege or other reasons. However, it is a leading practice to involve all stakeholders to the degree practical and advisable.

Some project managers may be tempted to exclude some stakeholders from communications because they think it too time consuming or not necessary. Communication represents, by some calculations, 80 percent of a project manager's activities. Without effective communication to stakeholders, project managers (1) may not benefit from the skills, knowledge, and input of the stakeholders; (2) may find that an issue has not been identified, thereby creating a risk; or (3) may find that the lack of communication has created conflict. Of course, if there is any suspicion that an individual could be involved in the fraud, he or she should not be a stakeholder in the project.

The level of detail and the number of areas to be covered by the project plan must be commensurate with the scope of the project. Although larger, more complex projects may require a very detailed plan in several documents, projects with a limited scope might require only a single document at a reduced level of detail.

Supervision is critical to ensuring compliance with the project plan and associated protocols, procedures, and activities. Without adequate management of compliance, participants may fail to act in a manner that supports the defensibility of the investigation processes and that demonstrates due professional care.

Sufficient Relevant Data

Obtain sufficient relevant data to afford a reasonable basis for conclusions or recommendations in relation to any professional services performed.[12]

With the ever-increasing volume of ESI that must be preserved, collected, and reviewed during an investigation, there comes a fundamental challenge: Have we applied our search and review processes, our tools, and our professional judgment to the right body of evidence? While no legal principle requires perfection in collection, review, and disclosures, counsel and investigators do have obligations to perform these processes reasonably and ethically, demonstrating due professional care and judgment.

Quality control processes employed prior to the review of electronic information are an essential element of demonstrating the "reasonableness" of a party's evidence management processes; they also support chain of custody documentation. Parties using well-designed evidence management processes are able to account for 100 percent of the electronic

---

11 Project Management Institute. A Guide to the Project Management Body of Knowledge, Third Edition (PMBOK Guides), 2004.

12 See www.aicpa.org/about/code/et_200.html.

information they collect, even though they may review and produce only a small portion of that information.

The complexity associated with multilocation collection, large numbers of custodians, different sources of live systems, archives, and forensic images makes effective quality control processes essential. Without them, parties are more vulnerable to potential challenges related to omission of potentially relevant data, spoliation, conversion of data, or productions.

Quality control procedures have two main purposes: data accountability and anomaly detection. In general, quality control steps and reports should be in place for each major phase of discovery processing, including data collection, data extraction and conversion (which may include elimination of system files or other high-level culling techniques), deduplication, data culling or searching, and data review.

Leading practices call for maintaining the relationship between the data, original source media, and custodian throughout each processing stage. A party can then report both the contents and file counts at each stage of processing for each piece of media (such as a hard drive), as well as the contents and file counts for each unique source for each custodian. Clear documentation of what was done and not done should be maintained. If Internet e-mail is not processed for review, that should be documented. If a party uses forensic tools to recover deleted e-mails from a custodian's mailbox, that should be documented, including the tool used and the result.

A cornerstone of data accountability is establishing the counts of files on media before processing begins. From this defined starting point, the party should make adjustments to file counts postexpansion of the original documents, reflecting processing results for each source:[13]

- Elimination of system files (for example, based on the National Software Reference Library filter)
- Deductions for certain file types not processed (such as databases)
- Deductions for items that could not be processed (for example, corrupt files)

- Deductions for duplicates not processed
- Deductions for items not selected by filters

These files may be accounted for as shown in figure 8-2.

Figure 8-2: *Indexed Media File Count Processing*

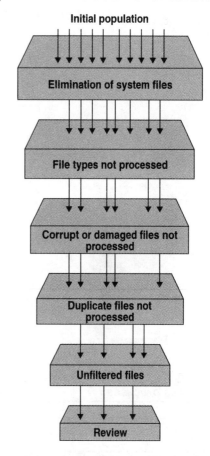

#	Category	Num. Items
1	**# Original items**	**64,748**
2	**Total files expanded**	**131,128**
3	**# of items filtered**	
a	# System Files	12,721
b	# File types not processed	47
c	# Corrupt or Damaged files	7,548
d	# Duplicates	18,745
e	# Items not selected by filter	38,748
	Total Filtered	**77,809**

---

13 Documents such as Zip archives may expand to two or more documents and should be expanded prior to the application of filters.

In addition, it also is important to note files processed but not indexed, such as encrypted files. Figure 8-3 demonstrates an approach to accounting for these files.

Figure 8-3: *Unindexed Media File Count Processing*

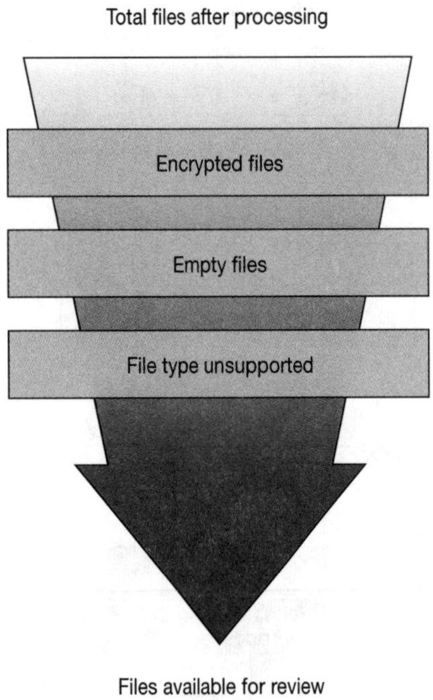

Total files after processing

Files available for review

#	Category	Num. Items
4	*Total files processed*	*53,319*
5	Error	
a	# Encrypted files	6,784
b	# Empty files	1,274
c	# File type unsupported	26,728
	Total	*34,786*

Using this approach, it will be possible to report the total number of items from all sources for each custodian, such as the server e-mail, e-mail archives, hard drives, network shares, and removable media. Searching the review database for all items associated with a custodian should yield a result that matches the total items reported for the custodian after the media has been processed. This enables a party to account for all the data that it collected for a matter. Subjected to the scrutiny of an independent or adversarial party, the evidence management process is transparent and can be defended as thorough and diligent.

The raw data regarding the electronic information that this approach generates also is useful for identifying anomalies in the evidence. Investigating and resolving anomalies and exceptions in the data serves as an additional quality control check that may discover errors or omissions in the collection process. At a minimum, investigating anomalies will answer questions that other parties may have about the collection process. Indexing exceptions that are not documented are of particular concern because the items are loaded into the database and appear to be available for searching, analysis, and review. Because they are not indexed, any keyword searches performed against the data will not include those items. Therefore, a review that is based at least in part on the results of keyword searches may overlook these items. Figure 8-4 demonstrates an approach to tracking data anomalies.

The quality control processes that enable data accountability must be incorporated into the overall evidence management process; late implementation of these processes will require a historical reconciliation of the data sources through each phase of the electronic evidence review process and will be both difficult and costly.

The Electronic Evidence Review Process

The review of electronic evidence is the process by which electronic documents are collected, processed, analyzed, and reviewed. Subjective and objective decisions about each document are recorded by reviewers, helping to paint a picture of fraud activities that may have occurred. Ultimately, documents that are not subject to a legal privilege are provided or "produced" to the government agency, auditor, or opposing party that requested them. The electronic evidence review process is described in figure 8-5.

Identification

Identification is the process of determining which data sources are in the scope of the investigation and should be preserved, collected, and processed for review.

Figure 8-4: *Data Anomaly Tracking*

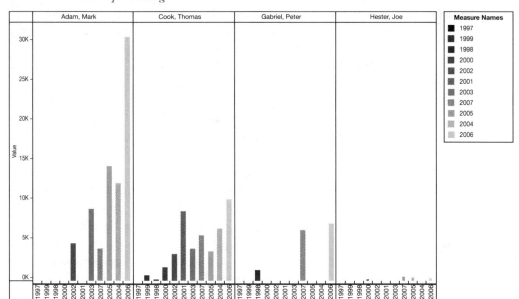

Figure 8-5: *Evidence Review Process*

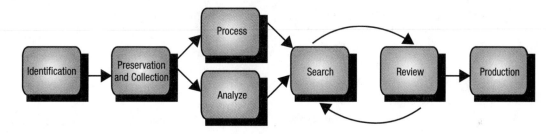

In order to establish the scope of the collection, outside counsel, the company, and its advisors will typically identify custodians who may have custody or control of relevant ESI, based on currently known information, as well as custodians whose work involves business processes relevant to the matter. The advisors, working with the company, will identify the business systems that support those processes and the data sources related to those systems.

One key tool in identifying potential evidence is a company's asset management system. These systems track and maintain a history of IT assets. An asset management system will help in determining what systems a custodian has access to now or had access to in the past. As an example, if a custodian has recently received a new laptop, important evidence may be on the old laptop as well. The asset man-

agement system will be essential in identifying what has happened to the old laptop. It may have been assigned to someone new, or it may be in storage. By using the asset management system, investigators can more thoroughly identify evidence that may be obtained.

Preservation and Collection

In many cases, it will not be feasible to collect all potentially relevant ESI as soon as it is identified. As a result, that ESI must be preserved from alteration or deletion (known as spoliation) until such time that it can be collected. ESI may be deliberately or inadvertently altered by a human action or an automated system process, such as scheduled purging or archiving of e-mail or documents by a computer system. Investigators and counsel must therefore alert custodians of potentially relevant ESI that they must refrain from altering or deleting it, or they must take specific action to prevent such activities, such as by deactivating a rule in their mailbox that deletes older documents. Preservation begins with notification to custodians that they must preserve ESI in their custody or control, which is a process known as a legal hold. As a part of the legal hold process, custodians will generally be issued written preservation notices informing them of the actions they must take or not take to preserve the ESI in their custody or control. The collection of ESI may take place at any time while data is under a legal hold, though it is advisable to collect data as soon as possible. The legal hold and collection processes are discussed in more detail subsequently.

Legal Hold

When ESI must be preserved, custodians should generally be notified that they must avoid deleting or changing potentially relevant electronic evidence. An organization's counsel should notify custodians of their duty to preserve potentially relevant ESI in their custody or control. Custodians also may be informed of their duty to preserve potentially relevant information created in the future, if applicable. The preservation notice should be understandable to custodians, actionable, and sufficiently detailed. Depending on the needs of the matter, counsel also may follow up to verify that the requirements of the legal hold are understood and honored by all custodians. The notification process should clearly establish procedures for the following:

(1) Notifying custodians of potentially relevant ESI of the need to preserve that information
(2) Tracking acknowledgements by custodians of these obligations
(3) Reminding custodians of their continuing obligations to preserve ESI
(4) Monitoring compliance with the notifications

It is important to note that one size does not necessarily fit all; the level of communication, tracking, and monitoring will tend to be defined by the scope and nature of the investigation triggering the hold.

The most effective method for communicating a preservation requirement to custodians is a written

preservation notice. This may not always be necessary, and, on occasion, no notification may be required. For example, if the relevant ESI is retained forever as a matter of policy and practice, if the ESI can be collected immediately, or if there is a suspicion that a custodian might delete ESI should he or she receive a notice, it may not be necessary or even judicious to provide notification.

Preservation notices will generally be issued from the office of the general counsel or some other department charged with responsibility for preserving records of the organization. If the company has implemented a legal hold management system capable of transmitting preservation notices by e-mail or another mechanism, then the notice may be transmitted by outside counsel or a technical advisor who manages the system. The e-mail should be formatted consistently with the company's internal e-mail system and indicate that it was sent from the general counsel's office, so that recipients do not consider the e-mail spam. The company's spam filtering systems also should be evaluated to ensure they do not block preservation notices originating from outside counsel or technical advisors.

The effectiveness of the notification process will depend, in part, on accurate identification of current and former business, IT, and records management personnel who have custody or control of information potentially relevant to the investigation. Non-employees also may be within the scope of a legal hold. For example, individual contractors may be in possession of potentially relevant information that is within the organization's custody and control. The company should consider such persons who have e-mail or other user accounts on the company's systems because they may possess information within the scope of the hold. Additionally, third parties, such as application service providers, may have physical custody of information that is within the organization's control and relevant to the legal hold.

Thorough documentation of the legal hold is necessary to demonstrate that reasonable efforts were made to comply with applicable rules and regulations. The following items should be documented:

• The hold trigger and date and personnel involved

- Scope and scope changes, including custodian lists, systems, and sources of ESI
- Systems inventory
- Preservation plan and protocol for custodians, systems, and repositories of ESI
- Record of notice and updated notices to custodians
- Custodians' acknowledgement of their obligation to preserve ESI
- Copies of the preservation notices
- Interview notes and memoranda
- Preservation questions and answers

The company should issue periodic reminders of the hold if it is of extended duration. Too frequently, a legal hold is treated as a one-time communication. Considering that legal matters often last for years, it becomes instantly clear how even the most diligent custodian could fail to remember the details of a legal hold notice sent months or years earlier. Thus, it is recommended that the legal department issue quarterly reminders to all affected custodians reminding them to continue to preserve documents as required by the hold.

Legal holds are iterative; the hold may be both refined and expanded as facts and information come to light. Those responsible for the hold should consider whether preservation notices should be updated and reissued as the litigation evolves. Furthermore, steps should be taken to ensure that new employees receive any notices obligating them to comply with a preexisting hold. Updated notices should take into account any sources of ESI that have emerged since the original notice was issued.

Depending on the scope and nature of the hold, it may be advisable to audit custodians' efforts to comply with the hold in order to demonstrate compliance and for the person responsible for the hold to document and certify ongoing compliance. The legal hold team will follow up with custodians throughout the process to verify compliance. A team of legal and IT personnel should be identified who can assist custodians who have legal or IT-related questions associated with the hold.

Advisors involved in a legal hold also should report regularly to the company and its outside counsel on the progress of the hold. Reporting typically includes status reports, formal meeting minutes, and regularly scheduled meetings to discuss the status of notice and preservation efforts. Summary documentation for each custodian or business unit should be prepared to provide a clear record of the representations the custodians made regarding ESI within their control and the actions they took to preserve ESI in response to counsel instruction. The summary typically includes a confirming signature by the custodian.

Timely and accurate reporting of holds is an important aspect of a well-designed, well-planned, and defensible hold. Depending on the nature of the legal hold, a standardized report template may be developed and reports regularly circulated to stakeholders that identify progress made on the implementation of the hold. Such reports might include the following:

- The number of preservation notices transmitted overall and by business unit
- The number of acknowledgements received overall and by business unit
- The number of unacknowledged notices overall and by business unit
- Data sources preserved overall and by business unit, data source, and type of preservation
- Noticing and preservation activities on an actual schedule versus planned schedule basis

The office responsible for transmitting the notification should define escalation procedures in the event that a custodian fails to respond to the preservation notice. Generally, in those circumstances, notifications should be sent to the recipient's supervisor advising the supervisor of the recipient's inaction and urgent need for compliance. This communication also should be tracked, recording the date the supervisor was notified and the date of that individual's response. Organizations should clearly establish the responsibilities of employee and supervisor in this process, and the results of noncompliance should be clearly communicated. For monitoring purposes, a report should be created detailing the delinquent recipients and the level of escalation implemented for the recipients, and it should be reviewed for appropriate action by the office responsible for the hold.

Preservation

An effective legal hold will help a company preserve ESI necessary for the investigation and as little unnecessary ESI as possible. It is not a requirement to maintain every e-mail or document in a company's possession when a legal hold is triggered, only those potentially relevant to the investigation. An effective preservation plan and process is not overly inclusive but preserves only relevant ESI, as far as possible. Companies can preserve ESI by more than one method. The following three methods tend to be used most commonly:

- *Preserve on tape.* The ESI is preserved by segregation of backup tapes from the disaster recovery or archival system.
- *Preserve in place.* This form of preservation relies entirely upon compliance by custodians with the preservation notice. It should not be used to preserve data in the custody or control of a suspected fraudster or coconspirators.
- *Preserve by collection.* Various methods are employed to create identical copies of the relevant data.

The facts of the specific investigation will influence the approach that the company takes to preservation. For instance, in an on-going preservation obligation (the legal hold is applied to information created or received today and in the future), some aspect of "preserve in place" will need to be incorporated into the preservation plan. Generally, collection should take place as soon as possible after the ESI is preserved, regardless of the method of preservation, though this may not be feasible depending on the number of custodians involved and the overall scope of the hold. Many methods of collection exist. Most importantly, the method of collection should capture the ESI in a forensically sound manner. It should not damage, modify, delete, or alter either the original ESI or the copy made for collection.

It may be necessary to design and perform a "sweep" for off-line media, such as backup tapes pulled out of rotation, hard drives, and other magnetic media. A sweep may require the development of a questionnaire that the company implements on its own regarding these media, or it may involve technology advisors performing a physical sweep (walk-through and collection of media) with counsel. A sweep should include thorough documentation of how the sweep was performed and the geographic, departmental, and physical (within a building or offices) locations that were searched. It also should result in a searchable inventory that categorizes, quantifies, and describes the materials found during the sweep.

Collection

Appropriate protocols are required during collection, preservation, and analysis of electronic evidence, if evidentiary integrity and value are to be preserved. Maintaining a chain of custody log will enable evidence to be traced from the point and time of original collection to the point and time when it is presented in a proceeding. Creating a clear and comprehensive chain of custody documentation is particularly critical, given the length of time that may elapse between data collection and the presentation of the results of a forensic analysis of the data.

Fundamentally, investigators need to be aware of the need to

- understand the physical environment within which the electronic evidence is located and document observations, interviews, and actions taken with respect to the data collection. For example, if it is believed that relevant data may be stored on an active e-mail server, it will be necessary to take appropriate steps to understand how data is stored on that server and if any automatic deletion policies are implemented on users' mailboxes. If interviews of IT personnel are conducted, the date, time, location, and interviewee names should be documented for future reference, along with the substantive information gathered.
- control the physical environment once it is understood. In the prior example, if e-mail of interest is located on a server, creating a forensic copy of user mailboxes can be undertaken by qualified personnel using appropriate tools and techniques. The copy can then be verified to ensure that it is an exact copy of the data required, and the verification procedures can be documented.

- log all detail pertaining to the handling of forensic copies. Continuing the example, the media used to store the e-mail copies should be clearly identified (for example, by bar coding), and the movement of that media to secure storage and in and out of storage during analysis must be documented. A chain of custody log will then present a chronological history of each time the media is physically touched, including where, when, by whom, and for what purpose.

Computer Forensics

The field of computer forensics encompasses a range of activities, from relatively straightforward tasks, such as searching a single computer system for evidence of unauthorized use, to searching for deleted e-mail messages that might remain on a computer network.

Computer forensics in the context of evidence gathering and electronic evidence review relates to the application of investigative processes and technical skills to find, secure, replicate or preserve, and chronicle or examine data within computers, electronic devices, and storage media, so that it can become admissible evidence in court proceedings.

Forensic Tools

Forensic tools capture a forensic or "mirror" image of the original evidence media. This "mirror" image is a bit-by-bit copy and will contain the active files found on the media along with the unallocated storage space, which is the location on the hard drive where erased or deleted files may be found. Forensic tools must not change either the content of the data or information used by the computer to classify a file or directory, such as the date and time the file or directory was created. This information is known as metadata.

Other data on a disk can include file slack, which is the remaining part of a deleted file after a smaller file is written over it, and unallocated space, which is space on the hard drive not currently allocated to a file and possibly containing a deleted file or fragments of a deleted file. These types of electronic information are frequently important to investigations. The forensic disk image may include the following:

- Files visible in Windows Explorer
- Deleted files
- File slack
- Unallocated space
- Metadata (both from the file system and specific applications)
- Operating system information

The tool used to create this forensic image should be able to verify that the output image matches the input media by using a verification hash comparison. A hash value is a "digital fingerprint" of a file or media. During the imaging process, the application will generate a hash value for the entire suspect media. Once the image is created, the application will then generate a hash for the forensic image and the two will be compared. If they match, the tool successfully created a duplicate. It is important to note that the tool selected to create a forensic image must not affect the original data.

Remote Collection Tools

Remote collection tools are enterprise applications that are permitted unrestricted access to most network machines. These tools can allow a company to seamlessly collect potentially relevant data, often without a custodian's knowledge. The key difference between these tools and other forensic tools is that a forensics professional does not need to physically be at the location of the machine to collect the data. An administrator can schedule a collection at a specific time or as a result of questionable activity on the network. The administrator also can preview a network machine before collection without altering any of the active file metadata, keeping the evidentiary integrity of the image.

Collecting Structured and Unstructured Data

Electronic evidence may be divided into two broad categories: (1) structured ESI and (2) unstructured ESI. Structured ESI is typically contained in databases, such as financial or accounting databases (that is, general ledger, accounts payable, and payroll) and other databases, such as customer relationship management, shipping, or inventory databases. Unstructured ESI includes e-mails, documents (that is, Word and Excel), instant messaging logs, and voicemail. The investigator will work with counsel to determine what type of electronic data should be obtained.

Structured data is stored in a highly efficient and organized form, such as a database or spreadsheet. Structured data is typically collected using functionality available in the application managing the data or by using other utilities. Once the data is exported from the application, it can be analyzed using specialized tools.

Unstructured data includes e-mail messages, letters, and memoranda. Unstructured data lacks a highly efficient and organized data structure and is most typically collected using forensic tools designed for this purpose. In some cases, unstructured data also can be collected using the application that manages it. For example, ExMerge, the Microsoft Exchange Server Mailbox Merge Wizard, is a utility that allows trained personnel to extract e-mail data from one or several server-based mailboxes. The extracted e-mail messages retain all of their metadata and are identical to the e-mail messages found in a user's mailbox.

Collecting Other ESI

ESI may be automatically created as the result of a particular activity. For example, when a computer user visits a Web site, the computer operating system will temporarily store some Web site information in the computer's memory and in temporary space on the computer's hard drive. These data fragments often can be observed with specialized forensic analysis software tools, but the fragments do not live on the hard drive as intact, complete documents, such as a letter, memo, spreadsheet, or e-mail message. They may contain some data from a specific Web site, but there will typically not be any discernable beginning or ending point to the data that is present. This data may be of interest to investigators and it is only through the use of specialized tools, techniques, and training that the data can be reviewed once it has been forensically preserved.

Leveraging Company Resources

Most organizations have systems administrators (for example, database server administrators, e-mail server administrators, network specialists, and desktop application support personnel) who have a specific expertise but are typically not trained in forensic disciplines. IT departments use hardware and software tools to support the business needs of the organization, such as to recover lost data. These tools may alter the data being copied, compromising the evidentiary value of the data.

Specialists in computer forensics have developed investigative methodologies and software tools to collect and analyze electronic information in a manner that is technically and legally consistent with its use for evidentiary purposes. Internal IT departments may not have personnel with the appropriate backgrounds, and they may not have the budgets to purchase, update, and provide ongoing training in the use of specialized tools. If an organization chooses to use its own personnel and tools, the organization runs the risk that evidence may be altered, damaged, or lost. The use of internal IT personnel in an investigation, for purposes other than support roles, also can compromise an organization's independence in an investigation. Box 8-3 identifies company resources that may provide critical assistance to investigative personnel.

Process and Analyze

Processing data for electronic evidence review has evolved over the past decade as the volume of data to review has increased and the tools that support it have become more sophisticated. Data processing includes all the steps necessary to prepare data to be loaded for review and analysis. Electronic evidence processing must accommodate a wide variety of unstructured data types (for example, e-mail, documents, presentations, and so on) as well as structured data types, such as databases and financial systems, if appropriate. Processing must always consider the review software that will be used because the review platform will generally have specific formatting requirements. Processing systems must be able to handle foreign languages, so they must be Unicode compliant.

Processing is the stage at which data may be filtered for content. For example, counsel may decide that duplicates should be removed, files that are not likely to contain useful data (such as system files)

Box 8-3: *Shared Organizational Resources for Personnel Investigation*

- Describe the technical infrastructure within a company, the location of specific hardware, and the function of various hardware devices.

- Describe the flow of data within the organization.

- Assist with the collection of structured and unstructured data from common applications and proprietary or legacy data systems.

- Describe specific application software policies and administrative procedures, such as tape backup cycles, data retention practices, and acceptable use (code of conduct) policies.

- Share information about user IDs, passwords, and rights and credentials on IT systems.

- Provide information regarding the timeframe in which applications were migrated (for example, when the company changed from one e-mail system to another).

- Provide information regarding the transition of computer equipment from one employee to another over time.

should be eliminated, and data that is outside the relevant date range should be removed from the collection. The investigator must be able to account for all data dropped from review because of filtering decisions and should be prepared to defend those decisions. Additionally, some data may be corrupt or encrypted and may not be loaded, or if it can be loaded, may not be properly searched. That data should be listed on an "exception list" and may be subject to further review and analysis.

The analysis of both structured and unstructured data may provide insights and understanding to an investigator. Because of the inherent differences between them, structured and unstructured data may require different analytic techniques. An investigator should consider each of these types of data and should be familiar with the tools and techniques necessary to analyze them. Frequently, the greatest value can be had by comparing information contained in structured data (such as questionable transactions) to that contained in unstructured data (such as oblique references to transactions in e-mail).

Structured Data Analysis

Because structured data is highly ordered and organized for efficient computing, it can be readily analyzed. Even though structured data comprises only approximately 20 percent of organizational data, it has historically been a prime focus of investigations.

Because the majority of data is not structured, investigations that focus solely on structured data may omit relevant evidence. Nevertheless, very useful information can be discovered by analyzing structured data.

Although each investigation is unique, many different techniques and methodologies can be applied to structured data to obtain useful results. First, because most organizations have some form of business intelligence (BI) system implemented, an investigator may be able to use the existing infrastructure to gather information pertinent to the investigation. Some BI systems that might be encountered during an investigation include Hyperion, Crystal Reports, Business Objects, and Cognos.

Data mining is an analytic technique that involves searching through large amounts of data to identify relevant information, patterns, trends, and differences indicative of fraud. Another useful data analysis technique is clustering or grouping data with similar properties. Clustering data can help uncover patterns that can identify fraud. Perhaps the most valuable analytic tool for structured data is the relational database, which is a type of database that supports very efficient analysis of structured data.

In a typical investigation, structured data is loaded into a relational database. Once data is available within the database, many advanced analytic techniques, such as data mining and cluster analysis, become practical. Relational databases provide powerful query capabilities that can help an investigator locate and focus on key information. Additionally, most of these databases support numerous reporting and export facilities that can help an investigator compile and present the relevant information. The most prominent database systems include Microsoft SQL Server, Oracle Database, IBM DB2, and PostgreSQL.

Several other software tools are available to assist the investigator with structured data analysis. Audit command language (ACL) software is one such tool that has many uses, including data extraction and transformation, statistical analysis, and identification of exceptions and irregularities. ACL also may be used to prepare data for analysis by other programs, such as statistical analysis products developed by SAS Institute Inc. and SPSS Inc., which can help analyze statistical trends in large data sets.

Unstructured Data Analysis

Leading electronic evidence review systems have evolved from tools that support queries using Boolean logic (such as term 1 and term 2) keyword searching to include technologies that categorize documents into groups without human intervention. As the amount of data collected in an investigation continues to increase rapidly, today's electronic evidence review systems must allow an investigator to find and review relevant documents faster and with higher precision.

Typically, 80 percent of data collected during an investigation is e-mail and other unstructured data. Investigators should consider the use of alternative search methods, such as concept clustering, social network analysis, and thread analysis, in order to facilitate the discovery of important evidence. Concept clustering groups data into sets with similar themes. Social network analysis captures the pattern and frequency of communications between custodians, and thread analysis groups together e-mails that are part of a chain, so that the investigator can more easily understand the entire "conversation."

Forensic Analysis

A variety of analytic methods can be employed with electronic information that has been collected in a forensically sound manner. A frequent question asked in many investigations is, *who knew*? A forensic analysis of data obtained from a specific person can ascertain if he or she possessed a certain electronic document, even if it has been deleted. Most computer operating systems do not actually erase data files when they are deleted. The operating system simply alters an entry in a table that points to that file's location on the hard drive. The space is then free to be used by other files. If no other file has yet been written to that particular space on the disk, the original file contents remain. A forensic analysis can recover the contents of the file. If another file has been written to that space, other indirect traces may still remain. For instance, if a document was printed, temporary files that contain portions of the document may be on the disk.

Another question frequently addressed by computer forensic analysis is, *when*? Computer systems create and maintain a number of logs during their operation. A time stamp on a file will indicate when it was created, last accessed, and last modified, though this information can be altered by other activities. System logs can indicate when a system was last turned on and when various forms of network activity occurred, and provide many other indicators of how a computer was used. Internet browsing history is typically of great interest not only for its content (what was looked at) but for its timing (When did he or she read the article about Foreign Corrupt Practices Act crackdowns, for example?). A forensic analysis can piece together a detailed time line of events using these clues found in the data.

Lastly, forensic examiners are often asked, *what did they do*? For example, a user may have utilized a commercial tool to "wipe" their drive (that is, overwrite all areas of the disk). A forensic analysis can very easily spot this activity. Establishing the fact that the custodian wiped his or her drive and how he or she did it may be of substantial evidentiary value.

Search

Recently, advances in e-mail and document analysis technology have allowed the electronic evidence review process to incorporate more advanced text analytics, in addition to simple Boolean logic keyword searching. These advances have given rise to the increased popularity of early case assessments (ECAs) prior to traditional keyword filtering and searching. ECA involves an analysis conducted soon after data is first loaded to the review platform, for the purpose of evaluating the collection of electronic evidence to determine potentially relevant information that may drive case strategy, such as key topics or themes of the case, dates and amounts, specific vocabulary and jargon, and people.

Performing early case assessments using advanced text analytics can assist the investigator in finding useful information quickly without having to sift through large volumes of documents. Having an understanding of the data before developing an extensive list of keywords can help minimize the number of "false positives" (or nonrelevant documents that contained keyword hits), which can significantly slow the investigation and increase review costs.

Once an early assessment of the matter has been completed and information has been gathered from interviews, documents, and other sources, a list of key words can be developed to search the data set. These key words may be developed by counsel, forensic accountants, and other consultants, and the syntax of the phrases may be refined by technical advisors, so that they can be executed within the review platform. Should the investigation come under review by a government regulator or shadow investigator, the final key word list and analysis logic applied will certainly be requested.

Review

The document review is the stage at which attorneys, forensic accountants, and other specialists review documents in order to determine whether they are potentially relevant to the investigation. Attorneys also will make a determination regarding whether a document is legally privileged and so may be withheld from production to a requesting party on that basis. The reviewer can usually categorize documents based on a predefined set of criteria, such as the issues to which they relate. Reviewers may review each document returned by searches for key terms or may review documents that have been identified by a system capable of grouping documents together that have a common theme.

More complex investigations have a greater need for effective project management of the review. The review team should be briefed on the background of the investigation, the types of documents in the collection, and the review protocol outlined for the case. It also is important for the review team to have an understanding of the taxonomy or "ontology" of related words or terms referenced in the evidence collection.

The review training will typically include a mock exercise in categorizing documents. The team will receive a sample set of documents from the evidence collection and discuss them as a group. After reviewing the material, the investigators apply the proposed categories to each document and discuss their selections as a group. The review facilitator will provide clarification and direction for the review team before moving forward with the review. Conducting an open dialog with the investigation team regarding the different types of categories available for review, the types of documents in the collection, and key case terminology will help ensure consistency and efficiency during the review process.

Production

Once data has been reviewed, it may be provided to a government agency, shadow investigator, or other party. The data will be exported from the system and produced in an agreed-upon format. The form of production will drive the choice of review platform. For example, if documents must be produced in their native format, a review platform that requires conversion of all documents to tagged image file format (TIFF) images would be entirely unsuitable. It is important that the investigators understand the ultimate specifications for the production and consider the ramifications of those specifications at the beginning of the process, not the end.

Conclusion

The review and analysis of electronic evidence is a critical component of a fraud investigation. Yet, just as the ability to derive meaning from electronic evidence has become an important tool in the arsenal of fraud investigators, the complexity of identifying, preserving, collecting, reviewing, and analyzing that data has greatly increased. The investigator needs to consider all potentially relevant sources of electronic evidence at the onset of the investigation. Once all sources have been identified, the investigator may want to consult a technology professional who possesses the expertise and tools to collect the electronic evidence without affecting the evidentiary value of the data. The investigator also should consider whether he or she possesses the expertise and tools to review, analyze, and gain an understanding of the story that properly understood evidence may tell.

9

Cross-Jurisdictional Issues in the Global Environment

Mike Savage, Partner/Principal
Ruby Sharma, Partner/Principal

Introduction

The globalization of business has increased the extent to which investigations are likely to be affected by legal requirements from more than one jurisdiction. In addition, fraudsters have long known that moving their assets (and themselves) to a different location and beyond reach of the "long arm of the law" is an effective strategy; for ease of reference, we'll call these cross-jurisdictional investigations. Differences and variations in laws, governing and regulatory bodies, accounting standards, business practices, governmental policies, litigation forums, and even languages can make cross-jurisdictional investigations quite complex.

Regulators and law enforcement bodies from countries around the world have responded to these complexities with commitments to shared law-making initiatives on issues such as anticorruption and anti-money laundering (AML), as well as encouragement of cross-border cooperation between enforcement agencies.

Multinational corporations also have had to respond to these complexities. Challenges exist in applying a corporate policy on a consistent global framework even, for instance, when acquisitions are effectively integrated. Companies are aware that damage is done when a news headline focuses on the multinational brand name and are concerned with *reputation risk*, which is the fear of global damage to their corporate reputation. This and many other factors drive many companies to consistent global compliance in preference to varying local standards.

Many investigations are precipitated by unexpected crises and are necessarily planned and implemented in a very short time frame. Contingency planning can significantly improve response time and effectiveness, enabling early escalation within management and allowing the investigative team to mobilize quickly to implement measures to preserve evidence and secure assets.

Cross-jurisdictional investigations can differ substantially from traditional domestic ones in a number of ways, including how and by whom the investigation will be conducted, the nature and sequence in which procedures are executed, the legal orders utilized, and the investigation objectives. For example,

local resources may be required when the issue requires competency in a different language or when privacy legislation limits the movement of personal information out of the jurisdiction. Although company staff will usually be available for an interview in the United States, in some cases and jurisdictions, trade union agreements or labor laws may allow employees to refuse to submit to such questioning.

The more common cross-jurisdictional considerations include the following topics:

- The global environment and issues
- Monetary judgments, arbitral awards, and restitution orders
- The differences in foreign countries' legal systems and the legal orders available
- Coordinating with government or local authorities
- Effective utilization of resources

The Global Environment and Issues

Over the past several decades, there has been increasing consensus and awareness that in order for there to be global prosperity and economic growth, business should be conducted on a level playing field, free from the damaging effects of fraud and corruption. This recognition has been an incentive for the development of regulatory systems that have moved toward more effective criminalization of fraud, particularly in areas such as money laundering and corruption. The leadership of governmental and nongovernmental institutions and their thought leadership have further bolstered and driven movement toward global consensus in assuring that fraud, which can cause damage on the larger economic scale, is reduced whenever possible and punished under the law.

The global economy has rapidly evolved over the past three decades. The evolution of regional markets, such as the EU; the emergence of new economies; and the urgency of the need for stabilization of markets worldwide in an increasingly interdependent business marketplace have created a need for consensus. Governmental and nongovernmental bodies have moved to meet that need with the creation of cross-jurisdictional conventions, agreements, and recognition of common laws and standards. However, challenges still remain as public policy, legal systems, and stages of progress toward convention and alliance in standards continue to evolve toward a common standard.

Countries and organizations worldwide have agreed to adopt a more comprehensive and integrated approach to compliance with international standards for fighting fraud and corruption. Efforts and focus have been increased on those countries whose financial systems are most at risk. More and more of these high-risk countries and regions are reaching ratification, agreement, and compliance, making the world a smaller place in which to hide assets or escape from the consequences of fraud.

However, areas of risks remain and businesses, and corporations with international or multinational operations fall victim to fraud. Conducting investigations for businesses with global operations or in multiple jurisdictions requires a broad understanding of the numerous governmental and legal systems, policies, and procedures. In an effective investigation, an understanding and knowledge of the regulatory and legal variances across jurisdictions must be utilized to effectively uncover the facts.

For example, in our case study[1], Grand Forge Company experienced a need for this broad understanding of global issues that are faced when conducting an investigation, which ultimately led Grand Forge Company to select Perusi & Bilanz LLP to conduct the investigation. What helped make the investigation more effective was when Perusi & Bilanz LLP allocated local resources from their Asia office to conduct the investigation in the Philippines, which led to a more comprehensive understanding and knowledge of local regulatory and jurisdictional issues. This allowed the investigative team to conduct, and Grand Forge Company to receive, a more effective and efficient investigation.

In many regions, law enforcement and regulators have strengthened their international cooperation. For example, INTERPOL, created in 1923 and the world's largest international police organization,

operates in 187 member countries. With this broad geographic enforcement authority, it facilitates cross-border police cooperation and supports and assists all organizations, authorities, and services whose mission is to prevent or combat international crime. Many countries have gone a step further and implemented mutual legal assistance treaty agreements, creating alliances between two foreign countries for the purpose of gathering and exchanging information in an effort to enforce criminal laws. However, the enforcement powers of these agreements are typically available only to prosecutors from the respective criminal justice departments, not to private sector investigators. As a consequence, information gathered by the police may only become available to investigators in the course of a public trial.

Because of these international alignments, when dealing with an investigation, a team might easily find itself dealing with parallel investigations not only by securities regulators and criminal justice prosecutors within a specific country but also by their counterparts in other countries.

It also must be taken into consideration that there may be differences in accounting standards. For example International Financial Reporting Standards are accounting standards that may differ from the standards applicable under U.S. generally accepted accounting principles. The correct accounting treatment of a particular transaction may differ, depending on the standard adopted for the accounting records under investigation. In many countries, the accounting standards have the force of law, and a difference in the standard could be a cross-jurisdictional issue that will require an understanding of those differences.

In addition, the number of formal international agreements or conventions by which different countries align themselves toward a common standard are increasing. Not all countries have adopted all or, in some instances, any of the conventions. Even when they have adopted the convention, the statute to bring the countries into compliance with the broad principles of the convention may vary between countries. As a result, rarely is a single

---

1 The reader is invited to read the detailed case study of Grand Forge Company earlier in the Introduction to this book.

over-arching convention or statute applicable in every jurisdiction. The United States is, however, a party to a number of key conventions, and the growing global acceptance of these is driving regulatory convergence. Many of the more important global conventions relevant to fraud investigations are those governing data privacy, corruption, and money laundering, as discussed in more detail subsequently.

Data Privacy and Moving Data Across Jurisdictions

Investigators frequently review data that includes personal information, such as e-mails or customer account information, to establish facts. The requirements for working with personal information can be different and much more restrictive in foreign jurisdictions than in the United States, and differing data privacy legislation can directly affect the investigation.

As an example and as was the case in the Grand Forge case study example, an investigator working with personal information in the EU should be aware that the EU considers the right to protection of personal data a fundamental right. In 1995, the EU issued Directive 95/46/EC on data protection, which governs all countries in the EU. The EU directive not only broadly limits the scope of data and information on individuals that may be processed, it also restricts the terms and conditions under which transfers of data to locations outside the EU may occur unless there are adequate safeguards for the protection of the personal information. Article 25 of the directive states, "The Member States shall provide that the transfer to a third country of personal data ... may take place only if ... the third country in question ensures an adequate level of protection."[2] The requirements for an adequate level of protection are quite formal and can significantly limit the transfer of data to the United States unless there is a "safe harbor" certification ensuring the privacy protections would be ensured as would be in the EU.

Other regions have their own privacy frameworks, and, in many instances, member countries have adopted privacy legislation to conform to those frameworks. For example, the *Asia-Pacific Economic Cooperation (APEC) Privacy Framework*[3] includes the following principles:

- Preventing harm
- Integrity of personal information
- Notice
- Security safeguards
- Collection limitations
- Access and correction
- Uses of personal information
- Accountability
- Choice

A common issue in investigations is that many statutes reflect a general principle that notice and consent of the individual is required before use of their personal data. More specifically, the trend is to require the following regarding notice and consent:

- *Notice.* Organizations must notify individuals about the purposes for which they collect and use information about them. They must provide information about how individuals can contact the organization with any inquiries or complaints, the types of third parties to which the organization discloses the information, and the choices and means the organization offers for limiting its use and disclosure.

- *Consent.* Organizations must give individuals the opportunity to choose whether their personal information will be disclosed to a third party or used for a purpose incompatible with the purpose for which it was originally collected or subsequently authorized by the individual (opt out). For sensitive information, affirmative or explicit choice must be given if the information is to be disclosed to a third party or used for a purpose incompatible with the purpose for which it was originally collected or subsequently authorized by the individual (opt in).

Because the preceding principles are not uncommon and have growing acceptance in the

---

2 See http://ec.europa.eu/justice_home/fsj/privacy/docs/95-46-ce/dir1995-46_part1_en.pdf.

3 See www.ag.gov.au/www/agd/rwpattach.nsf/VAP/(03995EABC73F94816C2AF4AA2645824B)~APEC+Privacy+Framework.pdf/$file/APEC+Privacy+Framework.pdf.

international community and newer regulations, investigators using information collected from other jurisdictions should be aware of the privacy legislation applicable in those countries. These laws can affect an investigation in terms of what data can be reviewed, whether the individual whose data is being reviewed must be notified, whether the data can be moved to another jurisdiction, and what can be done with the result.

Because personal data may be broadly defined in these statutes and can include any data associated with identified or identifiable natural persons, it may be impractical or difficult for the company to notify the individuals and secure their consent before using the information in an investigation. Seeking consent might even defeat the purposes of the investigation. In some countries, specific exemptions exist in the privacy statutes when information is being collected for the prevention and detection of fraud.

Please note that additional information on the management and transfer of personal data can be referenced in chapter 8, "Electronic Evidence."

Anticorruption

Corruption generally refers to a payment or offer of a bribe or anything of value to obtain or retain business or improper advantage. When the payment or offer is to a government official, the act is generally referred to as *public corruption*, which is distinct from private or commercial corruption. Anticorruption legislation can be both relevant and helpful to a fraud investigator. Many frauds include corrupt acts, particularly in jurisdictions where the government has a large role in the economy, either through state-owned enterprises or extensive regulations.

When undertaking an investigation, investigators and forensic accountants should understand the international or regional agreements and conventions that impacted the legal framework of the involved jurisdictions, be it one or many countries or regions. An awareness of the relevant law is helpful in understanding the country-specific enforcement frameworks and the resulting consequences for cross-border investigations.

For example, with respect to the Grand Forge Company case study, Jacob was familiar with the complicated intricacies of investigations and, there-fore, knew he needed investigators who understood international and regional agreements and the impact they might have on the investigation being conducted in the Philippines. Jacob felt more comfortable when Perusi & Bilanz LLP constructed the team that would conduct the investigation, which consisted primarily of experienced experts in international investigations, including individuals who have conducted investigations in Asia, with resources added to the team from the local and regional offices of Perusi & Bilanz LLP to assist in the investigation. These included individuals who spoke Filipino and were familiar with local accounting regulations.

International Conventions and Organizations

On a global scale, countries are now collaborating on their responses to corruption and have conventions seeking to align standards and practices across jurisdictions. These conventions seek to be more effective in repatriating the proceeds of corruption and extraditing the offenders when they flee to another jurisdiction or remit the proceeds of their crime to a different jurisdiction. In addition, these conventional standards and practices often provide the framework for anticorruption legislation within the signatory countries themselves.

In a similar manner, other important nongovernmental or industry-specific organizations have collaborated to focus on corruption across jurisdictions. These include Transparency International, the World Bank Group, the International Monetary Fund (IMF), and the International Chamber of Commerce (ICC). These organizations have publicly available information and insights that are often relevant to investigations in other jurisdictions.

Because of the influence of these organizations and the broad acceptance of the conventions put forth by them, two of the most influential and important international conventions that are focused on combating global corruption and bribery are the *United Nations Convention against Corruption* (UNCAC) and the *Organization for Economic Co-operation and Development (OECD) Convention on Combating Bribery of Foreign Public Officials in International Business Transactions*. Several other important government-sponsored initiatives, including the *African Union*

Convention on Preventing and Combating Corruption, continue to gain influence.

Other organizational initiatives also are working to align anticorruption conventions and standards globally, such as the initiatives of APEC. Many of these monitor the progress of a country's adherence to their agreements to conventions or produce reports and studies on issues, developments, or statistical information that can be useful in the planning of forensic investigations.

The most influential of the conventions and organizations and their objectives and roles in the global fight against fraud and corruption are summarized subsequently. A more complete listing of conventions can be referenced in box 9-1 at the end of this section.

Conventions

United Nations Convention against Corruption[4]

- Membership of over 113 countries.

- Adopted on October 31, 2003.

- Requires members to establish criminal and other offenses for specific actions, if such actions are not already crimes under that jurisdiction's own domestic law.

- Member countries agree to cooperate with one another in every aspect of the fight against corruption, including prevention, investigation, and the prosecution of offenders.

- Encompasses not only basic forms of corruption, such as bribery and the embezzlement of public funds, but also trading in influence, the concealment of corruption, laundering of the proceeds of corruption, and offenses committed in support of corruption.

- Members bound by the convention to render specific forms of mutual legal assistance in gathering and transferring evidence for use in court and to extradite offenders.

- Members required to take measures to support tracing, freezing, seizing, and confiscating the proceeds of corruption.

- Provides agreement on asset-recovery procedures.

- Several provisions of the convention specify how cooperation and assistance will be rendered, and, in particular, how embezzled public funds can be returned to the country requesting them.

Organization for Economic Co-operation and Development Convention on Combating Bribery of Foreign Public Officials in International Business Transactions

- Ratified by 37 countries

- Adopted on November 21, 1997

- Commonly referred to as the OECD convention

- Includes commitments from signatory countries to put national anticorruption laws in place

- Focuses on the global fight against bribery and corruption and the combating of bribery of foreign public officials in international business transactions

- Makes recommendations on the tax deductibility of bribes to foreign public officials

---

4 See www.unodc.org/unodc/en/treaties/CAC/index.html.

African Union Convention on Preventing and Combating Corruption

- 53 members (but as yet only ratified by 24 members)
- Agreed by the African Union in July 2003[5]
- Commonly referred to as the African Union convention
- Focuses on measures for prevention, criminalization, and prosecution in the fight against private- and public-sector corruption and bribery
- Provides consensus and guidance in international cooperation and asset recovery
- Provides a regional cooperative framework and covers an extensive range of anticorruption provisions, including prevention, education, enforcement, sanctions, criminalization, and mutual law enforcement assistance

Organizations

Asia-Pacific Economic Cooperation

- A forum for facilitating economic growth, cooperation, trade, and investment in the Asia-Pacific region.
- Principally from Asia but also includes the United States, Canada, and Australia.
- In 2007, the Anti-Corruption and Transparency Experts Task Force deliverables were adopted and approved by APEC leaders and ministers in Sydney.
- In 2004, APEC issued a document titled *APEC Course Of Action On Fighting Corruption And Ensuring Transparency.*

Transparency International

- A civil organization that seeks to fight corruption.
- Provides country-level information useful to the planning of investigations, including its *Global Corruption Report*, *Corruption Perceptions Index*, and *Global Corruption Barometer*.
- Produces a range of studies and reports on corruption, including reports on monitoring the implementation of international conventions, such as the following:
  - *Effectively Monitoring the United Nations Convention against Corruption (UNCAC)*[6]
  - *TI Progress Report 2007: Enforcement of the OECD Convention on Combating Bribery of Foreign Public Officials*[7]

  For example and with respect to the Grand Forge Company case study, as Perusi & Bilanz LLP prepared to conduct the investigation, the members of the team gathered information from Transparency International's *Corruption Perceptions Index* in order to educate themselves and gain an understanding of the local cultural issues in the Philippines This was deemed a tremendous asset to the team.

---

5 See www.africa-union.org/root/au/Documents/Treaties/Text/Convention%20on%20Combating%20Corruption.pdf.

6 See www.transparency.org/publications/publications/ti_pp_01_08_uncac.

7 See www.transparency.org/publications/publications/3rd_oecd_progress_report.

World Bank

- One hundred eighty-five member countries

- An international financial lending institution that provides financial and technical assistance to developing countries for infrastructure and development programs with the objective of reducing poverty.

- Views good governance and anticorruption, with a particular focus on emerging markets that are at higher risk for fraud, as centrally tied to its mission to alleviate poverty and establish healthy economic development

- Established the Department of Institutional Integrity with a mandate to investigate allegations of fraud and corruption in all World Bank Group operations and funding, assist in preventative efforts to protect World Bank Group funds and those funds entrusted to it from misuse, and deter fraud and corruption in World Bank Group's operations.

International Monetary Fund

- One hundred eighty-five member countries.

- Monitors global economic and financial developments, provides policy advice, and provides financing and loans to countries in crisis or with low income.

- Considers corruption and governance issues a part of its overall focus and monitors all lending programs.[8]

- Advocates policies and develops institutions and administrative systems that eliminate opportunities for bribery, corruption, and fraud in the management of public resources.

- In growing recognition of the adverse impact of poor governance (and the resulting corruption) on economic efficiency and growth, the IMF has turned its attention to a broader range of institutional reforms and governance issues in the reform programs it supports.

- Contributes to the international efforts to combat money laundering and the financing of terrorism by assessing its members' legal and regulatory frameworks, providing technical assistance to address shortcomings, and conducting policy-oriented research.

- To reduce the risk of IMF resources being misused by countries, the IMF executive board strengthened the IMF's existing safeguards on funding in March 2000 by specifying new requirements that each borrower's central bank publish annual financial statements audited to international standards by outside experts. The IMF will be able to carry out on-site checks by IMF staff, experts from other central banks, and accounting firms.

8 See www.imf.org/external/np/exr/facts/gov.htm.

International Chamber of Commerce

- Hundreds of thousands of member companies in over 130 countries.

- Three main activities are rules setting, arbitration, and policy.

- Close working relationship with the UN, the World Trade Organization, and other intergovernmental and global forums.

- ICC's International Court of Arbitration (ICC court) is an internationally trusted system of commercial arbitration with 86 member countries.

- ICC's Commercial Crime Services provides the world business community with a centralized crime-fighting body that
  - operates according to two basic precepts: to prevent commercial crime and to investigate and help prosecute commercial criminals.
  - works closely with international law enforcement officials, including INTERPOL.
  - includes the Financial Investigation Bureau, which focuses on detecting financial fraud before it is perpetrated.
  - provides banks and other financial institution members access to a vast database of shared information to assist in fraud-prevention measures.

- Established the Anti-Corruption Commission, which focuses on developing self-regulation by enterprises in prevention of extortion, bribery, and corruption and provides business input into these initiatives on a global scale.

In 2005, the ICC's Anti-Corruption Commission issued revised rules of conduct and recommendations on anticorruption for business and issued a supporting manual for companies titled *Combating Extortion and Bribery: ICC Rules of Conduct and Recommendations.*[9] The ICC's rules outline the basic measures companies should take to prevent corruption. Though without direct legal effect, these rules and recommendations are intended as a method of self-regulation and constitute what is considered good commercial practice in the matters to which they relate. The manual include nine rules or "articles" that cover bribery and extortion; political and charitable contributions; gifts, such as hospitality and expenses; facilitation payments; corporate policies; financial recording and auditing; and board of directors' responsibilities in ensuring compliance with anticorruption policies. The rules also include ensuring that all agents, intermediaries, joint ventures, and outsourcing agreements comply with companies' antibribery policies.

It is noteworthy that the anticorruption activities of the ICC can be particularly helpful to investigators in determining policy deficiencies and making recommendations aligned to practices in many jurisdictions.

---

9 See www.iccwbo.org/policy/anticorruption/id870/index.html.

Box 9-1: *Key Anticorruption Conventions and Instruments*

Global and interregional

- *United Nations Convention against Corruption*
- *United Nations Convention against Transnational Organized Crime*
- *Organization for Economic Co-operation and Development on Combating Bribery of Foreign Public Officials in International Business Transactions*
- *Revised Recommendation of the Council on Combating Bribery in International Business Transactions*

Africa

- *African Union Convention on Preventing and Combating Corruption*
- *Southern African Development Community Protocol against Corruption*
- *Economic Community of West African States Protocol on the Fight against Corruption*

Americas

- *Inter-American Convention Against Corruption*

Asia and Pacific region

- *ADB OECD Anti-Corruption Initiative for Asia-Pacific*

Europe

- Council of Europe *Criminal Law Convention on Corruption*
- Council of Europe *Civil Law Convention on Corruption*
- Resolution (99) 5 of the Committee of Ministers of the Council of Europe: *Agreement Establishing the Group of States against Corruption*
- Resolution (97) 24 of the Committee of Ministers of the Council of Europe: *Twenty Guiding Principles for the Fight against Corruption*
- *Treaty of the European Union on the Protection of Financial Interests of the Communities* and two protocols
- European Union *Convention on the Fight against Corruption involving Officials of the European Communities or Officials of Member States of the European Union*

(Source: http://www.transparency.org/global_priorities/international_conventions/conventions_instruments)

Anti-Money Laundering

Perpetrators of frauds may well utilize different jurisdictions to their advantage in their attempts to mask their crime. For example, corrupt officials may remit the proceeds of their crime to a different jurisdiction because local deposits are more likely to lead to questions by bankers more familiar with the officials' public role.

Money laundering is not just about drugs and terrorism; it also extends to the proceeds of fraud. Tracing the proceeds of fraud may well take the investigation into the ambit of the money-laundering statutes.

This has implications for the cross-jurisdiction fraud investigation. For example, some people are required to report suspicious transactions under the money-laundering regulations. In some jurisdictions, these may include local professionals on the investigation team.

Money laundering encompasses any financial transaction that conceals the identity, source, or destination of money and generates an asset or value as the result of an illegal act. International conventions on money laundering are often integrated into agreements in relation to the fight against organized crime and terrorism.

Fraudsters profit financially from their criminal activities, and the pursuit and recovery of the proceeds of the crime are considered the standard for effective deterrence and sanctioning of those activities. AML targets the proceeds of crime and can be relevant to investigators, particularly as a tool to secure and recover assets.

Money Laundering Conventions

Two important historical conventions have affected and given force to the investigation of money laundering. Although they have broad missions in other areas, their provisions in the areas of the investigation and the seizure of assets related to money laundering deems mention.

Entered into force in November 1990, the *United Nations Convention against Illicit Traffic in Narcotic Drugs and Psychotropic Substances* focuses on providing comprehensive measures against drug trafficking but includes provisions against money laundering and provides for international cooperation, including aspects of the transfer of proceedings of profits. It requires parties to empower its courts or other competent authorities to order that bank, financial, or commercial records be made available or seized. The convention further states that a party may not decline to act on this provision on the ground of bank secrecy.

Adopted in November of 2000, the *United Nations Convention against Transnational Organized Crime* also took a series of measures against transnational organized crime, including the creation of domestic criminal offenses (participation in an organized criminal group, money laundering, corruption, and obstruction of justice).

Both have been useful in the movement toward sanctions and deterrence against money laundering on a global scale.

The USA PATRIOT Act

A more recent and powerful tool in the investigation and sanctioning of money laundering is the USA PATRIOT Act, which was passed into law in 2001. The USA PATRIOT act is an enhanced law enforcement investigatory tool for responding to terrorist financing that has provided significant impetus to global AML initiatives. This has resulted in better client-level information collection and retention by financial institutions and more effective cross-jurisdictional cooperation between law enforcement and regulators. For instance, the USA PATRIOT Act provides for the facilitation of the government's ability to seize illicit funds located in foreign countries, the issuance of subpoenas or summonses to foreign banks with relationships to U.S. banks, the reporting of suspicious activities, and special due diligence efforts. As a result, institutions put into place reasonable steps to identify beneficial owners of bank accounts and those who are authorized to use or route funds through payable-through accounts. It also is now necessary that financial institutions must undertake enhanced scrutiny of any account that is owned by, or is being maintained on behalf of, any senior political figure (often referred to as a *politically exposed person*).

The Financial Action Task Force

In response to mounting concerns over money laundering, the Financial Action Task Force on Money Laundering (FATF) was created by the G-7 member states, the European Commission, and eight other countries. Since its inception, the FATF has spearheaded the effort to adopt and implement measures designed to counter the use of financial systems by criminals. The FATF has now expanded to 33 members.

In 1990, the organization established a task force and issued a list titled *The Forty Recommendations* that detailed specific measures to be taken by financial service and banking entities worldwide to assist in the fight against financial corruption. In 2001, the FATF issued a list titled *Special Recommendations on Terrorist Financing*, which included eight recommendations on the topic. In 2004, a ninth recommendation was added. The recommendations strengthened AML and counter-terrorism funding standards and are now commonly referred to as the *40+9 Recommendations*. Compliance with these principles, or at least the movement toward such compliance, is now generally seen as a requirement of an internationally active bank or other financial-service entity. The FATF 40+9 Recommendations have been recognized, endorsed, or adopted by many international bodies, including the IMF and the World Bank.

The 40+9 Recommendations provide for the institution of financial reporting systems that are now providing the basic framework for AML efforts and are intended to be of universal application. Recommendations include the institution of standards and practices of due diligence and record keeping; reporting of suspicious transactions; provisions for criminalization of money laundering activity; recommendations for measures that should be set in place to limit money laundering activity, including the sharing of information; requirements for ongoing scrutiny of financial business relationships and due diligence in "knowing your customer" when establishing accounts and transactions; and records keeping, records maintenance, and five-year minimum data storage requirements.

A major provision is the recommendation that financial institutions monitor, investigate, and report transactions of a suspicious nature, as well as large cash transactions, to the governing financial intelligence unit in their respective country. In the United States, for instance, financial institutions must report suspicious transactions to the Financial Crimes Enforcement Network, a division of the Department of the Treasury. The United Kingdom has its Serious Organised Crime Agency with a financial intelligence unit responsible for dealing with financial information concerning suspected proceeds of crime in order to counter money laundering.

Although financial intelligence units might refer these reports to government agencies for investigation, the reports may not be directly available to corporate financial investigators. The prime method of fighting money laundering is the requirement on financial intermediaries to know their customers and document that knowledge. In practice, the reporting institution is likely to have done reasonable diligence on clients giving rise to suspicious transaction reports, and the client file may well be relevant to the investigation and accessible through legal procedures in the course of following the trail of misappropriated assets.

In some jurisdictions within the EU, for example, the reporting requirements for suspicious transactions might extend beyond financial institutions and include "gatekeepers," such as accountants, lawyers, or others who may be involved in business transactions involving financial transactions or instruments. For instance, accountants managing securities or other assets involving financial institutions or lawyers involved in legal transactions involving the creation or selling of a business entity involving assets reaching threshold amounts of money may be required to report suspicious transactions or activities. When forming an investigative team or conducting an investigation, care should be taken to manage any risk that an investigator may come across. As a possible "gatekeeper," a member of the team may be required to separately file a suspicious transaction report to his or her countries' financial intelligence unit.

Police Cooperation: Anticorruption and Anti-Money Laundering

INTERPOL allows the police forces in member countries to assist each other. The organization allows for the facilitation of international police cooperation even when diplomatic relations do not exist between particular countries. In 1998, Interpol established the INTERPOL Group of Experts on Corruption, and it is currently in the process of developing the INTERPOL Anti-Corruption Office and the INTERPOL and United Nations Office on Drugs and Crime Anti-Corruption Academy. These components support anticorruption activities by establishing policies and standards, as well as conducting or assisting with education, research, training, investigations, and asset-recovery operations.[10] AML is an important priority for INTERPOL, and the organization includes corruption as one of its six priority crime areas. Individual countries also have strengthened their police forces' international cooperation. The UK Serious Fraud Office, for example, has produced a "Guide to obtaining evidence from the UK" and works to actively cooperate in the investigative process.[11]

---

10 See www.interpol.int/.

11 See www.sfo.gov.uk/international/evidence_uk.asp.

Although it may well result in delays and loss of control of the investigation, in some situations, it may be appropriate for the victim organization to lodge a criminal complaint and rely on the police criminal investigation to collect information from other jurisdictions that may ultimately become accessible through the criminal trial.

For example, as noted previously in the Grand Forge Company case study, it was determined that it was in the best interest of Grand Forge Company to notify INTERPOL of the crimes so it could assist in the investigation of the theft of assets. Jacob and Perusi & Bilanz LLP weighed the pros and cons of making this decision, and, in the end, the benefits far outweighed the potential for delays and loss of control of the investigation. Grand Forge Company was able to mitigate these potential concerns by having investigators on the team from Perusi & Bilanz LLP who had experience in working with INTERPOL.

Monetary Judgments, Arbitral Awards, and Restitution Orders

Financial recovery is an important investigation objective and may be achieved through several available avenues of legal recourse.

Several outcomes may ultimately lead to an opportunity for financial recovery or recourse. Civil courts provide a monetary judgment, arbitrations provide an arbitral award, and criminal courts provide a restitution order. Significant differences exist among these forums, including the degree of control over the process, the burden of proof, and the degree of publicity. In cross-jurisdictional investigations, a further difference is that the forum may not be located in the same jurisdiction as the asset and securing the judgment, award, or order is a completely separate matter from enforcing it. The type of proceeding under which the award is made can make a difference to how the financial recovery of the asset is enforced.

Monetary Judgments

Enforcing a monetary judgment granted by a court in a different jurisdiction is not necessarily a formality. To enforce monetary judgments, some U.S. states have implemented the Uniform Foreign-Country Money Judgments Recognition Act. Passed in 2005, this act updates the 1962 Uniform Foreign Money-Judgments Recognition Act previously implemented in some U.S. states and was recommended for adoption by the National Conference of Commissioners on Uniform State Laws. The conference recognized the strong need for uniformity between U.S. states with respect to enforcement of foreign country judgments and encouraged all states to adopt the act.[12]

Similarly, relying on a monetary judgment granted by a U.S. court to collect money in a foreign jurisdiction might have some challenges resulting from issues, such as differing cooperational agreements, international laws, differing treaty agreements, or even the current public policy concerns. Common obstacles to recognition and enforcement of U.S. judgments can be found in box 9-2. A number of other existing conventions may apply to enforcements of certain monetary judgments and can be useful to investigations.[13] These include the following:

- The *Brussels Convention on Jurisdiction and the Enforcement of Judgments in Civil and Commercial Matters*, which is recognized by the EU and the European Free Trade Association (EFTA)
- The *Lugano Convention on Jurisdiction and the Enforcement of Judgments in Civil and Commercial Matters*, which is recognized by the EU and EFTA
- The *United Nations Convention on the Recognition and Enforcement of Foreign Arbitral Awards* (New York Convention), which is a widely recognized foundation instrument of international arbitration, addresses arbitral awards and enforces them in accordance with specific procedural rules in international commercial disputes, and is recognized by most major trading nations
- The *Inter-American Convention on the Extraterritorial Validity of Foreign Judgments and Arbitral Awards*, which is recognized by the Organization of American States

---

12 See www.nccusl.org/.

13 See http://lectlaw.com/files/bul12.htm.

Box 9-2: *Judgment Recognition and Enforcement Obstacles**

- *Lack of jurisdiction.* Some countries (for example, Brazil, Switzerland, and France) will refuse to enforce a judgment against their nationals unless there is a clear indication that the national intended to submit to the foreign court's jurisdiction.

- *Special notice procedures.* Some recognizing countries require that the foreign litigant serve the local defendant party, in accordance with procedures not commonly employed in the United States.

- *Treaty requirements.* Several jurisdictions, including most of the Nordic countries, the Netherlands, and Saudi Arabia, will refuse to recognize a foreign judgment unless there is the specific existence of a judgments convention between the rendering and recognizing jurisdictions.

- *Confusion over the lack of uniformity of U.S. law.* Foreign courts often cannot discern a clear U.S. policy on recognition and enforcement because of the range of case laws.

- *Public policy concerns.* Foreign courts may view the public policy aspects of U.S. law, such as unrestricted jury awards, punitive and treble damages actions, and the use of long-arm statutes, as contrary to their own public policy.

* See www.osec.doc.gov/ogc/occic/refmj.htm.

Arbitral Awards

Arbitration is an alternative dispute resolution process discussed in more detail later in this chapter. The outcome of arbitration is an arbitral award, typically a monetary amount. Arbitral awards are enforceable through the civil court system.

Many frauds ultimately result in a breach of contract, and, in cases in which the contract includes an arbitration clause, the investigation objective might include an arbitral award.

Arbitral awards enjoy greater international recognition than judgments of national courts. One reason may be that both parties have contractually consented to abide by the final outcome of the arbitration.

Most countries have signed the 1958 New York Convention, facilitating enforcement of such awards. Under the New York Convention, the 144 participating states are required to recognize arbitral awards and enforce them, in accordance with specific procedural rules in international commercial disputes. As previously noted, most major trading nations, as well as many other countries, have ratified the New York Convention, giving the convention broad acceptance and making this an effective proceeding for financial recovery.

As previously noted, the ICC maintains the ICC court, a highly facilitated and endorsed arbitration forum with 86 member countries. In 2004, 561 requests for arbitration were filed with the ICC court concerning 1,682 parties from 116 different countries and independent territories. The court also has received new cases at a rate of more than 500 per year since 1999.[14]

Restitution Orders

Restitution orders are remedies intended to reverse unjust enrichment and prevent a wrongdoer from profiting from the crime. These remedies and principles are broadly accepted, and, therefore, most countries have some restitution mechanism in their criminal justice system. Restitution orders can be used in recovering assets.

All U.S. states allow for orders of restitution, but the processes for enforcement may vary. Restitution in the United States is normally a provision of sentencing in a financial fraud prosecution and can have an effect on other sentencing conditions, such as imprisonment, probation, or parole for the defendant. Similar provisions exist in many other countries.

In real practice, one of the most common obstacles to recovery is the time taken to effectively secure a criminal fraud conviction, which often allows the fraudster to dissipate or exhaust any assets before any restitution order is granted. It is because of this reason that recoveries from these orders may not be substantial.

14 See http://www.iccwbo.org/id93/index.html.

This was the concern in the Grand Forge Company case study. The company's concerns were due to the fact that the primary suspect was now living in Manila; had a luxury yacht and a residence in France, which is listed for sale; and may well seek to relocate his assets.

The company determines that an Anton Pillar and a Norwhich Pharmacal order should be issued in order to preserve documents necessary for further investigation and ensure that assets, such as the yacht, are not removed to an unknown location. The forensic accountants from Perusi & Bilanz LLP provide the accounting support and documentation for the company's legal representatives to support the issuance of both.

The Differences in Foreign Countries' Legal Systems and the Legal Orders Available

Set against the global environment and the variety of applicable U.S. and international laws and regulations, each cross-jurisdictional investigation offers a different scenario from its own facts and circumstances. Awareness of these differences and their implications on issues, such as how to discover evidence; how to trace, freeze, and recover assets; and when to sue, become critical.

Some more important differences and implications discussed subsequently include legal privilege, letters rogatory, insolvency, orders generally available in the Commonwealth, and alternative dispute resolution (ADR).

Legal Privilege

In conducting investigations, legal privilege is an important consideration. Legal privilege is intended to protect an individual's ability to access the justice system by encouraging complete disclosure to legal advisers without the fear that any disclosure of those communications may prejudice the client in the future. Investigative findings commissioned by legal advisors to provide advice to their clients also may well be legally privileged.

In the United States, communications between client and counsel are frequently privileged. Although the concept of privilege also exists in most international jurisdictions, the types and nature of such privilege may vary from the precedents set in the United States and due care should be taken by investigators to preserve legal privilege when possible and appropriate.

Letters Rogatory

Letters rogatory are a formal request from a court to a foreign court for assistance. Letters rogatory can be used to obtain evidence from a witness. Letters rogatory are utilized as a request from a court in the United States to the appropriate judicial authorities in another country to obtain evidence from a witness, either through testimony to answer questions or through the production of documents. The letters are used when the assistance of foreign authorities is required to compel a witness who is not willing to testify or produce evidence voluntarily.

Although the process can be very useful for compelling evidence in a cross-jurisdictional investigation, the process of letters rogatory is long and complex and delays of up to one year are common.

Insolvency and Receivership

Often, the financial stresses of a fraud can cause enough damage to a business or company that the fraud precipitates insolvency or receivership. For example, the fraud may have caused or concealed insolvency. Similarly, a fraud might give rise to a claim against a business. In some instances, an investigation or discovery of fraud may trigger financier covenants, leaving the entity unable to pay its debts in the ordinary course of business.

If the business is unable to pay the claim in the ordinary course of business or its liabilities exceed its assets, it becomes insolvent. If this is a result of the claim against the business, the victim (as creditor) may be able to use the insolvency to secure and appoint a trustee or liquidator to take control of the business. A *receivership* is a court action that places property under the control of a receiver during litigation so that it can be preserved for the benefit of all. When a trustee or liquidator has been appointed, he or she has the legal authority to further the investigation by recovering assets or compelling witnesses to provide information. Trustees, liquidators, or receivers also have broad powers to control the business; investigate missing assets; and, ultimately, distribute the assets.

Orders Generally Available in the Commonwealth

Many jurisdictions have legal systems based on English common law, including the 53 countries of the Commonwealth. These include countries such as Canada, the United Kingdom, India, and Australia. A complete list of Commonwealth countries is available in box 9-3. The common law offers some investigative options not ordinarily available to investigations in the United States If the facts and circumstances allow, there may be an advantage to commencing proceedings in one of these jurisdictions (such as Canada) to benefit from some of these options.

Box 9-3: *Commonwealth Countries*

Antigua and Barbuda	Jamaica	St Vincent and the Grenadines
Australia	Kenya	Samoa
The Bahamas	Kiribati	Seychelles
Bangladesh	Lesotho	Sierra Leone
Barbados	Malawi	Singapore
Belize	Malaysia	Solomon Islands
Botswana	Maldives	South Africa
Brunei Darussalam	Malta	Sri Lanka
Cameroon	Mauritius	Swaziland
Canada	Mozambique	Tonga
Cyprus	Namibia	Trinidad and Tobago
Dominica	*Nauru*[++]	*Tuvalu*
Fiji Islands[+]	New Zealand	Uganda
The Gambia	Nigeria	United Kingdom
Ghana	Pakistan	United Republic of Tanzania
Grenada	Papua New Guinea	*Vanuatu*
Guyana	*St Kitts and Nevis*	Zambia
India	St Lucia	*Gibraltar

(Italics indicate countries which are not currently members of the Commonwealth Foundation.)
(* Gibraltar is an associated member)
† Per the Commonwealth Web site, Fiji was suspended from the Commonwealth following a December 2006 military coup
†† Per the Commonwealth Web site, Nauru is a member in arrears

In jurisdictions that function under Commonwealth law, an investigative team could utilize a number of different types of orders to obtain bank account information or preserve and seize evidence and freeze assets.[15,16] Some orders can be secured without prior notice to the other party (referred to as ex parte orders). These orders are often referred to by the common law case in which the underlying concept was established (for example, Mareva injunctions, Anton Piller orders, and Norwich Pharmacol orders). Other orders relate to the recovery of stolen property.

---

15 Rubin, Sandy. "Competition and change: The Canadian legal landscape." *Managing Partner*, February 2006.

16 Caylor, Lincoln, Jim Patterson, and Maureen Ward. "Canada country focus: Fighting fraud across borders." *Managing Partner*, February 2006.

Ex Parte Order

In brief	Without the other party
About	Ex parte proceedings are brought from, by, or for one party in the absence of, and without the representation or notification of, other parties. An ex parte decision is one decided by a judge without requiring all of the parties to the controversy to be present.
Purpose	Ex parte proceedings are utilized very practically in cases in which a plaintiff has reason to believe that notification of the defendant may cause significant risk to the plaintiff's interests. For example, if a defendant knew that the plaintiff was going to file legal proceedings, the defendant could have the opportunity to move or liquidate recoverable assets. Ex parte proceedings would, in this case, grant the plaintiff some protection of his or her interests during court proceedings.
Risks and other	Courts are generally reluctant to grant orders because it is unfair to not hear from the other party. As a result, specific conditions are required and safeguards are built into the process to discourage abuse. These conditions generally include a strong case, significant urgency, undertakings concerning damages, and requirements for full disclosure of all relevant information. Orders discussed subsequently, such as the Mareva injunction, Anton Piller order, and Norwich Pharmacol order require an element of surprise to be effective. For this reason they are frequently requested on an ex parte basis.

Mareva Injunction

In brief	Freeze the asset
Case	Named for the precedent case *Mareva Compania Naviera SA v. International Bulk Carriers SA*, which was decided in 1975.
About	A Mareva injunction is a court order that freezes assets so that a defendant cannot frustrate a judgment by dissipating his or her assets from beyond the jurisdiction of the court.
Purpose	The purpose of a Mareva injunction is to restrain the defendant from disposing of his or her assets from the jurisdiction of the court and thereby protect the interests of the plaintiff until the trial ends and judgment is passed.
Risks and other	It is important to demonstrate that there would be a real risk of the assets being removed or dissipated before the due process can run its course. The order can be effective worldwide and often can include an ancillary disclosure order mandating that the defendants disclose the nature and location of their assets.

Anton Piller Order

In brief	Evidence preservation
Case	Named for the precedent case *Anton Piller K.G. v. Manufacturing Processes Ltd.*, which was decided in 1976.
Purpose	The purpose of the order is to secure and preserve documents or other evidence that might otherwise be disposed of by the defendant.
About	The order allows for the applicant to enter the respondent's premises and search for, inspect, seize, or make copies of documents or other evidence. This includes information on computers.
Risks and other	It is important to demonstrate the existence of incriminating documents or other evidence and that a real risk exists that the evidence might otherwise be destroyed. A safeguard that may be included is a requirement that the evidence seized be held by a neutral party until the plaintiff has had an opportunity to take legal advice on whether to contest the order.

Norwich Pharmacal Order

In brief	Discovery from third parties
Case	Named for the *Norwich Pharmacal Co. v. The Commissioners of Customs and Excise*, which was decided in 1974.
Purpose	The purpose of the order is to allow for the discovery of evidence from innocent third parties, such as financial institutions.
About	The principle underlying the order is that if, through no fault of his or her own, a person facilitates the wrongdoing of others, then that person comes under a duty to assist the victim. He or she can assist by giving the victim full information and disclosing the identity of the wrongdoers.
Risks and other	The financial institution incurs no liability for violating its client's confidences because it is complying with a court order. The financial institution may be ordered to not notify its client that the information has been provided.

Stolen Property

Stolen property is recoverable by the true owner under English common law and applies in cases in which the property can be traced and returned to the true owner.

A constructive trust may exist when a party has been wrongfully deprived of its rights due to unjust enrichment or interference by another person. When the assets have been transferred to a third party, that third party may be deemed to hold those assets for the benefit of the rightful owner under a constructive trust. Under a constructive trust, the third party becomes a trustee whose sole duty is to transfer the title and possession to the rightful owner.

A constructive trust claim can be established, for example, when the third party has been unjustly enriched by receiving funds fraudulently obtained or if the constructive trustee is recklessly or willfully blind to the conduct of the party that provided him or her with those funds.

It may be possible to effectively freeze property by notifying a third party (such as a land registry or financial institution) of the disputed ownership.

Alternative Dispute Resolution

ADR is relevant to the investigation process in many jurisdictions. Examples of ADR include arbitration, mediation, and negotiated settlements. Issues under investigation are not always resolved in public court. ADR may even be preferred to the court system in some cases, particularly when the parties have ongoing relationships or the issues are complex. For example, there may be insufficient evidence to support a claim but sufficient evidence to support a negotiated settlement, or the issues may be technically complex and better suited to determination by an arbitration tribunal with relevant expertise than a local court.

In some jurisdictions, ADR may be required as part of the due process for disciplinary hearings. For example, some jurisdictions require a specific ADR process to be followed when terminating an employee and failure to follow the process can result in procedurally unfair dismissal, irrespective of the merits of the case established by the investigation.

Financial recoveries might be possible on fraudulent transactions governed by contracts with arbitration clauses, particularly in jurisdictions in which the legal system is unfamiliar or inefficient.

In considering whether to use arbitration, some factors to be considered include the following:

- *Enforceability.* Arbitral awards rendered in one country can be relatively easily enforced in another country, allowing the successful party to pursue foreign assets.
- *Confidentiality.* The dispute and its resolution are confidential.
- *Choice of arbitrators.* It is possible to appoint available and suitably experienced specialists as arbitrators.
- *Final binding decisions.* Appeals or judicial reviews of arbitral awards are limited to very narrow circumstances and are generally not possible.

- *Flexibility in selecting place, language, and process.* The location, language, applicable law, and procedural rules (such as discovery) can be selected, if not already specified in the contract.

Arbitral institutions have tried and tested arbitration rules and can assist with administration of the arbitral process. Two prominent institutions are the ICC court previously mentioned and the American Arbitration Association. Both organizations do not arbitrate disputes, but they provide administrative support to the arbitration process.

Coordinating With Government or Local Authorities

The timing and extent of disclosures to regulators and law enforcement are an important consideration during an investigation. The priorities of regulators and law enforcement may not match the priorities of the business investigating the fraud. For example, although financial recovery of the financial losses may be the primary objective for the business, civil procedures for recovery may be placed on hold pending resolution of a criminal procedure initiated by law enforcement. Early disclosure may lead to premature allegations, a loss of control over an investigation, or delays in resolution of an internal investigation.

Generally, investigators prefer to complete their investigation of the facts before making disclosures to the U.S. government because it allows for an unimpeded investigation with the most complete and accurate disclosure of the facts and findings. When early disclosure is required or is chosen as an avenue to gain credit for voluntary cooperation, it may be possible to agree with the government that the internal investigation can run its course before the respective government agency takes a more active role, as discussed under the "Parallel Investigations" section in chapter 11, "Working with Regulators and Parallel Investigations."

When investigations cross jurisdictions, thoughtful consideration should be given to the need for the timing of disclosures to, and inclusion of, the foreign authorities who have applicable jurisdiction. If foreign authorities initiate an investigation on their own, they may view the investigation team as interfering with or even obstructing their work.

Effective Utilization of Resources

By their very nature, investigations are often perceived as crises. They can arise suddenly, preempt other activities, and place a significant burden on management. Generally, when a fraud or allegation of fraud arises, a company must respond immediately in order to minimize financial and legal damage to the company. The company should utilize internal resources, most importantly their internal legal, accounting, and auditing resources, as appropriate, and take advantage of their proximity and familiarity with the systems, processes, and issues.

In many cross-jurisdictional investigations, it may be necessary to balance the investigative team with external resources, particularly when objectivity is required for the integrity and credibility of the investigation or when specialist skills are not locally available. Coordination to a consistent standard and project plan across multiple locations can be a complex undertaking in and of itself. It may require that further resources be considered to assist in cases of international and cross-jurisdictional investigations, such as the following:

- Local legal counsel who may be able to take advantage of locally available court orders or prevent inadvertent breach of local statutes in the course of the investigation
- Local industry experts who are familiar with customary business practices normally conducted in the industry and region
- Local technical experts, such as computer forensics practitioners or investigative accountants, who could read documents and hold interviews more effectively than a translator

These resources should be selected based on criteria such as their competency and experience with the local language, customs, traditions, and laws. Further discussion on third party roles and responsibilities in a cross-jurisdictional investigation can be found in chapter 6, "Roles and Responsibilities: How Different Stakeholders Work During Investigations."

Conclusion

In the current global environment, awareness and focus has increased on the need for attention to the adherence to high ethical and practicing standards in the fight against fraud and corruption. Even now, as the global economy seeks to converge to a common forum in the fight toward stabilization in difficult economic times, the need for guidelines in the financial and banking sectors that prevent fraud and increase transparency in transactions to limit and prevent the possibility for fraud are at the forefront in global economic policy.

In an increasingly global and connected business economy, business transactions will increasingly cross borders and jurisdictions. Investigations of those transactions will follow accordingly. The alignment of governments and regulators continues to develop in the fight against fraud, bribery, and corruption of all types and, in so doing, lends direction; assistance; and, in some cases, support to the work of the fraud investigation.

A current understanding and awareness of the jurisdictional and cross-border issues will lead to more successful investigation outcomes.

Although risks are inherent to investigations in different and unfamiliar jurisdictions, opportunities also are provided to use tools not domestically available. The pursuit of offshore assets is no longer as difficult a task as it once was. Increasing cooperation and accountability now exist in the transparency of financial and business transactions. Businesses and financial institutions worldwide are increasingly focused on identifying and preventing fraud, bribery, and corruption. The world no longer has as many options for the fraudster seeking to escape accountability. Indeed, the "long arm of the law" is likely to get even longer.

Working With Attorneys: The Relationship With Counsel

Lynda Schwartz, Partner/Principal
Jeanine Colbert, Senior Manager
Rory Alex, Senior Manager

Introduction

Grand Forge[1] has recently learned about a series of separate allegations and issues that raise a variety of intertwined business, legal, and financial reporting challenges. Among Grand Forge's issues are a series of whistle-blower reports of improper accounting practices, inflated expense reporting, and a complaint and claim for damages from a significant overseas customer. As Grand Forge begins to grapple with these issues, it is likely that they will draw on the skills of both forensic accountants and attorneys. Whistle-blower allegations with more complex fact patterns and those involving legal or regulatory matters are usually addressed by a team of experts with financial, accounting, internal controls, and legal expertise, often working side-by-side to address all aspects of the problem. Typically, these professionals coordinate their efforts to investigate facts, analyze issues, advise their clients about potential courses of action, make recommendations, and assist their clients in implementing decisions.

For many litigation and investigation matters, it is essential to have both the legal and accounting perspectives to achieve the best possible outcome. Accounting, auditing, and finance skills are needed to help gather and develop an understanding of the underlying facts and determine the best course of action from a business and financial perspective. At the same time, companies need sound legal advice. Consider, for example, that one of Grand Forge's significant overseas customers has called to complain about the quality of a large volume of product that had been recently shipped. The customer states that Grand Forge's country manager has routinely pressured the customer to take product in excess of their needs, especially at the end of the quarter. The customer is now alleging that the product they received is substandard, unusable and outside the contract specifications and is claiming damages related to the substandard product. To address these issues, Grand Forge will need to gather the accounting books and records related to these allegations. It may also need a wealth of information that accountants are highly skilled in gathering including:

- a detailed understanding of the company's internal controls around production,
- order management,
- fulfillment,
- inventory management,
- revenue recognition,
- and analysis of the customer's financial situation.

At the same time, it will also need legal advice on conducting an investigation of possible channel stuffing, an assessment of the strength of the contract claims, and the possible approaches to resolving claims within that overseas jurisdiction.

This chapter focuses on the close and integrated working relationship between accountants and attorneys. It addresses the intersecting roles of accountants and attorneys in the investigation setting, including the typical structure of the engagement and the roles taken by these professionals during investigations. The chapter also touches on the various aspects of working with attorneys in a litigation setting. Using the Grand Forge scenario, the chapter articulates ways that practitioners can work most successfully together.

Working Together

Attorneys and accountants can both bring deep skills and training to bear, although their contributions differ widely depending on the individuals and issues involved. Both professions claim investigations, fact gathering, and the synthesis of data to be among their strong suits. Depending on the investigation, dispute, or business challenge, each offers unique strengths, but each may focus on different aspects of the problem.

In general, a team that comprises both accountants and attorneys will generate a better outcome, precisely because of the differences in the skills, training, experience, and responsibilities of the respective professionals. By working together on investigations, an integrated team of accountants and attorneys often develops a more well-rounded view of the issues at hand. For example, at the outset of an investigation, attorneys and accountants may influence the structure, scope and timing of an

---

1 The reader is invited to read the detailed case study of Grand Forge Company found in the Introduction to this book.

investigation. In Grand Forge's example, the company needs an investigation that will collect the data necessary for its decision making and will need to address the legal, accounting, and practice implications of a broad range of potential outcomes. An accountant might suggest a scope that includes a variety of business, financial and accounting procedures related to the allegations of channel stuffing and the financial analyses related to the potential extent of damages, if any. An accountant might also encourage the investigation team to think about the time that the company and its external auditors will need to consider and test any outputs of the investigation. Grand Forge's attorney will likely be attentive to the ways in which the information developed during the investigation may be legally shielded from external disclosure, permitting the company to better defend against litigation spawned by the underlying issues or investigation. Attorneys may also suggest scope and timing to ensure that contract and regulatory requirements are fully addressed. In situations like these, an integrated team of attorneys and accountants brings diversity of thought and approach and helps ensure that multiple avenues are explored, many sides of the issue are addressed, and the needs of a variety of stakeholders are considered.

Both attorneys and accountants also contribute during the fact-gathering stage. Usually, fact-gathering interviews are more fruitful when the interviewer's questions incorporate the approach of both the accountants and attorneys. During such interviews, attorneys help ensure that the rights of the company and those being interviewed are respected and often have a well-honed sense of how to fully exhaust a witness's recollection of a particular subject. The analytical strengths of attorneys and accountants tend to complement each other during fact gathering. For example, an attorney's line of questioning might gravitate to the contractual, transactional, and regulatory aspects of a problem. By contrast, an accountant might focus on (1) inconsistencies between a witness's description of events and the investigator's understanding of the business controls and processes or (2) the specific details of accounting records or financial reports. Although attorneys often take the lead, interviews by accountants can be highly fruitful, particularly during questioning

related to accounting books and records, financial transactions, or processes. Interviews by accountants can sometimes be disarming, compared to those conducted by an attorney, because they have the tone of the normal audit or advisory-related inquiry with which many business people are familiar. Because the people interviewed in business-related investigations often have some financial, control, or business-process responsibility, it is helpful that the accountant speaks the same language. Accountant-to-accountant interviews often yield specific and content-rich information.

In gathering documentation, attorneys and accountants also reach for evidence that is familiar in their lines of work. Attorneys tend to focus on words and narrative evidence, such as e-mails, contracts, regulatory filings, and the records in the corporate secretary's office. By contrast, accountants tend to be more comfortable with quantitative data and often reach for transaction paperwork, bookkeeping records, and accounting books and records. The auditing skills of testing, vouching, and tracing are second nature to accountants but may be less familiar to attorneys. Bringing together both the attorneys' and accountants' skills helps identify and gather all relevant documents and, therefore, permits better probing for inconsistencies. This helps develop a more complete picture of the situation.

In investigations of business transactions, the application of generally accepted accounting principles and generally accepted auditing standards may be as relevant as any legal principle. For example, if the investigation in our scenario is focused on whether the seller has breached its warranties to Grand Forge, a legal interpretation of the contract may set the framework for fact gathering. However, if an investigation is focused on whether a transaction was properly reported in the subject company's books, records, and financial filings or on whether such information would be relevant to the company's independent accountants, the accounting and auditing standards set that framework. In many investigations, as in our scenario, such issues intersect.

As the facts become known, legal and accounting analyses tend to diverge, but the work of accountants and attorneys remains intertwined. Along with financial reporting and related advice, accountants may be asked to analyze the underlying data, considering a variety of business-oriented metrics, damages, and other calculations. Attorneys may handle all aspects of the legal analysis. Accountants can provide attorneys with the facts that are needed to make good legal conclusions, including a nuanced view of the accounting and financial implications of various courses of action. By contrast, attorneys often help accountants understand the aspects of the attorneys' work that might be confusing and can provide valuable insights on the application of rules and standards to particular fact patterns.

By identifying issues that can affect financial statements or financial reporting and assessing the risk of misstatement, forensic accountants also may help the attorneys ensure that the attorneys' communications with external auditors regarding an investigation are appropriate and complete. Box 10-1 outlines the differences between attorney and forensic accountant roles and responsibilities during a fraud investigation case.

Accountants are usually well qualified to quantify damages or prepare financial models in litigation or in the context of efforts to resolve disputes.[2]

The structure and specialized skills of accounting and law firms provide the following additional reasons for successful working relationships:

Subject matter expertise and a cross-disciplinary team. Typically, a company such as Grand Forge that is addressing the various challenges of investigations and disputes rarely has expertise in all of the accounting, legal, and operational areas necessary to fully address the matters it faces. Companies facing such challenges deserve good advice and the best thinking of professionals with experience in addressing similar issues. They can benefit equally from the personal expertise or experience of an individual professional and from the ability of a large firm to draw on the skills of a group of specialists within a firm or professional network. Similarly, large firms can deliver teams of professionals to help expand a company's ability to

Box 10-1: *An Overview of the Possible Roles for Forensic Accountants and Attorneys*

Forensic Accountant's Role	Attorneys' Role
• Participate in discussions concerning investigation scope, data resources, and data retention	• Participate in discussions concerning investigation scope, data resources, and data retention
• Perform data acquisition, processing, review, and analysis	• Perform data acquisition, processing, review, and analysis
• Conduct interviews, with special focus on financial reporting, control environment, transactions, and their context	• Conduct interviews, with special focus on chronologies, accuracy of assertions, and assembling of relevant facts
• Assist company and external auditors with understanding and considering facts	• Assist company and external auditors with understanding and considering facts
• Quantify damages or prepare financial models for different scenarios	• Provide legal advice regarding legal rights and obligations
	• Defend regulatory proceedings
	• Bring claims on behalf of clients

---

2 For a listing of typical litigation services provided by accounting and forensic practitioners, see the AICPA Consulting Services Special Report 03-1, *Litigation Services and Applicable Professional Standards*, New York: AIPCA, 2003, app. A.

staff large or complex projects with independent, objective, and skilled resources.

Global reach. The largest accounting firms have global reach and can typically provide qualified professionals who are both fluent in the local languages and familiar with the business practices of almost any locality or specialized industry. Some of the large law firms have similar reach. Collaboration between the accounting and legal firms can ensure that an adequately staffed and well-integrated team balances the needs for various skills, expertise, language, nationality, or ethnicity. Particularly in investigations, it is helpful to have professionals who can empathize and communicate with interview subjects, identify the patterns unique to specific localities, and put the facts into context. Global reach also helps bring to light the unique legal and operational aspects of executing an investigation in various localities, including the requirements for employee rights and handling evidence.

Legal technology. It is becoming common practice to gather electronic evidence, such as e-mail and computer-based files, as part of investigations and business litigation. Legal technology professionals are now essential in the majority of such assignments, and most large accounting and legal firms have such experts in their organizations. They also are found at boutique professional services firms. Often, gathering electronic evidence is a first and critical step in the investigation. Having a legal technology team that is well integrated with the core investigation team is an increasingly important asset. For more information on electronic evidence, including discussion of types of evidence, please refer to chapter 8, "Electronic Evidence."

Roles and Engagement Structure

Let us return to Grand Forge's issue with alleged channel stuffing and a related claim for damages by its customer. Mindful of the need to explore and resolve these issues prior to submitting its financial

filings, Grand Forge may press its forensic and legal professionals to get started on any necessary investigation activities as soon as possible. Although Grand Forge may hope for the best, it must recognize that an investigation of the issues in the scenario may prompt a civil or criminal investigation by government or regulatory authorities or may lead to legal action by shareholders or outsiders. Grand Forge's ability to conclude such legal matters successfully may depend on its ability to resist disclosing to future adversaries the work products of its investigation. Similarly, Grand Forge's ability to demonstrate that its investigation was led by competent people who were sufficiently independent of those who may have committed wrongdoing may affect the degree to which the investigation is reliable and whether regulators and auditors will consider it to be reliable for their purposes. That, in turn, may affect how quickly any external audits or regulatory inquiries can be resolved.

For these reasons, a first question for those structuring the investigation is how the engagement should be structured. The forensic accountant will want to ensure that professional responsibilities are met and that any investigation work with the attorneys is competent, objective, and well coordinated. Attorneys will want to ensure that any legal privileges are available and that their client's ability to resist discovery of the investigation's work product is not compromised.

Another critical consideration is whether the investigation team is sufficiently competent, independent, and credible. For example, when it is reasonable to believe that an investigation may cast doubt on the integrity of a senior manager within a company, it also is reasonable to question whether that company's ordinary counsel or an attorney that has previously represented that senior manager should lead the investigation. Sometimes, the participation of a forensic accounting team that is truly independent may make others more comfortable with proceeding with ordinary counsel, particularly when the risk of an adverse finding against the senior manager seems remote. Similarly, investigations focusing on potential improprieties in the revenue recognized in a company's financial statements might be staffed differently than investigations focusing on tax reporting.

The credibility, objectivity, and reliability of the investigation are important to the company. They also are important to possible external parties, such as auditors and regulators who may wish to rely on portions of the investigation team's work in the context of their responsibilities. Having competent, credible, and independent investigations may reduce the overall time necessary to bring the matters to conclusion.

Early decisions related to whether to preserve and gather evidence, whether specific individuals will participate in the investigation, and whether management can influence the scope of the investigation may, in some instances, taint relevant data or witnesses and permanently impair the quality of an investigation.

Thus, early decisions regarding engagement structure are more than "who does what." They have significant ongoing ramifications because early decisions regarding roles and responsibilities also affect who is in charge, the viability of any claim of legal privilege, and the extent to which the output of the investigation is as valuable to the company as it can be. A well-structured investigation also helps to ensure that roles are clear, that team members are accountable for their work and responsibilities, and that work is efficiently conducted.

In investigative settings, attorneys and accountants work together in several different ways, with the accountant retained either directly by the same client as the attorney (usually a company, but sometimes an individual) or indirectly by the attorney in connection with the attorney's legal advice to the client. Functionally, the two professional firms can work in a variety of ways. Oftentimes, in the United States, the attorney is retained as a lead investigator by the client that is often a company, committee of a board, or individual. Then, the attorney retains the accountant as a coinvestigator or technical expert. The reason is that, in the United States, except for certain tax questions, no accountant-client privilege can be reliably asserted to prevent discovery of investigative work product by the government or litigants. Although some jurisdictions recognize such privileges, they are not generally respected in

federal court, where much enforcement activity takes place.

The formal structure of the retention arrangement between the attorney and accountant says little or nothing about the overall allocation of work steps among the team. For example, an attorney can be retained to direct an investigation into the propriety of accounting determinations that will require that the bulk of the work be done by the accountant. Even when the attorney is retained directly by a client and the forensic accountant is retained by the attorney, the forensic accountant often works closely with both of them. For example, even when retained by an attorney, the forensic accountant may be instructed to work directly with company representatives. That said, in order to preserve the viability of any assertion of a legal privilege, it cannot be the case that the attorney's role is an empty formality.

In adversarial proceedings or dispute settings, including litigation, arbitration, mediation, presentations to regulators about controversies or adversarial matters, and other such situations, the accountant's role may vary. Sometimes, the accountant plays a role in assisting the attorneys and their clients in investigating, analyzing, and communicating the factual matters relating to the litigation. Often, such work includes understanding and assembling the information gathered during the litigation, assisting in the discovery process, analyzing fact patterns, calculating damages, and developing presentation materials. At other times, the accountant testifies about facts or expert opinions about that work to a judge, jury, or another fact finder.

In litigation settings, the accountant also may help in gathering information and considering, critiquing, and rebutting opposing analyses. In such situations, the accountant is usually retained indirectly by the attorney in connection with the attorney's provision of legal counsel to the client, but this is not always the case. Usually, in such situations, the attorney is a litigator and the accountant may act as a forensic specialist, consulting expert, or testifying expert witness.

The accountant should consider the following critical questions before evaluating the structure of the engagement and accepting the engagement. It is helpful to document the answers as part of understandings reached with the client.

Who is the client? Accountants have particular professional responsibilities to their clients. These include, among other things, maintaining client confidentiality. Therefore, determining exactly which entity is the client of the accountant is essential to meeting one's obligations. At the outset, the parties should define the client and develop and document an understanding with that client. Even when the accountant has coordination, administrative, or other engagement-oriented communications with both the attorney and company representatives, defining the client at the outset clarifies the accountant's role and professional responsibilities. It is reasonable to anticipate that the accountant will develop professional relationships with both the client and any other stakeholders. Those professional relationships will be built on understanding and addressing the needs of the various stakeholders consistent with their roles and responsibilities in the engagement.

What is the arrangement, and how should it be documented?[3] Accountants establish a written or oral understanding with the client (who may be an attorney representing a litigant) about the responsibilities of the parties and the nature, scope, and limitations of services to be performed, and modify the understanding if circumstances require a significant change during the engagement.[4] Usually, such understandings are documented in a formal engagement letter. Because an investigation or litigation assignment can evolve as the accountants, attorneys, and their clients learn more about the issues, the scope is usually defined in terms of the issue, topic, or question to be analyzed.

When the company may desire to assert a legal privilege regarding communications with the accountant or investigative work product, the engagement letter should clearly identify the client and the relationship among the client, attorney, and forensic accountant. Without documentation of such relationships, legal privileges may not be available and work products may be subject to discovery. Even when an attorney will not be involved and no claim of legal privilege is advanced, an engagement letter will articulate the terms and conditions of the retention, set expectations, and memorialize understandings relating to timing, efforts, expected outputs, and costs.

Does the retention create a conflict of interest? A conflict of interest may occur if a significant previous or current accountant–client relationship could be viewed as impairing the accountant's objectivity in the performance of an engagement.[5] Therefore, prior to accepting an engagement, accountants should evaluate any previous or current relationships with parties in connection with an investigation or litigation matter, taking care to consider whether prior engagements with litigants represent a conflict. If there are potential conflicts, the accountant should take care to avoid an improper disclosure of confidential information gleaned from another engagement. In certain cases, the accountant may choose to decline the engagement.[6]

Is the proposed retention compliant with professional standards and regulatory requirements? Before accepting an engagement, the accountant should understand the pertinent professional standards. These standards are affected by the nature and scope of the engagement and its structure.[7] If the accountant or that accountant's firm provides assurance services to one or more parties involved

---

3 For a further discussion of engagement letters and other matters related to documenting the scope of work, see the AICPA Forensic and Valuation Services Practice Aid 04-01, *Engagement Letters for Litigation Services*, New York: AIPCA, 2004.

4 CS section 100, Consulting Services Definitions and Standards (AICPA, Professional Standards, vol. 2, par. 07).

5 AICPA Consulting Services Special Report 03-1, *Litigation Services and Applicable Professional Standards*, New York: AIPCA, 2003, par. 38.

6 For a further discussion of conflicts, see the AICPA Consulting Services Special Report 93-2, *Conflicts of Interest in Litigation Services Engagements*, New York: AIPCA, 1993.

7 For a decision tree to determine the application of professional standards, see the AICPA Consulting Services Special Report 03-1, *Litigation Services and Applicable Professional Standards*, New York: AIPCA, 2003, app. B.

in the matter, the accountant should give special consideration to independence requirements and whether the service would be prohibited under the Sarbanes–Oxley Act of 2002 or other professional standards or regulatory requirements.

What are the anticipated outputs of the work, and who will use them? Ideally, the intended outputs of the engagement and its intended users will be identified in advance. Doing so within the engagement letter is sound practice.

The accountant's consideration of the investigation outputs and the intended use of those outputs should be more expansive than a mere discussion of the distribution of whatever written report might be generated. It is helpful to think ahead about the possible ways the investigation or dispute could evolve and, in particular, about (1) whether such evolution would change any assessment, (2) whether the accountant had a conflict, (3) how different stakeholders might seek to use or rely on the output of the engagement for decision making, and (4) whether those situations would be acceptable if they were to occur. For example, when it is likely that a regulator will be interested in the results of an investigation, the independence of the investigation team may be more important than those instances in which the more probable result of the investigation is private civil litigation by the client against a former employee.

Considerations in Working With Attorneys

It is important for accountants to appreciate that their role differs in substance and responsibility from that of an attorney.

Attorneys are agents of their client. When they appear before a court, they have ethical responsibilities to that court. They have a professional responsibility to act with integrity and be consistent with the rules of the court or jurisdiction in which they represent their clients. For example, attorneys generally are required to take steps to prevent witnesses in an investigation from proceeding based on a misunderstanding that the investigating attorney

represents them, and failure to do so can severely compromise their client's ability to use information obtained from the witness in any action against the witness. Attorneys who are acting as advocates also may have a responsibility to advocate zealously on behalf of their clients.

Generally speaking, attorneys are conscious of the tension between ethical conduct and zealous advocacy and take care to do all that such advocacy requires, without stepping over the line to unethical conduct. Whether their approach is low-key or adversarial, cajoling or more calmly persuasive, attorneys strive to advance their clients' interests within the bounds of professional ethics and the law. Depending on the jurisdiction and the setting, attorneys may be limited in their ability to resign from representing a client, even when the client fails to pay.

By contrast, accountants are neither professional advocates nor agents for their clients. For certain types of engagements, they must be independent of their clients, consistent with professional standards and regulatory requirements. In all engagements, they should maintain professional objectivity. Unlike attorneys, accountants may be obliged to resign in certain circumstances and they have more freedom to do so, especially if that right is articulated in the engagement letter.

This distinction between being an advocate, which is the attorney's role, and being an objective advisor, which the accountant strives to be, is an important one. As articulated in the AICPA Consulting Services Special Report 03-1, *Litigation Services and Applicable Professional Standards*, all litigation services provided by AICPA members are classified as consulting services. Therefore, in such engagements, their adherence to the Statements on Standards for Consulting Services is required. CPAs engaged in litigation services also must comply with the general standards of the AICPA Code of Professional Conduct; they also must obey the relevant standards established by various state boards of accountancy, the professional standards of any other organizations to which they may belong, and any other licensing requirements to which they may be subject. Specifically, AICPA members must comply with the rules of professional conduct set out below in box 10-2.

Box 10-2: *AICPA Rules of Professional Conduct Relevant to Working with Attorneys*

- Rule 102, *Integrity and Objectivity* (AICPA, *Professional Standards*, vol. 2, ET sec. 102, par. .01).

- Rule 201, *General Standards* (AICPA, *Professional Standards*, vol. 2, ET sec. 201 par. .01). Such general standards include requirements related to professional competence, due professional care, planning and supervision, sufficient relevant data, assumptions, and documentation.

- Rule 202, *Compliance With Standards* (AICPA, *Professional Standards*, vol. 2, ET sec. 202 par. .01).

- Rule 301, *Confidential Client Information* (AICPA, *Professional Standards*, vol. 2, ET sec. 301 par. .01).

- Rule 302, *Contingent Fees* (AICPA, *Professional Standards*, vol. 2, ET sec. 302 par. .01).

- Rule 501, *Acts Discreditable* (AICPA, *Professional Standards*, vol. 2, ET sec. 501 par. .01).

In certain circumstances, the following also may apply:

- Rule 101, *Independence* (AICPA, *Professional Standards*, vol. 2, ET sec. 101 par. .01)

- Rule 203, *Accounting Principles* (AICPA, *Professional Standards*, vol. 2, ET sec. 201 par. .01)

(Source: AICPA's Consulting Services Special Report 03-1, Litigation Services and Applicable Professional Standards, New York: AIPCA, 2003.)

In the context of litigation or an investigation assignment, the accountant's responsibility for objectivity may exist in tension with the attorney's responsibility to represent client interests and advocate for the client. Although an attorney may advocate the outermost interpretation of what can be argued, accountants consider whether such a position is consistent with their objective professional opinion, based on the available information.

The Investigation Setting

To return to our Grand Forge scenario, although the customers' allegations and claims raise immediate questions, management's response to those questions depends largely on their understanding of the facts. Focusing on the channel-stuffing allegation, the relevant facts might include:

- the circumstances surrounding the customer's orders,
- any contractual agreements and relevant local laws or business practices,
- any evidence regarding whether the goods shipped were in excess of the customer's needs,
- revenue recognition policies and practices,
- whether the goods in question were of adequate quality,
- the impact of any substandard goods on Grand Forge and on its customer's business,
- and whether there are any other related regulatory issues or violations.

Whether internal or independent, formal or informal, Grand Forge will need an investigation of those facts.

In order to uncover and understand the facts, Grand Forge and, in some instances, its audit committee or a special committee of the board of directors should answer the following questions at the start of the investigation:

- What facts are known?
- Is an investigation warranted?
- What will be investigated?
- Who will sponsor and be responsible for the investigation?
- Who will investigate?
- What types of information will be preserved, gathered, and considered and from whom?

Evaluating Known Facts

The root allegation or concern prompting an investigation is sometimes called the *predicate of an investigation*. Plainly, someone at Grand Forge must decide whether an investigation is necessary. In the case of Grand Forge's prospective investigation, it will be helpful for management and the board of directors to be able to summarize the facts that are known about the predicate and have a general understanding of facts to be uncovered. It also is appropriate to consider the extent to which the predicate logically suggests that other problems exist.

Determining Whether an Investigation is Necessary

The next question is whether the available information suggests that an investigation is necessary. This is not always an easy decision. Sometimes, whistleblower allegations are clear and unambiguous, or relate to issues that clearly have significant potential impacts on the company and its financial reporting, underlying operations, or reputation. In other cases, an allegation might be vague, seem to spring from emotion rather than fact, or not appear credible. When balanced against the cost of a full-scale investigation, some predicates may be worthy of follow up. It also is human nature to discount the validity or importance of a complaint or allegation or the potential range of issues raised by an allegation.

Several considerations are relevant to the decisions regarding whether an investigation is necessary. First, it is helpful to have an independent or objective decision maker. Such decision makers may see more clearly than a person who may be affected by the outcome or upon whom the burden and distraction of an investigation might fall. It also is helpful to assess whether an investigation is required by law or whether an investigation might reasonably be considered appropriate in the circumstances. If the right people conclude that the allegations have some credibility, are not clearly frivolous or irrelevant, and warrant an investigation, then the next question is how the investigation should be structured.

Oversight of Investigations

The decision about who will bear the responsibility for an investigation depends on the initial assessment of the allegation. When the predicate is unlikely to involve management and management is sufficiently competent and objective, the company's managers may successfully sponsor or control an internal investigation. Depending on the facts and circumstances, either the company's internal counsel or the

external counsel might provide legal advice, and the company's financial experts, internal auditors, or external accountants might provide the accounting expertise.

Sometimes, the predicate appears to be more significant. Questions may arise about the involvement of the company's employees or regular advisers in a particular situation, or the audit committee or board may determine that those individuals lack the necessary competence, capability, objectivity, or resources to oversee an investigation. In such instances, an audit committee or special committee of the board may take responsibility for overseeing an investigation. In these cases, the committee typically engages outside professionals to manage the investigation, subject to oversight and direction from the committee. Such structures are routinely employed for significant financial investigations because they help ensure the objectivity and independence of the investigation and assure board members that the matter will be appropriately addressed from a corporate governance perspective. Typically, for privilege reasons, the committee will retain external counsel who may, in turn, retain accountants and other forensic specialists to work with them.

The sponsor of the investigation generally has responsibility, among other things, to retain and direct the investigators, approve the scope of the investigation, monitor the status of the investigation, consider its outputs, take responsibility for the adequacy of the investigation in the circumstances, reach findings of fact, and decide upon recommendations for remedial actions, if any. In some instances, the sponsor may be asked to make formal presentations and representations regarding the conduct and outcomes of the investigation to the public, auditors, and regulators.

Selecting an Investigator

The decision about who should investigate is similar to, and flows from, the decision about sponsorship of the investigation. Investigators should be independent of the people and transactions that they are investigating. Whether the individual team members are attorneys or accountants, members of the team need to be competent in the variety of skills required in the particular situation. In the case of our example at Grand Forge, these could include the following:

- *Potential legal issues and ramifications.* Legal counsel should be familiar with financial reporting regulations, understand the legal requirements in all the appropriate jurisdictions, and understand the potential regulatory requirements related to facilitation payments or bribery. For Grand Forge, this would include both China and the United States.

- *Language.* Either the attorneys or forensic experts should speak and read both English and the native language of employees and others who may have relevant information for the investigation.

- *Financial reporting expertise.* The investigative team needs to understand the underlying accounting and financial reporting issues required to assess which fact patterns are most relevant to financial reporting issues. Also, a working knowledge of the likely books and records, business processes, and local business customs is essential to quickly locating relevant evidentiary matter.

- *Electronic evidence expertise.* Few investigations can overlook electronic evidence because it is sometimes the primary form of business communications and transactions and the primary medium for certain types of books and records. Electronic evidence has the virtue of being objectively dated and readily available through the use of forensic technology. E-mails and other electronic messages also are a source of informal, unguarded, and occasionally highly incriminating communications, precisely because users often believe that such communications are private. Expertise in handling electronic evidence is needed because such evidence may be spoiled if not handled and analyzed properly and because the technology tools available and the standards for handling such evidence continue to evolve. In the case of Grand Forge, electronic evidence would likely include the company's accounting records, e-mail, and other user documents retained on laptops or servers.

- *Subject matter expertise.* It is difficult to recognize what is unusual and improper if one has never learned what is normal and customary. If the issue or business matter to be investigated requires specific industry or subject matter expertise, it is important to include such experts on the investigation team. For example, investigating the propriety of certain credit swap derivatives transactions would be informed by the input of financial services professionals who understand the transactions, industry jargon, and normal usage and documentation, among other things.

Typically, investigations are staffed with a team of resources, drawing on personnel with backgrounds in accounting, law, or other forensic expertise. As with any significant project, teamwork is essential to harness the benefits of the various professionals' skill sets.

Establishing the Scope of the Investigation

The scope of any investigation is set by its sponsor and is specified, at least generally, in engagement letters or at the direction of the sponsor. The scope should be sufficiently broad to fully address the matters raised by the allegation of financial impropriety. It is unusual in an investigation of any complexity for the scope to remain static from beginning to end. It is important to regularly reconsider the adequacy of the investigation's scope as additional information is collected.

Accountants and lawyers can provide critical advice to the investigation sponsors regarding the various issues implied by the predicate of the investigation to ensure that they are fully addressed. When appropriate, the allegations and proposed scope should be discussed with other potentially interested parties, such as a company's financial statement auditors or the appropriate regulators. Ideally, the outcomes of such conversations are anticipated at the outset, to avoid unnecessary rework to address all the various facets of the allegation. This prevents expensive rework that might have been more efficiently addressed had the requirements of all the potential audiences for the investigation's outputs been better understood at the outset. Box 10-3 outlines how the scope of an investigation may be evaluated from a variety of viewpoints.

Box 10-3: *Investigation Scope Evaluation Considerations*

- The issue, question, or topic to be investigated.

- Whether the investigation will be broad or be narrowed to a specific time period, geographic region, business unit, or issue.

- Whether investigators will merely gather facts or whether they might plan to include other activities, such as developing observations, assessments, or recommendations related to employee conduct; specific transactions or business practices; estimates of financial or financial reporting impacts, deficiencies, weaknesses, or improvements in internal controls; and other remedial actions.

- The factual conclusions needed by auditors, regulators, or clients who will be informed of the results of the investigation in order for them to conclude any steps that they will likely take. For example, when a possible result of an investigation is a financial restatement, the scope of the investigation may need to be sufficient to permit the external auditors to draw conclusions regarding the integrity of management. In addition, when the possible result of an investigation is a follow-up investigation by a regulator, the scope may need to be sufficient to permit the regulator to rely on the findings of the investigation, if he or she chooses to do so.

Sources and Preservation of Information

It is a legal judgment concerning when document preservation is required and the extent of preservation that is appropriate. Lawyers sometimes advise companies to preserve documentation as soon as there is reason to believe it might be relevant to an investigation or litigation. In the United States, federal law may require the retention of records relevant to a likely government investigation. Accountants and forensic specialists can provide critical input to the attorneys based on their understanding of business processes, including the organization's accounting and information technology systems. Accountants can help identify obstacles to proper preservation, provide insight regarding the nature and extent of preservation so that burdensome and overbroad preservation orders can be addressed, and help avoid miscommunications between lawyers and information technology professionals that may impair an investigation or litigation. When accountants, attorneys, and other specialists work together, the risk of miscommunications regarding the nature and extent of document preservation and collection is reduced.

Once evidence collection begins, accountants and lawyers often work together to identify individuals, both internal and external to the organization, who might be custodians of relevant paper or electronic evidence. Based on this review and the business processes being investigated, they will suggest appropriate people to interview. Ideally, the accountants help anticipate how the predicate of the investigation might affect the financial reporting process and the work of the auditors. They can help attorneys gather the relevant information for those secondary users during the investigation and thereby avoid unnecessary rework. In addition, the nature and extent of evidence collection and investigation interviews may be discussed with the external auditors to ensure that their needs are met in the context of the investigation.

Accountants often work side-by-side with attorneys in the interviewing process and sometimes take primary responsibility for conducting initial inquiries, collecting and evaluating documentary and electronic evidence, and offering preliminary observations based on that evidence. It may be appropriate for people being interviewed in connection with an investigation to be warned about any ambiguities regarding whether the attorneys involved are representing them. These so-called "Upjohn warnings" are named for the Supreme Court decision identifying the adverse consequences of failing to provide such a warning. Whether an Upjohn warning is necessary is a legal judgment. Similarly, particularly in non-U.S. jurisdictions, there may be legal restrictions on evidence gathering, and legal advice about such restrictions is sometimes necessary. For example, some European countries limit the ability to access or transmit electronic evidence during an investigation and often will limit any access to e-mails or documents stored on individual computers. Accountants should communicate proactively about legal requirements and limitations to ensure that the investigation remains within those parameters.

Executing the Investigation[8]

Suppose that Grand Forge's investigation team has taken all the preceding steps and has identified and gathered a large body of evidence. Synthesizing and considering that evidence, interviewing relevant witnesses, and communicating about the investigation and its findings in a coherent report are important next steps. Executing the investigation is particularly challenging when the investigation must be completed by a specific point in time, such as a date driven by financial reporting filing deadlines or pending strategic transactions.

Although planning is critical at the outset of an investigation, few work plans survive contact with the evidence. Usually, an investigation starts with a predicate and a defined set of theories or questions to be included in the scope, but the work plan then evolves based on the nature and extent of available evidence and the investigators' observations during evidence gathering. It is possible that a smoking gun will clearly identify wrongdoing, and the investigation might evolve to include an assessment of "What else could have been wrong?" In other cases, the early stages of an investigation may uncover information that disproves the initial allegation or resolves whatever misunderstandings or misconceptions led to it. In still other cases, information will not clearly prove or disprove the allegation. In such situations, the investigation's sponsors and investigators have to consider whether the nature and extent of their investigative procedures are sufficient to have addressed the issue or whether more forensic work is warranted.

One question that should be answered tentatively at the outset is whether the sponsors of the investigation want a written or oral report and to whom such a report will be made. Clients usually expect some form of report. If an allegation of impropriety relates in any way to the financial statements, at the least, the facts obtained in the investigation are likely to be shared with the external auditors. Depending on the facts and circumstances, the facts or a report also may be shared with regulators or the public. For example, a company might commission an investigation and written report in an effort to address public criticism of the company or its management.

The form of a report varies by the type of engagement, the client's requirements, the mandate from the investigation's sponsors, and the needs of outside stakeholders, such as auditors or regulators. Various considerations govern the form of the report. One concern is whether the company and its counsel desire to preserve any legal privileges regarding the attorney's legal advice or work product. Another is whether any of the stakeholders, such as sponsors, regulators, or auditors, require written documentation. Still another is whether the sponsor can avoid disputes with those who might like to read the report by not commissioning one. Investigators also consider the nature of the factual information to be conveyed and the medium which will be most effective in doing so. Some findings can easily be communicated orally. Others are so complex, detailed, or technical that written communication, sometimes with documentary support, is necessary to avoid misunderstandings. One consideration is the nature of any current or anticipated litigation in which such a report might be obtained through discovery.

The content of an investigation report depends on the facts and circumstances but usually includes information relevant to the work of both the

---

8 For a further discussion of executing an investigation engagement, see the AICPA Forensic and Valuation Services Special Report 07-1, *Forensic Procedures and Specialists: Useful Tools and Techniques*, New York: AICPA, 2006.

accountants and attorneys, including a description of the investigation process, the nature and extent of the evidence collected and considered, and the details of the facts discovered in the investigation.

If it falls within the scope of the investigation assignment, the report also may include assessments of the propriety of individual or corporate conduct, observations regarding internal controls and business processes, assessments of the cooperation, integrity and credibility of current or former employees, or recommendations regarding remedial actions, including those related to individual employees.

The report also should consider any internal control aspects of the findings. Investigators often recommend steps to mitigate or remediate gaps identified in the course of the investigation. For example, if the Grand Forge investigation team highlights the facts related to the allegation of channel stuffing its investigation report, then it might be reasonable to include recommendations on how to remediate business processes and controls to avoid recurrence. Such recommendations are often grounded in the detailed information gathered during the investigation. Here, as in most of the investigation, accountants, forensic specialists, and attorneys would work together to deliver the best thinking to their clients.

Dealing With Investigation Stresses

Investigations create tension, and the investigation process can place a great deal of stress on professional relationships and the individuals involved in the investigation. When a credible allegation of financial impropriety comes to light, virtually everyone involved is under pressure, including company management, the audit or special committee members, attorneys, internal accountants and auditors, and external audit teams. The investigation team itself will be under pressure to conclude the investigation quickly to avoid unnecessary expense and have adequate regard for the difficulty of assessing, in hindsight, the motivations and judgments of the subjects of the investigation. When it appears that some significant errors in judgment have occurred or that possibly fraudulent activity has taken place, many of these people will be facing this type of situation for the first time in their careers. Senior managers, even those who are not subjects of the investigation, also must grapple with the frustration associated with the fact that they do not control the investigation, and, instead, that the sponsor and investigators are making decisions that necessarily detract from the productivity of company personnel. Tensions are exacerbated by unexpectedly challenging workloads. When one or more members of management must be replaced as a consequence of an investigation, such strains are even more intense. Even veterans of previous investigations find that one investigation is likely to be very different from another.

Scheduling

If an investigation can be accomplished within the normal financial reporting schedule, that is all the better. Increasingly, however, when an investigation is needed because of a whistle-blower or other allegation that calls into question a company's financial reporting, a company will not issue additional financial statements and may withdraw previously issued financial filings until all the parties are in a position to stand behind the numbers.

In recent years, financial reporting deadlines have become increasingly tight. The need to respond quickly is a major source of stress, especially if the allegation arises around the time of a financial reporting deadline. Missing filing deadlines may be significant to a company and its shareholders because late filings raise the specter of regulatory violations, may result in possible delisting from stock exchanges, limit the company's ability to complete strategic transactions, restrict the availability of stock-based compensation, and interfere with the company's compliance with debt covenants or the ability to finance itself. Let's imagine that Grand Forge's management has reason to believe that its Shanghai revenue recognition has been improper and that the revenue in question is material to users of the financial statements. Grand Forge must then consider whether to advise the markets upon which its securities trade that its prior financial statements cannot be relied upon and that it may be unable to restate its prior financial statements or issue new financial reports until the facts are known. In such a case, the pressure to complete an investigation as quickly as possible will be keen.

Cognizant of the risk of such adverse impacts, investigation sponsors and company managers are usually eager to complete the investigation as quickly as possible. Those working with attorneys should be aware of the desire for speed and be ready to respond with focus and intensity. Accountants can help mitigate this stress by dedicating to the investigation a sufficient number of resources with the right expertise, helping to focus the investigation when appropriate, and communicating proactively to ensure a high degree of teamwork.

Knowledge Transfer

Knowledge transfer from the investigators to the company's management is critical, especially at the conclusion of fact finding. Although investigators have a specific role in fact finding, the company retains the responsibility for its own financial records and reports. In the haste to complete an investigation within the shortest possible time frame, some investigators fail to fully anticipate how investigation outputs can, or could, be used by those who will prepare, certify, and opine on the financial statements. The investigative teams (including attorneys, accountants, forensic specialists, and investigation sponsors) serve their clients well when, after their role in fact finding is complete, they proactively and attentively manage the transfer of factual information and findings to both management and the internal and external auditors. Gaps in fact finding or the lack of clear, careful, and complete transmission of the investigation's outputs to these secondary users can greatly lengthen the time necessary for managers, preparers of financial statements, and auditors to fully address all the relevant aspects of the findings in the financial reporting process.

Moreover, for external auditors, allegations of misconduct by management may call into question a broad array of management's representations. Auditors frequently gather as much audit evidence as possible during an investigation. They may receive status updates throughout the investigation, attend interviews, or execute some of their audit procedures side-by-side with investigators. Nonetheless, auditors may be cautious in articulating the necessary changes to their audit approach until all the facts are known. With their bird's-eye view and experience, forensic accountants involved in investigations can greatly reduce the stresses on various participants by helping them understand their respective responsibilities, roles, steps, and needs. In order to avoid time-consuming rework and reduce the stresses of the investigation on normal professional relationships, up-front communication of expectations and discussions regarding information needs at various points in the investigation are essential.

Working With Attorneys in a Litigation or Dispute Setting

Returning to Grand Forge, let us assume that the company has long since completed its investigation of the underlying facts related to the customer's claims of substandard products and channel stuffing. Now, assume that the customer has filed suit against Grand Forge, alleging lost profits and lost business value as a direct result of Grand Forge's substandard products. This time, let us assume that the attorney representing Grand Forge is asking the forensic accountant to analyze the customer's calculation of damages and anticipates the possibility that the forensic accountant also may prepare an expert report and testify as an expert witness in the legal proceedings. This means the accountant faces a new situation. Now the accountant's role is in the context of developing and testifying about an expert opinion in the litigation setting.

Understanding the Litigation Setting

In this text, litigation refers to a variety of adversarial proceedings for resolving disputes. Litigation can occur in a court setting or in one of a variety of forms of alternative dispute resolution (ADR). This chapter is not intended as a substitute for a legal treatise on the subject, but it is safe to say that accountants working in the litigation setting should familiarize themselves with the various forms of dispute resolution and the key milestones in the life cycle of a legal dispute. A brief and necessarily general description of the accountant's role in various types of litigation follows:

Criminal litigation. Accountants are sometimes asked to become involved in criminal litigation, generally in relation to a governmental or regulatory claim that an individual or corporation broke the law and should be punished. In such settings, accountants can play a variety of roles, including gathering or analyzing the evidence that might be used by the prosecutor or serving as an expert witness for the prosecution or defense. For example, accountants may help in tracing assets related to an allegation of criminal embezzlement, or they may opine on whether a difference in accounting judgment was reasonable in light of all the facts and circumstances.

Civil litigation. Accountants are frequently involved in civil litigation, which generally relates to claims between a plaintiff and defendant, with the goal of receiving redress from the court, which may take a variety of forms. Accountants can be involved in a wide array of business and financial litigation and claims and also can be involved in the calculation of damages, even in disputes otherwise unrelated to business. For Grand Forge, for example, the accountant may be asked to calculate damages associated with a breach of the warranties in the purchase and sale agreement related to Grand Forge's acquisition of the Shanghai operation.

ADR includes arbitration proceedings, mediations, and other dispute resolution processes.* As in civil litigation, accountants may be involved throughout the dispute's life cycle. They also may become involved in providing testimony or making less formal presentations to regulatory authorities. Examples of such situations are presentations to the U.S. Securities and Exchange Commission, the Federal Bureau of Investigation or other law enforcement authorities, and regulatory authorities regarding environmental compliance, health care marketing and reimbursement, defense contracting, or pharmaceutical regulatory compliance, among others.

Typically, the life cycle of a matter in litigation includes the initiation of the dispute, a claim within a particular dispute resolution forum by the aggrieved party (usually called the plaintiff in court or the claimant in arbitration settings), and a response from the opponent (usually called the defendant in court or the respondent in arbitration). After these initial steps, most types of litigation proceed to a discovery phase, during which the parties gather information related to the investigation from one another and third parties, and then to a process by which a final conclusion of the dispute is reached (such as a trial, summary judgment, or an arbitration proceeding).

Discovery tools include, among other things:

1. Written requests for admission
2. Written interrogatories
3. Subpoenas and other requests for production of documents, including electronic documents
4. Written reports
5. Depositions

Many cases are settled during discovery by mutual agreement. If cases are not settled, they typically continue to a trial or arbitration hearing, and the matter is adjudicated by a judge, jury, or arbitrator.

(continued)

(continued)

> An accountant's role in litigation will depend, among other things, on the setting, the current status of the matter, and what the accountant has been engaged to do. Because the accountant's role depends not only on the engagement but also on the jurisdiction and venue for the matter, along with a variety of other factors, it is essential that the accountant work with the attorneys to understand the legal requirements of the work being performed. Witnesses should ask about the venue and nature of the dispute, the status of the litigation in its life cycle, and the status and extent of discovery. Accountants benefit by working closely with attorneys to understand this work setting and also may need to seek their own legal advice in areas in which they are unfamiliar.

* For further discussion of an accountant's role in alternative dispute resolution, see the AICPA Consulting Services Practice Aid 99-1, *Alternative Dispute Resolution Services*, New York: AIPCA, 1999.

The Accountant's Role as Expert[9]

The role of an expert witness is to assist the trier of fact, usually a judge or jury. For example, the Federal Rules of Evidence, which govern litigation in U.S. federal courts, state the following:

> If scientific, technical, or other specialized knowledge will assist the trier of fact to understand the evidence or to determine a fact in issue, a witness qualified as an expert by knowledge, skill, experience, training, or education, may testify thereto in the form of an opinion or otherwise, if (1) the testimony is based upon sufficient facts or data, (2) the testimony is the product of reliable principles and methods, and (3) the witness has applied the principles and methods reliably to the facts of the case.[10]

Attorneys like to hire experts who will be persuasive and advance the interests of their clients. Although attorneys are zealous advocates on behalf of their clients, testifying experts should, by contrast, advocate only their own opinions, which should be formed objectively by considering the available facts. Some of the practical considerations of working with attorneys in the context of expert testimony are considered in box 10-4.

When the Opinion is Not as Desired

Sometimes, the expert's consideration of available information results in an opinion or factual observation that an attorney or the attorney's client does not perceive to be advantageous to their case. Almost all experienced witnesses have encountered situations in which their professional opinion, after consideration of the facts, was not as the attorney or the attorney's client had hoped. Perhaps the expert's calculation of damages yielded a figure that was lower than expected or perhaps the expert discovered flaws in the legal strategy or facts that were inconsistent with the hoped-for approach. In such situations, the experts, attorneys, and their clients should clearly communicate the reasons for the opinion and the differences identified. In some situations, such dialogue results in the suspension of the engagement. In every instance, however, the accountant, attorney, and client benefit from hearing an unvarnished assessment as early in the litigation process as possible. Many times, such discussions lead to a change in strategy or approach, such as commencement or acceleration of settlement negotiations. In every case, the attorneys and their clients can make better decisions if they have a transparent and complete understanding of the professional opinion and the bases for it.

---

9 Additional information regarding a CPA's responsibilities in the context of expert testimony can be found in the article "Expert Testimony: The CPA's Responsibilities" by Michael G. Ueltzen, CPA, CFE, and Robert H. Johnson, Esq., in *The Practicing CPA*, September 2001.

10 Federal Rules of Evidence (2006), Rule 702. For a comparison of AICPA professional standards and Federal Rule of Evidence 702, see the AICPA Consulting Services Special Report 03-1, *Litigation Services and Applicable Professional Standards*, New York: AIPCA, 2003, app. D-E.

Box 10-4: *Experts Working with Attorneys: Key Considerations*

- *Define the assignment.* Generally, the assignment is defined in terms of the area of inquiry or topic for development of an opinion. Defining the assignment in terms of a desired opinion or outcome might be an indication of an inappropriate lack of objectivity.

- *Understand the context of the testimony in the overall legal strategy.* Although accountants are not advocates, it makes sense for them to understand the legal strategy and ensure in advance that they are comfortable that the opinion, as positioned within the attorney's legal strategy, would not be misleading. The accountant, in articulating an expert opinion, can often assist the trier of fact and the attorney by bringing out salient information that gives context to the opinion. In addition, when appropriate and to avoid confusion, the accountant can carefully select words to be consistent with the nomenclature or phrases used by other participants in the process.

- *Ensure an adequate understanding of the status of the case and any deadlines.* Court-ordered deadlines are rarely flexible, and experts rarely have unlimited time to execute their work. The expert witness should understand what limitations are imposed by the litigation schedule. Sometimes, attorneys do not retain experts until late in the process. Sometimes, experts are retained after the close of the discovery phases or near the deadlines for submission of expert opinions. Before agreeing to be retained, therefore, accountants should consider whether the engagement can be completed in a competent matter within the required time frame. Once the engagement is underway, frequent status updates are essential to understand any revisions to the schedule and to understand the nature and extent of any information, any new evidence arising in discovery, and any changes in engagement needs.

- *Clarify in advance the areas about which the expert will testify, any assumptions the expert is being asked to adopt, and how any facts necessary to the opinion will be brought into the record.* Accountants' opinions should be focused and will be based on a variety of data and assumptions. Whether and how the factual basis will be presented at court should be clarified in advance to avoid opinions that lack adequate foundation.

- *Ensure adequate access to underlying evidence.* It is not at all unusual that an attorney working on a legal matter will pull together a series of key documents for the expert's consideration. To avoid "cherry-picking," or the appearance of it, the accountant should ensure adequate access to source materials and request and consider any materials that may be relevant to the opinion. Similarly, litigation attorneys often have most of the direct contact with the client. The accountant also should have adequate access to the attorney's client, not simply to avoid misunderstandings among the expert, attorney, and attorney's client but also to ensure complete understanding of whatever data and other information are being provided by that client.

- *Discuss with counsel the nature of the written work that the expert will prepare and the extent to which it is permissible to discard information relevant to the engagement.* A testifying expert may be required to produce in discovery the information provided to the expert in connection with his or her work, communications with counsel, and drafts of opinions. In some instances, the expert may be required to explain whether the information that has been considered has been produced. In some jurisdictions, discarding information may be grounds to exclude the expert from testimony. Accordingly, the expert should have a clear understanding with counsel about what materials will be produced and obtain advice from counsel about the extent to which it is permissible to discard information relevant to the engagement.

Assisting in the Discovery of Opponents and Third Parties

Accountants and attorneys frequently work together in the discovery phase. Accountants, with their rich background in business processes and analyzing business books and records, can help shape and focus requests for documents, requests for admission, or interrogatory questions in the discovery phase. Accountants can frequently help in crafting subpoenas and requests for production of documents to ensure that the most salient and informative information is requested and that requests are specific and narrow enough to receive a fruitful response. Early involvement of accountants has frequently saved attorneys and their clients both costs and aggravation because it focuses discovery on obtaining the necessary financial information the first time and ensures that necessary information for the case and expert opinion is provided on a timely basis for the litigation team.

In some types of litigation, discovery documents are accumulated in a physical or electronic document repository. Accountants may work with the attorneys to locate, evaluate, and assess the documentation obtained during the discovery process.

Accountants may be involved during interviews, depositions, and other inquiries related to financial and business topics. As with document discovery, the accountant can help focus the questioning and at the same time ensure that necessary topics are not omitted. Accountants are often most helpful when they assist the attorney in asking the probing follow-up questions in response to superficial or evasive answers to the attorney's line of questioning.

Preparing for the Discovery of the Expert

Depending on the evolution of a case, an expert's work, working papers, and communications may be shared with other litigants during the discovery process. Accountants serving as experts should anticipate this. Accountants' professional standards require adequate documentation of the work performed but may provide some flexibility regarding the nature and extent of documentation.[11] Accountants should normally avoid preparing or creating unnecessary documentation and should take care to avoid documenting incomplete or unfunded analyses or making flippant, extraneous, or unprofessional comments that could be embarrassing when read by third parties. To avoid destruction of documentation that should be produced during the discovery process, accountants should discuss their discovery obligations and document retention practices with the attorneys (or with their own legal counsel), particularly as they relate to drafts, information considered but rejected, and editorial revisions. To facilitate later discovery, it is sometimes helpful to segregate working papers from source documents and documentation of the administrative aspects of an engagement.

The nature and extent of discovery requirements is essentially a legal issue and depends on the facts and circumstances of the investigation. Various types of documents may be subject to different discovery requirements. At other times, the attorneys may be able to limit discovery to a subset of documentation. For example, the parties in a litigation matter might, for a variety of reasons, voluntarily agree to limit certain kinds of document production. The nature and extent of document production also differs by the venue of the dispute. For instance, document production requirements for litigation tend to be more limited in litigation outside the United States or in various alterative dispute resolution settings.

When thinking of expert discovery, do not forget electronic media, such as e-mail, instant messages, faxes, and certain types of voicemail. Depending on the subpoena or request, all of these may be subject to discovery by third parties. While executing the engagement, it is helpful to employ a working assumption that anything communicated in electronic format may later be made available to the opponents and, thus, would be available for cross-examination.

---

11 For additional detail regarding an accountant's responsibilities for working papers and documentation, see the AICPA Consulting Services Special Report 03-1, *Litigation Services and Applicable Professional Standards*, New York: AIPCA, 2003, app. C.

Preparing the Expert Report

Many good references exist for accountants preparing expert reports, including, among others, the AICPA Consulting Services Practice Aid 96-3, *Communicating in Litigation Services: Reports.* The opinion articulated in the expert report is that of a testifying witness, not that of an attorney or professional services firm. Usually, the expert personally signs the report and bears responsibility for it. When developing the content of an expert report, the expert should carefully consider the attorney's strategy, terminology, and suggestions but should take care to form an objective professional opinion. Similarly, the tenor of the expert report should be professional and straightforward, avoiding hyperbole and advocacy-oriented language.

The form of the expert report varies by jurisdiction and, indeed, by practitioner. The general rules for expert reports in U.S. federal courts are found in the Rule 26 of the *Federal Rules of Civil Procedure.* Generally, Rule 26 provides the following:

> Unless otherwise stipulated or ordered by the court, this disclosure must be accompanied by a written report—prepared and signed by the witness—if the witness is one retained or specially employed to provide expert testimony in the case or one whose duties as the party's employee regularly involve giving expert testimony. The report must contain:
>
> (i) a complete statement of all opinions the witness will express and the basis and reasons for them;
>
> (ii) the data or other information considered by the witness in forming them;
>
> (iii) any exhibits that will be used to summarize or support them;
>
> (iv) the witness's qualifications, including a list of all publications authored in the previous 10 years;
>
> (v) a list of all other cases in which, during the previous 4 years, the witness testified as an expert at trial or by deposition; and
>
> (vi) a statement of the compensation to be paid for the study and testimony in the case.

Chpater 12, "Reporting on Fraud" goes into greater detail on rules for expert reports. Ideally, the expert drafts the report. Questions during cross-examination occasionally focus on whether the expert, the expert's junior staff, or the attorney drafted the report. The forensic accountant retained as an expert witness should be prepared to testify about the development of the opinion, the process to draft and finalize the report, and any changes to it during its development. If the report goes through different drafts and the drafts are made available during the discovery process, the expert also should be prepared to defend the final conclusion and explain any differences from the prior drafts.

Quality Control Procedures

It is a good quality control practice to prepare a so-called "tied-out" copy of the report, which includes either by footnote or cross-reference all the support for each of the statements, data, or assumptions. This practice has multiple purposes. The process is effective because it forces documentation of the final opinion. It also becomes a study aid as the witness prepares to testify. The accountant can use this process to ensure that data in the report can be traced to valid sources, such as evidence obtained in discovery, established industry or public sources, or other evidential matter. Documentation of the bases for any assumptions and estimates should be adequate because these are common areas of attack.

It also is helpful to have a skilled quality reviewer, such as another competent accountant, read and consider the report. That person can assist in identifying undocumented assumptions, unsupported assertions, or areas of weakness in the approach. Another practitioner with a fresh eye is less likely to have become wedded to a particular approach and may suggest alternatives that would yield additional insight. Further, a quality reviewer can help identify areas of weakness in the report, including subtle biases and areas in which the accountant has taken more aggressive positions. These procedures are most helpful as early in the process as possible. They should be involved before the accountant has expressed an opinion, but they can be helpful throughout the engagement.

Privilege

Accountants can benefit from a candid, up-front discussion with internal or external counsel about any legal privileges that might attach to communications and work product arising during and from the engagement.

Although the definitions of privileges and the types of communications that qualify as being governed by privilege are themselves legal judgments, accountants should generally be familiar with the following two well-recognized privileges that are commonly asserted:

1. The *Attorney-Client Privilege* protects communications between attorneys and their clients when they are discussing legal advice given in the context of actual or threatened litigation. Such privilege may not attach to communications in which attorneys are dealing with a purely managerial activity or communications that are not kept private between the attorney and the attorney's client. For example, attorney-client privilege may attach to documents or analyses prepared by the client for the attorney to understand the client's assessment of financial damages.

2. The *Attorney Work Product Doctrine* protects an attorney's internal documentation of the work or analyses created in support of the attorney's legal representation of the client. Therefore, if the accountant is working at the attorney's direction to assist the attorney in providing legal advice, the accountant's work product may fall within this doctrine. For example, the accounting consultant's analyses related to financial damages and prepared solely for the attorney (and not as an expert witness) may fall under the attorney work product doctrine. As with materials protected under the attorney-client privilege, access to materials protected under the attorney work product doctrine generally must be restricted in order to retain such privilege.

Unfortunately, it is not always clear whether and to what degree a legal privilege will attach or whether such privileges might later be waived. Documents and communications are not privileged merely because they are labeled as such or even because they were intended to be privileged. Instead, whether the communication is privileged is based, among other

things, on the substance of the communication, the substance of the relationship between the attorney and the person to whom the communication was made, the nature of the matter to which the document relates, the rules within the specific jurisdiction of the matter, how widely the communication or documentation was circulated, and with whom it was shared. Parties sometimes contest assertions of privilege and sometimes do so well after the fact.

For the accountant, the following are a number of practical considerations in managing documents and communications that may be privileged or fall under the attorney work product doctrine:

- *Proactively discuss handling documents and communications with attorneys.* Whether privileges attach to documents and communications is, at its core, a legal conclusion. Accountants should not assume that they are aware of all the nuances of privilege-related law. Rather, they should discuss their document-handling practices with the attorneys with whom they are working and the modes that they plan to use for communication, so that the attorneys can give legal guidance when appropriate. In a non-litigation environment, an accountant might normally communicate directly with the company about issues and advice or disseminate information about an engagement to all appropriate stakeholders. For potentially privileged documents, it may be important to restrict distribution or preferable to have such communications come through the attorneys. Proactive communication about what should be communicated, and to whom and how, will help avoid the unintended waiver of potential privileges.

- *Label potentially privileged documents and communications.* Although documents and communications may not be privileged merely because someone labels them so, labeling can be helpful by expressing the intent of the parties to keep the documentation privileged. From a practical perspective, labeling also can remind accountants and their teams that documentation is intended to be privileged and should be handled appropriately. Discuss the appropriate label with the attorneys and follow their guidance.

- *Assume that work may someday be disclosed.* Operating under the assumption that their work products and communications are privileged, professionals sometimes feel free to draft e-mails that candidly describe their thinking, their preliminary work, the perceived strengths and weaknesses of the work, and their communications with attorneys regarding the engagement. Some, thinking that no one will ever see them, include embarrassing or flippant remarks in their writing or make statements that undermine their later testimony. Almost every experienced witness can tell tales of opponents who were questioned about unguarded and inappropriate comments after privileges were waived and their communications were exchanged in discovery. E-mails expressing preliminary conclusions, initial concerns, worries, or doubts also are classic fodder for cross-examination, if discovered. All professionals involved in litigation services should work as if the whole world will someday see their work product or read what they once thought were their confidential communications with their own teams or with the attorneys. Good working habits and discipline help prevent damaging disclosures.

- *The medium and tenor of communication*. The tenor of the communication and work product should be professional, thoughtful, and consistent with the thorough and objective analysis that the accountant has been retained to deliver. The mode of communication and documentation also can be important. Final documentation should be complete and adequately support the work performed. Preliminary work, however, might have limited or no documentation. For example, the accountant might meet for an in-person discussion of issues, questions, and approaches without leaving a permanent documentary record of preliminary results. A phone or conference call might appropriately report on the status, open items, and concerns without leaving the documentary trail of an e-mail. Not only will such foresight reduce the exposure to discovery, but it also will limit the risk that materials could be copied or forwarded in ways that might cause an unintended waiver of any privilege that might otherwise be available.

Preparing to Give Testimony[12]

Many investigations or litigation situations require the accountant to testify. Examples of testimony by accountants could include the following:

- Written expert reports or interrogatories
- Deposition testimony
- Direct examination in court or arbitration
- Cross-examination in court or arbitration
- Presentations in mediation or other alternative dispute resolution settings
- Testimony or presentations to regulators
- Testimony as a fact witness related to an engagement

The pressures of providing testimony are intense. It is prudent for accountants engaged in the matter to reconsider their role and the objectives of the case. Especially in preparing and giving testimony, the accountants should take care to remain objective, advocate only for their own opinions, and focus on the responsibility of assisting the trier of fact.

When meeting with attorneys, accountants may feel subtle pressure to assist the attorney in advocating for the client. Other times, pressure may come from within. For example, an accountant might feel a need to "help the team," want to excel at the role of expert witness, or begin to see the opposing attorney as a personal adversary. There may be both direct and indirect pressures from attorneys and their clients to adopt unreasonable assumptions, take aggressive positions, or phrase answers in ways that are advantageous to their positions. Time pressures also are common. All these elements can erode professional objectivity. Keeping one's own responsibilities in mind greatly helps the witness to remain centered, despite such pressures. Quality control procedures and quality reviews from other accountants, described earlier, also can bolster awareness of such pressures and create an environment that is supportive of ethical, objective, and quality-oriented work. Box 10-5 outlines the experiences of successful accounting-oriented witnesses and suggests several keys to successful testimony.

---

12 For additional information on expert testimony, see the article titled "Working with Attorneys, Juries and Judges" in the *Focus* newsletter of the AICPA Forensic and Valuation Services Section, January/February 2008 ed., vol. 4, no. 1.

Box 10-5: *Ten Keys to Successful Testimony*

1. *Know your own opinion.* A clearly stated professional opinion sounds simple, but, in practice, it can be profoundly difficult to craft. An opinion to be articulated in testimony is not a casual, everyday opinion of personal preference. A strong, expert opinion is limited to the topics and matters that the accountant was asked to analyze. A good witness avoids over-extending the opinion to vulnerable side topics. Testimony should be supported by the facts and circumstances, personal experience, research, analysis, and, if appropriate, clearly defined and articulated assumptions. Rule 26 requires that the expert report state all the opinions and the bases for them.

   Ideally, the expert states the opinion in a series of declarative sentences, with each statement supported by detailed explanations, calculations, or materials that articulate the bases for the opinion. Being able to articulate the opinion and its bases is usually required in the litigation setting and would be good practice, even if not required. Clear statements help the testifier remember, under the pressure of cross-examination, what the opinion is not. Skilled cross-examiners often try to lead a witness into over-extending testimony from his or her opinion into other, less well-considered statements. Then, a witness could easily fall victim to a critique of any ill-formed judgments. Similarly, many cross-examiners attempt to confuse a testifier with convoluted hypothetical questions, some of which may have little relevance to the matter at hand. Refocusing on one's own opinion and the bases for it can help a witness remain oriented.

2. *Communicate the opinion in the context of the themes and context of the case.* Although the core of an accountant's testimony is usually an accounting or financial judgment, accountants are ideal witnesses to help attorneys tell the story of their cases in the litigation context. Because of the unique professional role of accountants in developing, analyzing, understanding, and communicating about financial matters, their testimony includes the background of what happened or the business and financial context of specific transactions. Through that testimony, the judge, jury, or trier of fact may come to see the facts of the case from the accountant's viewpoint.

   The accountant's work is therefore strengthened by understanding the key themes of the attorney's strategy. The accountant should appreciate whether and to what degree the attorney anticipates using the accountant's testimony in building context for his or her legal arguments or establishing foundational elements of the case. Within the bounds of their own professional responsibilities, accountants also can be very helpful to judges and juries by helping them understand salient themes in the case, especially those involving matters such as money, damages, accounting, financial reporting and analysis, business processes and controls, the facts surrounding specific transactions, and quantitative analyses.

3. *Focus on the bases for assumptions.* In some types of damages analysis, informed and thoughtful assumptions are an integral and necessary element. Expert witnesses are permitted to employ assumptions in their analyses. Witnesses should know the assumptions embedded within their work and should be able to clearly articulate the bases for them. Many assumptions are selected by the accountants based on verifiable inputs. Others are given to them by the attorneys. Generally, to avoid misleading the trier of fact, the assumptions given to the witness should be articulated in a written report or direct examination. Sometimes, the nature of the assumption will be critical to the case. For example, if an accountant is asked to calculate damages assuming that the defendant is found liable, that testimony might become moot if the finder of fact decides the defendant is not liable. Similarly, if the witness were asked to calculate damages assuming that company revenues reached a stipulated figure, the expert opinion might be disregarded if that assumption were found to be unreasonable. Identifying assumptions and clearly communicating about them helps prepare the witness to successfully address the inevitable cross-examination

   (continued)

Box 10-5: *Ten Keys to Successful Testimony* (continued)

4. *Use a variety of modes of communication.* The expert may have an opportunity to use a variety of communication tools during the litigation process, including written reports and oral testimony. Depending on the facts and circumstances, the witness may use a variety of graphs, charts, diagrams, models, and other tools as exhibits. Because the goal is to help the trier of fact, it is worth investing the time to ascertain what mode of communication would help most in getting the message across and which modes of communication are permitted in that particular setting.

5. *Prepare.* Preparation for testimony is essential because the witness may be questioned in detail on any aspect of the opinion, the bases for the opinion, and about any expert report or prior testimony in the case. Witnesses also may be questioned on their prior writings, publications, or testimony in other matters or on documents they may have considered, their communications with the attorneys, and the approaches or data that they may have considered and rejected. Sometimes, cross-examiners ask questions far afield of the opinion for the sole purpose of making the witness look unprepared, biased, or careless.

   Witnesses should try to "over-prepare," if possible. Preparation for testimony cannot be delegated because only the witness will testify. Good preparation, even over-preparation, reduces the likelihood that the cross-examiner will be able to confound the witness.

   Among the techniques helpful in preparing for testimony is to hand-calculate all the critical calculations underlying the opinion. In this age of computers, this may seem archaic, but hand-calculations force witnesses to slow down and understand each step in the calculation, thus allowing them to recreate the calculation on the stand, if asked. Another technique, as alluded to earlier, is to create a "tie-out" expert report that includes a footnote or cross-reference from every fact, figure, and statement to its supporting documents. When embedded in the report itself, such cross-references fully document the basis for the opinion. They are also a great timesaver as the time for testimony nears.

6. *Clarify the message.* Although the issues in the case often are complex, it is worthwhile for the expert, while preparing his or her testimony, to consider how to articulate an opinion to someone lacking the expert's level of expertise and knowledge. If it can be done within the bounds of confidentiality, the witness might talk about the case with a person who is not skilled in accounting and finance. The witness can assess whether the key points are clear to the layperson, the listener understood the overall themes of the case, the examples or metaphors used in the testimony resonated, and the testimony left the listener with unanswered questions. In large cases, focus groups help attorneys and witnesses test their messages. For other cases, the witness can seek out the unvarnished feedback that will help the witness communicate more clearly during testimony.

7. *Anticipate cross-examination.* Another strategy is to consider talking through cross-examination with attorneys and other professionals who are knowledgeable about the case. Often, insufficient time is spent preparing for cross-examination of expert witnesses in the belief that experts can take care of themselves. Expert witnesses benefit by gaining input from others to help anticipate likely cross-examination questions and approaches. Sometimes, the best preparation is with an attorney on the team who knows the case but does not regularly interact with the witness. A less-experienced legal associate on the team might fill this role. An attorney's questions may come from a different perspective, which is a good way for the witness to "expect the unexpected."

(continued)

(continued)

8. *Narrow the testimony.* Testimony should focus on those topics about which the accountant has formed a professional opinion. Witnesses can further narrow their testimony by actively searching for ways to limit the points of disagreement. This usually benefits the client by focusing the dispute, and it benefits expert witnesses by minimizing the number of areas on which they can be cross-examined. For example, although the accountant could conceivably choose the "best" answer for all the inputs to a damages analysis, there may be a range of reasonable answers. Some inputs have little true impact on the overall opinion. One example is a hypothetical situation in which damages are calculated as the sum of discounted cash flows. The damages calculation might not be sensitive to the assumption regarding capital expenditures in the tenth year of a projection, but it might be highly sensitive to the assumption regarding the interest rate used to discount the projected cash flows. The witness might limit areas of dispute by utilizing agreed-upon or stipulated facts. Another way the witness might limit areas of dispute is by adopting the opponent's assumptions when there is no substantive difference between the data or assumptions adopted by the witness and the opponents or when such differences have little impact. This focuses the dispute on the key drivers of the analysis, which is where the details make a difference.

9. *Maintain composure.* Successful witness testimony depends, in part, on the witness's self-control and ability to communicate clearly in a stressful context, even when subject to intense scrutiny.

   First-time witnesses are sometimes surprised at how physically and emotionally grueling it can be to sit in the witness chair for seven or eight hours. Good witnesses recognize that testifying is hard work, and it requires them to manage a number of factors, including the following:

   - *Energy.* The witness needs to remain energized and focused throughout the testimony. Good witnesses make sure they are rested, well-fed, hydrated, and that they have addressed their physical needs, so that their minds can be fully engaged.
   - *Emotions.* Sometimes, cross-examiners bait the witness to elicit an emotional response. Within certain bounds, they can charm, challenge, tease, ridicule, and irritate the witness. Good witnesses stay focused, regardless of these tactics.
   - *Responses.* One rule of testimony is to listen to the question. If a question is unclear, the witness can ask for it to be repeated or clarified. Good witnesses answer what was asked and manage their responses to address the questions. Depending on the context, they avoid unnecessary disclosures, avoid opening new areas for examination, and maintain their credibility with the trier of fact.
   - *Message.* Strong, direct testimony puts the expert opinion in the context of an overall theme or message. Whenever possible, the witness can return to the key themes of the testimony to reinforce the message, even during cross-examination.
   - *Pace.* Good witnesses keep the pace of questioning and answering relatively constant under both direct and cross-examination. Skilled attorneys may try to disrupt or rush the witness by asking questions in quick succession trying, in cross-examination, to rile a witness who had been unruffled in direct examination; or letting silence stretch for an uncomfortably long time. Successful witnesses are aware of their own pace and keep themselves centered.
   - *Demeanor.* Successful witnesses conduct themselves in a competent, thoughtful, and objective way. They avoid body language or behavior that suggests bias or advocacy for their clients.

10. *Tell the truth.* Most testifiers take some form of the traditional oath to "tell the truth, the whole truth, and nothing but the truth." When a difficult question comes, the witness must answer truthfully, even if the truth is unappealing.

Strong Communication Builds Teamwork

To foster teamwork, focus on communication in the following areas:

- *At the outset of the engagement, it is especially helpful to discuss not only the roles, skills, and expertise of the individual practitioners but also the resources available to them. For example, most accounting and law firms have resources with a variety of technical skills. Global firms may be able to supply professionals with experience in far-flung localities or fluency in other languages. In addition to accounting skills, the Big Four accounting firms have a variety of specialized forensic resources. For example, an early offer of assistance with electronic evidence is frequently welcome and can enhance the overall project.*
- *During an engagement, non-attorneys may ask about the legal aspects of the matter and inquire about any legal terminology used by the attorneys. Although many attorneys have a strong working knowledge of accounting and financial reporting, it can be helpful to offer additional explanations or background, with respect to more technical topics. The opportunity to learn and share expertise is one of the benefits of working with attorneys.*
- *Communicate candidly about weaknesses in or questions about the engagement approach or the facts uncovered. Almost every professional benefits from looking at challenges with a fresh view. Because of their different backgrounds and skills, attorneys and accountants can help each other see issues from other perspectives.*
- *Communicate about commitments and timing. Given the short time frames and deadlines associated with such work, communication in this area is critical.*
- *Consider the viewpoints of the company, its managers, and other stakeholders. Accountants and attorneys need to focus on client service. Sharing information about client needs and concerns can help both sets of professionals reduce stress and manage expectations. In particular, accountants with experience in auditing and working with people in a variety of business roles can help the attorneys build relationships and understand the perspectives of the financial people within the company.*

Conclusion

Grand Forge, our subject, needs good lawyers to help them understand and resolve their legal exposures and help them benefit from their legal rights in disputes. The company also needs skilled accountants and forensic specialists to help uncover what happened and advise Grand Forge on necessary changes in business processes, financial controls, and financial reporting. Even more, the company stands to benefit from a synthesis of their work, drawing from both sets of skills to help the company make good business decisions. Grand Forge wants its attorneys and accountants to work cooperatively, avoid redundancy, and help them achieve their business objectives.

When lawyers and accountants work apart, each delivering their own specialized expertise in a vacuum, they miss a crucial opportunity to deliver to clients high-quality service that synthesizes the best approaches and skills of both the accounting and legal professions. Facing the unknowns that arise with allegations of financial impropriety and the very real challenges of claims, regulatory compliance issues, litigation, and disputes, clients deserve to realize the synergies that can be achieved when attorneys and accountants work cooperatively to address business problems.

Notwithstanding the pressures and challenges associated with investigations and litigation, such work is incredibly rewarding. When attorneys and accountants work together in appropriately structured and organized engagements, when they recognize and take into account their respective professional responsibilities, when engagement scope and communication are appropriate so that the professionals work together and not at cross-purposes, and when the work is done competently and skillfully, the benefits to clients are enormous.

Working With Regulators and Parallel Investigations

Dale Kitchens, Partner/Principal
Mike Sherrod, Senior Manager
David Laing, Partner, Baker & McKenzie LLP
Robert Tarun, Partner, Baker & McKenzie LLP

Introduction

In this age of heightened regulatory scrutiny, accountants find themselves working with company management, board members, federal and state regulators, lawyers, law enforcement officials, and other parties investigating potential wrongdoing.

In addition to the other allegations being investigated that have been addressed in the overall case study at the beginning of the book[1] consider the scenario that follows.

Nicole Evans, an accounting manager in Financial Reporting, was performing her normal closing procedures when she continued to be confused by entries made by Jon and Christopher and ultimately signed off on by Bill after the close process was completed each month. When she continually questioned Christopher, who was her boss, she was left with a feeling that something was unusual about these entries and, therefore, she continued to research by looking at the underlying supporting documentation. Still not satisfied with the entries' legitimacy, she was left with no other alternative but to draft and submit a whistle-blower letter to the Grand Forge fraud response hotline system.

Jacob Willis, the general counsel for Grand Forge, arrived to work on a Friday morning looking forward to his weekend. It has been a long three months as he had been dealing with the other allegations indentified in the original case study at the beginning of the book and it looked as if those were starting to be wrapped up. When he opened up his e-mail and saw the letter from Nicole, he quickly realized his weekend and the next few months were about to change dramatically. His first response after reading the letter was: What do I do now? What are the protocols and processes I need to consider throughout this process?

As Jacob quickly found out from our preceding hypothetical scenario, the roles for the parties involved, such as accountants and others within the organization, can become quite confusing, especially if they have no prior experience with regulatory investigations. Allegations can surface from numerous sources, including whistleblowers, lawsuits, external and internal auditors, media reports, and investigations conducted at other companies with which the company does business.

The more complicated investigations involve multiple regulatory and law enforcement agencies. For example, an alleged fraud scheme involving a bank and its publicly traded holding company may involve federal and state banking examiners, Securities and Exchange (SEC) enforcement lawyers and accountants, Department of Justice (DOJ) lawyers, FBI agents, IRS agents, and other regulatory officials.

Investigations of wrongdoing conducted by multiple regulatory and law enforcement agencies resulting from the same set of facts are commonly referred to as *parallel investigations*. Parallel investigations allow each regulatory agency to fulfill its individual oversight responsibilities. For example, in the allegations described in the case study for Grand Forge, the securities fraud may be investigated by the SEC for potential civil charges against the company or its employees, and the DOJ, with assistance from FBI agents, may investigate the same set of facts for potential criminal charges. It is common for such agencies to cooperate and share information and their investigative findings.

It also is common for a company to conduct its own internal investigation in parallel and in cooperation with a regulatory investigation. Both the SEC and DOJ frequently prefer that a company conduct its own investigation before determining how they will proceed in order to leverage the company's fact-finding results. In these situations, the regulators will closely monitor how the company is conducting its investigation and ask for periodic updates on findings and evidence.

Situations also arise in which company management or its board becomes aware of an allegation of wrongdoing on the part of one or more of its employees that has not been previously communicated to a regulatory authority. In these situations, the company will likely conduct its own internal or independent investigation and then determine, with

---

1 The reader is invited to read the detailed case study of Grand Forge Company found in the Introduction to this book.

advice from legal counsel, whether disclosure to regulatory authorities is required or desirable, based on the findings. Sometimes, disclosure is required even if not desirable; oftentimes, self-reporting is done because there is really no other option. This chapter is designed to assist accountants and other professionals not familiar with regulatory investigative processes by explaining some of the more important issues involved and describing some of the risks. This chapter also outlines considerations Jacob should be considering as he develops his course of action and as more information surfaces or government investigators get involved.

Internal Investigations

Receiving a grand jury subpoena or investigative demand, or learning that federal or state law enforcement agents and prosecutors have developed an interest in one's business or any individual officers or employees in that business, can cause instant alarm throughout an organization. At times, the alarm is warranted; federal law enforcement officials have been increasingly aggressive in investigating and prosecuting business crimes and even the collateral consequences of becoming a subject of an investigation, such as an adverse shareholder reaction, harm to one's business reputation, and even loss of business, can be severe.

At other times, the level of alarm is more a function of the unknown. Executives and board members at compliance-conscious, law-abiding business enterprises typically have no significant experience that will help them discern whether the investigation should be a cause of genuine concern.

At the same time (or prior to, as the case may be) that a regulatory agency conducts its investigation, a company will always want to be conducting its own internal review to make an informed determination about what happened and what remedial actions should be taken. In its conduct of this second, parallel investigation, the company must pay as much attention to how it conducts its own investigation and the results as it does to the government's investigation. An effective and efficient internal investigation helps the company reach a determination, based on the most accurate facts and understanding of the matter available. Understanding these facts should allow the company to make sound decisions about its succeeding course of action.[2]

Although some routine or less serious matters may be handled internally and less formally by the company's internal auditors, compliance officers, and in-house counsel, the current regulatory and law enforcement environment is not forgiving to corporations that underreact to evidence of internal misconduct. Boards of directors, senior management, and in-house counsel now frequently face situations that call for launching a vigorous internal investigation. Such investigations typically involve at least the assistance of outside professionals and often are conducted at the direction of such outside lawyers, including counsel experienced in not only conducting internal investigations but in negotiating with law enforcement personnel and regulators who have, or soon will, become aware of the circumstances leading to the investigation.

Jacob understood that a course of action was needed and that he would have to strongly consider outside assistance in order to properly assess and investigate the situation, due to the parties alleged to be involved in this scheme. Although inevitably costly and disruptive, beginning such an independent and thorough factual investigation promptly can often help allay the concerns of regulators, prosecutors, and shareholders about allegations of wrongdoing that have become publicly known. Irrespective of whether the allegations have attracted the attention of regulators or law enforcement investigators, embarking on an internal inquiry is often a critical first step in assisting management in dealing with potential law enforcement actions or regulatory intervention and girding the company for shareholder litigation. It also may help preempt subsequent litigation

---

2 The information in this and succeeding sections is intended to inform readers about internal investigations and working with regulators; nothing in these materials should be construed as legal advice. In situations in which a company faces an internal investigation or is potentially subject to a government inquiry, a range of legal and strategic issues can arise; every situation presents specific challenges. When such an investigation unfolds, it is imperative—for the reasons outlined in the succeeding discussion—that management consult and engage experienced counsel.

against individual board members that charges them with a failure to act prudently in the discharge of their fiduciary obligations.

When an investigation is initiated internally or by the government, several considerations come into play. These include trying to identify the potential violation and determining if the company is a victim or is potentially liable. Management or the board of directors also will want to determine whether the investigation warrants the creation of a group to oversee the investigation, such as a special committee of the audit committee or the board. Other considerations include the following:

- Will the fraud or alleged act of misconduct be investigated internally or externally?
- What is the company's existing document preservation policy and what issues should be considered with regard to the growing complexity of electronic document preservation?
- How does the company and its management team plan to ensure attorney-client privilege?
- Will a restatement occur as a result of the investigation into the fraud?

Additional considerations include devising a plan for making public statements and appointing a spokesperson who may possibly be an attorney. Lastly, in some cases, the possibility of leniency does exist. The regulatory agency may have a standard policy for fielding requests, providing some sort of regulatory safe harbor for voluntary self-reporting companies, or providing avenues to lessen sanctions if the company's full cooperation so warrants. These issues are covered in more detail in the succeeding sections.

Identifying Violations, Preventing Further Damage, and Determining Liability

A company's first goal is to identify whether it could be considered to have liability for a potential violation or whether the cause of the concern is an employee committing a violation and the company is a victim. A company will have criminal liability for the acts of its employees, officers, and agents only if (1) the employee, officer, or agent acted within the scope of his or her apparent authority granted by the company, and (2) the employee, officer, or agent acted for the benefit of the company.

In our scenario, the CEO, CFO, and Controller at Grand Forge created a plan to fictitiously manipulate the earnings over an 18-month period, and, therefore, Grand Forge could have criminal liability. In this case, the management team, led by Bill, Jon, and Christopher, and the company itself benefited by realizing more revenues from the manipulation of the reserve accounts. Bill and his team received bonuses directly related to the performance of Grand Forge, and Grand Forge's earning per share and stock prices increased dramatically as a result of the schemes; therefore, both could have criminal liability.

If a company is a victim of an employee's potential violation of law, the company should fully consider the repercussions of not cooperating fully with a government investigation, which could include the possible adverse publicity that could result. If the company may have liability as a result of the employee's potential violation, the company must carefully assess its liability and account for that liability in the strategic response to the potential violation.

In the preceding scenario, Jacob needs to determine what liability Grand Forge could suffer based on the potential violations of Bill and his team and, additionally, the pros and cons of cooperating with a government investigation into the matter.

Appointing Special Committees

For any internal investigation to succeed, it must have the support of a management team committed to seeing it through to its conclusion, wherever it may lead. To ensure its unencumbered success, after the initial decision is made to embark on an investigation, day-to-day decisions about its scope and direction should ordinarily be left to those responsible for the investigation. In the Grand Forge scenario, special consideration should be given to who is responsible for the investigation, in light of the fact that the highest levels of management are alleged to be involved, and who will receive the status update and results during the progression of the investigation.

Correspondingly, management should appoint to the investigative team an officer of the company with sufficient authority to effectively support the investigation and serve as management's liaison to counsel. When outside counsel has been retained, that liaison might be the corporation's general counsel or an attorney on his or her staff, the internal audit director, or the corporate compliance officer. If the matter is being investigated by in-house staff, management is particularly well advised to manifest full support for the investigation and provide complete cooperation. Based on these facts, Jacob decided to retain assistance from outside counsel to assist in the investigation, and Jacob was the liaison from outside counsel to the board of directors of Grand Forge.

The concept of an internal investigation is extremely flexible; it can be as formal or informal as the company chooses. It can be staffed entirely at the company's discretion, and its scope can be predetermined and later expanded or contracted at the company's will.

Notwithstanding this apparent flexibility in structure, however, the decision of whether and how to launch an internal investigation is a critical one and calls for the exercise of informed judgment by management, in-house counsel, and the board of directors. As Grand Forge dealt with in our hypothetical scenario, during the company's early grappling with what are often vague allegations of wrongdoing, there is substantial room (indeed, a need) for consultation with counsel experienced in conducting corporate investigations, as well as with the particular regulatory and government agencies who might later be involved. The perception by the government and public of how the company is handling the investigation can be critical, and obtaining the input of an outside professional, devoid of internal "protective" instincts, should be carefully weighed.

On receipt of information suggesting the existence of internal irregularities, it is appropriate that management or the person responsible for the investigation discretely obtain records and other documentation and conduct a limited number of informal "interviews" to help them decide how best to proceed. In that regard, care should be taken not to signal to employees that management has formed an adverse judgment; that employees are under suspicion; or, as in our case, the highest levels of management do not feel they are under suspicion. Documents, including employee e-mails and computer records, may need to be gathered and reviewed confidentially. Ultimately, answers to the questions found in box 11-1 will greatly influence management decision making.

Reviewing a Case With Regulators

Typically, the first concern of management upon receiving a subpoena or notice from a regulatory agency about a pending inquiry is to learn as much as possible about the allegations or circumstances giving rise to the regulatory scrutiny (the procedures for which have been addressed in the preceding "Internal Investigations" section of this chapter). The company will first want to determine for itself whether the allegations have merit; second, it will want either a member of the internal investigative team or the company's counsel to contact the governmental agency in charge of the investigation to obtain as much information as possible about their investigation and the issues surrounding it. Depending on the nature and extent of the regulatory inquiry, the company often will engage external lawyers and forensic accountants to assist the company in responding to the regulatory inquiries and conducting fact-finding procedures to determine what remedial actions are needed if the allegations prove to be true.

Although numerous federal, state, and local agencies conduct investigations of companies and their employees' activities, the agencies most frequently encountered by company financial executives and accountants are the SEC and DOJ. These two agencies monitor the activities of public companies, uphold the integrity of the financial markets, and investigate any wrongdoing. Although attorneys with these agencies will limit any disclosures to what is within the subpoena, additional information often can be gleaned from comments these government attorneys make about the subpoena and the company's expected response.

The SEC will neither confirm nor deny the existence of an investigation unless and until it becomes a matter of public record. Depending on the nature of the issues of concern to the SEC, it will either commence an informal or formal inquiry. Most SEC inquiries involving allegations of fraudulent financial reporting or other violations of securities

Box 11-1: *Special Committee Appointment Considerations*

- Is the allegation or controversy known publicly? Is it known to the government?

- If an allegation is substantiated, what is the potential for adverse regulatory action?

- Could the conduct lead to prosecution? Is it criminal in nature?

- What is the potential corporate liability for the acts of the company's employees?

- Who are the potential subjects of the investigation? How high in management are they?

- Once a wrongdoing is revealed and if it is substantiated, what is the potential that the conduct at issue will result in civil litigation and the imposition of liability?

- Could a failure to investigate lead to later civil liability of board members?

- Once employees understand that an internal investigation is underway, what is the potential that documents, e-mails, or other important evidence will be discarded, interfered with, or destroyed?

- Is there an obligation to report the allegation to an insurer under a directors' and officers' liability policy?

- What will be the cost of an internal investigation if external professionals (counsel, forensic accountants, and technical experts) are required?

- If the allegations are substantiated, what effect will they have on management's required certifications of its financial statements?

- What disclosure to outside auditors might be required?

- Will some restatement of income be required in this period or in prior years?

- If so, could such restatements trigger debt covenant defaults?

- Are the allegations the result of a whistleblowing complaint? Is there the possibility that there already exists a qui tam action?

- Could the conduct at issue lead to disbarment or exclusion from any government programs or contracts in which the company is engaged?

- What effect will a failure to appropriately respond have on the integrity of the company's existing compliance programs?

- What is the likelihood that existing audit or compliance systems are deficient?

laws commence as an informal inquiry. During the informal phase, the SEC will request that the company voluntarily produce specific information that typically includes documents (for example, company records, including electronic evidence such as employee e-mails), internal interview summaries, and other testimony. It is common for an informal inquiry to escalate into a formal investigation, provided the facts support further investigation. During a formal investigation, the SEC uses its subpoena and enforcement powers to conduct a thorough investigation of the issues of concern, leveraging the company's internal investigative findings.

As stated on its Web site, the SEC conducts its investigations confidentially for two main reasons.[3] First, the agency feels it can conduct investigations more effectively if its investigations are not announced publicly. One particular concern is the preservation of evidence conceived as necessary for investigation; for instance, important documents and evidence can be destroyed quickly if people hear of an investigation. Second, investigations are kept

---

3 See the "Division of Enforcement" section on the Securities and Exchange Commission's Web site at www.sec.gov/about/whatwedo.shtml.

confidential to protect the reputations of companies and individuals. If the agency finds no wrongdoing or decides that it does not have sufficient evidence to bring a successful action against the company or any of its employees, then it can close the investigation without further involving the company in a public debate.

The existence of an SEC investigation becomes public when the company under investigation makes a public disclosure or the SEC files an action in court as part of its internal administrative process. Information about public enforcement actions is posted on the SEC's Web site.

Along with the SEC, the DOJ also plays an essential role in the fight against sophisticated economic crime. The Criminal Division of the DOJ supervises enforcement of all federal criminal laws, except those specifically assigned to other divisions. However, the scope of the Criminal Division's jurisdiction is not limited to criminal matters; it extends to civil matters as well. The statutes currently administered by the Criminal Division are set forth in the United States Attorneys' Manual (USAM) Title 9, quoted as follows:

> The Criminal Division will provide assistance to a U.S. Attorney in any matter within the jurisdiction of the Division. The Division will also attempt to assist a U.S. Attorney in any matter related to the Federal Rules of Criminal Procedure or Speedy Trial Problems. Finally, the Division will serve as a conduit for a U.S. Attorney to a higher authority within or without the Department on matters within its jurisdiction. (USAM Title 9-1.000, "Department of Justice Policy and Responsibilities")

Depending on the agency conducting the investigation and the attorney in charge of it, some useful information can be obtained through an initial contact session. In particular, the company or its attorneys may be able to determine whether the company or only selected employees are the subject of the investigation and who are the proposed witnesses, subjects, or targets of the inquiry.

For example, it is the stated policy of the DOJ to advise a grand jury witness of his or her rights, if such witness is a target or subject of a grand jury investigation.[4] The DOJ defines a *target* as a person about whom the prosecutor or grand jury has substantial evidence linking him or her to the commission of a crime and who, in the judgment of the prosecutor, is a putative defendant. A *subject* of an investigation is a person whose conduct is within the scope of the grand jury's investigation.

Importantly, an officer or employee of an organization that is the target of an investigation is not automatically considered a target, even if such officer's or employee's conduct contributed to the commission of the crime by the target organization. The same lack of automatic target status holds true for organizations that employ or employed an officer or employee who is a target. Box 11-2 outlines three critical preparatory steps when a company is facing a governmental investigation, regardless of whether the investigation is being driven by the SEC, DOJ, or any regulatory other body.

Box 11-2: *Key Business Considerations when Working with a Governmental Investigation*

- The company should work with the regulatory agency as much as reasonably possible to understand the premise and objectives of the investigation. Even in the context of an ongoing investigation, the company being investigated may be able to guide or influence the agency's activities in some reasonable regard.

- The company should determine if it or its outside counsel will be permitted to attend interviews or meetings conducted by the attorneys or investigators retained by the agency.

- The company should advise both its current and former employees about the investigation, appropriately inform them of its scope and purpose, apprise them of their rights, and give them instructions on preserving all evidence in their possession or control, including electronic evidence such as e-mail.

---

4 United States Attorneys' Manual Title 9-11.000, "Grand Jury."

If the company makes an early determination during the period of its being investigated that cooperating with the investigating agency is in its best interest, or if it at least determines that it has not yet found sufficient information to conclude that it should not cooperate, then the company or some member of the investigative team should contact the lead attorney or investigator from the agency conducting the investigation to obtain as much information as possible about the investigation's premise, scope, and planned course. Because the company will want to demonstrate its willingness to cooperate, it would be helpful to obtain the following information as soon as possible:

- Who does the regulator or investigator want to interview? Learning this gives the company time to notify the relevant employees and determine if the employees should obtain outside counsel to assist them.
- From whom does the regulator plan to request documents for review? This is important so that the company can develop a plan to generate document production batches for the regulator within the requested time frame.
- What time periods are subject to investigation? What are the issues involved? By establishing what time periods are subject to the review, the company and its document production team can set up search terms to expedite the requests for information.
- How soon does the regulator want to start conducting interviews and reviewing documents?
- Will or should the company or its outside counsel plan to be present for interviews of employees or former employees? (On a side note, company management should be aware that its counsel or representatives will almost never be permitted to attend the interview of an employee represented by separate counsel.)

Once a company has made its best attempt to determine the scope and structure of the regulator's investigation, management needs to determine whether the affected current or former employees should have outside counsel.

Of course, a regulator's intent in conducting interviews is to gain as complete an understanding as possible of the pertinent facts and circumstances surrounding his or her investigation. For individual employees who have retained their own counsel, some consideration must be given to whether a joint defense agreement is necessary between company counsel and the separate counsel for employees. This consideration will be addressed later in this chapter.

Advising Employees About Investigations

The regulatory agency performing the investigation may choose to interview employees either at work or outside of work. The company also may choose to interview witnesses that the government is interviewing about their knowledge of the issues under investigation. In advance of such interviews, the company may want to ease their employees' concerns about the process, typically by sending a letter informing said employees that they may be contacted or by personally speaking with them. All written materials shared with company employees regarding an investigation must be written with the knowledge that it also will likely be read by government attorneys. The letter to these employees may include the following:

1. An overall description of the investigation
2. A general description of an employee's rights about what they can do if an interview is requested
3. A statement that either the company or separate counsel may assist the employee, usually at the employee's option, in the initial stages of an investigation, and that the company will pay for the employee's legal assistance
4. A recommendation that the employees ask for identification from any government agents asking for an interview and advising them to inquire about why he or she is being requested for that interview

Additionally, the letter should include reminders that, first, the employees should be honest in response to questions asked by a government investigator and, second, that the employee has the right to take notes during his or her interview.

How Interviews Are Recorded

Most investigative interviews conducted by government agents are relatively informal, and, typically, no formal record of the interview is made, other than notes taken by a nonattorney government representative. These notes and recollections form the basis for any false statement charge against an employee if the government determines that the employee had made false material statements during the interview. In some cases, however, the interview may be a more formal proceeding with a transcript made; certainly, all grand jury proceedings are recorded and transcribed. To the extent possible, an understanding about what type of recording will be done should be obtained for the employee by the company or counsel when it is trying to obtain the structure of the investigation.

Providing Documents: A Critical Process?

Only in rare situations will the government seize company documents and records under the authority of a search warrant. Not infrequently, however, full compliance with a document production request emerges as an early issue because practical difficulties can occur in fully complying with a request.

In the vast majority of investigations, the government agency issues a subpoena requiring the company to provide documents relevant to their investigation. Almost immediately after receiving a subpoena, the company needs to implement a document preservation and production plan and should quickly work with the regulatory agency to determine what documents are required to be turned over. It is critical to gain as complete an understanding as possible from the regulator of what issues the investigation is centered around and whose documents the government agency wishes to review. It is equally important for the company to ensure that documents are being produced in the time frame requested by the investigative agency.

Electronic document production is increasingly becoming the principal part, and in some instances the entirety, of a company's response to a government subpoena. Due to the number of technological issues regarding electronic document location, review, and production and the time required to manage these technical issues, the company must understand the scope of the electronic documents involved as soon as possible.

A number of considerations are important during this document production period. First, it is critical to determine what company documents may be responsive to the subpoena and establish their location. Of those documents, the company should determine how many are electronically stored. Second, company management should establish a useful document numbering and identification system, if such a system or an adequate litigation hold program is not in place. In those cases in which more than one regulatory agency is involved, the company will want to establish how documents are produced for all regulators. The scope of different regulatory agencies' investigations may differ, and the document organization and identification systems may vary accordingly. Third, someone will need to be responsible for overall maintenance of the hard copy master files that are being produced. Most importantly, the company should have the means to ensure that all employees comply with the subpoena and should consider using an independent law firm for obtaining and producing all documents requested by the subpoena.

Sarbanes–Oxley Requirements

The Sarbanes-Oxley Act of 2002 was passed in response to corporate scandals that severely damaged investor confidence in the United States. It is primarily intended to protect investors by enhancing and improving the accuracy and reliability of corporate disclosures made pursuant to the securities laws. Sarbanes-Oxley created new standards for corporate accountability and new penalties for acts of wrongdoing. It changed how the boards of companies and their executives interact with each other and changed their interaction with their external auditors.

The Sarbanes-Oxley Act specified new financial reporting responsibilities, including adherence to new internal controls and procedures designed to ensure the accuracy of companies' financial records. One section in particular, Section 302, "Corporate

Responsibility for Financial Reports," lays out specific requirements to address and report fraud, dealing primarily with the following assertions by management:

- The signing officers have reviewed the report.
- The financial report does not contain any untrue statements of a material fact or omission to be considered misleading.
- The financial statements and related financial information fairly present in all material respects the financial condition and the results of operations of the issuer.
- The signing officers are responsible for establishing and maintaining internal control, have evaluated the effectiveness of these controls within 90 days prior to the report, and have reported on their conclusions about the effectiveness of the internal controls.
- A list exists of all deficiencies in the design or operation of internal controls that could adversely affect the issuers' ability to record, process, summarize, and report financial data and has identified material weaknesses in internal controls for the issuer's external auditors.
- The company acknowledges any material or immaterial fraud that involves management or other employees who have a significant role in the issuer's internal controls.
- The company identifies any significant changes in internal controls or related factors that could have a negative impact on the internal controls.

Parallel Investigations

Internal or Independent Investigation: A Key Decision

Determining the composition of the investigative team is a critical early decision. When the investigation is initiated, it is important to consider whether to use an internal group within the organization or an external group that may be perceived as more independent. We focus here on selecting the individual or entity (external or internal) that will be primarily responsible for conducting the investigation and marshaling the resources available to staff the effort. In determining who will lead the investigation, the company must consider two sometimes competing objectives: first, the need for a quick, thorough, and independent investigation and one that is internally perceived as such and, second, the need for a confidential, effective, and efficient investigation.

Internal Group

If an internal investigation team is used to investigate the fraud, it is important for this team to understand that they represent the interests of the company and not the personal interests of any employee. If the internal team investigating the alleged fraud fails to adequately represent the company's interests, it could damage the credibility of the investigation and, in the end, cause more harm and risk to the company.

In reality, many complaints or allegations of wrongdoing that require an investigation can be handled internally, provided that the structure of the company allows the internal investigative team access to the necessary information needed to conduct a proper investigation. For example, in-house counsel may be a source of potential internal investigators; human resources professionals also often have the necessary skill set to conduct an internal investigation, given the proper support internally and the access to documents and company personnel. In some cases, a special committee of internal resources can be appointed as a team.

In the Grand Forge example, the special committee may consist of Jacob, Michele, and Judith, which are often the departments that get involved in the formation of this special committee.

External Group

If a company is under investigation from an external regulatory body, they may decide to use an outside group to conduct the parallel investigation of the alleged fraud. In such a case, the company must decide which independent counsel or forensic accountants should perform the investigation. Appointing an outside party to conduct an investigation has discrete advantages, including the perception of objectivity and independence, as well as gaining specific expertise for the subject matter of the investigation. The skills, experience, and objective and independent approach that an external investigation team brings to the investigation can lead to a more thorough approach; often, it can lead to a more effective investigation and clearer outcome. Potential external investigators can include forensic accountants, legal counsel, private investigators, and police enforcement agencies. When reviewing how it should assemble the investigative team, the company needs to thoroughly assess what is at stake and who will be the most likely outside entities, including not only the regulators and prosecutors but also shareholders and the media, to later assess how well management responded to the circumstances prompting the investigation.

Ultimately, several additional pragmatic factors should be considered, which are as follows:

- First is the desirability of using counsel to lead the investigation by providing the investigative effort with confidentiality privileges ordinarily attending communications between attorney and client (that is, the attorney-client and attorney "work-product" privileges) in an effort to discover facts in anticipation of litigation and ensure management's ability to control the extent of later disclosures of its results
- Second is the need to maintain the integrity of the investigation by insulating the effort from inappropriate influences of management and assuring actual independence
- Third is the importance of preserving independence
- Fourth is the completely reasonable and sensible desire to minimize the cost and disruption of an investigation to the fullest extent possible

In making a final determination of the investigative team, at least four separate staffing scenarios can be reviewed. These four alternatives are reviewed as follows:

Alternative One: Compliance, Internal Audit, or Human Resources Personnel

Companies often have highly experienced, well trained, and truly independent nonlegal professionals on staff that management will trust to conduct a thorough and independent inquiry. At certain times, particularly when dealing with relatively routine, "lower-exposure" cases of fraud, it is entirely appropriate for management to choose its own internal compliance, audit, or human resources staff to conduct an investiga-

tion. This team would then report its findings either to in-house counsel or directly to senior management or the board of directors.

This approach has its limitations. For example, it should be avoided if there is a risk that the suspected fraud or controversy will significantly expand or if it may invite public or government scrutiny at a later time. The results of an internal investigation and interview notes generated during its course may not be protected by privilege, creating the risk that at some future point the company may be compelled to disclose them in a government investigation or in private litigation. In the Grand Forge scenario, the company must avoid assigning personnel to the investigation who may have been involved in or contributed in some way to the relevant conduct, either through an affirmative act or inaction or oversight or supervision of the employees or conduct involved in the investigation. The personnel involved in the conduct of the investigation should not have a reporting obligation to managers potentially assigned to the investigation.

Moreover, there will always be the perception or speculation by outsiders, no matter how ill-founded, that an internal investigator is susceptible to influence by management; the investigator was directed, instructed, or supervised by persons involved in the underlying matter being investigated; or the internal investigator was influenced not to make adverse findings for career-advancement factors. This perception is particularly troublesome when the company anticipates that it will be important to later convince a prosecutor that the company acted promptly and responsibly to unearth evidence of internal misconduct in an effort to avoid, defer, or limit the scope of an otherwise enormously disruptive and costly government investigation. Most prosecutors are skeptical of the results of any purely internal inquiry, due to concerns about the lack of integrity and independence, and many are cynical toward the sincerity of management's early pledges of full cooperation.

It does bear noting, however, that this perception on the part of prosecutors is frequently ill-directed. Management's decision not to fully disclose the particulars of any given internal investigation to the government, relying instead on attorney-client privilege to limit or shape its disclosures, is often prudent and fully justified by factors having nothing to do with a desire to hide information from the government. Limiting dissemination of the full results of an investigation to the government reduces the risk of a "waiver" of the privilege that could later result in required disclosures to persons outside the government who have an interest in using it adversely against the company (for example, to plaintiff's counsel in class-action shareholder litigation). It also can strengthen the company's ability to report the results internally in a completely candid manner, in order to foster self-criticism and an open dialogue regarding the crafting of effective remedial measures and controls. Nonetheless, perception is often reality in the eye of the beholder, and management must be mindful of the suspicions that abound among agents and prosecutors regarding management's motives when launching an internal investigation that is staffed entirely by corporate employees.

Alternative Two: In-House Counsel

Precisely because of the concerns of impartiality, independence, and influence previously cited, tasking in-house counsel with lead responsibility for an internal investigation is commonly not advisable in anything other than routine settings. In-house counsel may suffer many of the perceived (or actual) limitations burdening the compliance officer or internal auditor. These include a lack of true independence and their potential involvement directly or indirectly in the events leading to the controversy, including their having given or not given internal advice regarding the matters at issue before they became the subject of the investigation. They also include the conception of the general counsel's self interest in not being critical of senior management.

Importantly, the privileged nature of the inquiry, which is one of the main benefits of using counsel to conduct the investigation, may be only illusory in this context because in-house counsel often serves management as business advisors, separately and apart from providing purely legal

advice, and it may be difficult to later turn back a challenge to the company's invocation of privilege to shield the results of the investigation during civil litigation. With the increasing frequency of global investigations in which a company's or employee's conduct could impact operations in multiple countries, the laws of privilege of all relevant countries also must be considered. Most European countries, for example, do not recognize attorney-client privileges for in-house counsel. Nevertheless, assuming that in-house counsel does not take the lead in the matter, there can be, as addressed subsequently, significant benefits to using in-house counsel as prominent members of the investigative team.

Alternative Three: Outside Counsel

In today's highly charged regulatory and litigation environment in which perception is often all-important, management frequently resorts to outside counsel to lead an internal investigation about any material controversy, whether or not litigation is expected.

The advantages of using outside counsel are numerous and most are obvious. Some of the advantages are as follows:

- Retained counsel often brings a greater sense of objectivity to its task. The advantage of being an outsider means the attorney can recognize and balance the needs of all corporate constituents, from regulators and shareholders to management and employees, rather than being conscious of reporting lines and internal chains of command.
- At the same time, the outside attorney can focus on the "end game" (that is, the civil litigation that might result or later regulatory or law enforcement consequences).
- Findings and recommendations, often viewed as coming from a fresh and unbiased view of the facts, can carry more authority internally among management and the board.
- Frequently, too, outside counsel is in a position to mobilize quicker, bring greater resources, and undertake the assignment without day-to-day operational demands that often impede in-house legal staff.

Management electing to use outside counsel to conduct the investigation has other benefits. Importantly, the use of outside counsel provides the greatest assurance that management will retain maximum flexibility in terms of its later decisions about disclosing the investigation's results to the government, shareholders, and others. Lower- or mid-level employees who know critical facts may be more willing to divulge these facts to an outsider than to an internal investigator for fear (well founded or not) that they might be viewed by management as disloyal long after the investigation is concluded. Using outside counsel provides a greater perceived assurance to shareholders that the company is acting responsibly and that the circumstances leading to the investigation will be discovered, disclosed, and addressed. Outside counsel also may be in a better position to provide expert legal advice about potential violations of law or potential liability, especially if those matters pertain to an area requiring highly specialized legal assistance.

Most importantly, as alluded to previously, prosecutors, agents, and regulators are typically skeptical about the results of purely internal efforts. Outside counsel can provide a greater demonstration of objectivity, particularly if the investigation by the outside law firm is being conducted by a team including one or more former DOJ attorneys, which is not uncommon. Former DOJ attorneys are presumed by the agency to be experienced in the investigation of complex financial and commercial criminal matters, knowledgeable about the decision-making processes of prosecutors and regulators, and capable of communicating effectively and clearly with law enforcement. Such former prosecutors or enforcement counsel, often with years of experience in investigating matters in a grand jury setting and in preparing for criminal trials, can bring a unique skill set to an investigation. Their training often further enables them to effectively plan and "sequence" interviews, assess evidence in a way similar to his or her counterpart in active government service, and be watchful for efforts by witnesses to conceal documents and other evidence or affirmatively mislead. They can be particularly adept at questioning witnesses who find themselves in a position in which their conduct may be at issue or could be questioned and who, therefore, suffer conflicting interests.

In addition, the government investigator or prosecutor heading the criminal investigation or regulatory inquiry is much more likely to presume that outside counsel experienced in conducting investigations, whether former prosecutors or regulators, will avoid investigative missteps that might later be seen as influencing the substantive accounts given by witnesses. Management needs to be careful to choose counsel who will not only maintain the integrity of the investigation but will be viewed by the government as being above reproach.

In-house counsel are, of course, intimately familiar with the company, its culture, and personalities; they are known to management and employees and are seen as less of a threat. As a result, in-house counsel can play an important support role as a liaison, leading efforts to gather hard copy and electronic documents, conduct preliminary interviews, brief outside counsel, and so on in a far less disruptive (and less costly) manner than if these tasks were all assigned to outside counsel. Also, in some limited circumstances, structuring a hybrid approach in which an investigation is conducted by the in-house staff, who are supervised by outside counsel, may be appropriate.

Alternative Four: Special Investigative Counsel

At certain times, controversies arise that are of such sensitivity and magnitude that the board will be convinced, for the sake of complete independence and the appearance of the same, to find and retain outside counsel who have never previously represented the company and who can serve on a one-time basis as "special counsel" tasked with conducting a top-to-bottom investigation. Such outside investigative counsel work under the supervision of the board of directors' audit committee or a special board committee responsible for the investigation and frequently engage forensic accountants to provide support. This is a particularly compelling alternative if the company's current principal outside firm is somehow involved in the matter under investigation, even if only peripherally. Occasionally, too, it makes sense in cases that dictate particularly specialized legal expertise.

For additional information about working with counsel during an investigation, see chapters 6 ("Roles and Responsibilities: How Different Stakeholders Work During Investigations") and 10 ("Working with Attorneys: The Relationship With Counsel").

Securing Information

Protecting and producing evidence is critical in any investigation, and the investigator must secure all pertinent physical evidence and documents. Counsel experienced in conducting investigations will have an inventory of items to be gathered (usually including e-mails, informal notes, calendars, expense reports, toll records, and other electronic records), and management should provide the support necessary to ensure that the task is accomplished fully and expeditiously. The company's normal document retention policy should be suspended along with the regular practice of recycling back-up tapes.

Once discovered, and assuming his or her intent to conceal, the destruction of records or data by a manager often assures his or her indictment. Individuals who might be viewed as subjects of the investigation should not be asked to gather documents; rather, uninvolved personnel should be enlisted. Document destruction can have disastrous results for the company as well. In more extreme cases, in which spoliation of evidence is possible, internal audit or compliance staff may be enlisted to secure documents, and IT professionals may be used to obtain electronic records and secure computer assets for review. Chapter 7, "Sources of Evidence," covers how to secure evidence in greater detail.

Document Preservation: Policy and Practice

The process of securing books, records, data, and other materials for an investigation can be disruptive, and in many circumstances, it can have adverse effects on morale. Moreover, employees are often quick to judge that an investigation means some

wrongdoing has occurred, which is not necessarily the case.

In these cases, the disruption and demoralization can be lessened if the company issues a memorandum that outlines the importance of preserving documents. The communication should point out that, even if no wrongdoing is discovered, having preserved documents helps the company to later convince the government and public of the integrity of the investigative process. In choosing to send such a notice, management should consult with counsel to ensure that the memorandum, or other internal communications to affected employees, does not have the opposite and inadvertent effect of encouraging destruction of documents and other evidence.

Another way to ensure the preservation of information and documentation that may later be relevant to an investigation is to have an effective, systematic process and formal policy for document retention and records management. The goal of such a policy is to achieve the following:

- Retain important documents for future use and reference.
- Delete documents that are no longer necessary for the proper functioning of a company.
- Organize important documents for efficient retrieval.
- Ensure that all employees are aware of the document retention policy and that, as a result of this understanding, each employee should know what documents should be retained, the length of their retention, their means of storage, and when and how they should be destroyed.

State and federal laws require companies to maintain certain types of records for particular periods. Failure to properly maintain the correct records for the correct amount of time could subject the company to penalties, fines, and obstruction of justice charges and have a negative effect on a company's position in a litigation matter. Chapter 7, "Sources of Evidence," covers how to preserve evidence in greater detail.

Protecting Attorney–Client Privilege

Everyone preparing documents during the investigation should assume that anything prepared can and will be used in subsequent legal proceedings. Whether legal counsel are asked to conduct the investigation themselves or instead are retained to advise those company employees who conduct it, the attorney-client privilege must be maintained in connection with documents produced for investigators or generated by them.

Government seizure of computers, servers, and hard copy files inevitably prompts questions about the agents' sensitivity toward the privileged nature of legally protected and highly confidential files, such as those containing communications between clients and their attorneys. Generally, a document is privileged and protected from disclosure (and seizure) if it constitutes or reflects any communication between the company and its lawyers that is intended to have been confidential and was made for the direct or indirect purpose of obtaining legal advice or assistance. Even records showing the transmittal of documents to lawyers may fall within the scope of the privilege. Of course, privilege can be waived; importantly, also, it does not extend to communications with counsel that have been shared with third parties.

From the perspective of the forensic accountant, investigator, or executive responsible for an investigation, it is important to recognize that financial records and mere "transactional documents" prepared by counsel are ordinarily not covered by the privilege. Records reflecting the payment of fees to counsel, for example, are not necessarily privileged; however, although attorney billing statements may reflect on their face the activities of your attorneys on your behalf, the detail on activities represented in the underlying records may be protected from disclosure, either as attorney-client privileged communications or on the strength of the attorney work product doctrine.

Under that doctrine, government investigators are typically not entitled to obtain so-called "work product" materials (that is, materials generated or prepared by counsel in anticipation of litigation or that reflect an attorney's independent thought

process, counsel's legal analysis, and the efforts of counsel in anticipation of litigation). Because counsel frequently task a corporate client's employees with gathering records and documents for attorneys' further review, those instructions and compilations also may be protected from disclosure, insofar as they effectively constitute the work product of the attorney (on a principal-agent theory) or are reflective of the attorney's mental impressions.

Both the attorney-client and work product privileges must be stringently guarded so they are not inadvertently waived. Protecting these privileges is even more important when the company has already commenced its own internal investigation about matters likely within the scope of the search warrant. The proliferation of e-mail communication between counsel and client virtually assures that company e-mail servers contain confidential work product and other privileged material. As a result, if company electronic records are seized by government investigators and some of the information seized is thought by the company or its attorneys to be privileged, it is important that the existence of privileged materials is immediately disclosed to the investigating agents, that those communications with the agents are promptly documented, and that the company catalogues for counsel the types of privileged documents that were likely seized so that appropriate relief can be obtained, if necessary.

Distinguishing between privileged and nonprivileged information in legal files demands some thought. When agents engaged in a search believe themselves authorized to seize nonprivileged materials in the company's legal files, a separate team is sometimes assembled to determine what materials are nonprivileged and therefore subject to seizure. In such cases, the agents will have been instructed to cursorily review only the headings of file folders or the captions of documents to ascertain whether those files are likely to contain privileged (and relevant) material. If this review occurs on the company's premises during the execution of a search warrant, it is important that these activities be closely monitored. Typically, in such circumstances, the agents involved permit counsel or senior management to be present to observe their conduct and the procedures employed by them to prevent inadvertent seizure of privileged materials and to protect against later claims that there was wholesale rummaging through legal files.

Obviously, if an internal investigation has already begun and interview memoranda and the like exists in the files, effort should be made to urge the agents to simply set those files aside (that is, not even review the documents for privilege) pending a negotiated review process agreed to by the prosecuting attorney and your counsel.

Protecting Proprietary Data

As a general proposition, U.S. courts are far less protective of proprietary data than they are toward protecting attorney-client privilege and confidential communications. The courts also are familiar with fashioning protective orders to prevent the further dissemination of proprietary information; these sorts of orders are granted daily in civil cases, and if the company subject to a search believes that its files or subfiles contain highly proprietary data, it should inform the government's investigating agents and their counsel. The government might not be required to return such data, but upon appropriate application by counsel, it can be prevented from sharing the data with competitors and witnesses.

Encouraging Employee Cooperation

Needless to say, employees are frequently upset by a search and investigation and seek assurances from company management about what the search might mean to them. However, it is not advisable to discuss the search, investigation, or any presumed implications with individual employees or groups of employees while the search is being conducted. Following an encounter as stressful as the intrusion of law enforcement officers into their place of work, employees will likely not accurately remember what a manager has told them or may misconstrue the manager's words.

Correspondingly, however difficult it may be to avoid such discussions, the recommended course is to inform the employees that the company has pledged its full cooperation to the investigation. The company may decide to hold a meeting with the employees in the days after the search to discuss it.

As difficult as it may be, company personnel should resist any inclination to talk substantively about the circumstances underlying the investigation or declare the company's innocence. Management should allow the situation to defuse, addressing employees only after having had time for reflection and counsel. The company's legal counsel can advise management precisely about what can and should be said to employees after the search. In most situations, days will have passed, allowing time for a script to be prepared.

Providing Legal Counsel to Employees

Conflicts occur frequently during internal investigations. An employee under investigation for sexual harassment, for example, may be subject to discipline by the company; the company, on the other hand, needs to protect itself from possible government investigation and private litigation. In such a case, the company's and the individual's interests obviously conflict. In many instances, therefore, the attorneys or law firm advising the company cannot represent both the company and the individual employees of the company during an investigation. Even in circumstances in which representing both parties is technically permissible, it may not be advisable. This applies equally to in-house and external counsel.

In circumstances in which a company is under investigation (such as investigations of accounting or customer fraud), the company and the individual employee appear to have a common interest— avoiding company liability. However, the employee's interests may diverge from the company's if that employee has or may have information that could create liability for the company. If made aware of an actual conflict of interest, a court would not allow an attorney to represent both parties; often, the court requires the attorney to withdraw from representing either party. Also, government investigators are inherently skeptical about one attorney or law firm representing both the company and individual employees.

In almost all circumstances, the same attorneys cannot represent both the company and individual employees because of legal reasons and the need to maintain the appearance of independence and uphold that independence in fact. As a result, in communications with employees, a company should inform employees that its attorneys represent the company, not the employees. Typically, this is most important in prefatory conversations before interviews of employees because the company will want to mitigate against future claims by an employee that company attorneys led him or her to believe that the attorneys represented the employee. Such a claim, if upheld, could prevent the use or disclosure of information that the employee provides during an interview.

Although informing employees about this policy is necessary, its communication need not be forceful, aggressive, or alarming in tone or substance; a simple statement that the company's attorney represents only the company for the purposes of the investigation is sufficient. Moreover, in some cases, the company may want to pay for separate legal counsel for one or more employees; under many state laws and employment agreements, companies are required to pay for employees' separate legal counsel. Of course, companies are not required to pay legal fees for employees who have violated a law that subjects the company to liability, and many state laws prohibit a public corporation from paying legal fees of an employee or officer who has been convicted of a felony. Until a conclusion has been reached that an employee has violated a law, however, the company should usually pay his or her attorneys fees and seek reimbursement if the employee is found to have violated the law.

Notwithstanding the preference—if not the requirement—for independent counsel, a company's attorneys often work closely with employees' attorneys. A common strategy of sharing information obtained during the company's investigation, and in the employee's separate interviews by his or her attorney, is frequently the best defense to a government investigation or civil litigation. Concomitantly, attorneys for the company and its employees may form a "joint defense agreement" to document their common interests and specify the conditions under which information will be shared. If the company and its employees have a common interest, the attorney-client and the work product privileges will extend to the separate attorneys' shared communications.

Planning for Public Statements

Imagine television cameras showing footage of government agents carting off box after box of a company's records, along with hard drives, laptops, work stations, and servers. Any executive faced with such a picture would feel the urge to defend themselves and his or her company immediately and publicly.

The executive should refrain from reacting quickly, consult with counsel, and urge the company to express its intent to fully cooperate with law enforcement and defer comment about the expected progress and outcome of the investigation. When the facts precipitating an investigation become known, management has an important role in managing the flow of information, both internally and externally. They should be prepared for the alleged fraud or its investigation becoming public and recognize that negative publicity about a suspected fraud or investigation of wrongdoing could trigger shareholder lawsuits. In such circumstances, it is advisable to retain a public relations firm that specializes in so-called "crisis communications." At the same time, the company should designate one spokesperson to respond to media requests and coverage.

External audiences are not the only concern. Premature disclosure of a controversy or investigation can trigger rumors and have disruptive effects, including the possibility that employees might tamper with or destroy evidence. This strongly suggests that, if the particulars of the matter are not generally known, information regarding the investigation be disseminated internally on a strict need-to-know basis. Legal counsel responsible for the investigation need the opportunity to quietly gather information and conduct preliminary interviews without un-due distraction. Further, because securing physical evidence is of critical importance, counsel should be given the full opportunity to do so before disclosure.

If internal disclosures are premature (that is, issued before management has been able to obtain a clear understanding about the magnitude of the controversy or issue), then the rumors can invite media inquiries, further spur the interest of regulators or law enforcement, and even prompt litigation. At some point, if for no reason other than to avoid speculation and rumor, management may deem it advisable to make a brief statement to employees, announce the commencement of an internal investigation, and express management's commitment to a prompt and thorough review and resolution. For obvious reasons, that statement should be crafted and delivered only upon consultation with counsel. Typically, no public statement regarding the results of the investigation should be disseminated until the investigation is complete.

Once a company sees the facts of an investigation made public, its initial reaction to anticipate and manage media inquiries is often to craft a statement that suggests how the company will manage and minimize the expected impact of the search and investigation of the company's business. At times, such statements are appropriate, but it is advisable to consult with legal counsel first. Frequently, the company will have little idea regarding the precise scope and direction of the investigation, and often, the less said the better.

Restatements: Managing the Process

Enron, WorldCom, Tyco. The list of multibillion dollar frauds over the past 10 years is a long one. In most of these cases, companies have made restatements of their financial statements. If a restatement of previously issued financial statements is necessary, the company should consider the following as it tries to get through this costly endeavor:

- Communicate with the media, analysts, and other relevant members of the public that there will be a restatement.
- Provide information through disclosure or other means to explain why the restatement is necessary without disclosing the findings of the investigation.
- Determine if any existing members of management were involved in the accounting decisions that led to the financial restatement and whether any action should be taken.
- Consider Section 304 of the Sarbanes-Oxley Act of 2002, which discusses forfeiture of CEO and CFO bonuses and profits.[5]

For more information regarding financial statement restatements, please review chapter 3, "Financial Statement Restatements: Protocols and Process."

Disciplinary Action

After any discovery of fraud or financial wrongdoing, some action must be taken to recover from the damage, revisit the control environment, and set a tone for the future. Disciplinary action is a necessity in such circumstances, especially because the employees should know the consequences of breaching the fundamental code of conduct at the company. That code, along with any other documents and policies in place, such as an ethics policy or fraud prevention policy, help establish the tone and culture in an organization. They also must be enforced; a company with a weak tone or culture that does not follow the code of conduct and other documents that spell out the disciplinary action in an organization can create an environment susceptible to management override, financial misstatement, and fraud.

In developing its disciplinary approach, the organization should consider all of the following:

- Executive management develops a clear and explicit message related to fraud and the organization's tolerance to such actions.
- The organization maintains a strong control environment.
- The organization explicitly discusses expectations related to fraud and acceptable behavior.
- The organization encourages reporting of unusual or fraudulent activities.
- The organization maintains formal programs to broadly and frequently communicate the code of conduct and other related documents that depict the disciplinary action of the company.
- The organization conducts formal training on fraud awareness and ensures that employees read and understand the code of conduct and other disciplinary items.
- Executive management and the audit committee take swift and decisive actions to address fraud, as well as appropriately communicate the lessons learned.
- Disciplinary actions are clearly communicated and consistently applied.

---

5 Sarbanes-Oxley Act of 2002, Section 304. Available at www.sec.gov/about/laws/soa2002.pdf, p. 34.

Additional discussion of post fraud investigation activities can be found in chapter 14, "Antifraud Programs."

Conclusion

As Jacob found out as a result of the investigation performed at Grand Forge, there are multiple factors to consider when faced with the issue of investigating a potential allegation of wrongdoing. A potential or actual criminal investigation or regulatory proceeding, receipt of a grand jury or administrative subpoena, a search warrant, document preservation issues, attorney-client privilege, and possible restatements are the most frequently recurring investigative scenarios. They are also the types of adverse circumstances companies always hope to avoid, and they require effective management responses and often difficult judgments. Faced with any or all of these, management is well advised to promptly enlist the assistance of a legal team that includes not only experienced counsel but also a forensic accountant with experience in investigating "white-collar" fraud, the defense of such investigations, and corporate compliance. The adverse appearances that can flow from management missteps are often hard to shake and they can significantly and negatively affect the outcome of an investigation or enforcement action. Not only can these professionals guide the company through the investigation, they also can help the company avoid errors that affect the perceptions that government officials form about the company or its individual managers.

Bibliography

The Sarbanes-Oxley Act of 2002. *Section 406, "Code of Ethics for Senior Financial Officers"* Baker McKenzie Draft Document from David Laing

The First 72 Hours of a Government Investigation, A Guide to Identifying Issues and Avoiding Mistakes, *Sheila Finnegan, Volume 10 Number 2 February 2006* Baker & McKenzie

12

Reporting on Fraud

Ruby Sharma, Partner/Principal
John Tsai, Senior Managerr

Introduction

As discussed in earlier chapters of this book, matters involving fraud often require forensic accounting services.[1] Forensic accountants provide litigation services, usually only acting as consultants to an attorney or expert witness. Fraud investigation is one of the many services considered litigation services. A forensic accountant is often retained to perform a wide range of consulting services, including litigation services.

After the investigation has been performed and data has been gathered, the forensic accountant may prepare a written report of his or her findings under the direction of in-house counsel or external counsel. The objective of the report often is to present the findings and observations to the client or opposing party in a litigation matter.

In addition, the Sarbanes-Oxley Act of 2002 states that all fraud findings should be reported to the client's audit committee. The report will usually provide a description of the work performed; interviews conducted; exhibits, data, and other documentation supporting the findings; and observations.

The accounting firm should ensure that the findings and observations detailed in the report follow the professional standards listed by the AICPA.[2] The professional standards used to provide the services, as well as the standards and guidelines followed to issue a report, are determined by the specific objectives set forth by the client.[3] For example, in the Grand Forge Company[4] case study, as in most fraud investigations, the client is seeking recommendations or advice about a certain matter involving fraud or allegations of fraud.

This chapter provides an overview of the various reporting standards that apply when an accounting firm is hired in a litigation services engagement. The chapter will further discuss in detail the types of standards that apply when issuing a report for a fraud investigation. The first part of this chapter discusses the standards used when issuing reports on fraud engagements and the circumstances under which these standards are applied. The second part of this chapter discusses in detail the various guidelines related to the preparation and distribution of such reports.

Reporting Standards

One form of communication between the accounting firm and the client is a written report. The practitioner from the accounting firm should be careful in his or her wording to avoid giving the impression that the report follows additional standards when it does not. For instance, words such as *assure, review, ensure,* and *assurance* could be associated with auditing standards and should be avoided when issuing a written report based on consulting standards provided to the client.

Statements on Standards for Consulting Services (SSCSs) are issued by the AICPA Management Consulting Services Executive Committee. This committee issues pronouncements in connection with consulting services. Consulting services provided to clients have broadened from just accounting-related matters to a range of services over various industries and practices, including tax services. For fraud investigations, specifically in the context of litigation, the SSCSs require the results of the investigation be communicated to the client. The SSCSs do not specify what form of communication; this decision is determined by the arrangement made between the client and its practitioner.

The client may request the practitioner perform procedures that are not categorized into one of the specific standards. The prescribed forms may require the accounting firm to report findings based on

---

1 According to the AICPA Forensic and Valuation Services Practice Aid 07-1, *Forensic Accounting & Fraud Investigations*, no specific standard terminology is used to name the accountant's litigation services assignment when fraud is suspected or alleged. Many terms are used interchangeably, including forensic or fraud audit, examination, investigation, or accounting.

2 Statements on Standards for Consulting Services issued by the AICPA.

3 Paragraph .03 of ET section 92, *Definitions* (AICPA, *Professional Standards*, vol. 2), defines the client as "any person or entity, other than the member's employer, that engages a member or a member's firm to perform professional services or a person or entity with respect to which professional services are performed."

4 The reader is invited to read the detailed case study of Grand Forge Company found in the Introduction to this book.

limited procedures applied to certain assertions. Under these circumstances, the rules and guidelines of a regulatory body or third-party user (for example, federal rules governing discovery) for which the reporting is intended may indicate to the practitioner the nature and extent of tests and other procedures required. In such circumstance, the procedures and guidelines set forth are effectively the agreed-upon procedures that will be the framework for the investigation. In an agreed-upon procedures engagement, the practitioner does not provide an opinion or negative assurance. Instead, the agreed-upon procedures report is in the form of procedures and findings. Because each party has a specific role in agreeing upon the procedures performed or to be performed, the use of the report is restricted to those specified parties.

The application of professional standards in an engagement that requires litigation services requires a deep understanding of the client's specific needs. In order to select the most applicable professional standard, the client and the accounting firm can use the decision tree in appendix A to determine the professional standards that apply.

Guidelines for the Preparation of the Report

Work Product and Report Formats

Communication with the client, attorney, and trier-of-fact about the results from work and events may take many forms. Generally, the practitioner would issue a written report to communicate the fraud investigation's results and findings. Although no standard proscribed formats are required, one should consider including certain basic elements in the written reports. In certain circumstances, the client may require the written report to be prepared in accordance with Rule 26 of the *Federal Rules of Civil Procedure* (Federal Rule 26) because the practitioner is serving as a testifying expert witness and is required to issue a written report to be submitted to the court. If that is the case, specific defined elements must be included in a Federal Rule 26 report. Federal Rule 26 reports will be discussed in more

detail later in this chapter and are also discussed in Chapter 10, "Working With Attorneys: The Relationship With Counsel."

General Written Report Format

The nature and format of reports in fraud investigations vary widely from case to case. This generally depends on the nature of the case, the counsel's recommendations, the practitioner's personal preference, and the needs of the client. As a result, no standard reporting format is appropriate for all fraud investigations. It is recommended that certain pertinent facts be considered for inclusion in the written reports. The minimum elements for written reports, such as a report to document the findings from a fraud investigation, should include the background, scope and objectives, findings and recommendations, restriction on the use of the report, date, and signature. Additional language may be used for specific circumstances that arise from the investigation.

Background

The background section provides a brief description of the engagement and, if necessary, a discussion about the client and the parties involved. The background forms the basis for the scope of the engagement and provides the reader the context on the subject matter to be covered in the body of the report. In our case study, Perusi & Bilanz LLP would provide a summary describing the pertinent parties, the current accounting procedures in the Shanghai office, and the allegations of wrongdoing.

Scope and Objectives

A section summarizing the scope and objectives of the work performed and any exclusion is an essential part of the accounting firm's report. The related activities not covered in the scope are described, if necessary, to clarify and delineate the boundaries of the investigation. The nature and extent of work performed also are described in this section. Alternatively, the accounting firm may reference the engagement letter (indicating the date of that letter) when a description of the scope of the engagement is included. When appropriate, the language specifying that the work product and report does not constitute an audit or review, in accordance with any generally accepted auditing or review standards, should be included in this section. An example of such language may be as follows:

> Unless otherwise noted, the information in this report is based on assertions made by individuals or contained in documents provided to Perusi & Bilanz LLP and has not been tested for veracity and accuracy. The procedures that Perusi & Bilanz LLP performed were advisory in nature and do not constitute an audit or other attest service, as defined by the AICPA. Further, they do not constitute an audit of Grand Forge Company's historical financial statements in accordance with generally accepted auditing standards, nor do they constitute an examination of prospective financial statements or an examination or review of a compliance program in accordance with standards established by the AICPA. The procedures were necessarily limited in scope and cannot be relied upon to detect fraud or other illegal acts.

This preceding statement is necessary to ensure that the reader understands that the work was performed in accordance with consulting standards and did not include an audit or review of the data noted in the report. This also assists to clarify that the consulting work does not offer any type of assurances on the financial data used in the written report or examined as part of the engagement.

In certain agreed-upon procedures engagements, the report should provide a detailed description of any agreed-upon materiality limits used during the engagement. Although engagements performed under agreed-upon procedures generally follow consulting standards, the guidelines are eventually set forth by discussions between the client and the practitioner. As a result, it is essential to include a list of the procedures performed and related findings.

In our case study, Perusi & Bilanz LLP would describe what they were engaged to do as agreed upon in their engagement letter with Grand Forge Company. Perusi & Bilanz LLP also would include a list of general procedures that were performed as part of their investigation (for example, obtained an understanding of Grand Forge Company's Shanghai office organization and accounting procedures, interviewed selected Grand Forge Company personnel, reviewed certain accounting transactions, and so on). This list of procedures should follow language stating that the procedures were performed under the direction of counsel, such as "At the direction of Grand Forge Company's Office of the General Counsel, Perusi & Bilanz LLP performed the following procedures as part of its investigation."

Findings and Recommendations

The results of the work also should be disclosed in the report. Issues or findings are pertinent statements of fact that outline significant items identified and documented throughout the engagement. The report should list issues in order of significance or risk to the client. Less significant or lower-risk issues may be communicated orally or through informal means of communication when agreed to by the client. It may be appropriate to include information about positive aspects of the client's business (for example, improvements since the last engagement) to fairly represent the existing issues and provide perspective and balance to the report. If applicable, based on the scope and objective of the engagement, general or specific recommendations are provided describing suggestions for action to correct existing conditions or improve operations. For example, in some circumstances, it may be desirable to recommend a general course of action and specific suggestions for implementing the recommended course of action. In other circumstances, it may be appropriate only to suggest further investigation or study. At times, the recommendations may be developed with the client.

In our case study, Perusi & Bilanz LLP would document its findings related to the allegations and quantify the accounting errors related to the abusive practices by Grand Forge Company's employees in its Shanghai operations. Prior to finalizing its documentation of the findings in the report, Perusi & Bilanz LLP shared its tentative findings with select Grand Forge Company senior management to confirm their understanding and quantification of the accounting errors. Grand Forge Company senior management pointed out that although two of the allowances for bad debt accounts were high, the amounts were reasonable and not part of the abusive accounting practices by its employees like the other accruals and allowance for bad debt accounts. Grand Forge Company senior management explained that, based on recent communications with these two clients, they do not expect to be paid in full. As a result, Perusi & Bilanz LLP adjusted their quantification of accounting errors. The practitioner may not always be aware of certain nuances due to his or her lack familiarity with the client's operations or certain communications with client personnel, and such a confirmation process with the client may explain certain irregularities.

Restriction on Use

Another section that should be included is the limitation and restriction on the use of the practitioner's report. The practitioner should advise the client that the report is not to be distributed to anyone outside the client, unless specified other users have been identified and the specified users have signed applicable third-party access letters. Specific language should always be included to restrict the use of the practitioner's report. Further details for this section can be found in the "Limiting the Use of Reports" section later in this chapter.

Date and Signature

Lastly, the report should be signed and dated. Generally, the report is dated the day it is signed and issued, which is different from the day the work was completed. For instance, the fieldwork for a fraud investigation may be completed on a certain date, but the accounting firm's report may not be issued until a week later. It is typical that the written report would not be issued until several days subsequent to the conclusion of the fieldwork. The practitioner would typically need time to complete his or her analyses, summarize his or her findings and recommendations, and draft the written report. The report also would need to pass through several levels of quality reviews by managers and partners of the accounting firm before it is issued to the client.

The date the work was concluded should be clearly specified in the body of the report. When management's responses are included, the report may be dated on the day that all of management's responses are received. When a signature is required on the report or cover letter, the practitioner is responsible for signing the report in the accounting firm's name, unless applicable professional standards or local legal or regulatory requirements dictate otherwise.

Additional Language for Specific Circumstances

For specific circumstances, other language may be included in the written report. One situation when additional language would be advised is when the engagement involves working as part of, or jointly with, a client team, and the client issues the report in a manner that associates the firm with the report. The accounting firm should consider requesting the client include a clarification statement, such as the following, which pertains to the case study:

> Perusi & Bilanz LLP assisted in a joint project, and the results of Grand Forge Company's work are included in this report. However, this report is the responsibility of Grand Forge Company.

Another situation when additional language would be recommended is when a client requests the engagement team include findings and recommendations from work prepared and reviewed only by client personnel. In such a case, it would be advised that a clarification statement, such as the following, which pertains to the case study, be included:

> These findings and recommendations, along with the underlying work, were performed and reviewed by Grand Forge Company personnel.

Federal Rule 26 Reports

According to Rule 26(a)(2)(B) of the *Federal Rules of Civil Procedure*, those experts who are "retained or specially employed to provide expert testimony in the case or whose duties as an employee of the party regularly involve giving expert testimony" must provide expert reports to the other parties in the case. The practitioner may be engaged as a consultant, an expert witness, or both. Sometimes, the practitioner may begin an engagement only as a consultant and then later be designated as an expert witness. If a Federal Rule 26 report is required because the report will be submitted to a court as part of a litigation matter, certain elements must be included in the expert's written report.

Federal Rule 26 requires experts to prepare written reports before delivering an opinion testimony at trial. The report must completely state the expert's opinions and include any exhibits that exemplify or support them. The basis, as well as substance, of opinions and conclusions and the methodology followed also should be in the report. Any other data and information that the expert considered must be included in the report, as well. In addition, details of the expert's qualifications should be disclosed in the report, including a list of publications from the past 10 years, a list of cases in which the expert testified during the past 4 years, and the compensation paid to the expert for his or her study and testimony. The Federal Rule 26 sections that the practitioner should include are as follows:

- *a.* Table of contents
- *b.* Executive summary
- *c.* Introduction and background
- *d.* Scope of the engagement that includes adopted assumptions or unaddressed issues, explanation of major work steps, or tasks and roles of any other parties who participated in the engagement
- *e.* References to source documents relied on to formulate the expert's opinion

For additional discussion of Federal Rule 26 reports, review Chapter 10, "Working With Attorneys: The Relationship With Counsel."

Written Work Product Other than a Report

If written work products other than the report are issued, the accounting firm should ensure that the information being provided to the client is information that can be included in the final report. These results can be are summarized in a presentation and the findings also should be referenced in the full report or work product that is ultimately provided to the client. The practitioner may be asked to provide any or all of the following:

- **(1)** A review of the client's procedures or control documentation
- **(2)** Summary presentations
- **(3)** Draft policies related to a business process
- **(4)** Strategy documents instead of a report

The client also may request formal or informal interim progress reports throughout an engagement. Interim progress reports, if the engagement letter included such provisions, also may be used to document potential scope changes. Interim progress reports and work products can be either written or presented orally. The reports are critical to communicate engagement issues. As a result, these interim progress reports generally should be included to form part of the engagement documentation and should be maintained, subject to the policies regarding retention of such reports agreed upon with the client.

Maintaining Confidentiality of Work Products

Rule 301, *Confidential Client Information* (AICPA, *Professional Standards*, vol. 2, ET sec. 301), of the AICPA Code of Professional Conduct refers to litigation services and states that, "[a] member in public practice shall not disclose any confidential client information without the specific consent of the client." The only situation in which this may not apply is when the accounting firm is ordered through a subpoena or court order to disclose confidential information. For certain engagements, information might be protected through protective orders. Protective orders can be as general as signing an agreement to maintain confidentiality of information, but they also can be as specific as keeping information from a particular party.

In a fraud investigation, the practitioner should consider being retained by the client's in-house or external counsel on behalf of the client. As an example, in our case study, Grand Forge Company would not engage Perusi & Bilanz LLP directly. Instead, Grand Forge's external counsel would retain Perusi & Bilanz LLP on behalf of Grand Forge Company. The attorney-client privilege protects communication between a client and its attorney, thereby maintaining confidentiality. This privilege is available to both corporate clients and individuals and applies to communications between attorney and client and vice versa. In the case of a fraud investigation requiring forensic accountants, the attorney-client privilege is then extended to the forensic accountants who are retained by the attorney on behalf of the client.

Privilege is maintained if all information gathering is performed at the direction of the client's in-house or external counsel. In our case study, if Perusi &

Bilanz LLP was retained by Grand Forge Company's external counsel, all information gathered by Perusi & Bilanz LLP in its investigation could be considered privileged and may not be readily available to the opposing side in the event of a subsequent civil lawsuit. However, if a criminal prosecution arises, access to the information may be granted, regardless of whether the material is marked "attorney-client privilege working paper." For instance, if the Department of Justice (DOJ) issues a subpoena or simply a request to the corporation to waive its attorney-client and work product protection, the work products may have to be turned over, regardless of the privilege that may have existed.[5,6] To further preserve privilege for working papers and reports, the working papers and reports should be marked as "attorney work product" and should not be disseminated without discussing the situation with the client's external counsel. This includes updating the client's senior management with an interim status report regarding the investigation.

Specific communications pertaining to the practitioner are protected via attorney-client privileges insofar that the practitioner is retained by the client's external counsel on behalf of the client. Certain communications, such as the final written report and the intermediate working papers, are a main concern for protection. A written report prepared by the accounting firm is protected under the attorney-client privilege if the report is only delivered to specific relevant parties, such as the board of directors, the audit committee, or certain individuals of management. However, should the report receive wider distribution, the client may appear to be voluntarily waiving their privileges. In certain circumstances when the client loses privilege due to providing the report to a government agency, the client could procure an agreement with the government agency to keep the report confidential. Nevertheless, this does not guarantee complete confidentiality.

Likewise, the working papers supporting the practitioner's written report also are protected. Some examples of working papers include interview notes, memorandums, affidavits, declarations, analyses that support the written report's conclusions but are not included in the written report, and so on. These are protected by the work product doctrine that states that tangible material or its intangible equivalent that is collected or prepared in anticipation of litigation is not considered discoverable and is protected from disclosure. Nevertheless, it is possible that the privilege could be waived by virtue of disclosure.[7]

In some instances, the client or its external counsel, or both, may prefer not to have a written report even when the practitioner's work is protected by the attorney work product doctrine. The attorney work product doctrine is not absolute and can be readily challenged. For instance, by showing undue hardship, the opposing party can obtain an order exempting an accounting firm's work from the attorney work-product privilege. As a result, a chance still exists that a written report containing possible negative implications for a client's case may be turned over to the opposing party.

Indicating Document Status

Any expert witness retained to present evidence at a trial or other evidentiary proceeding and any personnel working at the direction of such expert witness are required to preserve all documents, including draft reports and electronic data, which have been reviewed or created by or at the direction of the expert witness. It is important to ensure that during the preparation of the report, the phrase "Draft—Subject to Change" is clearly indicated on each page. The term "Draft—Subject to Change" should only be removed when providing the final report to the client.

It is common for legal disputes to go through several rounds of settlement conferences before they are settled in court. For this purpose, the

---

5 January 20, 2003, memorandum titled *Principles of Federal Prosecution of Business Organizations* from former Deputy Attorney General Larry D. Thompson to Heads of Department Components and United States Attorneys.

6 October 21, 2005, memorandum titled *Waiver of Corporate Attorney-Client and Work Product Protection* from Acting Deputy Attorney General Robert D. McCallum Jr. to Heads of Department Components and United States Attorneys.

7 There has been significant controversy within the legal community surrounding recently enacted policies and regulations regarding the mandatory waiver of attorney-client privilege and work product doctrine in the context of corporate investigations conducted by federal agencies.

practitioner may provide analyses strictly for the settlement discussions and have that information precluded in court should the settlement fall through. In this situation, documents should be labeled with language, such as "Prepared at the direction of counsel for settlement discussion purposes only." This label is important to clarify the purpose and use of the accounting firm's analyses or report so that it will not be misconstrued later on if the settlement talks fall through and the parties go to trial.

Working Paper Documentation

Although the consulting standards do not have any specific working paper requirements, preparing and maintaining working papers are still important because they are the basis for forming opinions, as well as any advice provided to the client. One specific area in which one's working papers are closely examined is litigation. In litigation matters, working papers are not subject to discovery unless the role of the practitioner is an expert witness. The AICPA *Professional Standards* apply to expert testimony and require that the opinion expressed be reached using reliable principles and methods properly applied to the source data and facts of the case. However, regardless of the role, the working papers should be prepared and kept under the belief that they will be scrutinized by others.

A number of factors need to be considered when preparing working papers. The main purpose of the working papers is to support the analyses and conclusions stated in the report, so the information in the working papers should reflect the results of the investigation. The working papers should exclude extraneous information that was not relied upon when forming one's opinion and not used to arrive at the conclusions. In addition, one should be sensible in any annotations and markings, including highlighting, on working papers because they become part of the working papers. When considering annotations, watch for conclusions that may have become superseded as the engagement progressed. The working papers also should follow the methodology applied to the data set to arrive at the opinion.

Working papers that support the opinion generally are not introduced as exhibits at a trial because the trier-of-fact usually has neither the inclination nor the ability to review the working papers. However, the opposing party may use the working papers as evidence of carelessness or erroneous conclusions if the opposing party finds errors or inconsistencies in them. The opposing party also may introduce the working papers as evidence if the opinions they support are contrary to those of the expert.

In order to guard against such use of working papers, the contents of the working papers should be carefully controlled and avoid the inclusion of irrelevant materials. The working papers supporting the opinions should be retained and properly organized so that the practitioner can find the source materials that are the bases for the opinion. It should be noted that the practitioner cannot remove anything after receiving a subpoena. Any relevant documents prepared by the accounting firm, whether they support the opinions stated in the report, must be produced in response to a subpoena.

It is worth nothing that working papers labeled as "subject to the attorney-client privilege and/or attorney work-product doctrine" may lose the privileges if the practitioner's role changes to that of an expert witness and the practitioner's working papers become subject to discovery.

Review of Reports and Work Products

The typical investigation is usually led by a partner from the accounting firm. On large scale investigations or investigations that span multiple countries, the accounting firm may deploy multiple partners to handle different work streams or different countries. The lead partner on the engagement (engagement partner) should always review each report and work product, including interim progress reports and interim work products, prior to providing the report to the client. Evidence of timely review by the engagement partner should be noted in the documentation. For example, the engagement team may prepare memorandums to the file or make annotations that should be reviewed and signed off on by the engagement partner. All required review procedures should be completed prior to issuance of the reports or work products. These review requirements also apply to the final input the engagement team provides to a client-owned report, even though the client may continue to alter the document after the team ceases its involvement.

A formal quality assurance program should be in place to ensure the quality of the work products that are submitted to the client and external parties. Appendix C contains an example of a quality assurance procedure. The example shown is a template that can be used to assist engagement teams in the effective qualifying, planning, delivering, and closing of an engagement. Appendix D contains another form that assists engagement teams to ensure quality is maintained for all deliverables and work products. The example shown is a form that could be filled out whenever the accounting firm issues a report or work product. The practitioner(s) responsible for the deliverable or work product represents that quality has been ensured throughout. The six objectives of a quality assurance program include identifying and mitigating risk on projects that are:

(1) unusually complex.

(2) designated as high risk during the engagement acceptance process.

(3) expected to last significantly longer than average (for example, longer than six months).

(4) expected to result in the issuance of a large number of reports or work products during the course of the engagement.

(5) led by an engagement partner who has joined the firm within the preceding six months.

(6) utilizing a new service (that is, a service not previously used to deliver a client engagement).

Once the engagement partner reviews the report or work product and is satisfied with it, the report or work product should be submitted for a preissuance review. A preissuance review also should be a component of the accounting firm's quality assurance program. A quality assurance partner (sometimes known as an independent review partner), who is another partner of the accounting firm other than the engagement partner, generally will function as a preissuance reviewer. The preissuance reviewer, at a minimum, reads the report or work products and summary memorandum, refers to the engagement

letter to confirm the scope of services provided, and discusses significant matters with the engagement partner. The preissuance reviewer also may read selected engagement documents (for example, project descriptions, procedure summaries, and memorandums describing significant findings) to objectively evaluate significant engagement execution and reporting matters.

The engagement partner should schedule the preissuance review as early as possible to avoid delays in providing the report to the client. The engagement partner also should consider involving the preissuance reviewer at various interim stages of the engagement to facilitate a timely final preissuance review. In addition, the involvement of the preissuance reviewer is more extensive when the engagement is higher risk, more complex, or employing an unconventional methodology.

In certain situations, if counsel and the client permits, the practitioner and the suspected wrongdoer could review the draft report. This allows the suspect to counter any findings, recommendations, or conclusions. However, for these meetings, the presence of the client or counsel is often requested by the practitioner.

Guidelines for Deliverables to the Client

Communicating the Conclusion of the Engagement

The nature of some engagements is such that the completion date is not evident (for example, those engagements that do not result in the delivery of an oral presentation or written report to the client). In these situations, the completion date might be specified in the engagement letter. If the completion date is not specified in the engagement letter, it may be communicated in a cover letter accompanying the final bill, or the practitioner may obtain acknowledgement from the client that the engagement has been completed.

Report Audience

An accounting firm that is involved in a civil fraud investigation should be aware that a parallel proceeding, such as a criminal investigation, may also be underway. As a result, the accounting firm's findings of the case may be presented to law enforcement authorities or subpoenaed. Examples of law enforcement agencies or personnel include the FBI, the SEC, the DOJ, the Office of Inspector General, the U.S. Attorney General, the CIA, and other federal and state regulatory agencies. Because dealings with law enforcement agencies and personnel are likely to involve highly sensitive, confidential, and even classified information, a heightened sense of confidentiality is recommended in such cases.

Presenting findings to law enforcement is highly specific to individual engagement circumstances, and consultation with senior management of the accounting firm who are familiar with legal issues, law enforcement, regulatory, and governmental procedures is strongly advised. In certain circumstances, the accounting firm's Office of the General Counsel should be involved. In all cases, the law firm retained by the client should be involved in this process. Similarly, if a meeting with a law enforcement or regulatory agency is requested or arranged, all appropriate authorization must be obtained from the senior management of the accounting firm prior to such a meeting. This also applies to any decision making or final determination of disclosure to law enforcement. Again, the law firm retained by the client should be involved and be an integral part of this process.

Returning to our case study, the abusive accounting practices resulted in a material error in accruals accounts, and a restatement of Grand Forge Company's financial statement was required. As a result, Grand Forge Company notified the SEC of the issue and worked with its financial statement auditors to begin the preparations for a restatement. The SEC requested specific analyses and supporting documentation, as a result of this disclosure. Perusi & Bilanz LLP has agreed to assist Grand Forge Company in preparing some the requested analyses. Now that the SEC is involved, Perusi & Bilanz LLP decided that a preissuance reviewer with SEC experience should be involved in the engagement.

Limiting the Use of Reports

Another section of the report would its use. Typically, fraud investigations are conducted for the benefit of the client. Accordingly, the practitioner should advise the client that the report is not to be distributed to anyone outside the client, unless specified other users have been identified and they have signed applicable third-party access letters. In addition, the accounting firm should not agree to the inclusion or referral of its report in a public document (for example, an offering circular or registration statement). For instance, in our case study, Perusi & Bilanz LLP's report would contain language, such as the following:

> This report is intended solely for the information and use of the management of Grand Forge Company and is not intended to be and should not be used by anyone other than these specified parties. Perusi & Bilanz LLP, therefore, assumes no responsibility to any user of the report other than Grand Forge Company. Any other persons who choose to rely on our report do so entirely at their own risk.

In certain instances, it is encouraged to limit the use of disclaimer language for a variety of reasons. Instead, the accounting firm might prefer to use an annotation, such as a header, footer, or title, to convey the limitations in the analyses. An example would be to include a more specific title, such as using the name of the case or dispute on the pages of the report.

If it is determined that the audience should expand beyond the client, the practitioner should work with the client to specify the audience for the report, so that the findings can be properly communicated. When the report is to be distributed outside the client, the consent of the client (or former client) is requested before making the engagement documentation available to others. Unless the accounting firm is precluded from doing so under the terms of a subpoena or other legal process, the review of the documentation is part of a peer review or quality review performed by a regulatory authority, and the right to review by designated third parties is included in the engagement letter or designated by a process of law.

Such consent is obtained in writing and signed by the executive in the client's organization who has the authority to provide the consent. In obtaining the client's consent, the accounting firm should determine whether the client has an adequate understanding of what has been authorized, and the practitioner should inform the client about sensitive matters contained in the documentation. In addition, the practitioner should consider offering the client the opportunity to read the documentation before obtaining consent.

Issuance of Report

The report is considered issued when it is printed, signed on firm letterhead, and the final copy has been sent to the client (or meets other completion criteria agreed upon with the client in the engagement letter). When the report is in the form of a presentation or other written work product by the accounting firm, it is considered issued when the transmittal letter is signed on firm letterhead and sent to the client. If the client agrees to electronically formatted reports, the final report is typically prepared in a format that retains the original source image of the document (for example, an Adobe Acrobat PDF file) and sent via an appropriate transmission method with consideration of the confidentiality and sensitivity of the information. Further guidelines for electronic formats of a report are discussed subsequently.

Sending Electronic Reports

The practitioner should consider creating documents in a format that retains the original source image of the document to decrease the risk of inadvertently including confidential client or accounting firm metadata information to third parties. When the client requires an electronic copy, the practitioner should convert the file, whether it is a docu-

ment (Microsoft Word), spreadsheet (Microsoft Excel), or presentation (Microsoft PowerPoint), to a format that retains the original source image of the document (Adobe Acrobat PDF) and transmit that file rather than the source file. Such transmission removes the possibility of disclosure of nonvisible historical data and metadata information. The format that retains the original source image of the document is more secure because it prevents the alteration of critical documents by the recipient.

Reissuance of Reports

Reports are typically issued shortly after the completion of the work or in accordance with the timing or other protocols agreed upon with the client. Delays due to disagreement with the client regarding factual matters should be promptly communicated to the client. Delays due to internal matters should be resolved as soon as practical. If the engagement team determines that a progress report, interim report, or the final report contains a significant or material error or inaccuracy, the accounting firm should determine whether the matter is significant enough to warrant issuing an amended report. When an amended report is issued, the accounting firm identifies the information being corrected and distributes the report to all individuals included in the original report distribution. The amended report should be dated contemporaneously and reference the date of issuance of the original report.

Conclusion

Reporting under different fraud litigation services requires an understanding of the applicable standards and guidelines. These standards help safeguard and minimize the practitioners' exposure regarding fraud engagements. An investigation into fraud or allegations of fraud is necessary to determine whether the allegations are true, who is responsible for what alleged wrongdoing, and how far back the fraudulent activities have been committed. Litigation services associated with fraud include investigations of suspected fraud, investigations of specific assertions of fraud, or quantifying losses due to fraud.

Fraud investigation is one of many services considered litigation services.[8] Litigation services are classified as transaction services in SSCS No. 1, *Consulting Services: Definitions and Standards* (AICPA, *Professional Standards*, vol. 2, CS sec. 100), and are subject to SSCSs and the professional standards embodied in the AICPA Code of Professional Conduct. Appropriate adherence to applicable standards ensures that the practitioner is always mindful of the fact that the work is properly performed and documented and avoids the risk of public embarrassment and loss of professional reputation.

---

8 Litigation services and applicable professional standards are discussed in AICPA Consulting Services Special Report 03-1, *Litigation Services and Applicable Professional Standards.*

Appendix A
Decision Tree to Determine the Application of Professional Standards

Practitioners can use the following decision tree to determine which professional standards apply in a litigation services engagement.[9] The Grand Forge Company case study is applied to illustrate the application of the decision tree in appendix B.

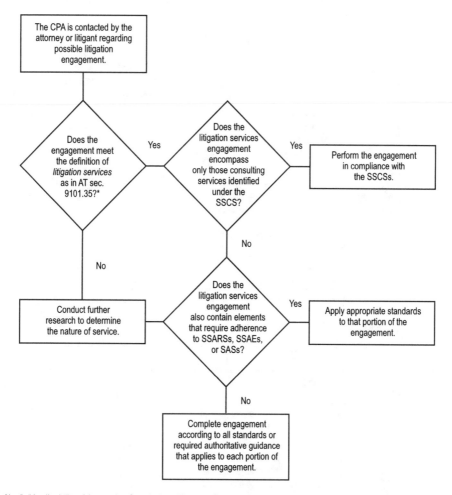

* Interpretation No. 3, "Applicability of Attestation Standards to Litigation Services," at section 100 *Attest Engagements* (AICPA, *Professional Standards*, vol. 1, at sec. 9101 par. 35)

9 AICPA Consulting Services Special Report 03-1, *Litigation Services and Applicable Professional Standards.*

Appendix B
Professional Standards Application for the Grand Forge Company Case Study*

The following questions and answers illustrate the process of determining which professional standards must be complied with in the Grand Forge Company case study:

Question: What form of service is being requested?

Answer: The answer to the question can be determined by applying the decision tree in appendix A, as follows:

Step	Criteria	Decision
1.	Does the engagement meet the definition of litigation services?	Yes. Grand Forge Company requires a forensic accounting investigation, and forensic accounting is a litigation service.
2.	Does the litigation services engagement encompass only those consulting services identified under the Statements on Standards for Consulting Services (SSCSs)?	Yes, Perusi & Bilanz LLP is requested to perform consulting services.
3.	Does the litigation services engagement also contain elements that require adherence to the Statements on Standards for Accounting and Review Services (SSARSs), Statements on Standards for Attestation Engagements (SSAEs), or Statements on Auditing Standards (SASs)?	No. See the following.
Exemption from the SSARSs, SSAEs, and SASs require a "No" answer to question (a) or a "Yes" answer to any questions from (b)-(e).		
	a. Will the practitioner issue a written communication that expresses a conclusion about the reliability of a written assertion that is the responsibility of another party?	No.
	b. Will the service comprise being an expert witness?	No.
	c. Will the service comprise being a trier-of-fact or acting on behalf of one?	No.
	d. Is the practitioner's work, under the rules of the proceedings, subject to detailed analysis and challenge by each party to the dispute?	No.
	e. Is the practitioner engaged by an attorney to do work that will be protected by the attorney's work product privilege, and is such work not intended to be used for other purposes?	Yes.
4.	Determine the nature of the elements not covered by the SSCSs, SSARSs, SSAEs, or SASs and adhere to appropriate standards or refer to available guidance.	
5.	Complete the engagement.	

Question: Would the answer be different if no formal report was requested and the results were to be supported only by Perusi & Bilanz LLP's working papers?

Answer: No, the answer would be the same. The written report is not a criterion for distinguishing engagements.

Question: If Perusi & Bilanz LLP constructs the engagement as an agreed-upon procedures engagement, would the firm be governed by AT section 201, *Agreed-Upon Procedures Engagement* (AICPA, *Professional Standards*, vol. 1), on agreed-upon procedures or by the attestation standards?

Answer: Neither. The answer would be the same. Agreed-upon procedures can be used in a consulting engagement, and the practitioner can look to AT section 201 for guidance but should not indicate, imply, or construe the engagement as falling under the attestation or auditing standards (including AT section 201).

---

*Adapted from AICPA Consulting Services Special Report 03-1, *Litigation Services and Applicable Professional Standards.*

Appendix C
Engagement Quality Procedures: An Example

This document is designed to assist engagement teams in the effective qualifying, planning, delivering, and closing of an engagement. It serves as a reminder of key engagement processes that should be completed. The work steps contained in this document should not be altered or deleted; however, engagement teams may supplement or customize this checklist with additional procedures that are specific to their respective engagements.

Each work step is manually signed off on and dated by the individual completing the task or, if the procedure is not applicable, noted with an "N/A" and an indication why it is not applicable. As indicated in the engagement quality procedures (EQPs), certain steps are required to be manually signed-off on and dated by the executive in charge (EIC) of the engagement. The EIC need not necessarily complete these steps personally but signs to indicate that he or she is satisfied the steps have been completed. It is indicated in the form when the EIC must complete the step, in whole or in part. The completed EQP is retained in the engagement documentation along with other documents supporting the completion and resolution of the applicable steps.

Client Name: _____

Engagement Name: _____

Preparer: _____

Date Completed: _____

I have reviewed the engagement quality procedures and determined that they have been completed appropriately and accurately (*provide manual signature*):

Engagement Executive or Manager: **Date:**

_____   _____

Engagement Executive in Charge: **Date:**

_____   _____

Brief Engagement Description:

Identify Applicable Professional Standards Under Which This Engagement Is Being Performed.

AICPA Consulting Standards   _____

AICPA Attestation Standards   _____

Other (must provide explanation of standards)   _____

Describe Expected Report(s) or other Work Product(s):

(continued)

Engagement Procedure	Date Completed	Completed by	Comments or References
QUALIFY			
Proposal			

1. Prior to submitting a proposal to the client (or potential client), the team should
   a. consult with and obtain approval from the engagement partner.
   b. review that appropriate terms and titles were used for non-CPAs
   c. review that appropriate verbiage, language, and terminology were used within all aspects of the proposal document or presentation.
   d. review that an adequate description of the scope and services, as well as professional fees, if applicable, are evident.
   e. review that client logos, names, trademarks, or references were used appropriately and with permission from the client.			

Client Acceptance			
2. Perform background checks on the client prior to client acceptance. *a.* The executive in charge (EIC) of the engagement signs off that client acceptance has been completed and approved if this is a new client.			
Engagement Acceptance			
3. If significant changes in client circumstances were identified during the engagement, an evaluation needs to be performed on the client.			

4. Determine if there are any potential conflicts of interest regarding any other clients the firm has at the present time.
   a. Perform conflict checks of other known parties.
   b. If there are any potential conflicts of interest identified, the firm should take steps to manage the conflict. The firm needs to document the steps taken. The firm also must obtain a signed consent letter from the client acknowledging the potential conflict of interest.
   c. The engagement partner should sign off that any potential conflicts of interests with the other clients have been appropriately considered and documented.			

5. Evaluate any engagement independence requirements. Such evaluation should include engagements performed under AICPA attest standards. Perform the following, when applicable:
   a. Confirm the status of the ultimate parent or controlling entity of the client.
   b. Confirm the approval from the engagement partner and determine that the services to be provided are not prohibited, for independence purposes, under applicable regulatory or professional standards, including Interpretation No. 101-3, "Performance of Nonattest Services," under Rule 101, *Independence* (AICPA, *Professional Standards*, vol. 2, ET sec. 101, par. .05), for nonattest services to audit clients.
   c. Have the EIC of the engagement sign off that all applicable independence matters were appropriately considered and documented.			

Engagement Procedure	Date Completed	Completed by	Comments or References

6. Perform and document engagement acceptance in order to consider and approve potential risks of the engagement. The following procedures should be performed prior to issuing an engagement letter:
  a. Determine that the proposed services are within the approved guidelines for the applicable service offering.
  b. Complete the forms to estimate engagement economics.
  c. For any engagement in which a business relationship with a third party (for example, subcontractor, contract employee, alliance partner, third-party subject matter resource, and so on) is used, obtain approvals.
  d. Have the EIC of the engagement sign off that the engagement acceptance was completed and approved and that all required engagement acceptance approvals have been obtained and documented.
  e. Have the EIC of the engagement sign off that the other required approvals mentioned in step 6(c) were completed, approved, and documented and that the use of such business relationship was disclosed to the client.			

7. Develop and issue the engagement letter (EL) or statement of work (SOW).
  a. Determine that the EL or SOW
    (1) includes the objectives, scope, and limitations of services to be performed.
    (2) restricts the use and distribution of the report, if appropriate.
    (3) addresses the responsibilities of both the firm and client staff.
    (4) discusses the work products and, if applicable, the timing.
    (5) provides for a fee arrangement, including appropriate description of the calculation methodology.
    (6) provides for a payment schedule and adequately describes the fee arrangement.
    (7) was reviewed and approved by the engagement partner prior to delivery to the client.
    (8) incorporates or references the standard terms and conditions included in the overall approved master service agreement, if issued under a SOW.			

Enter any additional comments needed relating to the EL or SOW in the following space:			
8. Obtain approval signature on the EL from the appropriate client representative. *a.* The EIC of the engagement signs off that an appropriate, approved EL or SOW was developed and executed with the client and included in the engagement files.			
PLAN			
9. The EIC understands and agrees with the client about the expectations, protocols, expected work products, and timing of the engagement.			
10. Plan and staff the engagement with the appropriate team. Discuss engagement goals, objectives, and expectations with the engagement team, including the nature, extent, form, and content of the planned engagement documentation.			
11. Develop a written work program that includes descriptions of key work steps.			

(continued)

Engagement Procedure	Date Completed	Completed by	Comments or References
12. Finalize the detailed scope of the engagement and update the EL or SOW, if appropriate.			

13. Determine that the client has designated an appropriate management-level individual to be responsible for overseeing the services, in accordance with Interpretation No. 101-3.
    Identify the individual designated by management to be responsible for overseeing the services, including his or her functional position.
    Document the procedures performed to assess and conclude whether the designated individual possesses the suitable skills, knowledge, or experience for such oversight.			

14. If this is an attest engagement under AICPA attestation standards, determine that the engagement executive who will be signing the attestation report is a CPA licensed to practice in the state in which the office issuing the report is located.			
15. Plan and perform the engagement in accordance with the applicable attestation policies and procedures. Assurance or agreed-upon procedures engagements require the participation of professionals experienced in providing these services. (*Note:* Certain attestation engagements, such as agreed-upon procedures, are subject to additional guidance.)			
16. If applicable, review and approve the quality assurance plans and programs.			
17. Review and approve additional risk management procedures, if the engagement was classified as other than low risk in engagement acceptance or continuance.			
DELIVER			
18. Create engagement documentation throughout the engagement to provide sufficient evidence to support the results of the work communicated to the client and document critical advice given.			
19. Document the software used on the engagement. Describe procedures used to evaluate the adequacy of the software or application.			

20. In regard to the work of a third-party contractor or specialist or the firm's subject matter resource
   a. evaluate and document the work performed, if the engagement involved the work of an external third-party specialist or other contractor or the internal subject matter resource.
   b. confirm that the industry sector subject matter resources and tax and other professionals were consulted, when appropriate, and that these consultations were appropriately documented.			

21. Continually assess the engagement for significant changes in engagement scope, progress (timelines), or economics (fees). Document agreed changes as an amendment to the EL or SOW and obtain approval signature of the appropriate client signatory.			
22. Determine that adequate engagement supervision of work is performed, including documentation thereof.			
23. Provide adequate client updates and project communications to an extent consistent with the timeframe and complexity of the project.			

Engagement Procedure	Date Completed	Completed by	Comments or References
24. Prepare or review appropriate documentation for consultations on significant issues, including being satisfied that those individuals consulted were informed of the relevant facts and circumstances on a timely basis and that the conclusions reached are reasonable and consistent with professional standards. 　Memorandums that address significant issues on which consultation occurred are included in the engagement documentation with written evidence of approvals by those consulted.			
25. Obtain any signed access letters, consent letters, third-party report access letters, nondisclosure agreements, acknowledgement and consent letters for any potential conflicts of interest, or letters of representation, when applicable. 　a. The EIC of the engagement signs off that all appropriate, signed external letters have been obtained.			
26. Prepare a summary memorandum.			
27. Complete required reviews, including second-level reviews and preissuance reviews (when applicable) of engagement documentation, report(s), or work product(s).			
CLOSE			
28. Draft any required engagement report(s) or other work products based on applicable professional standards and the terms of the engagement letter. Determine that the report is appropriately worded based on the nature and scope of the engagement and avoids inappropriate words. 　a. The EIC of the engagement signs off on the compliance of all applicable firm reporting requirements.			
29. Communicate the final results of the work to the appropriate client personnel. 　a. The EIC of the engagement signs off that the final results of the engagement have been communicated to the appropriate client personnel.			
30. Complete and obtain all required signatures on the engagement quality review form, when applicable. The form should be used for all engagements, unless another form has been approved for the engagement. 　a. The EIC of the engagement signs off that all required approvals have been obtained and documented on the form.			
31. Finalize and archive the engagement in accordance but not limited to • clearing and deleting review comments and to-do lists. • destroying superfluous engagement documentation, including e-mails. • not sharing draft copies of reports with the client.			
32. Communicate with the engagement team their responsibilities for conducting procedures to determine that the document retention policies have been followed. This includes determining that confidential client or personally identifiable information has been removed from the engagement documentation and other collateral devices and either returned to the client or disposed of in a secure manner when such information is not required to be retained as engagement documentation. 　Indicate in the comment column how the preceding was communicated to the engagement team.			

(continued)

Engagement Procedure	Date Completed	Completed by	Comments or References
33. Initiate an assessment of the quality of service provided, if applicable. Request that the client complete the survey, as deemed appropriate.			
34. Complete performance assessments for engagement team members, if applicable.			
35. Complete knowledge submissions, if applicable.			
36. Communicate the results of the project to the engagement partner of the client.			
37. Conduct a postengagement team meeting to debrief the team on the engagement.			

Appendix D
Engagement Quality Review Form for Engagement Reports or Work Reports

Name of Client: _____

Name of Engagement: _____

Description of reports or work products, including date: _____

This engagement quality review form must be completed on every engagement.

ENGAGEMENT TEAM'S REPRESENTATIONS

Based on my role and responsibilities on this engagement, I make the following representations:

I have completed my assignments and duties, including

- supporting engagement documentation preparation, review, retention, and filing.
- supervision and review of engagement team members' documents and associated outputs.
- preparation and quality assurance of engagement reports or work products.
- compliance with professional standards and firm policies, procedures, and practices.
- resolution of differences of professional opinion, if any.

List Quality Procedures to Be Completed Before Reports or Work Products Are Released	Completed by	Date

Representations and Conclusions	Name	Signature	Date
Staff or Senior Staff			
Manager(s) and Senior Manager(s)			

Executive in Charge*			
Preissuance Reviewer			

* The Executive in Charge and Preissuance Reviewer do not sign the engagement quality review form prior to the satisfactory completion of the open items.

13

Recovering From Fraud: Fidelity Claims and Directors and Officers Claims

Joe Galanti, Partner/Principal
Bruce Zaccanti, Partner/Principal

Introduction

The post-Sarbanes-Oxley era has seen a significant expansion of companies' and stakeholders' awareness and reporting of all three primary categories of occupational fraud: asset misappropriation, financial statement fraud, and corruption. Certainly, since Sarbanes-Oxley and even before it, the incidence of fraud is distressingly high. Recent estimates suggest that two particular types of business fraud—embezzlement and employee theft—cost American businesses an estimated $1.5 trillion each year.[1]

Although the number of fraud investigations has grown considerably in past years, and notwithstanding the heightened regulatory scrutiny of corporate financial reporting, many involved in the investigative process sometimes overlook important follow-up procedures after conclusions are drawn about the fraud hypothesis. The focus of investigations is often on whether a fraudulent act occurred, rather than on how to recover potential losses. This is understandable, but in some instances, business unit operational managers are not aware of investigative protocols or potential recovery options, such as insurance.

A typical fraud investigation involves the following seven basic steps:

1. Identification and classification
2. Planning and deployment
3. Gathering evidence and documentation
4. Concluding
5. Reporting
6. Insurance Recovery (if applicable)
7. Prosecution and litigation or negotiation and settlement (if applicable)

The focus of this chapter will be the sixth step in this process: insurance recovery. To the extent that they touch on the insurance claims and recovery process, the other steps in the typical fraud investigative process also will be discussed.

In the wake of a discovery of fraudulent activity and with a determination that fraud has actually occurred, it is incumbent on company management to ensure that such fraud does not continue and appropriate controls be implemented to prevent such fraud in the future. In addition, although often overlooked by many in the company, more work needs to be done (for example, filing an insurance claim or identifying other venues to recover losses).

Addressing fraud risk only after the fact by claiming on a policy is insufficient. Company management and fraud investigation professionals need to ensure that they consider recovery options both before and after a fraud has occurred. Insurance coverage is available for certain fraud-related risks but not all. In addition, companies might also seek recovery from the fraud perpetrators via civil and criminal prosecution. Assessing the potential fraud risks facing a company and estimating the likelihood of their occurrence and possible severity can assist management in determining what insurance coverage it might seek for additional protection against certain risks, beyond traditional controls and monitoring.

This chapter addresses the various types of insurance coverage available to mitigate fraud risk and reviews frequent requirements under such policies, along with some consideration of the process of filing a claim for recovery and related aspects of insurance. The chapter comprises three major topics:

1. Fidelity insurance coverage
2. Fidelity claims process
3. Directors and Officers (D&O) insurance liability protection

Fidelity Insurance Coverage: Types and Claims

Fraud is an unfortunate fact of life. Although companies can seek to reduce the potential risk of fraud by establishing rules and guidelines for behavior, setting a zero-tolerance tone at the top policy, instituting well-conceived internal control policies, and monitoring controls rigorously, fraud risk cannot be entirely eliminated.

Fraud is one of the primary crimes against which companies seek to protect themselves through purchasing insurance. Fidelity insurance coverage provides policyholders with protection against the risk of certain crimes, including ones committed against

---

1 Zurich commercial crime and fidelity coverages, August 2006, 2.

the insured by employees and outside parties. The surety and fidelity industry is over 100 years old and currently generates approximately $3.5 billion and $930 million in annual premiums for surety and fidelity bonds, respectively.[2]

The Surety & Fidelity Association of America (SFAA) is the U.S.-based organization that comprises insurance companies that underwrite surety and fidelity bonds. Such bonds are intended to facilitate commerce, enhance economic development, and protect consumers and policyholders from a variety of risks. The two primary types of insurance coverage available to protect companies against fraud-related risk are financial institution bonds (FIBs) and commercial crime policies (CCPs). Below, each of these is described in turn.

As with all insurance policies, each policy is different and should be reviewed carefully to determine what specific coverage is afforded therein. Policyholders should work with their carriers, brokers, and other insurance professionals to develop comprehensive programs covering specific fidelity risks against which they wish to protect themselves.

Financial Institution Bond

The FIB was introduced in 1986 as a tool for financial institutions to insure against fraud risks. It evolved from the bankers blanket bond, which was created in 1916; however, the FIB is quite different than its forerunner because the financial services industry and relevant risks significantly changed during the interim period. The FIB risk management tool is unique to the financial services industry, but the CCP is used across many industries.

The FIB covers losses discovered during the policy period, and it is subject to an aggregate limit of liability per policy period, as well as limits for each occurrence during the policy period. When the aggregate policy limit is reached, the bond is cancelled. The FIB can be terminated immediately when requested in writing by an insured or with 60 days' notice when terminated by an insurer. It also can be terminated with 60 days' notice when the insured is taken over by a receiver, a liquidator, or

the government or when the insured is involved in a merger.

To claim against a FIB in the aftermath of discovering a loss, the insured must provide notice of a loss as soon as practicable but in no event later than 30 days after the loss is discovered. A detailed proof of loss must then be filed within 6 months of discovery, unless an extension is agreed on in order to fully investigate and document the loss. Legal proceedings against the insurer cannot be filed until at least 60 days after the original proof of loss is filed and not subsequent to 24 months thereafter. The average basic deductible is generally approximately 1 percent of the total limit of liability, although all policies are different and carriers set prices commensurate with the specific risks insured. The insurer is liable under the FIB for the amount that a single loss exceeds the deductible.

Insuring Agreements and Riders

In its current form, the FIB consists of seven separate insuring agreements, each of which provides coverage for different fraud-related risks. The insuring agreements are enumerated A-G, as originally introduced in 1941 as Standard Form No. 24, a bankers blanket bond. The basic bond coverage afforded under Standard Form No. 24 comprises insuring agreements A-C and F. The remaining insuring agreements, as well as other potential riders, provide optional additional coverage.

Following are descriptions of each insuring agreement, as well as several popular riders:

Insuring Agreement A—Fidelity

Insuring agreement A provides coverage for losses directly attributable to intentionally dishonest or fraudulent acts committed by an insured's employees. It is noteworthy that unauthorized acts by an insured's employees are usually not covered unless the employee had a manifest intent to cause harm and benefit financially, which will warrant further discussion subsequently.

Certain other characteristics of the fraud also must be present for coverage to respond. Unless

---

2 See the "About the Industry" section on The Surety & Fidelity Association of America Web site at www.surety.org.

committed in connection with a loan loss claim, the illegal acts can be committed alone or in collusion with others. The insured is not required to give the insurer notice when hiring or terminating employees, although those employees' actions may trigger coverage under the policy.

The central questions that generally require affirmative answers to confirm coverage under insuring agreement A are as follows:

1. Was a loss incurred by the insured?
2. Did the loss result directly from certain acts by an employee?
3. Were these acts committed by an employee?
4. Were these acts dishonest or fraudulent?
5. Were these acts committed with the manifest intent to cause the insured to sustain a loss and to obtain a financial benefit for the employee or another?
6. Was financial benefit intended to be received by the employee or another?
7. In connection with a loan loss claim, did the employee act in collusion with one or more parties to the transactions?
8. In connection with a loan loss claim, did the employee receive a financial benefit of at least $2,500 in connection with these transactions?[3]

One of the most disputed coverage-related questions involves the term *manifest intent*, as used in the preceding question 5, and the meaning of that clause in the insuring agreement. Establishing manifest intent clearly implies the ability to assess an employee's state of mind in committing a purported fraud; thus, it is not surprising that disagreements between policyholders and carriers are fomented by this provision to secure and exclude coverage, respectively. Some believe the clause was intended to limit coverage only to acts that were truly dishonest or fraudulent, rather than those resulting from negligence, misman-

agement, or ineptitude. A company's ability to clearly establish that fact in every circumstance is not easy, and enjoining the agreement of the insurance carrier to such a claim is not always straightforward either.

Other areas frequently occasioning disputes are the preceding questions 7–8, which relate to loan loss claims. The FIB defines a *loan* as "all extensions of credit by the Insured and all transactions by which the Insured assumes an existing creditor relationship."[4] However, because claims associated with loan losses involve additional requirements, such as collusion and a financial benefit of at least $2,500 to the employee, a policyholder might seek to demonstrate that the losses it sustained related to something other than loans. Demonstrating collusion or evidencing that an employee obtained a financial benefit of at least $2,500 can be difficult, even if such activity was characteristic of the loss. For example, cash bribes can sometimes be impossible to document. If an insured cannot satisfy the additional coverage requirements related to loan losses, then only that portion of the aggregate loss not related to loans, if any, can be recovered. Thus, if a policyholder can evidence losses attributable to some nexus outside the definition of a loan, then that claim may avoid the additional requirements for coverage.

Third-party claims are one further area of potential dispute that deserves mention in connection with insuring agreement A. Generally, such claims are covered if they relate to actual payments made to third parties by the insured to settle claims attributable to dishonest acts of the insured's employees. Conversely, carriers are generally not required to afford coverage to third parties that seek claim payments directly from a separate insured's carrier, regardless of whether the dishonest acts of the insured's employee gave rise to the claim.

---

3 Keeley, Michael, and Harvey C. Koch, "Employee Dishonesty: The Essential Elements of Coverage Under Insuring Agreement (A)." In *Financial Institution Bonds*, edited by Duncan L. Clore, 28–29, American Bar Association, 1998.

4 Financial Institution Bond, Standard Form No. 24, Conditions and Limitation—Definitions, Section 1(m). In *Financial Institution Bonds*, edited by Duncan L. Clore, 683, American Bar Association, 1998.

Insuring Agreement B—On Premises

Insuring agreement B covers the loss of property on the insured's premises that results directly from robbery, burglary, misplacement, mysterious unexplainable disappearance, theft, false pretenses, and common-law or statutory larceny. It also covers loss or damage to the insured's office itself and loss or damage to furniture, fixtures, supplies, and equipment resulting from theft, burglary, robbery, malicious mischief, larceny, or vandalism, as long as the insured is the owner of such property or liable for such loss or damage. Notably, insuring agreement B specifically excludes coverage for losses caused by fire.

Coverage issues that may arise in connection with the on premises provision often involve whether the loss actually occurred on the premises, as required for coverage. For example, if a fraudster calling from a location other than the premises of a bank convinces a bank employee to purchase fictitious bonds, the bank would likely be denied coverage under the on premises provision. Because at the time of loss the fraudster was able to effect the fraudulent transfers from the bank to his or her account by telephone from a remote location and not on the premises of the bank, the loss would not satisfy the physical presence requirement of this provision.

Insuring Agreement C—In Transit

Insuring agreement C covers the loss of property resulting directly from robbery, common-law or statutory larceny, theft, misplacement, and mysterious unexplainable disappearance when the property is in transit anywhere in the custody of a messenger or transportation company (or as a replacement thereof in an emergency situation). Coverage begins upon receipt of the property by the messenger or transportation company and ends on its delivery to the designated recipient.

Insuring Agreement D—Forgery or Alteration

Insuring agreement D covers losses resulting directly from the forgery or alteration of any negotiable instrument, acceptance, withdrawal order, receipt for the withdrawal of property, certificate of deposit, or letter of credit specified in the insuring agreement. Such losses include the unauthorized transfer of funds as well as the creation of unauthorized credit lines.

Coverage issues that may arise in connection with the forgery or alteration provision involve the question of what constitutes forgery and alteration. First, the definition of forgery encompasses "the signing of the name of another person or organization"[5]; it is unclear whether this would extend to fictitious persons or payees. Second, alteration is undefined in the policy; however, courts often look to Uniform Commercial Code §307-407(a) for meaning in order to determine whether certain acts meet the threshold definition for coverage.

Insuring Agreement E—Securities

Insuring agreement E covers losses resulting directly from the insured having acquired, sold, delivered, given value, extended credit, or assumed liability for a financial instrument, based on the insured's belief that the original financial instrument obtained was authentic but which was later determined to have a forged signature or been altered, lost, or stolen. The loss can occur in the insured's account or the account of a third party. The transaction must have been entered into in good faith and the insured must have relied on the authenticity of the original financial instrument for the insured to seek coverage.

Insuring Agreement F—Counterfeit Money

Insuring agreement F covers losses resulting directly from the receipt of any counterfeit money of the United States, Canada, or any other country in which the insured maintains a branch office. The transaction must have been entered into in good faith for the insured to seek coverage. Relatively high deductibles typically accompany such coverage, so claims are rare.

---

5 Michael R. Davidson, *The Other Insuring Agreements of Commercial Crime Policies*, in *Commercial Crime Policy, Second Edition*, edited by Randall I Marmor and John J. Tomaine, 288, American Bar Association, 2005.

Insuring Agreement G—Fraudulent Mortgages

Insuring agreement G covers losses resulting directly from the acceptance by the policyholder of any real property mortgage that proves defective due to a fraudulent signature.

Computer Systems Fraud Insuring Agreement (Rider)

This rider covers losses resulting directly from fraudulent electronic data entry or a change of electronic data or computer program within a computer system covered under the rider.

Extortion—Threats to Persons Insuring Agreement (Rider)

This rider covers losses resulting directly from the surrender of property by the insured due to a threat to the insured to do bodily harm to one of its directors, trustees, employees, or partners, or a relative of any of the preceding, when such an individual or individuals have been kidnapped or allegedly been kidnapped.

Extortion—Threats to Property Insuring Agreement (Rider)

This rider covers losses resulting directly from the surrender of property by the insured due to a threat to the insured to do damage to any of its premises or properties.

General Agreements

In addition to the specific insuring agreements and riders previously enumerated, FIBs also contain the following six general agreements:

Nominees

In the event of an assignment of some or all of the insured's employees to a specific entity created to handle business transactions for the insured, any losses sustained by that entity would be treated in the same manner as if they were sustained directly by the insured.

Additional Offices or Employees: Consolidation, Merger, or Purchase of Assets—Notice

In the event of a change in the risk profile of the insured due to growth in its business through consolidation, purchase, merger, or acquisition, written notification from the insured to the insurer is required before the effective date of such combination. Written consent related to the expanded coverage must be obtained from the insurer, and any additional premium must be paid prior to securing coverage. Notice and additional premium payments are not required for organic growth until the next policy period.

Change of Control—Notice

In the event of a change in control of the insured, the insured is required to provide written notice to the insurer upon the insured's learning of the change. *Control* is defined as "the power to determine the management or policy of a controlling holding company or the Insured by virtue of voting stock ownership."[6] A change in direct or indirect ownership of 10 percent or more of the voting stock is considered a change in control for this notice provision.

Representation of Insured

The representations of the insured made in its application for the bond must be complete, true, and correct. "Any misrepresentation, omission, concealment, or any incorrect statement of a material fact" can result in rescission of the bond by the insurer.[7]

Joint Insured

In the event that multiple insureds are covered under the bond, the first named insured will act for all insureds. If the first named insured ceases to be covered, the next named insured will act for the remaining insureds. Aggregate losses for all insureds are limited to the amount that would have otherwise been sustained if there was only one insured. In addition, knowledge of one of the insureds is deemed to be possessed by all of the insureds.

Notice of Legal Proceedings Against Insured—Election to Defend

In the event a legal proceeding is brought against the insured, it should notify the insurer as soon as practicable but in no event later than 30 days

---

6 See the "General Agreements" section of Financial Institution Bond Standard Form No. 24.

7 Ibid.

after notice thereof. Legal proceedings requiring notice are those that might constitute a loss under the bond. The insured also must provide copies of all relevant pleadings and documents to the insurer when giving notice. If the insurer elects to defend the insured in whole or in part, any settlements, judgments, and legal expenses will be deemed to be covered losses under the bond.

Conditions and Limitations

Conditions and limitations are located in the FIB immediately after the general agreements previously described. There are 21 definitions in the "Conditions and Limitations" section of the FIB. The following two key definitions can be the subject of differing coverage interpretations:

Employee

An *employee* is defined as

(1) an officer or other employee of the Insured, while employed in, at, or by any of the Insured's offices or premises covered hereunder, and a guest student pursuing studies or duties in any of said offices or premises;

(2) any attorney retained by the Insured and an employee of such attorney while either is performing legal services for the Insured;

(3) a person provided by an employment contractor to perform employee duties for the Insured under the Insured's supervision at any of the Insured's offices or premises covered hereunder;

(4) an employee of an institution merged or consolidated with the Insured prior to the effective date of this bond; and

(5) each natural person, partnership or corporation authorized by the Insured to perform services as data processor of checks or other accounting records of the Insured (not including preparation or modification of computer software or programs), herein called Processor. (Each such Processor, and the partners, officers and employees of such Processor shall, collectively, be deemed to be one Employee for all the purposes of this bond, excepting, however, the second paragraph of Section 12. (A Federal Reserve Bank or clearing house shall not be construed to be a processor.)[x]

Because coverage generally depends on the acts of the insured's employees, the definition of an employee can be an important determinant of whether a loss is covered. Most policy language does not require that specific employees committing a dishonest act be identified in order to recover losses, despite the legal threshold that fraud be proven with particularity in the criminal context. Contractors and agents generally do not fall within the definition of an employee but part-time employees generally do. Courts look at the level of control the insured has over the person committing the dishonest act when seeking to determine if that person is an employee. Persons controlling their own actions typically do not meet the definition of an employee.

Loan

A *loan* is defined as "all extensions of credit by the Insured and all transactions creating a creditor relationship in favor of the Insured and all transactions by which the Insured assumes an existing creditor relationship."[9]

As previously discussed in the section on fidelity insuring agreements, additional coverage requirements arise if a transaction is considered a loan, as previously defined—specifically, the need for the insured to prove collusion and demonstrate that the employee committing the wrongful act received a financial benefit of at least $2,500. Accordingly, determining whether a transaction is a loan can determine whether a loss is wholly covered.

Exclusions

The "Exclusions" section of the FIB follows the definitions in the "Conditions and Limitations" section and lists 26 specific exclusions. Some of the more relevant exclusions are discussed subsequently.

8 See the "Conditions and Limitations" section of Financial Institution Bond Standard Form No. 24.
9 Ibid.

Several of the exclusions limit coverage to the conditions described in the "Insuring Agreements" section. For example, the FIB does not cover losses attributable to forgery or alteration unless covered under insuring agreements A, D, E, or F. Similarly, losses attributable to civil unrest are not covered in transit unless, firstly, they meet the criteria of insuring agreement C and, secondly, no knowledge of the unrest was present prior to initiating transit. Losses caused by an employee also are excluded unless covered by insuring agreement A, B, or C.

Income not realized by the insured also is excluded because such losses are typically unknown at the time of underwriting, and they represent future costs generally not intended to be covered. The potential income exclusion usually results in coverage for only direct, out-of-pocket losses. Unpaid interest income on fictitious loans, for example, would generally not be covered; however, inconsistent court rulings exist on this issue.

Damages of any type for which an insured is liable, other than compensatory damages, are not covered. Thus, punitive damages are not covered even if the insured is found liable to pay them by a court. In addition, damages resulting from any legal proceeding in which the insured allegedly violated the Racketeering and Influencing Corrupt Organizations Act statutes are not covered unless the insured establishes that the acts giving rise to the violations were committed by an employee and caused a loss under insuring agreement A.

Fees and expenses related to investigating, quantifying, and documenting the loss are not covered in the standard form. Neither are indirect or consequential losses. However, additional coverage for such costs is usually available and often obtained by the insured.

Commercial Crime Policy

The current coverage provisions of the CCP are generally the same as those found in the rudimentary form of the policy that originated back in 1940, unlike the FIB, which underwent significant revisions since its inception in 1986. Most CCPs cover losses sustained during the policy period as long as they are discovered within one year after the termination date, unlike the FIB, which covers only losses discovered during the policy period. Most other provisions of the FIB generally mirror those of the CCP. The SFAA offers five coverage forms under the CCP, and they are detailed in box 13-1.

Box 13-1: *Commercial Crime Policy Coverage Forms*

Coverage Form A—Blanket Employee Dishonesty

This form provides coverage for losses caused by the dishonest acts of all of the insured's employees.

Coverage Form A—Schedule Employee Dishonesty

This form provides coverage for losses caused by the dishonest acts of only the insured's employees listed on the schedule of the coverage form.

Coverage Form B—Forgery or Alteration

This form provides coverage for losses caused by the forgery of checks and other financial instruments issued by the insured.

Coverage Form O—Public Employee Dishonesty (per Loss)

This form provides coverage for losses caused by the dishonest acts of an employee of a governmental entity. The coverage limit applies to a single occurrence, regardless of the number of employees who may be involved in the loss.

Coverage Form O—Public Employee Dishonesty (per Employee)

This form provides coverage for losses caused by the dishonest acts of an employee of a governmental entity. The coverage limit applies to each employee involved in a single occurrence.

In addition to the CCP, the SFAA also offers the crime protection policy (CPP), which contains fidelity, forgery, burglary, and theft coverage in a single, all-inclusive policy form. The six insuring agreements of the CPP are very similar to those previously described in connection with the FIB, namely employee dishonesty, forgery or alteration, loss inside the premises, loss outside the premises, computer fraud, and money orders and counterfeit paper currency. Although the coverage may be similar, the FIB, as its name connotes, is for financial institutions, and the CCP and CPP have broader application for other industries. Two additional available insuring agreements beyond the basic form are loss of clients' property resulting from employee dishonesty and funds transfer fraud; each of these additional agreements can be added by endorsement. The SFAA's CPP may contain between one and eight of the specific insuring agreements previously enumerated.

The CPP covers all losses discovered during the policy period, regardless of when the dishonest acts giving rise to the loss occurred. The CPP is available only to mercantile entities, not government entities. The employee dishonesty and forgery provisions of the CCP are basically identical to those in the CPP.

The Insurance Services Office (ISO) offered the following four stand-alone crime policies shortly after the SFAA introduced the CPP on March 1, 2000:

1. CCP (discovery form)
2. CCP (loss sustained form)
3. Employee theft and forgery policy (discovery form)
4. Employee theft and forgery policy (loss sustained form)

The most significant difference between the crime forms of the ISO and those of the SFAA's CPP is the ISO's use of employee theft language in the fidelity insuring agreement, as opposed to employee dishonesty. This is important because under the theft language provided in the ISO's forms, the insured is not required to prove the employee's intent to cause the insured a loss and obtain a financial benefit, as required under the dishonesty language used by the SFAA. Instead, for the ISO form, the claimant is required only to demonstrate that a theft occurred to the detriment of the insured.

In summary, two general categories of fidelity policies have been reviewed here: those with loss sustained coverage and those with discovery coverage. Loss sustained coverage provides coverage for losses that occur during the policy period and are discovered either during the policy period or within a limited time thereafter. Discovery coverage provides coverage for losses that are discovered during the policy period or within a limited time thereafter, regardless of when the acts or events causing the loss occurred. Table 13-1 outlines the different crime policy categories and their attributes graphically.

Fidelity Claims: The Process

As anyone familiar with preparing an insurance claim knows, several elements are key to success. Chief among these are timeliness of reporting and communications and thoroughness in documenting the claim or claims. Another vital component is having the right investigative and claims teams in place. Lastly, management must have the willingness to work cooperatively, not only with the insurer and broker but also with outside advisors and the internal personnel necessary to ensure that all aspects of the claim are appropriately reviewed, evidenced, and submitted.

Every policy is different; insureds must first review their policy and understand their specific requirements for coverage in order to determine if they should file a claim. If the policy language is ambiguous, it will be interpreted by the courts in favor of the insured; however, such a determination of coverage is made based on a review of the policy as a whole.

Notice

Providing timely notice of a suspected or proven loss can be the first step to a successful claim; failure to give adequate or timely notice, on the other hand, can seriously impede a settlement and even negate coverage. As previously noted, in the event of a loss, the insured is required to give notice to its carrier "as soon as possible" after discovery of a loss.[10] In this context, discovery occurs when the insured "first become[s] aware of facts which would cause a reasonable person to assume that a loss covered by this policy has been or will be incurred,

---

10 *The Commercial Crime Policy,* Master Appendix Exhibit B, Commercial Crime Policy (Discovery Form) Standard Form No. CR 00227, 695.

Table 13-1: *Financial institution bonds (FIBs) and commercial crime policies (CCPs)*

| Financial Institution Bond | | Commercial Crime Policy* | | Crime Protection Policy | |
7 Insuring Agreements:		5 Coverage Forms:		6 Insuring Agreements:	
A – Fidelity	Losses attributable to intentionally dishonest/fraudulent acts of employees	Form A – Blanket Employee Dishonesty	Losses caused by the dishonest acts of any of the insured's employees	Employee Dishonesty	Losses attributable to intentionally dishonest/fraudulent acts of employees
B – On Premises	Robbery, burglary, misplacement, theft, and certain other losses of property occurring on the insured's premises	Form A – Schedule Employee Dishonesty	Losses caused by the dishonest acts of certain of the insured's employees listed on the coverage form	Forgery or Alteration	Losses attributable to forgery or alteration of any negotiable instrument specified in the insuring agreement
C – In Transit	Robbery, burglary, misplacement, theft, and certain other losses of property occurring while property is in transit (in custody of a messenger or transportation company)	Form B – Forgery or Alteration	Losses caused by forged checks and other financial instruments issued by the insured	Loss Inside the Premises	Robbery, burglary, misplacement, theft, and certain other losses of property occurring on the insured's premises
D – Forgery or Alteration	Losses attributable to forgery or alteration of any negotiable instrument specified in the insuring agreement	Form O – Public Employee Dishonesty, Per Loss	Losses caused by dishonest acts of a government employee with an occurrence coverage limit, regardless of the number of employees involved	Loss Outside the Premises	Robbery, burglary, misplacement, theft, and certain other losses of property occurring while property is in transit (in custody of a messenger or transportation company)
E – Securities	Losses attributable to forged, altered, lost, or stolen securities believed to be authentic by the insured	Form O – Public Employee Dishonesty, Per Employee	Losses caused by dishonest acts of a government employee with an employee coverage limit for each occurrence	Computer Fraud	Loss or damage caused by fraudulent preparation, modification, or input of electronic data
F – Counterfeit Money	Counterfeit money received by the insured in a good faith transaction			Money Orders and Counterfeit Paper Currency	Counterfeit money received by the insured in a good faith transaction
G – Fraudulent Mortgages	Acceptance of defective real property mortgage by insured that has fraudulent signature				
Discovery Coverage – Covers losses discovered during the policy period, regardless of when the dishonest acts giving rise to the loss occurred		Loss Sustained Coverage – Covers losses sustained during the policy period as long as discovered within a year after termination date		Discovery Coverage – Covers losses discovered during the policy period, regardless of when the dishonest acts giving rise to the loss occurred	
Used in the financial services industry		Used across various industries		Used across various industries	

* Surety and Fidelity Association of America (SFAA) form described above; the Insurance Services Office (ISO) also offers similar crime policies with either loss sustained or discovery coverage. Primary difference is definition of employee dishonesty of SFAA (which requires intent) v. employee theft of ISO (which does not).

even though the exact amount or details of loss may not then be known."[11]

Thus, a reasonableness test is what dictates the triggering of the notice provision. Alternatively, discovery can occur in connection with a third-party claim when the insured "receive[s] notice of an actual or potential claim [ ] alleging facts that if true would constitute a covered loss under [the] policy."[12] Mere suspicion is generally insufficient to qualify as discovery and actual knowledge is generally too stringent. Therefore, the reasonableness test in determining the trigger of discovery generally falls somewhere between mere suspicion and actual knowledge.

The standard for providing notice after discovery is a reasonable time. Although a typical policy does not provide for any specific type of notice, the notice should be sufficient to enable the insurer to protect its interest. For example, the insurer should generally be afforded the opportunity to initiate its own investigation when witnesses to the facts of a loss are still presumed to be largely available. Detailed information on the quantum of the loss is not necessary at the time of notice, although it can be helpful to the carrier in setting reserves. Importantly, communicating notice using the telephone is typically not sufficient; some formal issue of a written notice must be provided by the claimant to the insurer.

Investigation Protocol

Fraud investigations most often begin with tips from employees or anonymous sources.[13] Such investigations usually concern specific allegations from which one or more fraud hypotheses are developed and tested. Because of whistle-blower hotlines, some organizations are inundated with allegations of fraud and other improprieties. Accordingly, developing a protocol for properly investigating such claims is important so management, internal audit, or an investigative unit can sift through allegations and reasonably evaluate which may have merit and which do not. Having a formal protocol can help ensure

that all allegations are thoroughly addressed and management's fiduciary responsibility to shareholders is met. An investigative protocol that is properly developed, implemented, and applied can improve consistency in the investigative approach and the response to the alleged wrongdoing. It also can serve as a deterrent to future fraudsters because the perceived opportunity to commit fraud is reduced. Moreover, because litigation is always a potential when prosecuting fraudsters or otherwise recovering monies, those investigating fraud should conduct their inquiries under the direction of internal or outside counsel to protect any legal privileges or confidentiality that may apply.

The Investigative Team

Many fraud investigations begin internally by using company resources. Depending on the gravity of the allegations and their potential severity, the investigations can escalate and external professional resources are often engaged to independently examine allegations. Such resources should be experienced in both fraud investigations and fidelity claims and recovery. From the opening moments of the investigation, the team should include a claims professional to help plan and execute the project and ensure that insurance considerations are appropriately addressed. That claims professional can assist with the following:

- Assessing possible recovery options and identifying potential coverage that may respond
- Complying with notice and proof-of-loss provisions in the relevant policies
- Developing a claim strategy
- Managing and accelerating the claim process
- Providing preliminary loss estimates to help the adjuster with reserve setting
- Obtaining and preserving evidence, including requesting or conducting computer forensic analyses (for example, imaging hard drives, querying e-mails, and conducting other electronic discovery)

---

11 Ibid.
12 Ibid.
13 See the "Initial Detection of Occupational Fraud" chart on page 18 of the 2008 Association of Certified Fraud Examiners *Report to the Nation on Occupational Fraud & Abuse.*

- Interviewing parties relevant to the investigation
- Responding to information requests from the carrier(s)
- Coordinating the communications among, and efforts of, internal departments involved in claim preparation (for example, Legal, Risk Management, Finance, Accounting, Internal Audit, Marketing, Operations, Human Resources, and so on) within the insured's company
- Coordinating communication with external parties (for example, outside counsel, insurers, adjusters, insurer's accountants, brokers, lenders, and so on)
- Managing expectations of the insured and the carrier
- Preparing a well-documented proof of loss
- Obtaining partial payments on segmented claims
- Working toward a fair and timely claim settlement

Failure to utilize an experienced claim professional on the investigative team can result in an undesirable outcome—chief of which is an unsupported claim, which could result in denial of said claim or a delayed or inadequate claim settlement due to inadequate claim support and insufficient cooperation with the carrier's adjusters and accountants. Other oversights that can place limitations on the claims team include overlooked sources of recovery, spoliation of evidence, and voided coverage due to noncompliance with provisions governing timely notice and proof of loss. One other potential danger is inadequate reserves on the part of the carrier, though this is a circumstance over which any individual insured has less control. In addition to the claim professionals, who are often focused on the quantum portion of the loss, outside counsel should be considered to assist with the coverage or liability portion of the loss. Counsel is especially important if coverage issues are complex or the insured believes the claim will be contentious.

Despite the prevalence of fraud and corruption throughout business over time, large-scale financial fraud remains rare enough that one individual company is unlikely to face it frequently, which is a fact that surely gives management some small comfort. However, in the case of a significant investigation, both the examination of the fraud and the ensuing claims process can be new to many on the internal team. In the case of a significant and potentially damaging fraud risk (sometimes alluded to as a "bet-the-company" case), it is therefore worth remembering that management and its claims team will likely be on unfamiliar ground. In the case of a public company, for example, a company's obligations to shareholders and the board should be managed by counsel. The protocols for a successful insurance claim also will depend on the advice of outside experts.

Consequently, it is helpful for the insured to use independent resources. Often, the insurance company will rely on a team of experienced loss adjusters, third-party accountants, and, sometimes, external counsel. These are practical and prudent resources for the insured to rely on, as well as to mirror the expertise of the carrier team. In addition to potential external consultants and attorneys, the insured's claim team also should include key stakeholders from its Legal, Risk Management, Finance, Accounting, Operations, and Human Resources departments and from any other relevant departments, as needed. A cohesive team helps ensure adequate internal communication, representation of all constituents, accurate claim development, optimal claim strategy, departmental accountability, and accelerated claims. Company management should appoint a designated leader of the claim team to manage the claim process and establish a single point of communication with the carrier.

Comparing Fraud Investigation Reports to Other Types of Claims

Fraud Investigation Versus Fidelity Claim

Conducting fraud investigations and preparing insurance claims are not identical. A fraud investigation often identifies potentially illegal acts and quantifies the resultant losses, but a typical investigative report of findings for management may not be sufficient support for a fidelity claim, which must conform to policy provisions. In contrast to a findings report for management, which may not have a specific threshold of proof, fidelity claims must be well documented and must usually pass a reasonableness test for full recovery. Different thresholds of evidence are relevant to each, and depending on the nature of the investigation and desired level of diligence directed by those leading it, an investigative report for management or a company's audit committee may or may not contain suitable documentation for a fidelity claim.

For example, if management sought a high-level understanding of an alleged fraud and a ballpark estimate of resultant losses, the attendant report of findings would likely not be adequate for recovery under a CCP. Alternatively, if a company with unlimited resources conducted a thorough investigation that left no stone unturned and had contemporaneous supporting documentation, then such report might be suitable for a fidelity claim, even though that may not have been its intended purpose.

It is therefore critical to determine the purpose of a fraud investigation before it starts. The purpose should be based on intended or possible outcomes. For example, if a company does not have crime insurance coverage and does not plan to prosecute fraudsters, then it may opt to avoid expensive and time-consuming investigations. Companies should balance the necessary thoroughness of a fraud investigation and its corresponding cost with what they perceive will be the benefit of knowing the full story. They should consider this in light of their apparent options for recovery, through insurance claims, and with the desire that most companies share—to establish and uphold a zero-tolerance policy for fraud with absolute prosecution of fraudsters.

Fraud Investigation Versus Civil and Criminal Prosecution

As previously noted, a high-level fraud investigative report for management is likely not suitable support for a fidelity claim. It also is not likely to be suitable support for a civil action or criminal prosecution. The burden of proof in civil matters, similar to the reasonableness test for fidelity claims, requires plaintiffs to prove their claims by a preponderance of the evidence or a more likely than not standard. Criminal prosecution, as to be expected, requires an even higher standard of proof, requiring plaintiffs to prove their claims beyond a reasonable doubt. If an insured conceives that it may eventually seek to prosecute fraudsters civilly or criminally, it should

plan the fraud investigation to ensure that relevant evidentiary requirements of both proceedings will be met without significant rework. This is particularly important with regard to electronic evidence and fraudster confessions. Quantifying losses in connection with a fraud investigation may require several different iterations that comport with the relevant evidentiary requirements of a management report, fidelity claim, civil matter, or criminal matter.

Phases of a Fraud Investigation

Depending on how suspicion of fraud arises, the circumstances of an investigation and its conduct can differ widely. Some investigations end shortly after they begin, such as those involving allegations that clearly lack merit. Fraud investigations that involve fidelity claims generally have five constitutive phases, including identifying what type of fraud may have occurred; planning an investigation and deploying the necessary resources gathering evidence, including electronic documentation; drawing conclusions from the investigation; and reporting to management.

Following these come the two compensatory phases in which a company seeks redress, firstly, through actual recovery and restoration of property that has been fraudulently obtained or through previously described insurance claims and, secondly, through prosecution, litigation, or settlement. Although insurance is sometimes not considered as an option for recovery until after a fraud investigation has concluded, it is important, as previously discussed, to plan and execute the investigation with a possible claim in mind when coverage may exist. If a company cannot, through negotiation, recover losses from the fraudsters who caused them, then the company should consider seeking to prosecute those individuals. Other avenues of recovery for the victim organization, assuming it has crime coverage and its claim gets denied, include litigation against its carrier to determine coverage for insured losses and pursuing potential bad faith claims.

The ensuing section, therefore, describes the typical elements of the insurance recovery phase, although some components may occur in earlier phases. Figure 13-1 depicts the six primary elements, which occur in order.

Figure 13-1: *Typical Fidelity Claim Process*

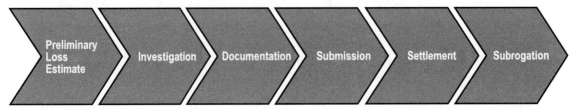

Preliminary Loss Estimate

The claim team should endeavor to develop a preliminary loss estimate shortly after discovery and typically within 30–60 days after providing notice of a potential claim to the insurer. Some investigations, especially those involving complex fraud schemes, may obviously require longer than 60 days for even preliminary loss estimates; however, estimates should be formulated and communicated to the insurer as soon as practical. The preliminary loss estimate is very important to the claims process because it establishes a potential claim range that the insurer can use to set an appropriate reserve.

The preliminary loss estimate must be presented appropriately and be based on the limited information available at the time it was prepared. It also should be stressed that the preliminary loss estimate will change as the investigation progresses and as additional information and supporting documentation is obtained. Unlike property claims, in which losses can be both substantial and more easily verified (that is, visible) and under which insureds can seek and obtain cash advances based on a preliminary loss estimate, fidelity claims generally require full investigation by the insurer prior to their issuing any payment.

Loss Investigation

Investigating a loss usually begins immediately on its discovery and continues during formulation of the preliminary loss estimate. This preliminary loss estimate is a high-level task because it often is developed by making some significant assumptions; the investigation phase, therefore, seeks to thoroughly delve into the details and identify the pertinent facts surrounding the loss. During this more detailed phase, the forensic accountant or investigator must pay particular attention to what caused the loss (that

is, to link the insured's loss with fraudulent acts of its employees). Interviews and data collection should typically start with those most distant from the fraudsters and work inward toward the fraudsters, gathering facts and understanding the loss prior to interviewing them.

The investigation also should develop and support a reasonable fraud hypothesis, based on the facts ascertained. Investigating fraud is an iterative process in which individual hypotheses should be formulated and either proven or disproven prior to developing and testing a new hypothesis. Developing and testing multiple hypotheses at the same time can render the investigation ineffective and cause it to drag on, often leading to no definitive conclusion. Although fraud is a legal conclusion that requires proving liability, losses can be quantified and recovery can be sought based on reasonable assumptions and facts that support the fraud hypothesis.

Loss Documentation

Data that documents a loss should be compiled throughout the investigation and corroborating evidence should support the hypothesis from the perspective of both liability and quantum. For obvious reasons, confessions are considered the most probative evidence of dishonesty. A report of findings should include detailed, cross-referenced exhibits, including confessions (if available) that state with specificity the facts underlying dishonest employee involvement. All such documentation should be compiled, referenced, and provided to the carrier as part of the claim. Copies are acceptable and originals should be returned to the insured to preserve chain-of-custody for potential use in prosecution of the wrongdoers. The report should contain only facts, not opinions, and the loss documentation should support those facts. Adequate supporting documentation is often key to a successful claim, both in terms of timeliness of payment and amount of recovery. However, many claims can be difficult to support, particularly those involving cash payments, complex schemes, poor financial records, or experienced fraudsters. Creativity, investigative skills, and technical prowess can sometimes overcome supporting documentation challenges. Aside from coverage issues, documentation challenges are often primary drivers of claim reductions (see subsequent sidebars).

Developing and Submitting a Claim

The next step is to combine the results of an investigation and supporting documentation into a comprehensive report of findings or formal proof of loss. There is no standard proof of loss form; most carriers prefer their own. In addition, there is generally no specific requirement on the part of the insured in preparing the proof of loss, other than enabling the carrier to fairly and correctly assess its rights and liabilities. In that context, it is prudent to itemize losses and open financial records to the extent possible to satisfy reasonable requests from the carrier so they may fully investigate the loss. Periodic meetings with the carrier and its claim team to explain the background of the loss, as well as the loss methodology and supporting documentation, will help facilitate understanding of the carrier, manage expectations, and expedite settlement of the claim.

Negotiating and Settling Claims

After the insured submits a fidelity claim, the carrier verifies the particulars of the claim. During this period, the carrier conducts its own due diligence and investigation to verify both its obligation to pay a claim and the amount of said claim. The length of this period can vary significantly depending on multiple factors, including the complexity of the claim, amount of supporting documentation provided, and experience and diligence of the carrier's and insured's claim teams. Once the carrier is satisfied with its obligation to pay and has determined the amount it believes it owes under the coverage afforded by its policy, negotiations typically occur with the claim teams and a settlement is reached.

Subrogation

Subrogation is the right of the carrier to be put in the position of the insured in order to pursue recovery from third parties who may be legally responsible to the insured for the loss paid by the insurer. Subrogation often occurs after the claim is paid by the carrier, although it may occur sooner. Recovery efforts from the fraudsters should be concurrent with the claims process. If the fidelity claim is denied, the insured still benefits if some level of recovery is successful against the fraudsters. If the claim is paid by the carrier, the carrier benefits with an offset to the claim payment. Most importantly, prosecuting fraudsters sends a message throughout the insured's organization that those who commit fraud will be pursued and prosecuted. This can serve as a significant deterrent to would-be perpetrators in the future.

D&O Insurance Liability Insurance Protection

D&O insurance coverage provides D&O with indemnity and defense coverage for claims related to the management of the organization. Arguably, the 1990s saw the largest increase in the procurement of higher limits of D&O coverage. Premiums for such coverage rose about 10 percent annually during the mid-1990s before another dramatic upswing in premiums occurred, coupled with a reduction of insureds' capacity to take on more risk after the Enron, Tyco, Adelphia, WorldCom, and Parmalat debacles.

However, although there was a large spike in the number of D&O claims reported in the early part of the 21st century, their volume is beginning to decrease. The direct cause for this decrease is difficult to pinpoint but likely involves a combination of the following factors: the distraction of plaintiffs' counsel to focus on a few very large cases, as a result of a spate of options backdating cases; the rigorous involvement of regulators; relative stock market stability in a growth market; and some of the recent high-profile settlements and punishments in fraud cases.

Fidelity Claim in Focus: Documentation Challenges in a Shipping Industry Payroll Fraud

A shipping company discovered a multimillion dollar payroll fraud that had been occurring aboard its ships for several years. The fraud scheme was discovered by an internal auditor through a tip from a crew member on one of the company's ships. All payroll payments to crew members were paid in cash onboard the ships. The fraudsters responsible for counting and distributing the cash to the crew colluded on each ship to inflate the cash payroll primarily through a ghost employee scheme. When payroll was funded, the fraudsters simply retained the excess cash that was purportedly to be paid to the ghost employees. Because the payments were made in cash on the high seas, it was difficult to demonstrate that the loss occurred, as well as determine the size of the loss. Unless one was involved in the fraud or physically present to witness the entire cash payment process, it would be difficult to identify and trace the excess payments because they were made in cash and, thus, there was no audit trail. The investigation and fidelity claim required a creative approach to quantify and support the shipping company's losses with contemporaneous documentation.

Payroll records were used to determine what cash was funded for each crew member. Such records were then compared to crew manifests to determine whether the crew members enumerated in the payroll records were present on the ship to collect their cash payment. Physical presence on the ship is a requirement for crew members to receive payroll payments. The payments to crew members that were not on the ship were deemed to be fraudulent. This approach to the quantification was corroborated by the fraudsters during investigative interviews.

In the final analysis, however, the enactment of Section 404 of the Sarbanes-Oxley Act may be the biggest contributing factor. Targeting corporate disclosures and establishing criminal liability for their misrepresentations, the act has the explicit goal of eliminating expense abuses, off-balance sheet investment vehicles, and other corporate misdeeds.

Wrongful Acts Committed by D&O

Although the frequency of D&O claims has recently begun to wane, the severity of those claims, especially those against Fortune 100 companies, has consistently increased over the last decade, and there are no indications that this trend will soon change. These lawsuits and claims are spurred by many causes, including allegations of inaccurate disclosure, stock options backdating, employee discrimination, and wrongful termination. Of these, the majority of claims over the past decade, especially those involving large, publicly-traded companies, have been triggered by inaccurate financial reporting and deceptive accounting practices that were designed to give the impression that the company was performing much better than it actually was. The following sections summarize these types of claims, explaining their causes.

Inaccurate Disclosure (Including Financial Reporting)

D&O insurance coverage is frequently provoked by a claim of some form of inaccurate disclosure or irregular accounting practices. In these situations, companies and their directors or officers are alleged to have misled their investors by overstating their earnings or the values of organizations they have acquired in order to improve the appearance of their financial success and growth. Once discovered, the inaccurate financial reports are corrected with a restatement of the affected years' reports, usually leading to significant loss in historical revenue and a corresponding drop in stock price.

Options Backdating

Exposure to a claim against D&O coverage from options backdating occurs when a company executive receives their stock options in the company at a retroactive, favorable price (sometimes right after the release of negative news or before a sharp gain in stock price), which results in an added financial gain for the holders of said options at a later time. Not only does this expose D&O to claims of fraudulent or illicit behavior, it also amounts to a violation of security laws and further likely triggers tax liability for the company (because in retroactively revaluing the stock awards and accounting for their value, the company's tax basis may change). In essence, backdating allows for the use of hindsight when determining the grant date for stock options and, therefore, the price. Also, backdating gives the appearance that the contract was issued "at the money" in the past, when the contract is actually "in the money."

According to data from Bloomberg L.P., as of April 2007, more than 200 companies had been investigated by the Securities and Exchange Commission (SEC) or announced their own inquiries into how they had set options prices.[14] Eighty D&O have lost their jobs and companies face more than 400 options-related lawsuits. Although this conduct typically does not result in prison time, an executive recently was sentenced to over 1 year in jail, raising the stakes for all those involved.

Employee Discrimination

This additional D&O exposure arises from situations in which employees of the company sue a director or officer of the company due to allegedly unfair or harassing treatment based on race, gender, age, and so on. Grievances usually are based on what the plaintiff believes is unfair treatment in regard to being passed over in the hiring process, promotional opportunities, or a salary increase, and claims are made under Title VII of the Civil Rights Act of 1964. This act states that an employer acts in an illegal and discriminatory fashion when it

1. fails, refuses to hire, discharges, or otherwise discriminates against any individual with respect to his or her compensation, terms, conditions, or privileges of employment because of some protected characteristic, such as race, color, religion, sex, national origin, age, or disability.

2. limits, segregates, or classifies employees or applicants in any way that would deprive or tend to deprive any individual of employment opportunities or otherwise adversely affect his or her status as an employee because of some protected characteristic.

Fidelity Claim in Focus: Documentation Challenges in an Auto-Leasing Fraud Scheme

Management of an auto-leasing company colluded with a lease broker to engage in a fraud scheme to divert monies from a $400 million lease portfolio. The head of the auto-leasing company effected over $50 million in fidelity losses through fictitious leases, improper payment transfers, retained lease payments, multiple-funded leases, and other tactics. The scheme occurred over numerous years and was uncovered by an internal auditor. The fraud scheme was very complex so it took a considerable amount of time and effort to determine what had happened and how much damage had been done. Preparation of the claim required deep technical skills in computer forensics and data analysis because there was scant hard copy documentation available as support.

Various data sources, such as customer payment histories, caller notes, and account origination files, were obtained and uploaded into a centralized database so that account summaries could be created for each lease. The data in the database was analyzed and each lease in the portfolio was categorized into one of numerous fraud schemes, as appropriate, based on query results. For example, if the caller notes evidenced an improper payment transfer or if two different leases had identical vehicle identification numbers, then the leases would be categorized into those two respective classifications. Reviewer notes describing the fraud scheme and supporting data available for each account summary were then created to support the losses. This facilitated understanding of the aggregate loss and accelerated the ultimate claim settlement.

---

14 Torbenson, Eric. "Tangled in Stock Scandal: Several Area Firms Feel Effects of Options Backdating Inquiries." *Dallas Morning News*, April 23, 2007.

Wrongful Termination or Discharge

An allegation and suit based on a claim of wrongful termination is initiated by former employees when they believe that they were terminated for illegitimate or discriminatory reasons. Wrongful termination claims encompass any unfair or illegal dismissal and can include breach of contract (regardless if a formal employment contract exists) or breach of implied covenant of good faith and fair dealing (a subset of breach of contract), whistle-blower claims (in which an employer dismisses an employee for reporting the employer to a regulatory agency), and retaliatory discharge (in which an employer discharges an employee for exercising a statutory right).

Other Events That Trigger a Claim

Typical sources of D&O claims include shareholders, shareholder-derivative actions, customers, regulators, competitors, employees, and other third-party organizations, such as environmental activists. Along with the acts committed by D&O, a number of so-called "resulting events" can indicate that a misrepresentation or illegal act has been committed within a company. Indeed, a host of attorneys monitor these situations and act quickly if they believe illegal or inappropriate acts have occurred.

These situations, which can precipitate legal action brought by plaintiffs' counsel or current or former employees, shareholders, and outside parties, include a significant decline in stock price, the failure of a company, a corporate reorganization, and the discrimination against and dismissal of one or more employees. Box 13-2 outlines these further special situations.

Box 13-2: *Potential D&O Resulting Events*

- *Significant decline in stock price.* claims over the past decade have been triggered by rapid, significant declines in the stock price of a company. Although the stock market has been rather unstable over this time period (which has helped inflate the number of D&O claims that are occurring), most of these price drops have been followed by important corporate announcements admitting to accounting inaccuracies and the required restatement of financial figures from previous years.

- *Failure of the company.* As in the cases of Enron, WorldCom, Adelphia, and many others during the early 2000s, many D&O lawsuits were triggered by company failures following announcements of fraudulent accounting practices and the resulting collapse of the company's stock price.

- *Corporate reorganizations (for example, a merger, acquisition, or divestiture).* Some D&O exposures and subsequent claims have occurred following a company's acquisition of another firm or its takeover by an outside entity. Litigation resulting from mergers, acquisitions, or divestitures typically originates from the shareholders' desire for the company to not participate in the merger, a perceived loss-of-value from the proposed terms (that is, the acquisition stock price is lower than key shareholders believe is appropriate), or the disclosure that the financial reports of one of the corporations involved in the transaction had been adjusted to improve the appearance of the acquisition to the public. In rare cases, a D&O claim may be brought because the purchaser has assumed some unanticipated and unwelcome liability (for example, legal, financial, environmental, and so on) during an asset purchase and such liability threatens the acquirer's balance sheet, its market capitalization, and its perceived value going forward.

- *Discrimination or dismissal of employee.* Another major trigger of D&O claims is the manner in which D&O interact with their employees. If an employee believes that he or she has been treated in a discriminatory manner or was terminated from his or her position for reasons beyond the normal scope of employment, the employee may initiate litigation against the firm or individual directors or officers the employee perceives to be the cause the action.

D&O Coverage

Corporations and senior executives may find themselves subject to allegations, claims, and lawsuits even when they make decisions with the best intentions of ensuring legal compliance, taking ethical action, and making appropriate disclosures. D&O liability insurance has become an integral feature of risk management programs at many U.S. corporations and trusts and is a requirement for recruiting and retaining board members and senior executives.

D&O liability policies generally provide coverage for the alleged wrongful acts of the insured company and D&O. Generally, such coverage is broad, and the actions of the insured are covered unless excluded or not defined within the policy as a loss. Similar to other types of insurance policies, D&O policies contain several sections, including declarations; the insuring agreements, definitions, exclusions, and limit of liability; and a retention clause. Depending on the insurer's policy, there may be over 20 sections detailing policy requirements or provisions that impact how claims must be reported, payment of defense costs, cancellation of the policy, and more. As a result, each of these sections requires a thorough understanding of its components, and policyholders often will benefit from reviewing each section's elements with their corporate risk manager or insurance broker. Knowing a D&O policy's carrier is vital because it will guide the insured in how the carrier will respond to any given claim.

CFOs, treasurers, and general counsel often will be present when the risk manager discusses D&O insurance coverage options with underwriters or brokers. The discussion normally will include contemplating limits, retentions, and exclusions and the side agreements A–C, which offer an expanded set of specialized coverages that can help protect the company and individual D&O. These so-called "sides" can be an important set of provisions for protecting the company and its D&O, including those who are meeting with the risk manager. They are worth explaining in some detail:

Insuring Agreement A (Side A)

A common coverage in U.S. companies, this side agreement generally provides coverage for defense costs and liability payments for D&O

for any allegations of wrongful acts. It provides a layer of coverage exclusively for individual D&O and is a method to address potential severability issues. Side A is important for individual D&O because it provides coverage when the company does not or cannot indemnify them against a covered claim. The attractiveness of side A coverage is that it protects the personal assets of D&O and generally does not have an associated retention or deductible.

Another variation on the side A coverage is for the company to purchase excess coverage, which is referred to as *side A—difference in conditions*. This option usually has fewer and less restrictive coverage exclusions than a traditional side A–C policy. In the event of a company's insolvency, individual D&O remain covered.

Side A policies that are stand-alone are attractive to many D&O because a traditional D&O policy that includes side A runs the risk of exhausting its coverage limits due to payments of indemnified claims and defense costs. Stand-alone side A coverage, however, is not used to pay claims against the company or reimburse the company for such indemnified claims. Along with its evident attractiveness to covered D&O, depending on market conditions, stand-alone side A coverage also may be viewed as a good risk for the insurers, which traditionally have viewed traditional D&O coverage as more likely to incur the payment of claims as opposed to a pay-out on stand-alone side A coverage. Because of their perception of a lower risk position, insurers also may offer favorable language relating to exclusions and severability.

Insuring Agreement B (Side B)

This coverage reimburses the corporation, not its D&O, for the company's indemnification responsibilities for its individual D&O, including the cost of claims, settlements, and legal defense. Commonly, side B coverage entails a retention deductible. Thus, side B coverage protects the balance sheet of the company.

Insuring Agreement C (Side C)

This coverage reimburses the company for securities claims made against the corporate entity.

For public companies, side C coverage responds to securities law claims, such as shareholders asserting a claim against the company in conjunction with the purchase or sale of securities. Side C coverage usually has a retention deductible similar to that of side B coverage.

Risk Management Using D&O Coverage

D&O coverage is offered and purchased on a claims-made basis. Simply stated, this means that insurance companies write D&O policies with the requirements that (1) the claim must be made against the insured during the policy period and (2) the incident giving rise to the claim must occur within the policy period. Importantly, with regard to this second requirement, an organization will face a gap in coverage any time it changes insurance carriers. As a result, many insurers will extend the policy period retroactively by providing prior acts coverage or will extend the retroactive date to the date of the initial policy's inception. Prior acts or retroactive coverage is critically important with claims-made coverage.

For the corporate CFO or risk manager seeking to transfer risk by using D&O coverage, a number of considerations come into play. Some issues to review internally, as well as with the corporation's insurance broker (preferably before the policy is bound) can be found in box 13-3.

Box 13-3: *Risk Transfer Assessment Considerations*

- What is the corporation's philosophy toward retaining and managing risk, as opposed to transferring it?
- How has this philosophy been validated by the past history of risks, exposures, and claims?
- What is the risk appetite of the board and its individual members?
- How much coverage should be purchased? What is the cost of coverage for "optimal" scenarios? What is practical?
- What is the cost of coverage of various retentions deductibles, and what are the retentions?
- What is the financial rating of the insurance company issuing the policy?
- What will the policy pay for (that is, claims, defense costs, SEC investigations, or informal inquiries)?
- Who is covered under the policy and who is excluded? What is the definition of an insured person? Are spouses covered?
- How are outside directors covered and to what extent?
- Are nonprofit or outside activities of the directors on behalf of the organization covered under the policy?
- What are the stipulations for reporting a claim, and when must a claim be reported to the insurer?
- What are the change in control provisions of the policy if a change in ownership occurs? How might a merger or acquisition related to the company and its subsidiaries affect coverage?
- Should stand-alone side A coverage be purchased in addition to traditional side A–C coverage?
- What are the insolvency provisions of the policy?
- Is so-called "tail coverage," which extends the policy a number of years beyond the original expiration date, a consideration?
- What information is required in the application for coverage, and how are the warranty provisions defined, related to disclosure of potential future claims?

Applying for D&O Insurance

Companies are required by insurers to complete a D&O insurance application as part of the underwriting process, so they may fully review and understand the risks and exposures of the proposed insured. The application also provides written protection to the insurer insofar as it documents the activities germane to the type of coverage, exclusions, or exceptions to those exclusions. D&O underwriters usually want to meet with company executives to discuss their claims and litigation history and gain an understanding of who they are insuring.

Certain of the information necessary for filing an application is readily available and immediately obvious; it includes identifying the company's corporate addresses, the names of the insured, and the officer of the company to be designated as the representative to receive notices from the insurer on behalf of entities and persons proposed for D&O insurance.

Insurers largely rely on the applicant's statements and disclosures in establishing and then underwriting risk. Rightly, D&O insurers require a great deal of information about the applicant seeking to purchase coverage and require that the application be true, accurate, and complete. To apply for insurance and prepare for such a meeting and review, the company seeking coverage also should plan to have the following information and disclosures available:

- A detailed list of recently completed large divestitures of stock, along with a list of anticipated divestitures
- A list of past merger and acquisition activities, along with some reasonable detail on acquisitions and divestitures pending or anticipated
- A list of ongoing litigation involving antitrust actions, copyrights, or patents
- Details on any civil, criminal, or administrative proceedings alleging or investigating violations of any securities regulations
- A list of past or pending class action or derivative suits
- A list of and detail about any claims made against persons or entities
- A copy of the company's latest SEC 10-Q and 8-K reports, proxy statement, Form 10-K, and most recent annual report
- A copy of the company's prospectus and offering circular
- Audited financial statements, including all notes and schedules
- Copies of all provisions of the applicant's charter and bylaws relating to indemnification of its D&O

During a review of the insured for setting policy limits, coverage, and endorsements, insurers also may ask somewhat more probing questions about the current situation of the company and current intent of the company's management in seeking insurance. This can involve management consenting to policy language, including a statement such as "No person or entity proposed for this insurance is cognizant of any fact, circumstance or situation which they have reason to suppose might afford grounds for any claim such as would fall within the scope of the proposed insurance." If the applicant has such information or knowledge, then some description of that information or knowledge is required in the application. If the information disclosed is new or previously unknown to the underwriter or broker, the underwriter will likely want to discuss the disclosed information, in addition to simply reading the disclosure on the application.

False Statements: The Warranty in the D&O Application

A warranty statement in the application asserts that no insured person is aware of any matter that may give rise to a future claim, unless such matter is disclosed to the insurer on the application. Warranty statements vary among insurers, and due care must be taken to appropriately disclose potential future claims related to the D&O coverage. For example, some warranties may require disclosure of information that "might" or "may" give rise to a future claim. Other applications may include language that requires disclosure of information if it is "reasonably likely" to give rise to a D&O claim. For example, if the applicant has been provided notice of a threatened securities claim against the company and fails to disclose such notice, then the applicant has failed to provide information that "might" give rise to a future claim.

Insurers routinely consider any documentation or filings attached to an application to be part of that application, including audited financial statements and any public filings, such as reports required by the SEC. In some cases, companies completing the application will include a statement that refers the insurer to the applicable SEC document. At that point, the referred public filing is considered "attached" to the application, and it will be considered by the insurance underwriter along with other information disclosed in the application.

If information in an application submitted to the insurer is false, the strongest action the insurer can attempt is a rescission action. Rescission voids the coverage from the beginning; in effect, the insurer asserts that the D&O coverage never existed. In such cases, the insurer must demonstrate that the insured made a false statement or representation. Generally, for an insurer to successfully win a rescission action, the insurer must prove that the insured made a false representation; that the false representation was "material"; that the insurer relied upon the false representation; and, further, that the insured had knowledge of the false representation, called *scienter* (this standard is not required in all states). Because insurance companies are regulated on a state basis, case law varies depending on the jurisdiction.

A false representation is usually considered material if it influenced the insurer's decision to accept the risk or if it affected the amount of the premium calculated by the underwriter. The burden of proof in such cases falls to the insurer, which must prove it would not have been bound to the coverage and would not have issued the policy had it received accurate information at the time of entering the contract. The insurer also could assert that the terms or endorsements would have been different if true information had been provided during the underwriting process.

Materiality is often established by reviewing the insurer's process of collecting and reviewing information for underwriting and by analyzing the data received by the underwriter. This does not mean that the insurer will automatically prevail in court against the insured. In a New York case, *Chicago Ins. Co. v. Kreitzer & Vogelman*, 210 F. Supp. 2d407 (S.D.N.Y. 2002), the court refused to grant summary judgment based on materiality for an insurer in which only subjective testimony was provided by the underwriter.

Above all, to move for rescission, an insurer must show that the underwriter relied on the false information in the application to determine its coverage. Insurers are usually not required to independently validate the information in an application if such validation would exceed the bounds of normal due diligence in their underwriting processes. However, if the insurer can prove that the false information was relied upon to approve the coverage, then the insurer may indeed prevail. If an insurer is successful in rescinding a D&O policy, then the premium paid is returned to the previously insured.

Some states require a higher standard to rescind the policy: to wit, that insurers establish that the insured intended to deceive the insurer in the application. Depending on the jurisdiction, scienter can include the insurer's establishing that the insured acted in bad faith by providing false information in the application. Scienter also can be established if the applicant did not take reasonable efforts to ensure that the information contained in the application was correct. Because state laws vary on the necessity and interpretation of scienter related to insurance polices, you should consult with legal counsel for your specific situation.

In some jurisdictions, it is presumed that an insurer would have simply charged a higher premium had it known the accurate information; in such cases, the insurer would not prevail in a rescission action, though its responsibility for full payment of a claim may be moderated or reduced by the court.

Rescission is a harsh measure and not always necessary. In some instances, insurers may instead seek to exclude coverage rather than exercising the rescission option. A warranty exclusion allows insurers to exclude certain coverage with language, for example, such as "the circumstances or wrongdoing which could give rise to a future claim exists prior to inception of coverage, and any subsequent claim arising from such wrongdoing is excluded from coverage." This exclusion allows the policy to remain in effect, at least for the nonexcluded items. The insurer also keeps the premium that was paid by the insured. For the insured company and D&O, a warranty exclusion can substantially dilute coverage.

In summary, whenever a corporation or other organization seeks D&O coverage, the organization's

CFO, chief risk officer, insurance manager, or other key members of the management team will want to carefully prepare and review available coverage; terms; side agreements; policy provisions and endorsements; and, of course, premiums. In preparing their application for said coverage, they should carefully consider what information is presented, ensuring its thoroughness and reviewing with legal counsel its disclosures, admissions, and asseverations. Every effort should be made to answer questions in good faith to mitigate the possibility of rescission or a warranty exclusion.

The D&O Claims Process

To succeed in the D&O claims process, any individual claim needs to be prepared and managed based on its specific facts of the alleged wrongful act, case law, and whatever slight nuances in insurance policy language may apply under the circumstances.

This section discusses the general processes to be followed in preparing and submitting D&O claims. These processes include the wrongful act, notice of claim, policy reporting requirements, claim confirmation, the requirements of duty to defend versus duty to pay, choosing representation, reimbursement of expenses, duty of association, and settlement. Given the complexity of D&O insurance and claim handling, it is always advisable to consult with an attorney that specializes in this area.

Claim Notification

The D&O claim process starts with notification of the alleged wrongful act to the insured in the form of a written demand seeking either monetary or nonmonetary relief. Once notice has been received, the insured has a duty to notify its insurance company in accordance with the terms outlined in the policy provisions. A typical policy will have explicit provisions that call for this notice, such as language like the following:

> The Directors and Officers shall, as a condition precedent to their rights under this Policy, give the Insurer notice, in writing, as soon as practicable of any Claim first made against the Directors and Officers during the

> Policy Period or Discovery Period, but in no event later than ninety (90) days after such claim is made, and shall give the Insurer such information and cooperation as it may reasonably require. [15]

The insured need be mindful of reporting requirements and understand the specific definitions of *wrongful act* and *claim* in the policy.

Claim Reporting

The language used for reporting requirements in D&O policies varies, and these requirements can consist of the following:

- As soon as practicable
- Reporting during the policy period
- Reporting not more than 90 days after the policy termination
- Reporting not more than 90 days after the claim is first made. [16]

Certain policies specify which individuals at the insured must receive notice of the claim in order for the clock to start on notice requirements. This provision might list the risk manager, chief legal counsel, CFO, and CEO. Having clear and explicit language of this type in the policy provision governing notification is helpful and preferable to the insured because it helps them avoid a situation in which a claim may be reported to someone at the insured's organization but not correctly reported to the specified individuals and, thus, is not reported to the company's insurer.

Sound practice dictates that a claim be reported in writing to both the insurance broker and insurance carrier. Many insureds have arrangements in place to report claims to the broker, leaving the broker responsible for reporting to the primary and excess insurance carriers. However, reporting the claim to the insurance broker alone leaves open the possibility of the report being late and even scenarios in which the company and its broker fail to fully or correctly report the claim. By reporting directly to the insurer, the insured can be confident that it has met its reporting requirements.

---

15 International Risk Management Institute, Inc., 2008.

16 Monteleone – Tressler, Soderstrom, Maloney & Priess (IRMI 2007).

Claim Confirmation

Once a claim is reported to the insurer, the insured should request written confirmation of their claim. This confirmation, which can be in the form of a claim acknowledgement, coverage letter, or reservation of rights letter, also can be a denial. In whatever form this written acknowledgement arrives, the confirmation from the insurer provides the insured with evidence that their claim was filed.

Duty to Defend Versus Nonduty to Defend

When considering how a claim is to be managed, the policy offers guidance about who is responsible for defense and choosing defense counsel.

There are two types of provisions in D&O policies: duty to defend and nonduty to defend. Duty-to-defend provisions require the insurer to provide the defense of the claim, giving the insurer choice of defense counsel and the ability to manage the claim. Under the nonduty-to-defend provisions, the insured has the right to manage the defense of the claim and choose defense council, subject to the insurer's approval. Insureds that have a level of sophistication with D&O coverage or want to be involved in the management of their claim would most likely not be well served by the duty-to-defend provision and would more likely choose a nonduty-to-defend provision.

Under policies with a nonduty-to-defend provision, the insured begins to incur defense costs from the onset of the claim. There are two ways to structure how D&O policies address the reimbursement of these defense costs: reimbursement during the claim or reimbursement once the claim has settled.

In the past, D&O policies did not advance defense costs until the resolution of the claim. Now, however, the majority of policies have provisions that allow for advancing defense costs. The advancement of defense costs does come with conditions associated with meeting the retention and the reduction of the limit of liability; moreover, such advances do not alter the intent of any reservation of right letter and are repaid if it is found that the costs are not insured under the policy.[17]

Permission to Incur Expenses

Prior to incurring any expenses on the claim, it is always a sound practice to obtain permission from the insurer to do so. Obtaining such permission helps avoid potential disputes.

Duty of Association

Under the nonduty-to-defend provisions, the insured has a duty of association with the insurance company. This duty requires the insured to keep the insurer current on the status of the claim and any potential settlements and, moreover, to not settle the claim without the insurer's consent.

Claim Settlement and Allocation

With the settlement of the claim comes the allocation process in which the insured and its insurer negotiate how to allocate monies received in the settlement. Allocation issues usually arise in two instances. First, when there are parties to the claim that do not have coverage under the policy (for example, attorneys and accountants) and, second, when certain aspects of the wrongful act are not covered under the policy (for example, professional services). The typical areas of discussion surrounding allocation with the insurer are insured versus noninsured parties, insured versus noninsured claims, and insured versus noninsured capacity.[18]

The typical allocation structures in D&O policies are predetermined allocation and methodology. In predetermined allocation, which is exactly as it sounds, the insurance policy predetermines the allocation. In methodology, the policy sets forth how the allocation will be determined.

Areas of Dispute in D&O Claims

Predictably, given the complexity of D&O insurance policies and litigation, disputes between the insured, insurer, and insurance broker can arise in numerous areas. The most common of these areas are described in box 13-4.

---

17 International Risk Management Institute, Inc., 2008.

18 Allocation, Dan Bailey, Bailey Cavalieri LLC.

Box 13-4: *Common Areas of Dispute in D&O Claims*

Late Notice

In almost all D&O insurance policies, specific guidelines determine when notice of claims must be made. Notwithstanding the clarity of the language in such guidelines, disputes can nevertheless still arise surrounding when the claim first occurred, the insured first had notice of the claim, and the insured reported the claim to the insurance company. Although policy language varies, notice to the insurer within the policy period or immediately thereafter is usually a condition precedent to coverage. The insured should therefore pay careful attention to the notice provisions in the policy form.

Choice of Defense Counsel

The insured and insurer should agree prior to binding the insurance policy how counsel will be selected if it becomes necessary to exercise a claim against the policy. If panel counsel is provided for in the policy, the insured should determine if they are allowed to go outside of the panel counsel for certain types of claims, such as nonsecurity claims, and whether multiple attorneys can be used when conflicts between insureds arise.

Failure to Report

The insured should avoid the error of reporting the claim to the insurance broker with the expectation that the broker will unfailingly report the claim to the insurer or report the claim in a timely manner. Notice should always be given concurrently to both the broker and insurance company, and the insured should request confirmation of receipt from each.

Allocation Issues

Allocating claim expenditures can occur at two points in the claim life cycle. First, allocation of defense costs and expenses can occur during the period in which the underlying claims against the director or officer are pending. Second, allocation of indemnity payments occurs at the time of settlement or judgment. When a policy makes no reference to issues of allocation, insurance companies can attempt to allocate costs of defense and indemnity on a 50-50 basis, even when little or no investigation of the surrounding facts has taken place. Allocation is an example of the potential for insurance company claims handling to erode the scope and quality of coverage.

Cooperating With the Insurer

The insured has a duty of association with the insurance company; however, at times, insureds can be concerned about disclosing confidential information to the insurer that the insurer feels is relevant to the claim. These types of issues, especially when they pertain to matters of competitive advantage or intellectual property, should be openly addressed between the insured and insurer in advance of pursuing a claim. Failure to do so can mean compromising coverage, especially when an insured chooses not to divulge information that the insurer feels it has a right to learn.

Fraud in the Application

Many policy forms require the insured to complete an application that will be included in the policy form. That form may include a clause whereby the insurance carrier incorporates all of a company's public statements into the policy application, including statements filed with the SEC, such as Forms 10-K and 10-Q. In securities cases, the truth of the company's public statements are arguably always at issue. In restatement claims, specifically, plaintiffs' counsel can allege that a restatement rendered the company's prior SEC filings false. In those cases, carriers might use the "Incorporation by Reference" clause in their policies to argue that coverage should be rescinded because the policy was induced by a misstatement of a material fact in the insurance application.

(continued)

Box 13-4: *Common Areas of Dispute in D&O Claims (continued)*

State Insurance Codes Can Cause Coverage Problems

State insurance codes and regulators can complicate insurability for claims brought against D&O. For example, many state laws prohibit insurance companies from providing coverage for liability due to willful conduct. Carriers may not be held responsible for providing coverage to the insured to cover liability for securities fraud because courts may find securities fraud liability required a finding of willful conduct.

Public Policy Concerns

Courts may agree with a carrier's defense and refuse to order coverage for claims that otherwise appear to meet the definition of covered claims. The allegation is that a claim for securities fraud did not constitute a loss under the terms of the policy because the court found that the plaintiffs were essentially seeking restitution from an ill-gotten gain. The court may reason that it was against public policy for an officer or director to lose an action requiring restitution of ill-gotten gains to plaintiffs and then may expect an insurance company to cover the costs.

Conclusion

In conclusion, D&O insurance coverage provides D&O with indemnity and defense coverage for claims related to the management of the organization. The late 1990s and early part of the 21st century saw policy procurement and claim severity increasing while claim frequency was decreasing. The enactment of Section 404 of the Sarbanes-Oxley Act is the likely driver behind this reduction.

Potential triggers to D&O claims are inaccurate disclosures, options backdating, employee discrimination, wrongful termination or discharge, significant decline in stock price, and corporate reorganizations.

The D&O insurance policy has three coverage parts: side A, side B, and side C. Side A coverage indemnifies the individual D&O when the corporation is prohibited by law or unable to do so, typically as a result of insolvency. Side B coverage provides reimbursement to the corporation for its costs associated with the indemnity and defense of the D&O. Side C coverage reimburses the corpora-

tion for the indemnity and defense of claims against the corporation.

Applying for D&O insurance typically requires completion of an application and providing information, such as public financials and details of mergers, acquisitions and divestitures, and litigation. It is important to remember that false statements under an application can lead to the policy being voided back to its inception date.

The D&O claims process needs to be prepared and managed based on the individual claim circumstances. The general claim process includes claim notification, claim reporting, claim confirmation, permission to incur expenses, duty of association, and claim settlement and allocation.

Common areas for dispute between the insurer and insured are late notice, choice of defense counsel, failure to report, allocation, and fraud in the application.

It is important to engage legal counsel to assist the organization in the D&O application process because unintended mistakes can prove to be quite costly to the individual D&O and corporation.

14

Antifraud Programs

Mike Sherrod, Senior Manager

Introduction

Given the economic crisis in the United States beginning in 2008, which includes unemployment reaching 30-year highs of from 9 percent to 10 percent, the continued decline in the housing market, foreclosure rates continuing to increase, the daily evaporation of consumer confidence, constant comparisons of this recession to that of the Great Depression, and the recent uncovering of several major fraud schemes, management and other key stakeholders are being constantly challenged to proactively think about fraud before it occurs. The continued impact of the current global economic downturn has created a robust environment for fraud. As internal and external pressures mount for individuals within organizations, some may resort to committing various fraud schemes to maintain their jobs; to continue to live a lifestyle to which they have grown accustomed; or due to other personal factors. The robust environment for fraud is magnified by the fact that many companies continue to downsize and reduce spending on nonmission-critical objectives, which may create tremendous strains on internal controls and create more opportunity for fraud. As Roland Brasky, the Chairman of Audit committee for Grand Forge Company and Grand Forge[1] found out in the opening case study, the identified allegations of fraud and the internal and external pressures that are increasing in the current marketplace are contributing factors that may be creating the perfect storm for increased corporate fraud (see figure 14-1).

Figure 14-1: *The Perfect Storm is Brewing*

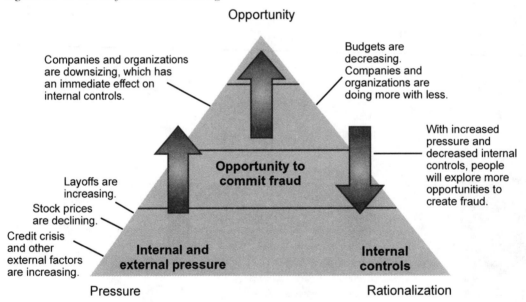

Roland asked his Internal Audit Director, Michele Hart, what the company was currently doing proactively to address this potential increase in fraud in the current economy. Michele contacted Perusi & Bilanz LLP, to determine options she should be considering to address fraud.

Perusi & Bilanz LLP's recommendation was that Michele work to implement a holistic antifraud program for Grand Forge Company.

Due to the fact that this was a new concept for Michele, she naturally had questions for Perusi & Bilanz LLP on the structure of this program. Michele asked the following questions:

---

1 The reader is invited to read the detailed case study of Grand Forge Company found in the Introduction to this book.

1. What should the overall framework for the antifraud program look like?
2. Describe for me in detail the elements of an antifraud program.
3. How do I implement the various elements and develop action items? Specifically, how do I conduct a fraud risk assessment?
4. What are the benefits of implementing an antifraud program?
5. If I take the lead in implementing this antifraud program, as directed by Roland, who should ultimately own the process and what should Internal Audit's role be?

As is the case with Grand Forge Company, the challenge for most companies is the lack of a formal antifraud program to address their rising concerns about fraud. Even within their Sarbanes-Oxley Act of 2002 (SOX) compliance activities, many companies have not implemented a program that addresses the risk of fraud holistically (that is, SOX compliance relates to internal controls around financial reporting; therefore, fraud risks related to corruption or asset misappropriation and the related factors of pressure, rationalization, and opportunity may not be addressed). In addition, many companies continue to address fraud through reactive investigations rather than proactive measures. As a result, companies can incur significant expenses, strained resources, and unwanted exposure due to fraud investigations.

Another challenge facing clients is determining what their duty is regarding fraud prevention within their organization. Chapter 8 of the *2007 Federal Sentencing Guidelines Manual*[2] provides the following seven points management should consider when establishing an antifraud program:

1. The organization must have established compliance standards and procedures that are to be followed by its employees and other agents and that are reasonably capable of reducing the prospect of criminal conduct.
2. Specific individual(s) in high-level positions in the organization must have responsibility to oversee compliance with such standards and procedures.
3. The organization must have used due care not to delegate substantial discretionary authority to individuals whom the organization knew, or should have known through the exercise of due diligence, had a propensity to engage in illegal activities.
4. The organization must have taken steps to effectively communicate its standards and procedures to all employees and other agents.
5. The organization must have taken reasonable steps to achieve compliance with its standards.
6. The standards must have been consistently enforced through appropriate disciplinary mechanisms, including, as appropriate, discipline of individuals responsible for the failure to detect an offense. Adequate discipline of individuals responsible for an offense is a necessary component of enforcement; however, the form of discipline that will be appropriate will be case specific.
7. After an offense has been detected, the organization must have taken all reasonable steps to respond appropriately to the offense and prevent further similar offenses, including any necessary modifications to its program to prevent and detect violations of law.

Regulations, such as the *2007 Federal Sentencing Guidelines Manual* previously mentioned, SOX, and the 1997 Organization for Economic Co-operation and Development Anti-Bribery Convention, require companies to be much more vigilant in their efforts to prevent and detect fraud. As a result of both the acts of fraud and the heightened regulatory environment, board members, independent auditors, and other stakeholders are asking executive management pointed questions about how the company is responding to these risks and regulations.

This chapter will outline an approach to addressing fraud proactively and reactively through the design and implementation of a holistic antifraud program.

---

2 *An Overview of the Organizational Guidelines*, Paula Desio, Deputy General Counsel, United States Sentencing Commission.

Antifraud Program Basics

Companies are continuing to look for ways to mitigate the potential for fraud from occurring. Having the ability to address fraud more proactively is an initiative that is now being pursued more often, due to the increased concern of fraud by internal audit directors, general counsel, chief risk officers, and other members of management within organizations.

Roland asked Michele what Grand Forge Company had done to respond to the allegations of fraud identified in the original case study and asked her to perform an assessment of this process. More specifically, Roland wanted to know what the organization is doing to ensure it has a consistent and documented approach in the way it investigates the potential allegations of fraud. Michele again was tasked with determining what the company is currently doing and how this process could be improved. Management can set the proper tone, execute a robust fraud risk assessment, and design internal controls to prevent and detect fraud, but, unfortunately, at some level fraud will still occur. Recent studies done by the Association of Certified Fraud Examiners (ACFE) estimate that as much as 7 percent of U.S. companies' revenues are lost each year due to fraud.[3]

Perusi & Bilanz LLP described in detail for Michele the elements of the overall antifraud program, which are grouped into the following three categories:

1. Tone at the top
2. Proactive
3. Reactive

Michele was eager to start the design and implementation of a holistic antifraud program. Michele looked to Perusi & Bilanz LLP for guidance about how to get started with creating and implementing this program and the various elements that are involved.

As previously indicated, Michele wanted to know what the overall framework for the antifraud program should look like because she was tasked with creating and implementing a program at Grand Forge Company.

The key to an antifraud program is to provide the framework for an organization to prevent, detect, report, and investigate both internal and external fraud. As a framework, an antifraud program cannot provide absolute assurance that a fraud will not occur within a company. However, a strong antifraud program will provide management and its employees with the opportunity, guidance, and support needed to understand the expectations of the company, what types of behavior are considered unacceptable, what procedures should be followed if fraud is suspected, and what actions will be taken if fraud is detected.

The key to an effective antifraud program is its communication to and understanding by all stakeholders. Understanding the roles and responsibilities of all stakeholders regarding the antifraud program is paramount to its success. Some factors to consider for roles and responsibilities with respect to the antifraud program can be found in box 14-1. These factors also will be described in more detail later in the chapter.

Antifraud programs are designed to provide management with a framework to mitigate their organization's exposure to fraud and also assist in creating, developing, and improving the organization's culture and how management reacts and responds to fraud-related issues. The three main aspects of a holistic fraud prevention program include the following:

(1) Setting the proper tone at the top within the organization
(2) Proactively identifying fraud risks and monitoring internal controls to prevent or detect the fraud risks
(3) Developing reactive protocols in the event that fraud is suspected

---

3 Association of Certified Fraud Examiner's (ACFE's) *2008 Report to the Nation on Occupational Fraud & Abuse.*

Box 14-1: *Antifraud Program Roles and Responsibilities*

- *Audit committee.* Responsible for overseeing the procedures established by management for the antifraud program, ensuring any reported matters are communicated to the appropriate body, and reviewing the potential for management override of controls or other inappropriate influence over the financial reporting process.

- *Executive management.* Responsible for providing management sponsorship and coordination of the antifraud program. Report to the audit committee the status of current investigations, completed investigations, results of the fraud risk assessment, and action plans to mitigate the risk of fraud within the company.

- *Managers and line supervisors.* Responsible for overseeing the implementation and ongoing effectiveness of the antifraud program. Report to executive management any indicators of suspicious activity.

- *Employees.* Responsible for the implementation of the antifraud program. Report suspicious activities or violations of the code of conduct via the various communication tools established by the organization (for example, whistle-blower hotline, general counsel, chain-of-command, internal audit, and so on)

- *Other stakeholders (for example, vendors, customers, joint venture partners, and so on).* Responsible for awareness of the company's antifraud program and understanding how to report issues.

Figure 14-2 depicts an illustrated view of the framework for an antifraud program.

Setting the Proper Tone at the Top

People commit fraud; therefore, setting the proper tone at the top and the way in which management reinforces its message regarding fraud have a pervasive impact on the company. The starting point for any antifraud program is the tone at the top of the company. Setting the proper tone within a company is a critical step in preventing and detecting fraud. To create a culture of constant integrity, management must go beyond stating that they hire good people or they operate their company with integrity and demonstrate how tactically their tone

is embedded into the company's day-to-day operations. Adopting a code of conduct, formalizing fraud policies and procedures, and conducting fraud awareness training are key elements to a successful tone-setting fraud prevention program. The tone of the organization can be defined as the integrity, ethical values, management philosophy, and operating style within the organization. The tone of the organization influences the control consciousness of its people, provides the foundation for all other components within the organization, and helps determine the discipline and structure of the organization. The tone at the top of the organization can be split into the following areas: code of conduct, culture, governance, fraud prevention policies, and fraud awareness training and communication.

Figure 14-2: *Holistic Antifraud Program Framework*

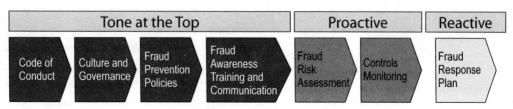

Code of Conduct

The code of conduct is the clear set of business rules set forth by an organization, and it can provide a framework to guide the response of the organization in the challenging and sometimes difficult choices that are presented to members of the organization. The purpose of a code of conduct is to promote the following:

- Honest and ethical conduct
- Full, fair, accurate, timely, and understandable disclosure in reports and documents
- Compliance with applicable governmental laws, rules, and regulations
- Prompt internal reporting of violations of the code
- Accountability for adherence to the code and the sanctions to be imposed for failure to adhere to the code

The code of conduct is typically approved by the audit committee and reviewed on an annual basis. The code of conduct should be part of the new hire practice (that is, all new employees must read and sign the code as part of their condition of employment) and periodically reaffirmed by those in positions of confidence.

Culture

As Michele continued to learn more about the various elements of the antifraud program and, specifically, the fraud risk assessment element, she started to identify the benefits of conducting a fraud risk assessment, which would allow her to prioritize her efforts and, perhaps, the efforts of others within Grand Forge Company to address fraud risks more effectively and efficiently.

During the fraud risk assessment and the controls monitoring exercise, Roland wanted to address some issues that had been found in the surveys done as part of the fraud risk assessment. He was alarmed that employees did not know how to access the hotline in the event they discovered a fraudulent action. He was troubled by the responses received when assessing the employees' understanding of fraud. He indicated that he wanted to strengthen the message around fraud and raise the overall awareness of fraud. He indicated to Michele that he wanted her to assist in creating a fraud awareness and com-

munication plan that would strengthen the overall tone and culture within the organization concerning fraud.

Culture is the personality of the organization. What do the employees of the organization do in response to the message from the tone at the top? Culture can best be defined as the values and beliefs that shape the behavior and determine the process by which things get accomplished within an organization. The following factors must be considered when determining the culture within an organization:

- Is the organization driven by earnings results and organization achievement or internal and external relationships with its employees, customers, and other stakeholders?
- How effective is the knowledge sharing within the organization that may undermine the performance of the antifraud program?
- Is there a rigid or flexible structure?
- Does the organization have an inclusive environment embedded within its organization?
- How does the culture change with respect to the different geographies within which it operates?
- How tactically is the tone embedded into the company's day-to-day operations to create a culture of constant integrity?

Culture can tell you a lot about an organization. This includes the messages that executives send with not only their words but their actions, how behavior within the organization is reinforced, the organization's appetite for risk, the communication throughout the company, and how the organization embraces change.

Understanding culture often creates uncomfortable situations for the executives within an organization because they are not entirely sure what it is, how to measure it, and if change to the culture is needed and how that is accomplished. Typically, an assessment of culture is the first step, and it is often-times accomplished through a series of interviews and surveys.

Governance

Governance specifies the relationship and the distribution of rights and responsibilities among the main groups of participants within an organization. Governance is the set of processes, customs, policies, laws, and institutions affecting the way a corporation is directed, administered, or controlled. Corporate governance also includes the relationships among the many stakeholders involved and the goals for which the corporation is governed. An important aspect of corporate governance is to ensure the accountability of certain individuals in an organization through mechanisms that try to reduce or eliminate the potential problem from occurring. It is helpful to consider if the strategy, objectives, and plans of the antifraud program are aligned with the business's strategy and plans.

Fraud Prevention Policies

Fraud prevention policies and procedures provide knowledge and support regarding what conduct is acceptable and how to report suspected violations.

Fraud prevention policies are a framework for an organization to prevent, detect, report, and investigate internal and external fraud. Formal fraud prevention policies should

- be specific to the individual organization and its operations.
- guide employees through complex issues, including facilitation payments, commission fees, gifts, and conflicts of interest.
- provide a channel for employees or third parties to report fraud.
- establish procedures to govern the escalation of fraud allegations and guide important resource decisions.

The fraud prevention policies are typically reviewed and approved at the appropriate level within the organization, such as audit committee or executive management. Additionally, the fraud prevention policies are maintained in such a way that the most current version(s) are readily available to the appropriate employees. Finally, the fraud prevention policies are periodically updated to reflect the changes in the business environment.

Examples of fraud prevention policies include the following:

- Hiring and promotion practices
  - Prehiring screenings and effective background checks
  - Promotion of those that demonstrate the organization's values
  - Performance evaluations

- Segregation of duties
  - Reassignment of incompatible duties (that is, separation of authorization, custody, recording, and control activity)
  - Position rotation
- User or physical access
  - Removal of incompatible user access
  - Limitation of physical access

Fraud Awareness Training and Communication

Proper policies and procedures set the expected standards for behavior by employees. Virtually all organizations have a code of conduct as a mechanism for disciplining employees who are behaving inappropriately and below a minimum expected standard of conduct. Codes of conduct are a necessary but not sufficient condition for setting expected behavior.

Many organizations have other policies providing guidance to employees on appropriate conduct. These can include, for example, topics such as the following:

- Assignments of authority and responsibility
- Ethical conduct guidance
- Accepting and giving gifts
- Fraud response plans
- Ethics hotlines or whistle-blower programs
- Hiring, promotion, and retention
- Incentive compensation

Fraud awareness training reinforces management's message and provides stakeholders with information regarding the latest issues, challenges, and concerns of the company.

Fraud awareness training is another significant and often overlooked aspect of an antifraud program and a key element in setting the tone within an organization. Lack of understanding and reinforcement of a company's antifraud policies, procedures, reporting protocols, and fraud risks exposes a company to employees, vendors, customers, and other stakeholders not knowing what is considered acceptable behavior or how to effectively report suspected fraudulent activities.

A fraud awareness training program is only as effective as the audience it reaches. All employees should receive annual fraud awareness training, which should be part of the company's annual training program. Fraud awareness training also should be part of the new hire orientation process and part of the integration process for newly acquired companies, joint ventures, or subsidiaries. Additionally, significant vendors and customers should be trained regarding specific aspects of the company's antifraud polices (that is, communicate to customers or vendors the company's policy regarding gifts, entertainment, whistle-blower hotline, and so on). The results of the training (that is, who attended, when, and where) should be recorded and summarized for the audit committee.

Fraud awareness training should include the following:

- Background and understanding of the company's overall antifraud program
- Options for reporting any suspicious activities to management via the chain-of-command or whistle-blower hotline
- An overview of the company's whistle-blower protection program
- Understanding the disciplinary process for those who violate the code of conduct or ethics
- Understanding and review of fraud risks most applicable to the company's business

Additionally, the fraud awareness training program should contain examples of what could be considered violations of the code of conduct or suspicious activity for which to be on the lookout, such as insider trading, receiving or giving gifts, consulting fees, and so on. As we will describe in more detail subsequently, the fraud awareness training should include specific examples of identified fraud risks that are relevant to the organization.

Employees cannot be reasonably expected to follow policies of which they are unaware. Policies may be communicated in many ways, either in hard or soft form or through provision of access to the policy. Some policies and procedures are particularly important or complex and may require more active communication. For example, specific training or certification on technical revenue recognition accounting might be more appropriate than passive provision of access to the policy in which revenue recognition financial statement fraud is a significant risk. Three key fraud awareness program policies that are often overlooked by employees but should be reinforced are:

- The offer of employment and orientation program provides an early opportunity to communicate behavioral expectations to new hires.
- The tone at the top is an important communication channel because leadership by example is a powerful communication tool.
- Whistle-blower channels are often the last resort considered by employees before turning outside the organization. For this reason, a disproportionately large effort is often made to communicate the existence and availability of the whistle-blower channel.

When breaches of the policy are tolerated without consequence, even adequate, well-communicated policies will become ineffective. Absent consistent enforcement, policies become "paper tigers" and their ability to regulate behavior is eroded.

Adoption of a code of conduct or ethics, formalizing fraud policies and procedures, and conducting fraud awareness training are key elements to a successful tone-setting element of the antifraud program. The code of conduct or ethics establishes the guiding principles of the company. Fraud policies and procedures provide knowledge and support regarding what conduct is acceptable and how to report suspected violations

Codifying formal antifraud policies is an element often overlooked by many companies. On a global basis, according to recent surveys done by Ernst & Young, over 40 percent of companies do not have a formal antifraud policy. Among larger companies with revenues greater than $1 billion, 30 percent do not have any antifraud policy, and 18 percent of Securities and Exchange Commission (SEC) registrants, regardless of size and location, do not have a formal antifraud policy.[4]

---

4 Ernst & Young's 10th Global Fraud Survey *Corruption or Compliance—Weighing the costs.*

Proactive

As illustrated in this cartoon, companies are finding it much more efficient, from a cost perspective, to be proactive with respect to fraud than to incur the costs, damage to reputation, and other negative effects of going through a fraud investigation. The ACFE indicates that the average fraud schemes last approximately 24 months, so there is an opportunity to become more diligent in efforts to address fraud proactively and to attempt to eliminate schemes in their early stages versus the latter stages, which are unquestionably more costly. The proactive element of an antifraud program allows management to actively assess what fraud type their company is susceptible to and identify internal controls to prevent or detect those risks. Although this process does not provide absolute assurance that all frauds will be identified, prevented, and detected, it should provide management with the opportunity to address significant fraud risks and consciously implement controls, such as IT analytics, delegation of authority, and user-restricted access, to reduce the likelihood and impact of those risks.

The fraud risk assessment can be based on potential schemes or focus on specific fraudsters who could commit significant fraud. The key is to understand the vulnerabilities a company may have regarding the way fraud could occur and management's ability to override business processes. According to recent studies done in the industry, 55 percent of corporate frauds were committed by management, and various schemes were used to circumvent internal controls.

Many fraud risk assessments focus on two questions: what is the most common fraud that could occur within any company or organization (for example, revenue recognition, conflict of interest, kickbacks, and so on), and what are the most common frauds that could occur within the industry or geographic location in which the organization operates?

If management decides to go through the exercise of performing a fraud risk assessment, then, upon completion of the identification and prioritization of the fraud risks, the next step within this proactive element is to identify and monitor internal controls to mitigate those risks. Action plans should be developed to identify, document, and evaluate the controls to mitigate those fraud risks that were identified and prioritized within the fraud risk assessment. The action plans should specify who will be responsible for identifying, documenting, and testing the controls, as well as who will review the results of their work. In most cases, objective, independent, and well-qualified individuals should be tasked with identifying and testing internal controls.

Specific reporting channels should be established for reporting the results of the fraud risk assessment and internal control monitoring. The reporting channels should include a line to the audit committee so they are informed about fraud risks, action plans to mitigate those risks, and the results of the testing efforts. Additionally, any control failures or suspected fraudulent activity should be communicated to the audit committee as soon as practical.

Execution of a robust fraud risk assessment is the first proactive step management should undertake. The purpose of the fraud risk assessment is to identify areas (for example, business processes, location, transaction types, geographic locations, and so on) that pose a higher risk of fraud. It is important to keep in mind that people commit fraud, not IT systems, business processes, or the heating system in the corporate office. Therefore, when executing a fraud risk assessment, it is imperative that management understand vulnerabilities and the causes of fraud, which are commonly referred to as the fraud triangle and illustrated in figure 14-3. The fraud triangle is discussed at length in chapter 1, "Basics of Investigations."

Figure 14-3: *Fraud Triangle*

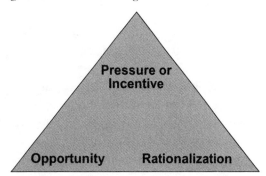

In our hypothetical Grand Forge Company case study, Roland specifically asked Michele to identify relevant industry-specific exposures that have affected or could affect Grand Forge Company. Michele set out to gain a better understanding of the allegations that were being raised in the original case study and of the fraud triangle and how they might assist her in her quest to implement and conduct the fraud risk assessment process at Grand Forge Company.

The fraud triangle concept is relevant to identifying and understanding the importance of fraud risk factors that may be present in an organization. These are the three conditions usually present when people commit financial fraud, misappropriation of assets, or corruption-type schemes. Internal audit directors and others involved in a fraud investigation must be alert for the following conditions:

- Incentives or pressures on management to perpetrate fraud to achieve desired financial results
- Opportunities (for example, control weaknesses) to carry out fraud without being detected
- Personnel who are able to rationalize to themselves a need for the fraud (that is, convince themselves the fraud is justified)

In addition to factoring in the fraud triangle, a good place to start designing and implementing a comprehensive fraud risk assessment is with the ACFE's fraud tree, which organizes fraud into the following three broad types:

- *Fraudulent financial reporting.* Most fraudulent financial reporting schemes involve earnings management arising from improper revenue recognition, the overstatement of assets, or the understatement of liabilities.
- *Misappropriation of assets.* This type involves external and internal schemes, such as embezzlement, payroll fraud, and theft.
- *Corruption.* This type refers to commercial and public bribery, as well as other improper payment schemes.

Upon identification of the three main areas, it is useful to review these fraud risk types in relation to the organization's business and determine the fraud risks that are relevant for your organization. It also is important to develop an initial point of view of those relevant key fraud risks that are more significant than others, based on your knowledge of the client, input from your industry, and subject matter resources and other sources (for example, partner(s) who have previously worked in this industry).

Creating and Conducting a Fraud Risk Assessment

When creating and conducting a fraud risk assessment, it is encouraged to focus a fraud risk assessment with a risk-based approach and top-down view of corresponding controls, as deemed necessary. Stakeholders within the company are generally aware of the areas of the organization most vulnerable or prone to the risk of fraud, based on factors such as industry experience, the organization's own prior experience, current issues in the organization's regulatory environment, and the facts and circumstances unique to the organization at that point in time.

A fraud risk assessment is used to identify and manage fraud risks. On June 20, 2007, the SEC published Interpretive Release No. 33-8810, which provides interpretive guidance for management's report on internal control over financial reporting. The following guidance indicates the importance of creating the fraud risk assessment:

> Management's evaluation of the risk of misstatement should include consideration of the vulnerability of the entity to fraudulent activity (for example, fraudulent financial reporting, misappropriation of assets and corruption), and whether any such exposure could result in a material misstatement of the financial statements. The extent of activities required for the evaluation of fraud risks is commensurate with the size and complexity of the company's operations and financial reporting environment.

> Management should recognize that the risk of material misstatement due to fraud ordinarily exists in any organization, regardless of size or type, and it may vary by specific location or segment and by individual financial reporting element. ... [E]ffective fraud risk assessments will require sound and thoughtful judgments that reflect a company's individual facts and circumstances.

The relevant fraud risks would be drawn from a universe of fraud risks. An example of a universe of fraud risks is the fraud tree, which we described earlier. The tree is useful in that it identifies a range of fraud risks, categorized within the categories of fraudulent statements, asset misappropriation, and corruption. The relevant risks, based on the factors in the preceding paragraph, would be identified for prioritization.

When creating and implementing a fraud risk assessment, it is very important to determine how the organization will define fraud. In other words, what does fraud mean to your organization, and how do you define fraud? Both of these questions will assist you greatly when determining fraud risks during the assessment phase. Fraud is generally a misrepresentation intended to secure an unlawful benefit.[5] Fraud is not a new phenomenon. There have been many instances throughout history in which fraudsters have unlawfully and intentionally prejudiced others to their own advantage. The Bernard Madoff issues come to mind when considering a recent example of this concept. The renegade Wall Street financier faces a possible sentence of up to 150 years in prison after being formally charged with a list of crimes, including laundering millions of dollars in ill-gotten gains through London. Federal prosecutors in Manhattan detailed 11 criminal charges against Madoff, including fraud, perjury, theft, false statements, and international money laundering. The U.S. Department of Justice described his alleged crimes as "extraordinary" and "unprecedented" in scale,

orchestrated through an alleged $50 billion Ponzi scheme dating back to the 1980s.

Similarly, our recent experiences have shown that general assumptions with respect to fraud and its definition and related controls may, in certain circumstances, be invalid. For example, segregation of duties is generally relied upon to ensure appropriate checks and balances over the behavior of any individual, but the quality of segregation of duties at the level of the CEO can be inadequate to effectively control the risk of management override. Although management would be responsible for the antifraud program, the directors, particularly the audit committee, would have some responsibility for managing the risk of management override. Additional information on segregation of duties during a fraud investigation can be found in chapter 6, "Roles and Responsibilities."

In the case of our Grand Forge Company example, Perusi & Bilanz LLP assisted Michele in creating, designing, and implementing the fraud risk assessment by asking the questions found in box 14-2, among others, to gain an understanding of how she and Grand Forge Company wanted to structure their fraud risk assessment and when and where they wanted to get started within the organization. Perusi & Bilanz LLP also asked other thought-provoking questions to assist in designing a tailored fraud risk assessment for their needs. Questions like these are critical to address up front as a company begins the process to create a more comprehensive and, therefore, more effective fraud risk assessment.

Box 14-2: *Grand Forge Company Fraud Risk Assessment Questions*

1. **Is the organization decentralized?**
This will determine if you want to structure your fraud risk assessment by business unit or conduct an assessment over the entire company.

2. **Does the organization have international interest?** This will determine how you want to structure your process (for example, in person interviews, facilitated sessions, or surveys). Do you need to consider fraud risk specific to that area of operations (that is, Foreign Corrupt Practices Act and so on)?

(continued)

---

5 *Black's Law Dictionary* defines fraud as "An intentional perversion of truth for the purpose of inducing another in reliance upon it to part with some valuable thing belonging to him or to surrender a legal right; a false representation of a matter of fact, whether by words or by conduct, by false or misleading allegations, or by concealment of that which should have been disclosed, which deceives and is intended to deceive another so that he shall act upon it to his legal injury."

Box 14-2: *Grand Forge Company Fraud Risk Assessment Questions (continued)*

3. **Does the company want to conduct interviews, facilitated sessions, or surveys as a means to gather information from participants in determining what fraud risks affect the organization?** This is critical as you start to determine how broad your fraud risk assessment will become.

5. **Has the organization experienced fraud previously?** Did the company do anything to mitigate this risk from happening again? Previous frauds that actually occurred should be identified as a fraud risk in the future and evaluated with the other potential fraud risks that have been identified.

7. **Has the organization recently restructured, acquired, merged, or announced a business unit disposal?** Fraud oftentimes occurs in units that are being disposed because the focus is no longer on them, with respect to controls. Acquisitions can be ripe with fraud because companies that are being acquired try and make their company appear stronger or more profitable to increase the purchase price.

4. **How will results be compiled? Will a report be issued to the board and so on?** This is important as you start to develop the work plan to accomplish the fraud risk assessment.

6. **Are there new accounting or statutory regulations?** Would there be an incentive to manipulate the numbers if these new regulations may have an area for manipulation in their implementation (that is, a "gray area")?

8. **Is the organization's industry competitive with declining margins or customer demand?** This can be a potential fraud risk because individuals may try and make the external reports appear better or stronger than they are, which affects other contracts.

Based on Grand Forge Company's structure with international operations, Michele indicated that she wanted to conduct a company-wide fraud risk assessment that focused on issues relevant to the corporate headquarters and international operations. Using the previous questions as a guide, she determined that she wanted to conduct the fraud risk assessment using all three of the following methods:

(1) Interviews

(2) Surveys

(3) Facilitated sessions

Typically, these three methods are used to conduct a fraud risk assessment because they are valuable tools and mechanisms for capturing information from participants in order to understand where fraud risks or exposures are located within an organization. Determining what method to use is based on how members of the company tasked with completing the fraud risk assessment feel that process would be received within the organization and how the company wants to structure the fraud risk assessment. In the case study example with Grand Forge Company, Michele started the process by conducting 25 interviews of key members of management at the corporate level to obtain an overall understanding of where they felt exposures to fraud risk were located within the organization. She performed similar interviews with selected members of management at each of the international locations. While Perusi & Bilanz LLP was assisting Michele conduct the interviews, she also sent out a 40-question survey to randomly selected employees (no one that was interviewed completed a survey) throughout the organization to gain insight into what the tone at the top of the organization was like; additional fraud risks from different perspectives within the company; awareness of fraud within the company; and also to gain an understanding of how fraud is handled, talked about, and dealt with internally.

Upon compiling the results from each interview and the results of the surveys, Perusi & Bilanz LLP assisted Michele in preparing for each facilitated session. Sessions were conducted at the corporate headquarters and each manufacturing facility within the company. The facilitated session is a process in which selected members of management are presented the ideas gathered and then asked to obtain consensus among themselves about the likelihood of fraud occurrence and the significance of its impact. As Michele prepared for the facilitated sessions, Perusi & Bilanz LLP indicated that she should group the fraud risks obtained into the three main areas of fraud, which indicated earlier and are as follows:

1. Misappropriation of assets schemes
2. Financial statement schemes
3. Corruptions schemes

The schemes are discussed in greater detail in chapters 2-4 of this book. The primary reason to group the fraud schemes into the three main areas of fraud is because, when voting on likelihood and significance of impact, it is valuable to view these schemes in the same category, rather than comparing all schemes together from the three categories previously mentioned. The following quick example demonstrates this point by illustrating the loss values associated with each main category of fraud. To further illustrate, if one was looking at travel and entertainment reimbursement fraud on the same scale as a fraudulent financial statement scheme, such as revenue recognition manipulation, the results would be skewed because the median results are so different. Therefore, when prioritizing efforts to address these identified risks, it is helpful to keep this concept in mind. Table 14-1 is based on information from the ACFE's *2008 Report to the Nation on Occupational Fraud & Abuse* and further describes the point of the differences in the three types of fraud from a median loss perspective.

Table 14-1: *Types of Occupational Fraud and Abuse*

Category	Description	Examples	Median Loss
Asset Misappropriations	Any scheme that involves the theft or misuse of an organization's assets	• Fraudulent invoicing • Payroll fraud • Skimming revenues	$ 150,000
Corruption	Any scheme in which a person uses his or her influence to obtain unauthorized benefit contrary to that person's duty to their employer	• Acceptig or paying a bribe • Engaging in a business transaction in which there is an undisclosed conflict or interest	$ 375,000
Fraudulent Statements	Falsification of an organization's financial statements to make it appear more or less profitable	• Booking fictitious sales • Recording expenses in the wrong period	$2,000,000

Loss is defined as the total amount of money or decrease in reported revenues attributable to the scheme being committed.

(Source: 2008 Report to the Nation on Occupational Fraud & Abuse. Copyright 2008 by the Association of Certified Fraud Examiners, Inc.)

Michele agreed to use the three main areas of fraud and the breakdown by median loss as a basis to structure the fraud risk assessment, which she considered a logical and useful method. Although these don't represent materiality levels for the financial statements, they do represent a point in which to gauge losses from a rating perspective when considering significance of impact.

One of the most critical elements when conducting the fraud risk assessment is how to compile the results. Perusi & Bilanz LLP indicated to Michele that she should consider using a "heat map" model to plot each fraud risk learned from the interviews and surveys, based on an assessment of likelihood of occurrence and severity of impact from the facilitated sessions. Michele agreed that this was an excellent way to pictorially show the results of the fraud risk assessment.

The relevant fraud risks are generally prioritized based on likelihood of occurrence and severity of impact. The likelihood of occurrence can be a factor in either the inherent or residual risk of fraud after the impact of internal controls. When creating a fraud risk assessment, an important decision to make is how to factor in the likelihood of occurrence. Do you review the fraud risks with the knowledge of the current controls in place to potentially mitigate those risks, which is residual risk, or do you assume the absence of controls, which is inherent risk? The severity should allow for both the quantitative and qualitative impact of the fraud. In practice, a relatively immaterial dollar amount might have a severe impact. For example, a fraud with regulatory consequences involving misrepresentations by senior management would have a severe impact, even when amounts involved were not a material dollar value, with respect to the overall financials.

In the Grand Forge Company case, a manipulation of earnings through management override by executives within the company could cause Michele tremendous concern about the tone and culture of the organization. A fraud committed from this perspective could be material, irrespective of the dollar amounts associated with the scheme, given the significance of those involved.

The individual facts and circumstances of the organization are relevant to determining the priority of fraud risks. The model most commonly used to identify the relevant individual facts and circumstances is the fraud triangle, which considers the following three conditions generally present when fraud occurs:

- An incentive or pressure providing a reason to commit fraud
- An opportunity to commit fraud through missing, ineffective, or overridden controls

- An ability to rationalize the commission of the fraud

The individual facts and circumstances within an organization can differ widely across geographies. For example, concerns of corruption are stronger in emerging markets, and concerns of financial statement misrepresentation are stronger in developed markets. Similarly, they can differ across the operations of the entity (for example, the conditions may be significantly different at a recently acquired operation).[6]

Figure 14-4 provides an example of a "heat map" chart to illustrate the power of compiling the results in this manner. Perusi & Bilanz LLP assisted Michele in compiling three individual "heat maps," one for each major area of fraud previously described (misappropriation of assets, fraudulent statement, and corruption schemes). Perusi & Bilanz LLP took the information obtained from the surveys and interviews of each business unit and selected a group of 25 members of management to sit in a 6-hour facilitated session and rank each of the identified fraud risks, based on a predefined scale for likelihood of occurrence and severity of impact (See figure 14-5). The scale used during the session and the output for fraudulent statement schemes from one of the sessions is detailed in figure 14-6. Each number on the "heat map" pertains to a corresponding fraud risk identified during the interviews, survey, and facilitated session.

As a result of the fraud risk assessment performed and the identification of the fraud risks identified, Michele, with assistance from Perusi & Bilanz LLP, set up a communication and training program. She ensured that the most relevant information and highest risk fraud schemes identified from the fraud risk assessment were portrayed in the training program.

Studies done by the ACFE suggest that the number one way in which fraud is caught is by a tip, so companies are exploring ways to ensure that their employees are educated on fraud schemes that are relevant to their organization.[7] Therefore, it is helpful to use the fraud risk assessment as a starting point in creating a fraud awareness training program. This

---

6 Ernst & Young's 10th Global Fraud Survey *Corruption or Compliance—Weighing the costs.*
7 ACFE *2008 Report to the Nation on Occupational Fraud & Abuse.*

Figure 14-4: *Risk Rating Criteria: Severity of Financial Impact*

Score	Fraudulent Financial Statements	Misappropriation of Assets	Corruption
5—Critical:	Critical Loss > $2,000,000	Critical Loss > $150,000	Critical Loss > $375,000
4—Severe:	Severe Loss $750,000–$2,000,000	Severe Loss $75,000–$150,000	Severe Loss $375,000–$250,000
3—Significant:	Significant Loss $250,000–$750,000	Significant Loss $25,000–$75,000	Significant Loss $250,000–$175,000
2—Moderate:	Moderate Loss $75,000–$250,000	Moderate Loss $10,000–$25,000	Moderate Loss $175,000–$50,000
1—Minor:	Minor Loss < $75,000	Minor Loss < $10,000	Minor Loss < $50,000

Figure 14-5: *Risk Rating Criteria: Likelihood of Occurrence*

Score	Fraudulent Financial Statements	Misappropriation of Assets	Corruption
5—Highly Likely:	The event will or has occurred once or more on an annual basis.		
4—Likely:	The event has occurred several times and could easily occur 3–4 times every 2–3 years.		
3—Possible:	The event has occurred or might be likely to occur every 3–4 years.		
2—Rare:	The event has occurred or might occur once or twice during the last 5–7 years.		
1—Very Rare:	Have heard of this happening or it could happen, but likely only once or twice in the last 10-year period.		

Figure 14-6: *Fraudulent Statement Schemes Chart*

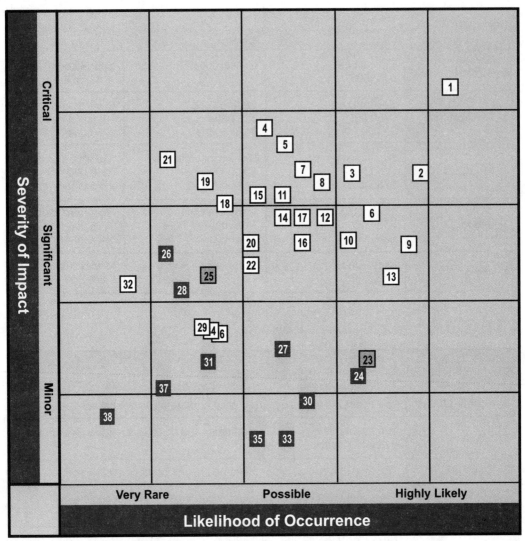

will give the organization the ability to identify and potentially strengthen areas of concern identified during the fraud risk assessment process and will ultimately assist in determining what type of training the employees within an organization should receive.

Controls Monitoring

Upon identification of the fraud risks relevant to the organization, it is critical to evaluate the controls currently in place to mitigate these fraud risks. Management's evaluation of the effectiveness of the processes and related controls in managing the fraud risks can indicate opportunities for improvement of the processes or controls in managing the fraud risks or management's planned actions to monitor or improve the processes or controls.

Control monitoring begins by listing the processes and initiatives that address the areas of focus identified as high-assessed fraud risks, followed by moderate-assessed fraud risks, and then low-assessed fraud risks. In some instances, there may be so many high- or moderate-assessed fraud risks or associated processes and initiatives that it becomes necessary to further prioritize to streamline the process.

Ultimately, management or the audit committee are responsible for determining which of the identified risks will result in performance of controls monitoring or improvement activities, after considering the potential impact of the fraud risks and the cost to execute such procedures.

Gap Analysis

As we indicated in the overview of the case study, the next logical question to ask is "What does the organization do with the results?"

Through a controls mapping process, identification of gaps in the controls structure is needed to determine the location of controls that were not in place to mitigate the risk identified from the fraud risk assessment. This also will help validate the placement of the fraud risks on the preceding "heat map," from a likelihood of occurrence and severity of impact perspective.

The following are the two main types of controls:

1) Entity-level controls
2) Transaction-level controls

Entity-Level Controls

These controls span the breadth of the organization. Entity-level controls set the tone and establish the expectations of the organization's control environment. Entity-level controls can be used to monitor the extent to which that tone and those expectations are being fulfilled. In short, entity-level controls help management deliver on its promise to stakeholders to run their companies effectively and efficiently.

The benefits of effective and efficient entity-level controls can be significant and may include the following:

- Reduction of the likelihood of a negative risk event by establishing and reinforcing the infrastructure that sets the control consciousness of the organization.
- A broad risk coverage over financial reporting and operations. For companies conducting evaluations of internal controls, the presence of effective entity-level controls can contribute to a more effective and efficient evaluation strategy.
- Generation of efficiencies in other businesses and operational processes.
- Reinforcement for all stakeholders of the importance of internal controls to the success of the business.

Entity-level controls generally have a wide-scope impact on the achievement of the company's objectives for internal control. Entity-level controls are organized in categories consistent with the basic components of internal control (monitoring, information and communication, control activities, risk assessment, and control environment), as defined by the Committee of Sponsoring Organizations of the Treadway Commission.

The impact that entity-level controls can have on an organization may vary, based on the control and the company. Some entity-level controls help define the overall control conscience of the organization but do not directly mitigate specific financial statement or operating risks. Other entity-level controls are implemented at the sub-process, process, location, business unit, or company-wide level. These controls are generally used to monitor specific business and financial risks and operate at the level of precision necessary to directly detect and correct breakdowns in the application of a company's policies and procedures. Example areas within an organization where entity-level controls may typically be found are outlined in box 14-3.

Whether compelled by governmental regulation, industry guidelines, or business executives seeking accountability, companies around the globe are evaluating the effectiveness of their internal controls. As part of a top-down fraud risk assessment, which helps identify and prioritize relevant business and financial fraud risks, the identification and evaluation of effective entity-level controls may be used to understand how identified risks are mitigated and redirect evaluation and other resources toward priority-risk areas. This helps increase both the effectiveness and efficiency of management's risk assessment and controls evaluation.

The benefits of entity-level controls can be further enhanced by focusing on those controls that are most effective at mitigating identified risks.

Leading companies are constantly striving to increase the effectiveness and efficiency of their internal control structure. They want improved internal control along with, not in place of, an increase in efficiency. In addition, they desire an internal control environment that helps generate improved business

Box 14-3: *Entity-Level Control Process Levels*

Monitoring

- *Ongoing monitoring activities.* Periodic review of processes and controls using relevant management reporting tools. For example, these would include a monthly review of aging of accounts receivable to determine the extent of reserves required for doubtful debts.

- *Independent assessment mechanism.* Use of external specialists or professionals to review and assess internal controls. For example, this might include the use of external tax professionals to review the controls around tax positions developed by the in-house tax team.

- *Variance analysis reporting.* Comparison and reporting of actual performance against predetermined benchmarks, if used appropriately, can serve as an early-warning mechanism. For example, a steady increase in debtor turnover might indicate varying levels of collection-related issues.

- *Remediation mechanism.* This refers to a systematic approach to resolving identified internal control issues. Although an issue could be identified by either an internal or external monitoring mechanism, the remediation mechanism is usually management owned.

- *Management triggers embedded within IT systems.* Most enterprise applications configure business rules in a manner to prevent undesired access or entries, require preapproval for access or entries, or alert relevant management personnel in the event that certain preset thresholds are not observed. For example, a sales application could deploy a control preventing sales transactions above the specified credit limit of a customer. As another example, an application may allow the same transaction but only after having secured certain approvals. As a final example, the same application could be set to simply alert the relevant management personnel after such a transaction has been recorded.

Information and Communication

- *Internal communication and performance reporting.* This refers to the lines of communication that run through an organization's structure, both top down and bottom up, including peer communication. Performance reporting is part of internal communication and usually involves a two-way process of setting expectations and monitoring performance against agreed-upon expectations.

- *Tone setting.* Tone setting refers to various components of the tone at the top, which are the building blocks of the character of an organization. Having set the right tone, it is equally important to have open channels of communication so that those within and outside the organization understand and act upon it. Examples of such components of tone include a code of ethics and corporate governance practices.

- *Board or audit committee reporting.* Board members, including independent directors, assume fiduciary responsibilities that require them to have access to accurate and relevant information. Although most countries have enacted laws regarding formal reporting to the board of directors and the audit committee of the board, these usually constitute baseline procedures and requirements. Companies are free to adopt more stringent measures regarding board or audit committee reporting, such as holding more frequent formal audit committee meetings than required by law.

- *External communication.* This refers to the communication to the shareholders, stock market, customers, regulators, vendors, and other entities outside the company's formal boundaries. The annual report is an example of external communication about the company's performance, financial statements, vision, goals, and targets.

Control Activities

- *Policies and procedures.* Policies are the business rules and formalized practices that the organization and its employees need to observe. These policies and procedures are governed by both legal and regulatory requirements and management philosophy. For example, accounting policies are typically aligned to prevailing accounting standards, whereas credit policy is dependent on management's risk appetite.

(continued)

(continued)

- *Internal Audit reviews.* Internal Audit serves as a tool for both the audit committee and management to dive into identified high-risk areas for identification of issues and recommendations on their remediation. Internal Audit frequently reports to the audit committee and can be either internally- or externally-staffed.

- *Segregation of duties.* This concept requires an independent review of the work performed by an individual to prevent him or her from being able to both start and complete a critical transaction. Segregation of duties is a key antifraud control.

- *Accounts reconciliations.* Periodic reconciliation of accounts helps identification of errors, omissions, and even fraud. For example, a reconciliation of customer accounts could identify payments received but not applied to the correct customer account.

- *System balancing and exception reporting.* System balancing refers to a built-in system of checks to verify the integrity of data transferred from another application. Examples include a mechanism for comparing batch totals between an original data source and data transferred into a new application. Exception reporting relates to the reporting of exception items to management so that management can use its time more effectively. For example, the sales manager could potentially review all sales transactions for a day, but it is more time efficient if the review and approval process is focused on transactions that are not sold at the list price or sold above a certain predetermined discount percentage.

- *Change management.* This refers to management of changes to processes, people, organizational structures, and so on in a manner to minimize business disruptions that might otherwise harm overall business performance.

Control Environment

- *Code of conduct.* This refers to the norms to which the organization voluntarily agrees to comply. For example, the company's code of conduct might include a policy prohibiting employees from accepting gifts from vendors.

- *Governance.* Governance is a mechanism for monitoring how the resources of an organization are being put to an efficient use by management, with an emphasis on transparency and accountability.

- *Assignment of authority and responsibility.* The term *authority* refers to the right to perform the organization's activities. The term *responsibility* refers to the obligation to perform assigned activities. It is important for the achievement of control objectives that authorities and responsibilities be consistent with the goals of the organization's business activities and be assigned to appropriate personnel.

- *Hiring and retention practices.* Hiring and retaining skilled resources is critical to an organization's success. Policies and procedures regarding job definition, recruitment, training, performance appraisal, employee retention programs, and management of employee exits are important components of managing human resources.

- *Fraud prevention, prevent and detect controls, and analytical procedures.* This refers to the antifraud controls and procedures used by management to prevent, detect, and mitigate fraud. Examples might include segregation of duties, setting up an ethics hotline, and periodic job rotation.

and operational performance. Entity-level controls can provide a foundation upon which companies are able to build a more effective and efficient internal control environment, and they allow management to establish expectations, provide guidance, and develop communication channels by which they can more effectively reach all levels of the organization. Entity-level controls provide management with a tool it can use to monitor adherence to the company's expectations.

Working in concert with each other, well-designed and effective entity-level controls help management better meet business and financial objectives and should be considered a key element of a leading-class internal control structure.

Transaction-Level Controls

These controls tend to have a narrower scope. They are important because they may be sufficiently specific to prevent or detect fraud on a timely basis. At the specific transaction level, internal control refers to the actions taken to achieve a specific objective (for example, how to ensure the organization's payments to third parties are for valid services rendered). Internal control procedures reduce process variation, leading to more predictable outcomes. These controls could be identified to specifically address one of the identified fraud risk schemes.

As is often the case, Michele indicated she wanted to focus on entity- and transaction-level controls already in place or those that needed to be put in place to mitigate the identified fraud risks. Perusi & Bilanz LLP developed an approach to complete the gap analysis with Michele in which she would list

- the fraud risks identified during the assessment.
- the corresponding controls in place to mitigate the fraud risks and the potential controls that could be implemented to mitigate each identified fraud risk.
- a process owner who would follow up on this fraud risk.
- the potential incorporation of data analytics into the process to help prevent, detect, and monitor each identified fraud risk.
- the timeframe for desired follow up.

Monitoring Activities

Monitoring controls to prevent or detect frauds are the means by which the organization develops a sense of the level and location of potentially irregular activity. The controls might be as simple as periodic conversations between people who might reasonably come across red flags, such as security, internal audit, and general counsel.

Common monitoring controls include the following:

- The results of exit interviews
- Internal audit reports
- Period end financial reporting processes, including reconciliations, executive reviews, and certifications

In more sophisticated environments, the controls might include real-time transaction validation controls, integrated compliance monitoring systems, or automated reporting of whistle-blower activity to multiple parties, including the chair of the audit committee.

Following this approach allows for the opportunity to push the process forward, rather than own the process, and treat the control monitoring exercise almost like an internal audit finding, which allows the Internal Audit department to remain independent from the process so that it can continue to audit the process from an effectiveness standpoint.

Reactive

The final step in a cohesive antifraud program is the establishment of reactive elements. Management can set the proper tone, execute a robust fraud risk assessment, and design internal controls to prevent and detect fraud, but fraud will still occur. As mentioned earlier, recent studies done by the ACFE estimate that as much as 7 percent of U.S. companies' revenues are lost each year due to fraud[8]. As a result, management should establish various protocols to react to those situations in which fraud is suspected.

Maintaining a fraud response plan is the cornerstone of any reactive element in an antifraud program. Policies and procedures should be established, reviewed, approved, and maintained regarding the company's response to potential fraud threats. The

8 ACFE *2008 Report to the Nation on Occupational Fraud & Abuse.*

fraud response plan should encompass investigations, remediation, and uniform disciplinary processes.

Investigation protocols should be established so that management has a framework from which to operate if a fraud is suspected. The protocols should state that all suspected frauds, regardless of source, will be investigated; management will lead the investigations; and the results of the investigations will be communicated to the audit committee in a timely manner. The setup of policies and procedures that establish the uniform practice of disciplining any individual, regardless of position, who commits fraud, fails to comply with federal or state regulations, or fails to comply with the organization's code of conduct or ethics is considered a best practice. Additionally, any disciplinary action that is taken against an employee, vendor, or customer should to be communicated to the audit committee.

Results of the fraud investigations will be reviewed to determine what remediation, if any, is required to eliminate the potential for reoccurrence (for example, changes in policies, procedures, or processes). Management should be required to report the status of the remediation plans to the audit committee.

In order for the fraud response plan to be effective, upon identification through the whistle-blower hotline, a tip, or otherwise, the fraud response process should allow for this alleged potential complaint to escalate properly and enable an appropriate investigation of the facts. In some circumstances, an investigation of the facts would be appropriately conducted by line management, but, in other circumstances, it might be more appropriate for the investigation to include a broader internal or even external team.

In our Grand Forge Company case study example, Michele worked with Perusi & Bilanz LLP and the general counsel, Jacob Willis, to create an outline of what the fraud response plan should look like and include. Jacob then worked to draft the document and, once completed, the company used an internal webcast to ensure all employees were aware of the newly developed policy. The fraud response plan that was created for Grand Forge Company may look something like figure 14-7, which captures all of the key fraud prevention elements necessary in a response plan.

Figure 14-7: *Fraud Response Plan*

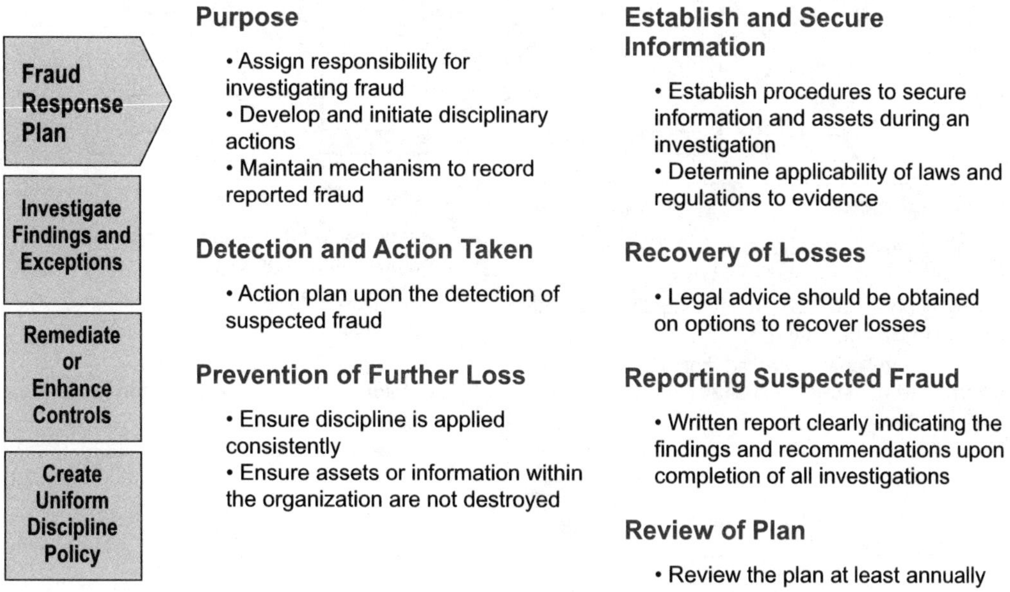

Fraud Response Plan

Investigate Findings and Exceptions

Remediate or Enhance Controls

Create Uniform Discipline Policy

Purpose

- Assign responsibility for investigating fraud
- Develop and initiate disciplinary actions
- Maintain mechanism to record reported fraud

Detection and Action Taken

- Action plan upon the detection of suspected fraud

Prevention of Further Loss

- Ensure discipline is applied consistently
- Ensure assets or information within the organization are not destroyed

Establish and Secure Information

- Establish procedures to secure information and assets during an investigation
- Determine applicability of laws and regulations to evidence

Recovery of Losses

- Legal advice should be obtained on options to recover losses

Reporting Suspected Fraud

- Written report clearly indicating the findings and recommendations upon completion of all investigations

Review of Plan

- Review the plan at least annually

Ownership of the Antifraud Program

Ownership of the overall antifraud program is not something Internal Audit can do alone, and, quite frankly, it should not have overall ownership of the program due to the fact that it will want to audit the individual elements and the overall effectiveness of the program once it is implemented. The key to designing and implementing an effective antifraud program is getting support from higher levels of management within an organization. This allows the employees to understand this is a key initiative, and it further strengthens the tone and culture within a company. It sends the message that fraud is something the company takes very seriously.

Michele was feeling more comfortable in her understanding of an antifraud program and the benefits to designing and implementing such a program. However, she was concerned that she couldn't ultimately own the process and remain independent and eventually audit the effectiveness of the program if Internal Audit was the driving force for putting the program in place. Perusi & Bilanz LLP agreed with Michele and offered a chart depicting the various roles that are typically involved in the design and implementation of an antifraud program (see figure 14-8). The key to implementing an antifraud program is determining what role each individual and department will play, with respect to the overall program.

Figure 14-8: *Roles and Responsibilities for the Grand Forge Company Antifraud Program*

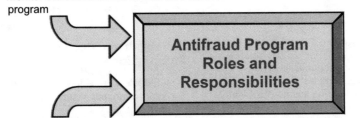

Board of Directors

— Setting the proper tone
— Ensure management designs effective fraud risk management policies
— Establish mechanisms to ensure it receives accurate and timely information
— Monitor the effectiveness of the Anti-Fraud program

Audit Committee:

— Comprises indendence board members
— Active role in the risk assessment process
— Monitors fraud risks via internal auditing
— Direct reporting channel for external audit

Antifraud Program Roles and Responsibilities

Internal Audit:

— Ensures fraud prevention and detection controls are sufficient for identified risks
— May be responsible for investigating suspected instances of fraud
— Company charter should dictate Internal Audit's role with respect to antifraud development

Management:

— Responsible for design and implementation of the Antifraud program
    — Setting the proper tone
    — Reactive
    — Proactive
— Reinforces setting the proper tone at the top
— Helps to create a culture of zero fraud tolerance

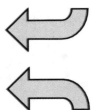

As previously described, for the antifraud program to be truly effective and properly implemented into the company it needs to have support from the various members of management.

Benefits of an Antifraud Program

Upon creating an antifraud program, the following points are considered to be benefits for designing and implementing the various elements of the antifraud program:

(1) Provide tangible evidence of a culture of integrity

(2) Allow Internal Audit to use to the results from the fraud risk assessment to drive the internal audit plan for the year

(3) Help prevent fraud and facilitate early detection

(4) Improve controls monitoring

(5) Increase fraud awareness

(6) Limit unpleasant surprises that affect reputation, credibility, and stock price

(7) Increase confidence of major stakeholders

(8) Reduce potential for class action lawsuits

Conclusion

Fraud is a significant threat facing businesses all over the world. According to Ernst & Young's *9th Global Fraud Survey: Fraud risk in emerging markets*, one in five companies surveyed has experienced a significant fraud in the past two years. Although organizations cannot be imprisoned, they can be fined, sentenced to probation for up to five years, ordered to make restitution and issue public notice of conviction to their victims, and exposed to forfeitures. The consequences of a financial statement fraud often result in bankruptcy, significant changes in ownership, financial penalties, and possibly delisting by national exchanges.

For these reasons, management should implement a strong antifraud program that helps prevent fraud

or detect it in its early stages and improves fraud awareness among the organization's employees, vendors, and customers through training and commitment to ethical behavior. Additional benefits of a strong fraud prevention program include improving the business by reducing surprises, increasing the external auditor's and board of directors' satisfaction with the internal controls environment, and reducing the potential of a class action lawsuit.

Enron; WorldCom; Tyco; Adelphia; Societe Generale; the Satyam fraud; and, recently, the Ponzi scheme perpetrated by Bernard Madoff are just a few examples of frauds that have occurred and caused devastating effects on their organizations, employees, and investors. These events continue to alter the public's perception of fraud in Corporate America and are causing management within organizations to explore ideas on how to proactively deal with fraud. All organizations are subject to fraud schemes occurring within their organization, and, as we noted earlier, 7 percent of organizations' revenues are lost each year due to fraud.[9]

With the continued onset of one of the worst economic downturns in the history of the United States and internal and external pressures on employees, a perfect is storm brewing for the potential for fraud to reach an all-time high. This is further magnified by the fact that companies continue to downsize and reduce spending on nonmission-critical objectives, which is creating tremendous strain on internal controls, such as segregation of duties, just by reductions in people alone. Millions of dollars lost each year to fraud; actual incidents of fraud, like the examples previously listed; the fear of an increase in potential frauds occurring due to the downturn in the economy; and the heightened regulatory environment are causing board members, independent auditors, members of management, and other stakeholders to ask pointed questions about how their company is responding to fraud risk.

Due to these factors, more and more exposure in the industry is currently being given to the concept of antifraud and fraud risk management and how to incorporate a holistic antifraud program within

---

9 ACFE *2008 Report to the Nation on Occupational Fraud & Abuse.*

an organization. As previously indicated, more and more companies are designing and implementing antifraud programs to help raise the awareness of fraud and proactively deal with fraud risk management. Antifraud programs should be viewed as a continuous process; all the elements of the antifraud program are interrelated and support each other and are fully represented as a holistic antifraud program in figure 14-9.

Figure 14-9: *Antifraud Program Cycle*

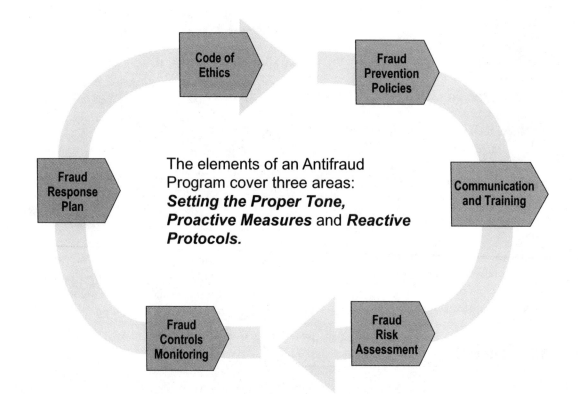

Glossary

1997 Organization for Economic Cooperation and Development Anti-Bribery Convention. An organization that establishes legally binding standards to criminalize bribery of foreign public officials in international business transactions and provides for a host of related measures that make this effective.[19]

40+9 Recommendations. The Financial Action Task Force's (FATF) 40 Recommendations set out a comprehensive framework for anti-money laundering efforts, and encompass criminal justice and law enforcement, the financial system and its regulation, and international cooperation. The Financial Action Task Force 40 lay out principles for countries to implement according to their particular circumstances and constitutional frameworks. In a related initiative, FATF identifies countries and jurisdictions that do not cooperate in the international fight against money laundering. After the events of September 11, 2001, FATF adopted 9 Special Recommendations on Terrorist Financing. Adopted on October 31, 2001 and updated on October 22, 2004, Recommendations on Terrorist Financing, when combined with the FATF 40, set out a comprehensive framework to detect, prevent, and suppress the financing of terrorism and terrorist acts.[1]

Accounting Principles Board (APB) Opinion No. 20, *Accounting Changes.* A statement that changes the requirements for the accounting for and reporting of a change in accounting principle. This statement applies to all voluntary changes in accounting principle. It also applies to changes required by an accounting pronouncement in the unusual instance that the pronouncement does not include specific transition provisions. When a pronouncement includes specific transition provisions, those provisions should be followed.[12]

accounts payable disbursement fraud. The payment to vendors for goods and services never provided or procured at excessive amounts usually due to bribes or kickbacks being paid by the vendor. The fraud also includes paying fictitious vendors who were set up with the intention of perpetrating a fraud.

active online. Information stored on magnetic disks, such as hard drives, attached to a computer or server.

adversarial proceedings. Or dispute settings, which include litigation, arbitration, mediation, or presentations to regulators about controversies or adversarial matters.

advocate. A person who pleads for the cause of another.[17]

African Union Convention on Preventing and Combating Corruption. A practical policy approach to enable accountability in the flow of data while preventing impediments to trade. It provides technical assistance to those Asia-Pacific Economic Cooperation (APEC) economies that have not addressed privacy from a regulatory or policy perspective.[4]

agreed-upon procedures engagement. An engagement in which a practitioner is engaged by a client to issue a report of findings based on specific procedures performed on subject matter. The client engages the practitioner to assist specified parties in evaluating subject matter or an assertion as a result of a need or needs of the specified parties. (AICPA—Statements on Standards for Attestation Engagements, *Agreed-upon Procedures Engagements* 2602.03.) In the context of a fraud investigation, the procedures and guidelines agreed to with the client effectively describe in detail the framework for the procedures that will be performed in an investigation.

AICPA Code of Professional Conduct. The code consists of two sections—(1) the Principles and (2) the Rules. The Principles provide the framework for the Rules, which govern the performance of professional services by members. The Council of the AICPA is authorized to designate bodies to promulgate technical standards under the Rules, and the bylaws require adherence to those Rules and standards.

AICPA Management Consulting Services Executive Committee. The committee designated to promulgate standards under Rule 201 (*General Standards of the Code of Professional Conduct*) and Rule 202 (*Compliance with the Standards*) with respect to the offering of management consulting services.

alternative dispute resolution (ADR). Refers to any means of settling disputes outside of the courtroom. ADR typically includes arbitration, mediation, early neutral evaluation, and conciliation.

American Arbitration Association (AAA). A not-for-profit organization that provides time- and court-tested rules and procedures.

American Institute of Certified Public Accountants (AICPA). A national professional membership organization that represents practicing CPAs. The AICPA establishes ethical and auditing standards as well as standards for other services performed by its members. Through committees, it develops guidance for specialized industries.

analytics. An efficient and reliable method of analyzing large sets of unstructured or structured data in a variety of fields, or a variety of ways for more in-depth analysis.

annotation codes. Symbols included in the e-mail review tool so that the e-mail review team can code the documents as they review them. The codes will typically be established for two reasons: first, to indicate the level of relevancy of a particular e-mail and, second, to put e-mails into meaningful categories.

anti-money laundering (AML). A term mainly used in the financial and legal industries to describe the legal controls that require financial institutions and other regulated entities to prevent or report money laundering activities. Anti-money laundering guidelines came into prominence globally after the September 11, 2001 attacks and the subsequent enactment of the USA Patriot Act.

anton piller order. An order that secures and preserves documents or other evidence that might otherwise be disposed of by the defendant. The order allows for the applicant to enter the respondent's premises and search for, inspect, seize, or make copies of documents or other evidence.

appeal level. A request made after a trial by a party that has lost on one or more issues that a higher court review the decision to determine if it was correct.[5]

arbitral award. The outcome of arbitration, typically a monetary amount. The awards are enforceable through the civil court system.

arbitration. The hearing of a dispute by an impartial third person or persons. The third person is chosen by the parties, whose decision and award the parties agree to accept.[5]

archiving systems. A system frequently used to alleviate space issues on the active e-mail servers by removing information regarding past e-mail communications regarding previous engagements.

Asia-Pacific Economic Cooperation (APEC) Privacy Framework. The framework promotes a flexible approach to information privacy protection across APEC member economies, while avoiding the creation of unnecessary barriers to information flows.[4]

asset management system. A system that tracks and maintains a history of assets. An asset management system will help in determining what systems a custodian has access to now or had access to in the past.

asset misappropriation. Comprises any scheme that involves the theft or misuse of an organization's assets. Typical examples would includes, theft of assets such as fixed assets, inventory, cash, intellectual property and other assets, travel and entertainment reimbursement fraud, fake vendor fraud, and payroll manipulation fraud.

asset tracing. Tracking the true economic substance of the transactions used to move the assets, as well as identifying the location of the assets.

Association of Certified Fraud Examiners (ACFE). An anti-fraud organization that provides anti-fraud training and education. The ACFE has nearly 50,000 members. The goal of the ACFE is to reduce business fraud world-wide. They offer and administer the designation of Certified Fraud Examiner.

attorney work product doctrine. A policy that protects an attorney's internal documentation of the work or analyses created in support of the attorney's legal representation of the attorney's client.

attorney-client privilege. The protection of communication between a client and its attorney, thereby maintaining confidentiality.

audit command language (ACL). A tool used to prepare data for analysis from other programs. The software has many uses, including: data extraction and transformation, statistical analysis, and identification of exceptions and irregularities.

audit committee. A committee established by and amongst the board of directors of an issuer for the purpose of overseeing the accounting and financial reporting processes of the issuer and audits of the financial statements of the issuer.[25]

audit committee of the board of directors. A committee (or equivalent body) established by and amongst the board of directors of an issuer for the purpose of overseeing the accounting and financial reporting processes of the issuer and audits of the financial statements of the issuer; and if no such committee exists with respect to an issuer, the entire board of directors of the issuer. [25]

authorization level. Those threshold levels that require certain signatures or other forms of approval for desired use.

backup protocols. The process and methodology of storing live electronic data and software onto tapes or other media.

balance sheet. The statement of financial condition at a given date which lists the organizations assets, liabilities and owners or stockholders equity. Assets = Liabilities + Equity.

bankers blanket bond. Covers losses as a result of dishonest or fraudulent acts by officers and employees, attorneys retained by the bank, and nonemployee data processors while performing services for the insured.[8]

bid-rigging. Bid-rigging occurs in the procurement process generally when a member of the offering organization that has placed a "request for proposal" fraudulently assists a vendor or contractor in winning a sale or contract through some form of manipulation of the offering organization's bid process.

big bath adjustments. When a company takes a large charge in a quarter in which the company knows that it will not make its earnings target. The idea is that a company will incur a "big bath" charge in a bad year in order to artificially inflate its earnings in future quarters.

bill and hold arrangements. A situation that arises when a company completes the manufacturing of a product, but the customer is not, in reality, ready to take delivery of the goods, due to lack of space, and/or delays in customer production schedules; therefore, the bills are held until a future date.

blog. A Web site that contains an online personal journal with reflections, comments, and often hyperlinks provided by the writer.[17]

bonus scheme. When someone within the organization intentionally creates a bonus payment and that payment is improperly entered in the organizations' payroll system and paid to a non deserving employee.

books and records provisions. As part of the Foreign Corrupt Practices Act (FCPA), issuers are required to keep books, records, and accounts, which, in reasonable detail, accurately and fairly reflect the transactions and dispositions of the assets of the issuer; and devise and maintain a system of internal accounting controls sufficient to provide reasonable assurances that transactions are executed in accordance with management's general or specific authorization.

Boolean logic. Relating to, or being a logical combinatorial system that represents symbolically relationships between entities.[17]

Boolean syntax. A way of searching electronic databases (indexes, catalogs and Web search engines) that allows users to indicate relationships between search terms by using the words "AND", "OR", and "NOT".

bribe. A scheme that falls under the corruption category. It involves the promise to pay money or some other form of compensation or favor to someone in a position of power or decision making, with the hope of intentionally influencing that individuals' judgment or behavior.

business drivers. Employees that take responsibility for finding solutions to business problems.

business intelligence (BI). A system implemented infrastructure used to gather information pertinent to investigations. Some BI systems include Hyperion, Crystal Reports, Business Objects, and Cognos.

business systems. Systems containing the online financial and operational transaction records for a company. These systems may be multitiered with a presentation layer running on one computer system, a database layer on another system, and a business logic layer on yet another system.

capitalizing expenses. Intentionally and inappropriately capitalizing costs as an asset on the balance sheet that should be correctly expensed in the income statement, such as research and development charges.

cash flows. The net of cash receipts and cash disbursements relating to a particular activity during a specified accounting period.[3]

cash in bank accounts. The total sum cash and cash equivalents in the organizations financial accounts.

cash larceny. The actual theft of cash on hand or from daily receipts. Attempts to conceal cash larceny are typically undertaken in one of three ways: by making no record of cash received, altering supporting documents to conceal theft of cash, or by falsifying journal entries to cover up the fraud.

cash on hand. All money, cash, and cash equivalents in the organizations cash registers and safes on the premises; as opposed to cash in the bank.

Central Intelligence Agency (CIA). An independent U.S. Government agency responsible for providing national security intelligence to senior U.S. policymakers.

chain of custody. Refers to the chronology of who has had possession of physical evidence and where that evidence was stored.

chain of custody log. A record that will enable evidence to be traced from the point and time of original collection to the point and time when it is presented in a proceeding.

channel stuffing. Occurs when a company offers large discounts and other incentives to a distributor or retailer to take large orders late in the reporting period in order for the company to meet the designated sales or profit targets.

chart of accounts. A list of accounts in the general ledger, systematically classified by title and number. The account number can be referred to as the GL code. The financial transactions are posted to these GL codes.

check fraud. A type of misappropriation of asset fraud scheme. It involves the manipulation of checks in such a way as to deceive victims expecting value in exchange for their money.

civil investigation. Providing and seeking information needed for a court case involving citizens who are disputing an issue that relates to their rights.

civil penalties. A fine assessed as a result of a violation against an individual by a state or government agency.

Civil Rights Act of 1964. An act that made racial discrimination in public places, such as theaters, restaurants and hotels, illegal. The act also required employers to provide equal employment opportunities.

claim. A legal action to obtain money, property, or the enforcement of a right against another party.

claimant. The aggrieved party in an arbitration setting.

clustering. Grouping data with similar properties. Clustering data can help uncover patterns that can identify fraud.

code of conduct. The clear set of business rules set forth by an organization. The code can provide a framework to guide the response of the organization in the challenging and sometimes difficult choices that are presented to members of the organization.

collaborative systems. A system that allows users to collectively share and search a body of information typically related to a single project.

Commercial Crime Policy (CCP). In 1986, as a part of the movement in the insurance industry to simplify policy forms, the Surety Association of America and the Insurance Services offices introduced this policy. This policy contained "simplified language" and was designed to be more "user friendly."[16]

commission scheme. A plan perpetrated by either falsely reporting sales or other activity for which a commission is to be paid or the rate at which the commission is to be paid.

Committee of Sponsoring Organizations of the Treadway Commission (COSO). Sponsored by five major professional associations in the United States, the American Accounting Association, the AICPA, Financial Executives International, The Institute of Internal Auditors, and the National Association of Accountants (now the Institute of Management Accountants). It is a voluntary private sector organization dedicated to improving the quality of financial reporting through business ethics, effective internal controls, and corporate governance.

commonwealth countries. A voluntary association of 53 independent states working together in the common interests of their citizens for development, democracy and peace.

compliance audits. The review of financial records to determine whether the entity is complying with specific procedures or rules.

compliance culture. Sometimes referred to as *tone of the top*, this represents the vision to identify the specific risks that could arise within each strategic area or the organization, establishes controls for each of these risks, is well documented, and makes sure key members of the organization are accountable for managing each specific element of the compliance system.

compliance officers. A person or function in a corporation responsible for the company's agreement with relevant legal requirements and regulations and responsible for assessing and understanding the compliance culture.

compliance programs. Set of procedures and methodology implemented by an organization to ensure that the rules and regulations are being met by the organization.

computer forensics. Encompasses a range of activities, from relatively straightforward tasks, such as searching a single computer system for evidence of unauthorized use, to searching for deleted e-mail messages that might remain on a computer network.

conclusion. A reasoned judgment, usually containing the summing of a point regarding statements of opinions and decisions reached.[17]

confidential process. Procedures or steps that are implemented to keep sensitive/privileged information and/or communication secretive throughout the duration of the event.

consent. Agreement as to action or opinion; voluntary acceptance of the wish of another.[17]

constructive trust. An agreement where the third party becomes a trustee whose sole duty is to transfer the title and possession to the rightful owner.

consulting fees. The amount of money spent for information and services provided by an expert.

control. Power or authority to guide or manage.[17]

***Control Objectives for Information and Related Technology* (COBIT).** An information technology governance framework and supporting toolset that allows managers to bridge the gap between control requirements, technical issues and business risks. The framework enables clear policy development and good practice for IT control throughout organizations. It emphasizes regulatory compliance, helps organizations to increase the value attained from IT, enables alignment and simplifies implementation.[6]

controller. An individual within an organization who is responsible for the accounting activities of the organization.

controls mapping process. The process of identifying gaps in the control structure. Identification of gaps in the control structure is needed to determine the location of controls that were not in place to mitigate the risk identified from the fraud risk assessment.

Convention on Combating Bribery of Foreign Public Officials in International Business Transactions. Establishes legally binding standards to criminalize bribery of foreign public officials in international business transactions and provides for a host of related measures that make this effective. The 30 Organisation for Economic Co-Operation and Development (OECD) member countries and eight nonmember countries—Argentina, Brazil, Bulgaria, Chile, Estonia, Israel, the Slovenia and South Africa—have adopted this convention.[19]

conventions. Event or session where different countries align themselves toward a common standard.

cookie jars. Slang term used to represent a contingency or liability that is placed on the balance sheet in anticipation of a future expense or loss.

corporate crises. A dramatic event such as an accident, scare, damaged product or scandal that sparks widespread and tremendous public attention, disrupts a company's regular operations, and damages its culture and reputation.

corporate intelligence professional. An employee or consultant tasked with the collection and analysis of public and nonpublic information that has strategic business value.

corrupt intent. The objective to perform corrupt acts.

corruption. Refers to a payment or offer of a bribe or anything of value to obtain or retain business or improper advantage. This is one of the three main types of fraud schemes.

counsel. A lawyer appointed or retained to advise and represent a client in legal matters.

crime protection policy (CPP). Offers fidelity, forgery, burglary and theft coverages in a single, unified policy form. The CPP is an all-inclusive policy that contains six basic insuring agreements, declarations page and policy conditions. Two additional insuring agreements may be added by endorsement.[7]

criminal investigation. Performing a process to gather necessary information to determine what criminal violations were violated by an individual or organization to potentially convict.

criminal liability. A liability imposed on a company for the acts of its employees, officers, and agents only if (1) the employee, officer, or agent acted within the scope of his or her apparent authority granted by the company, and (2) the employee, officer, or agent acted for the benefit of the company.

criminal penalties. The suffering in person, rights, or property that is annexed by law or judicial decision to the commission of a crime or public offense.[17]

crisis communications. The practice of communicating with key stakeholders in a documented consistent manner during times of crisis such as material fraud allegations that may warrant a financial restatement.

cross-jurisdictional conventions. When investigative activity on a case needs to be conducted outside the geographic jurisdiction of the primary regional office, the primary regional office may request the regional office having jurisdiction over this area (auxiliary office) to perform the work.[9]

cross-jurisdictional investigations. The investigations into fraudsters who have long known that moving their assets (and themselves) to a different location and beyond reach of the "long arm of the law" is an effective strategy for trying to cover up fraud.

culture. The personality of the organization.

custodian. Key individuals within an organization with whom to collect documents from in obtaining sufficient evidence to conduct an investigation.

data mining. An analytic technique that involves searching through large amounts of data to identify relevant information, patterns, trends, and differences indicative of fraud.

de minimis. An investigation that is deemed immaterial in momentary amount as well as complexity and therefore would not require significant outside experts to assist.

deduplicating. The process of removing duplicate components of data, such as addresses or names or entire exact duplicates of documents from a database.

defendant. The individual, company, or organization who defends or is asked to respond to the a legal action taken or complaint made by a plaintiff and against whom the court has been asked to order damages or specific corrective action redress some type of unlawful or improper action alleged by the plaintiff.

delaying expenses. The failure to accrue for goods and services at the period end or creating a prepayment for an expense for which the good or service has already been received by the end of the period.

Department of Commerce (DOC). The cabinet department of the United States government concerned with promoting economic growth.

Department of Justice (DOJ). The primary federal criminal investigation and enforcement agency. Their primary mission is as follows: to enforce the law and defend the interests of the United States according to the law; to ensure public safety against threats foreign and domestic; to provide federal leadership in preventing and controlling crime; to seek just punishment for those guilty of unlawful behavior; and to ensure fair and impartial administration of justice for all Americans.

departmental share. Repositories for user-created documents used by multiple custodians.

disclaimer language. A denial or disavowal of legal claim.[17]

discovery. A pretrial process in which each side requests relevant information and documents from the other. Parties must provide the requested information or documents or show good cause to the court why they should not have to do so.[15]

discovery phase. The time during which the parties gather information related to the investigation from one another and third parties.

dispute settings. Or adversarial proceedings, including litigation, arbitration, mediation, presentations to regulators about controversies or adversarial matters, and other such situations.

document holds. A legal notice that is generated when litigation or an investigation is pending or in progress and there is a requirement to preserve information and prevent or suspend destruction of paper documents and electronic data that must be retained during a litigation hold.

document preservation and production plan. A process that occurs after receiving a subpoena. The company should quickly work with the regulatory agency to determine what documents are required to be turned over.

document repository. The place where discovery documents are accumulated physically or electronically.

domestic criminal offenses. Participation in an organized criminal group, money laundering, corruption, and obstruction of justice.

duty to defend. Insurers are required to defend the insured against all actions brought against them which are, judging by the allegations of such actions, potentially within coverage of the policy.

early case assessments (ECAs). An analysis conducted soon after data is first loaded to the review platform, for the purpose of evaluating the collection of electronic evidence to determine potentially relevant information that may drive case strategy, such as key topics or themes of the case, dates and amounts, specific vocabulary and jargon, and people.

electronic data environment. Key systems and sources of electronic evidence.

electronic evidence. Electronic records such as computer network logs, e-mails, word processing files, and ".jpg" and picture files. Typically, depending on the particular circumstances of an investigation, there are two types of electronic evidence commonly analyzed, e-mail correspondence of key individuals and financial records of the company.

electronic evidence review process. The process includes discovery processing, including data collection, data extraction and conversion (which may include elimination of system files or other high-level culling techniques), deduplication, data culling or searching, and data review.

electronically stored information (ESI). Information stored on backup tapes, in e-mail messages, and in trace remnants of deleted electronic files on a laptop.

embezzlement. A type of fraud that would be classified as a misappropriation of asset scheme. It is an act where someone within the organization inappropriately and intentionally takes assets typically financial in nature, for their own use.

employee. A person who has agreed by contract or other form of agreement to perform specified services for an organization, in exchange for money or other forms of compensation.

employee theft. The intentional stealing, use, or misuse of an employer's assets without permission. This type of fraud would be classified as a misappropriation of asset scheme.

enforcement lawyers. The division of enforcement for the U.S. Securities and Exchange Commission (SEC) have lawyers on staff to investigate possible violations of securities laws, recommend SEC action when appropriate, either in federal court or before an administrative law judge and negotiate settlements.

engagement partner. The lead partner on each engagement.

engagement plan. A document used to help plan, organize, and guide the engagement.

English common law. English common law is made by judges sitting in courts, applying their common sense and knowledge of legal precedent (stare decisis) to the facts before them. A decision of the highest appeal court in England and Wales, the House of Lords, is binding on every other court in the hierarchy, and they will follow its directions.[17]

enterprise applications. Software designed to integrate all aspects of a firm's operations and processes.

EU privacy law. The rights that stem from The European Union Directive on Data Protection of 1995, which mandated that each EU nation pass a national privacy law and create a Data Protection Authority to protect citizens' privacy and investigate attacks on it.

European Commission. The executive branch of the European Union. The body is responsible for proposing legislation, implementing decisions, upholding the Union's treaties and the general day-to-day running of the Union.

European Union (EU). Economic, scientific, and political organization consisting of Belgium, France, Italy, Luxembourg, Netherlands, Germany, Denmark, Greece, Ireland, United Kingdom, Spain, Portugal, Austria, Finland, Sweden, Cyprus, Czech Republic, Estonia, Hungary, Latvia, Lithuania, Malta, Poland, Slovakia, Slovenia, Bulgaria, & Romania.[17]

European Union Directive 95/46/EC. A directive that limits the scope of data and information on individuals that may be processed and restricts the terms and conditions under which transfers of data to locations outside the EU may occur unless there are adequate safeguards for the protection of the personal information.

evidential matter. The support collected through inspection, observation, or confirmation and other selected procedures ordinarily performed during an audit.

ex parte. Something done on behalf of only one party, without notice to any other party. For example, a request for a search warrant is an ex parte proceeding, since the person subject to the search is not notified of the proceeding and is not present at the hearing.[5]

exception list. A list that must be able to account for all data dropped from review because of filtering decisions and should be prepared to defend those decisions.

executive management. A team of executives responsible for providing management sponsorship and coordination. The team among other responsibilities, reports to the audit committee the status of current investigations, completed investigations, results of the fraud risk assessment, and action plans to mitigate the risk of fraud within the company.

expert reports. The report that contains the opinion articulated by the testifying witness, not that of an attorney or professional services firm. Usually, the expert personally signs the report and bears responsibility for the report.

external auditors. Independent CPAs who are retained by organizations seeking qualified professionals to perform independent audits of their financial statements.

external resources. A source or supply of support that is used outside of the particular firm or corporation.

facilitating payments. Payments known to expedite or obtain a routine government action.

false statement charge. The statute criminalizes one who "knowingly and willfully" falsifies, conceals, or covers up by any trick, scheme, or device a material fact; makes any materially false, fictitious, or fraudulent statement or representation; or makes or uses any false writing or document knowing the same to contain any materially false, fictitious, or fraudulent statement or entry.[26]

Financial Accounting Standards Board (FASB) Statement No. 5, *Accounting for Contingencies.* The statement that establishes standards of financial accounting and reporting for loss contingencies. It requires accrual by a charge to income (and disclosure) for an estimated loss from a loss contingency if two conditions are met: (a) information available prior to issuance of the financial statements indicates that it is probable that an asset had been impaired or a liability had been incurred at the date of the financial statements, and (b) the amount of loss can be reasonably estimated. Accruals for general or unspecified business risks (reserves for general contingencies) are no longer permitted.[11]

FASB Concept Statement No. 2, *Qualitative Characteristics of Accounting Information.* The purpose of this statement is to examine the characteristics that make accounting information useful. Those who prepare, audit, and use financial reports, as well as FASB, must often select or evaluate accounting alternatives. The characteristics or qualities of information discussed in this statement are the ingredients that make information useful and are the qualities to be sought when accounting choices are made.[10]

Federal Bureau of Investigation (FBI). A federal agency that is designed to protect and defend the United States against terrorist and foreign intelligence threats, to uphold and enforce the criminal laws of the United States, and to provide leadership and criminal justice services to federal, state, municipal, and international agencies and partners.

***Federal Rules of Civil Procedure* (Federal Rule 26).** Parties may obtain discovery regarding any nonprivileged matter that is relevant to any party's claim or defense including the existence, description, nature, custody, condition, and location of any documents or other tangible things and the identity and location of persons who know of any discoverable matter.[28]

Federal Sentencing Guidelines Manual. The manual that contains the federal sentencing guidelines and policy statements effective November 1, 2008.

fictitious vendor. Commonly also referred to as a *fake vendors*, this type of fraud can be classified into the misappropriation of assets category of fraud schemes. The situations arises when fake or falsified vendor enters into the system and invoices for products or services that the company is not receiving but subsequently is paying for.

fiduciaries. A person who occupies a position of special trust and confidence.

FASB Statement No. 154, *Accounting Changes and Error Corrections—a replacement of APB Opinion No. 20 and FASB Statement No. 3.* This statement applies to all voluntary changes in accounting principle. This statement requires retrospective application to prior periods' financial statements of changes in accounting principle, unless it is impracticable to determine either the period-specific effects or the cumulative effect of the change. When it is impracticable to determine the period-specific effects of an accounting change on one or more individual prior periods presented, this statement requires that the new accounting principle be applied to the balances of assets and liabilities as of the beginning of the earliest period for which retrospective application is practicable and that a corresponding adjustment be made to the opening balance of retained earnings (or other appropriate components of equity or net assets in the statement of financial position) for that period rather than being reported in an income statement.[12]

Financial Action Task Force (FATF). An intergovernmental body whose purpose is the development and promotion of national and international policies to combat money laundering and terrorist financing.

Financial Crimes Enforcement Network (FinCEN). Established by the U.S. Department of Treasury in 1990 to provide a government-wide multisource financial intelligence and analysis network. The organization's operation was broadened in 1994 to include regulatory responsibilities for administering the Bank Secrecy Act, one of the nation's most potent weapons for preventing corruption of the U.S. financial system.

financial institution bond (FIB). A special form of bond designed to insure banks and other financial institutions against loss from employee dishonesty, burglary, robbery, larceny, theft, forgery, misplacement, and certain other perils. Previously called a "bankers blanket bond."

financial intelligence unit. A central, national agency responsible for receiving (and, as permitted, requesting), analyzing, and disseminating to the competent authorities, disclosures of financial information (i) concerning suspected proceeds of crime, or (ii) required by national legislation or regulation, in order to counter money laundering.[22]

financial intermediaries. Financial institutions that borrow from consumers and savers and lend to companies that need resources for investment.

financial statement fraud. That act of deliberate misstatements or omissions of amounts or disclosures of financial statements to deceive financial statement users, particularly investors and creditors. This is one of the three main types of fraud schemes. Examples could include falsification, alteration, or manipulation of material financial records, supporting documents, or business transactions.

financial statement restatements. The restatement of a previously issued financial statement due to an error or omission, this can be due to a mistake or a fraudulent act that has occurred and subsequently corrected.

flash drive (or thumb drive). A small, portable flash memory card that plugs into a computer's USB port and functions as a portable hard drive.

Foreign Corrupt Practices Act (FCPA). An act that generally makes it a federal criminal offense for any U.S. person, issuer, or domestic concern, or any foreign person while in the United States, directly or indirectly, to make a corrupt payment to any foreign government official to obtain or retain any business advantage (the anti-bribery provisions). The FCPA also requires companies with securities registered under the Securities Exchange Act of 1934 to make and keep appropriate books and records and to maintain a system of adequate internal controls. This fraud can be classified as one of the corruption fraud schemes examples.

forensic accountant. Accountants that act as fact gatherers and investigate allegations of fraud or the lack of management integrity. The accountants are trained specifically in fraud prevention, deterrence, data collection and analysis, interviewing, investigation, and detection.

forensic professionals. Workers in a wide variety of different disciplines who ultimately focus on applying science to the practice of law.

forensic tools. The tools that capture a forensic or "mirror image" of the original evidence media. This mirror image is a bit-by-bit copy and will contain the active files found on the media along with the unallocated storage space, which is the location on the hard drive where erased or deleted files may be found. Forensic tools must not change either the content of the data or information used by the computer to classify a file or directory, such as the date and time the file or directory was created.

forgery. Relates to the unauthorized use a purported maker's signature. Making, altering, uttering, or possessing, with intent to defraud, anything false in the semblance of that which is true. Attempts are included.[24]

form K-8 filings. The "current report" companies must file with the SEC to announce major events that shareholders should know about.[13]

formal inquiry. A more in-depth than an informal inquiry but also requires notification to the target that such an investigation is taking place, resolving doubt, or solving a problem.

formal interview. The interview of employees significant to an investigation. These interviews should be conducted at the outset of the investigation to gather information and relevant facts. Follow-up interviews of these individuals can be conducted as needed, based upon new information obtained further into the investigation.

formal investigation. An investigation where the SEC uses its subpoena and enforcement powers to conduct a thorough investigation of the issues of concern, leveraging the company's internal investigative findings.

fraud. Intentional deception by one or more individuals among management, employees, or third parties where one individual or group of individuals have received a direct or indirect gain and one individual, group of individuals or organization has suffered a loss.

fraud awareness training. The training that increases awareness and understanding of fraud and corruption.

fraud prevention policy. A framework for an organization to prevent, detect, report, and investigate internal and external fraud.

fraud prevention procedure. Procedures focused on protecting the company's assets and information by stopping fraud from occurring or identifying it in the earliest stages.

fraud risk assessment. The process and methodology performed to identify areas (for example, business processes, location, transaction types, geographic locations, and so on) that pose a higher risk of fraud and then prioritize those fraud risks indentified for follow up procedures to attempt to mitigate the risk from occurring.

fraud tree. A process used to organize fraud into the following three types: fraudulent financial reporting, misappropriation of assets, and corruption.

fraud triangle e-mail analytics. Advanced analytic technique using an objective list of key words that are specific to each component of the Fraud Triangle (Opportunity, Pressure, Rationalization) to look for co-occurrences of these terms to identify potential areas of concern from a fraudulent perspective. The co-occurrence of these terms is supported by the Fraud Triangle, which indicates that all three factors are present when fraud occurs.

full investigation. To conduct a comprehensive and systematic examination; to conduct an official inquiry of an allegation of potential wrong doing.

fuzzy searching. The text retrieval technique based on fuzzy logic. The technique finds matches even where the keywords (search words) are misspelled or only hint at a concept.

G-7 member states. A meeting of government bodies subject to international law, whose competences are limited basically by the will of the participant states and whose means of action are those permitted by international law.

gap analysis. Identification of gaps in the controls structure is needed to determine the location of controls that were not in place to mitigate the risk identified from the fraud risk assessment. This also will help validate the placement of the fraud risks on the "heat map," which attempts to prioritize from a likelihood of occurrence and severity of impact perspective.

gatekeepers. Accountants, lawyers, or others who may be involved in business transactions involving financial transactions or instruments.

general ledger. The central repository for transactions for an organization's accounting transactions with offsetting debit and credit entries. This is the main accounting record for an organization.

generally accepted accounting principles (GAAP). Accounting principles based on a framework of concepts determined by local legislation, by rules issued by professional bodies, and by the development of general practice within a country or other defined region.

generally accepted auditing standards (GAAS). Standards that management is responsible for adopting for sound accounting policies and for establishing and maintaining internal controls that will, among other things, record, process, summarize, and report transactions (as well as events and conditions) consistent with management's assertions embodied in the financial statements.

ghost company. A company that has been created for the sole purpose of creating fraudulent documentation to deceive an organization to pay money for these services or product that the organization did not receive. Sometime referred to as a *fake vendor scheme.*

ghost employees. Falsification of employees on the payroll list that result in overpayment, fraudulent commission or bonus schemes, and false workers compensation claims. This is one of the most common types of payroll schemes.

global reach. A characteristic that accounting firms exemplify when they can provide qualified professionals who are both fluent in the local languages and familiar with the business practices of almost any locality or specialized industry. Collaboration between the accounting and legal firms can ensure that an adequately staffed and a well-integrated team balances the needs for various skills, expertise, language, nationality, or ethnicity of executing an investigation in various localities, including the requirements for employee rights and handling evidence.

governance. The set of processes, customs, policies, laws, and institutions affecting the way a corporation is directed, administered, or controlled.

grease payments. A payment to a foreign official, political party or party official for "routine governmental action," such as processing papers, issuing permits, and other actions of an official, in order to expedite performance of duties of nondiscretionary nature, that is, which they are already bound to perform.[17]

hand search (field search). Hand search involves the examination of original, hard copy, or source records.

handheld personal devices. A personal digital assistant (PDA) is a handheld computer, also known as a palmtop computer. Many PDAs can access the Internet, intranets, or extranets via Wi-Fi, or wireless wide-area networks (WWANs).[17]

hash value. A "digital fingerprint" of a file or media.

heat map. A graphical representation of data used to display the fraud risks in certain areas of the organization. The heat map is an excellent way to show each identified fraud risk plotted from a likelihood of occurrence and significance of impact perspective. This allows the organization to prioritize the fraud risks and follow up in a more efficient manner.

hold (preservation notice). An order that seeks to ensure the preservation of any and all documents presumed to be pertinent to any given investigation. The order is issued to all employees of the company whose records are being reviewed and employees are bound to adhere to it.

International Criminal Court (ICC). A highly facilitated and endorsed arbitration forum with 86 member countries.

identification. The process of determining which data sources are in the scope of the investigation and should be preserved, collected, and processed for review.

impairment charges. The charge associated with writing-off fixed assets or inventory that has become obsolete or otherwise declined in value.

improper advantage. The advantage gained from the illegal actions in violation of the FCPA.

independent directors. A director who has not been employed by the Company or its related parties in the past five years.

independent investigation. An investigation performed by an independent third party.

informal inquiry. An investigation during the informal phase. The SEC will request that the company voluntarily produce specific information that typically includes documents (for example, company records, including electronic evidence such as employee e-mails), internal interview summaries, and other testimony.

informal meeting. Meetings are typically held between forensic accountants and employees for a particular purpose, potentially to gain information regarding a certain document or transaction at hand. Relevant information obtained from these meetings would be captured in the forensic accountants' working papers, as deemed necessary.

information leaks. The process by which information, through rumors, external publicity, and other forms of unintended communication arrives to parties not intended to receive this information.

Information Systems Audit and Control Association (ISACA). An association dedicated to the audit, control, and security of information systems.

information technology (IT). The technology involving the development, maintenance, and use of computer systems, software, and networks for the processing and distribution of data.

initial triage. The process of making a rapid assessment of the currently available information and making critical initial decisions on the nature and extent of the response.

initiation. A claim within a particular dispute resolution forum by the plaintiff and a response from the opponent, usually called the defendant.

insolvency. The situation where the business is unable to pay the claim in the ordinary course of business or its liabilities exceed its assets.

Institute of Internal Auditors. An institute that conducts an independent, objective assurance and consulting activity designed to add value and improve an organization's operations.

insurance recovery. The act of an insured attempting to recoup damages from an insurer for losses covered by a policy.

insurance recovery phase. The period after damages are inflicted on an insured entity in which the insured attempts to recoup losses.

Insurance Services Office (ISO). An organization that supplies data, analytics, and decision-support services for professionals in many fields, including: property/casualty insurance, mortgage lending, healthcare, government, human resources, and information for risk managers in all industries.

insuring agreements. Part of every insurance policy; specifies what the insurance company has agreed to pay for or to provide in exchange for the premium.

intangible assets. Long-lived assets without physical substance that are used in business, such as licenses, patents, franchises, and goodwill.

integrated team. A team of attorneys and accountants that brings diversity of thought and approach and helps ensure that multiple avenues are explored, many sides of the issue are addressed, and the needs of a variety of stakeholders are considered.

intellectual property. Usually a patent, trademark, service mark or copyright, or any concept, idea, or invention that a person or entity can claim to have created. Inventions are protected by patents. Brand names are protected by trademarks. Advertising slogans, as well as product and service descriptions, are protected by service marks. Written documents (including software) are protected by copyrights.

interim progress reports. Unaudited financial statements or report on a specific issue issued periodically, monthly, quarterly, or biyearly, by a company in order to give shareholders or board members up to date information on company performance.

internal audit department. A department that is an independent, objective assurance and consulting activity designed to add value and improve an organization's operations. It helps an organization accomplish its objectives by bringing a systematic, disciplined approach to evaluate the effectiveness of the controls put into place by management.

internal audit director. The executive responsible for the internal audit team, and responsible for reporting to the audit committee.

internal certification process. A process in which financial and other individuals throughout the company are asked to provide a certification to the CEO and CFO in order to provide them with some comfort of the accounting and financial information and controls system at the lower levels. The certifications generally have a section where individuals can write in concerns or items noted during the year that could help the investigation team identify potential risks that have previously been identified or other concerns employees have raised.

internal controls. A process, effected by a client's board of directors, management, and other personnel, designed to provide reasonable assurance regarding the achievement of operating, financial reporting and compliance objectives. It consists of all the policies and procedures adopted by the management of a client to assist in achieving management's objective of ensuring, as far as practicable, the orderly and efficient conduct of its business, including adherence to management policies, the safeguarding of assets, the prevention and detection of fraud and error, the accuracy and completeness of the accounting records, and the timely preparation of reliable financial information.

internal counsel. Also known as "in-house" counsel or the legal team employed by an organization.

internal executives. People that have administrative or managerial authority within an organization.

internal investigation. An investigation of an organization led by the organization itself.

internal reporting. Data accumulated by people within an organization to be communicated to someone else within the organization, not for use outside of organization. Generally this information is utilized by management in order to make more informed decisions.

internal resources. The resources within a company that are used during different situations to reach a conclusion on a matter. Most importantly a company's internal legal, accounting, and auditing resources, are used as appropriate, and take advantage of their proximity and familiarity with the systems, processes, and issues.

Internal Revenue Service (IRS). The federal agency that administers the Internal Revenue Code. The IRS is part of the United States Treasury Department.

International Accounting Standard (IAS) No.1, *Presentation of Financial Statements*. This standard prescribes the basis for presentation of general purpose financial statements to ensure comparability both with the entity's financial statements of previous periods and with the financial statements of other entities. It sets out overall requirements for the presentation of financial statements, guidelines for their structure and minimum requirements for their content.

International Accounting Standard (IAS) No. 8, *Accounting Policies, Changes in Accounting, Estimates and Errors*. Prescribes the criteria for selecting, applying, and changing accounting policies. In addition it deals with the accounting treatment and disclosure of changes in accounting policies, changes in accounting estimates and the correction of errors.

International Chamber of Commerce (ICC). The voice of world business championing the global economy as a force for economic growth, job creation, and prosperity. ICC activities cover a broad spectrum, from arbitration and dispute resolution to making the case for open trade and the market economy system, business self-regulation, fighting corruption or combating commercial crime.

International Financial Reporting Standards (IFRS). A set of accounting standards, developed by the International Accounting Standards Board (IASB) that is becoming the global standard for the preparation of public company financial statements.

International Monetary Fund (IMF). An organization of 186 countries, working to foster global monetary cooperation, secure financial stability, facilitate international trade, promote high employment and sustainable economic growth, and reduce poverty around the world.

International Crime Police Organization (INTERPOL). The world's largest international police organization. The organization operates in 187 member countries.

INTERPOL and United Nations Office on Drugs and Crime Anti-Corruption Academy. The world's first educational institution dedicated to fighting corruption was established yesterday. An agreement was signed between the International Criminal Police Organization (INTERPOL) and UNODC to establish the International Anti-Corruption Academy.

INTERPOL Anti-Corruption Office. INTERPOL established the INTERPOL Group of Experts on Corruption (IGEC) in 1998, and is currently in the process of developing the INTERPOL Anti-Corruption Office (IACO) and International Anti-Corruption Academy (IACA). These components support anti-corruption activities by establishing policies and standards, as well as conducting or assisting with education, research, training, investigations, and asset-recovery operations.

INTERPOL Group of Experts on Corruption (IGEC). A multidisciplinary group representing all of INTERPOL's regions which facilitates the co-ordination and harmonization of the different national and regional approaches to combating corruption. In addition, the group includes a host of other international stakeholders in the global anticorruption campaign. The rationale underlying this structure is the general belief that law enforcement should combat corruption as a phenomenon holistically, in cooperation with all major players and the community at large.

interview memorandum. A record or written statement summarizing an information finding meeting.

interviews. A process that seeks to obtain information regarding various areas, including an individual's current and past roles at the company and his or her knowledge of certain business practices.

investigation sponsor. The person or persons who will take responsibility for and/or oversee the investigation.

investigative demand. A demand issued in writing prior to the institution of a civil or criminal proceeding. The demand is served upon such person or enterprise that may be in possession, custody, or control of any documentary materials relevant to a racketeering investigation. The demand requires such person to produce such material for examination.[27]

investigative interview. A questioning session conducted where notes are made and they form the basis for any false statement charge against an employee if the government determines that the employee had made false material statements during the interview.

investigative public record researcher. People who are familiar with all aspects of public records, including knowledge of sources and proper protocol in obtaining the information. These individuals can assist forensic accountants in managing all aspects of identifying the various sources of information, the jurisdictions in which they reside, and the process of record retrieval.

investigative settings. When attorneys and accountants work together in several different ways, with the accountant retained either directly by the same client as the attorney (usually a company, but sometimes an individual) or indirectly by the attorney in connection with the attorney's legal advice to the client.

investigative team. A group of people tasked with performing a close examination and systematic inquiry.

iron curtain approach. An approach that quantifies the misstatement based on the effects of correcting the misstatements existing in the balance sheet at the end of the current year, irrespective of the year of origination of the misstatement(s).

issuers. The entity whose securities are being sold circulated.

joint defense agreement. The agreement formed between attorneys for the company and its employees to document their common interests and specify the conditions under which information will be shared. If the company and its employees have a common interest, the attorney-client and the work product privileges will extend to the separate attorneys' shared communications.

journaling systems. A system that captures all predetermined incoming and outgoing information which users do not control only administrators of systems control.

kickback. A kickback can take many forms but it is typically a form of money, gift or some other form of compensation that is given to an individual in return for performing a desired task. This fraud is classified as a corruption type scheme. An example would be someone that has inappropriately steered a contract or other form of business to a vendor in return for a gift of money or other non-monetary compensation.

lapping. Practice of concealing theft of cash, whereby an employee steals cash from one customer's payment and covers it up by crediting that customer's account with the next customer's payment. While this process is occurring at least one customer's account will always be overstated.

legal hold. In affect a do not destroy memo, which is an order to cease destruction and preserve all records, regardless of form, related to the nature or subject of the legal hold.

legal privilege. A right intended to protect an individual's ability to access the justice system by encouraging complete disclosure to legal advisers without the fear that any disclosure of those communications may prejudice the client in the future.

legal technology professionals. People who gather electronic evidence, such as e-mail and computer-based files, as part of investigations and business litigation.

letters rogatory. A formal request from a court to a foreign court for assistance; utilized as a request from a court in the United States to the appropriate judicial authorities in another country to obtain evidence from a witness, either through testimony to answer questions or through the production of documents.

liable. Obligated according to law to be held responsible to perform some action based on a result of an outcome.

likelihood of occurrence. The probability that an event will take place potentially based on qualitative and quantitative factors.

line supervisors. With respect to antifraud implementation and oversight—these individuals are responsible for overseeing the implementation and ongoing effectiveness of the antifraud program. The supervisors report to executive management any indicators of suspicious activity.

loan. All extensions of credit by the Insured and all transactions creating a creditor relationship in favor of the Insured and all transactions by which the Insured assumes an existing creditor relationship.

logistics companies. Companies that regularly transport goods in and out of countries that may be subject to customs, duties, or other charges.

management's liaison to counsel. The officer of the company appointed to the investigation with sufficient authority to effectively support the investigation.

manifest intent. The intent to cause the injured to sustain loss and therefore obtain benefit financially.

mareva injunction. A court order that freezes assets so that a defendant cannot frustrate a judgment by dissipating his or her assets from beyond the jurisdiction of the court.

master file. Source of relatively authoritative collection of related data or information stored as a single unit with single name.

materiality. The magnitude of an omission or misstatement that individually or in aggregate, in light of the surrounding circumstances, makes it probable that the judgment of a reasonable person relying on the financial statements would have been changed or influenced by such omission or misstatement.

materiality threshold. The cutoff point of the information that if its omission or misstatement occurred, could that influence the economic decisions of users taken on the basis of the financial statements.

mediation. A form of alternative dispute resolution aimed to assist two (or more) disputants in reaching an agreement. The disputes may involve states, organizations, communities, individuals or other representatives with a vested interest in the outcome.

metadata. The embedded electronic data about the data.

monetary judgment. A formal order issued by an authoritative body that one party to the disagreement is to pay the other party a sum of money.

money laundering. The process where proceeds generated from criminal or illegal activity are "cleaned" to intentionally disguise their illegal origin. This cleaning process involves circulating the money through legitimate businesses which ultimately disseminate the funds into the local economy, knowingly or unknowingly as the case may be.

monitoring controls. A process that assesses the quality of internal control performance over time and determines the effectiveness of the controls for their stated objective. It is accomplished through ongoing activities, separate evaluations, or by a combination of the two.

mutual legal assistance treaty. A treaty creating alliances between two foreign countries for the purpose of gathering and exchanging information in an effort to enforce criminal laws.

NASDAQ. The National Association of Securities Dealers Automated Quotations is a United States stock exchange. It is the largest electronic screen-based equity securities trading market in the United States.

National Conference of Commissioners on Uniform State Laws (NCCUSL). A conference that provides states with nonpartisan, well-conceived and well-drafted legislation that brings clarity and stability to critical areas of the law. NCCUSL's work supports the federal system and facilitates the movement of individuals and the business of organizations with rules that are consistent from state to state.

National Software Reference Library. A library designed to collect software from various sources and incorporate file profiles computed from this software into a Reference Data Set (RDS) of information. The RDS can be used by law enforcement, government, and industry organizations to review files on a computer by matching file profiles in the RDS.

monitoring controls. Various types of physical or network security device logs used to collect information. These may include card swipe logs, closed circuit video, Internet logs, remote access logs, and intrusion detection server logs.

mutual legal assistance treaty. A treaty creating alliances between two foreign countries for the purpose of gathering and exchanging information in an effort to enforce criminal laws.

NASDAQ. The National Association of Securities Dealers Automated Quotations is a United States stock exchange. It is an electronic screen based equity securities trading market with approximately 3,800 companies and corporations.

National Conference of Commissioners on Uniform State Laws (NCCUSL). A conference that provides states with nonpartisan, well conceived and well drafted legislation that brings clarity and stability to critical areas of the law. NCCUSL's work supports the federal system and facilitates the movement of individuals and the business of organizations with rules that are consistent from state to state.

National Software Reference Library. A library designed to collect software from various sources and incorporate file profiles computed from this software into a Reference Data Set (RDS) of information. The RDS can be used by law enforcement, government, and industry organizations to review files on a computer by matching file profiles in the RDS.

near-line. Information stored on removable media, such as optical discs, that can be made available by a device, such as an optical "jukebox."

negotiated settlements. An agreement composing differences.[17]

New York Convention. A meeting of the 144 participating states that are required to recognize arbitral awards and enforce them, in accordance with specific procedural rules in international commercial disputes. Most major trading nations, as well as many other countries, have ratified the New York Convention, giving the convention broad acceptance and making this an effective proceeding for financial recovery.

New York Stock Exchange (NYSE). Operates six cash equities exchanges in seven countries and eight derivatives exchanges. It is a world leader for listings, trading in cash equities, equity and interest rate derivatives, bonds, and the distribution of market data.

nonduty to defend. A situation where the insured has the right to manage the defense of the claim and choose defense council, subject to the insurer's approval.

non-reporting issuer. An issuer that is not subject to the Securities Exchange Act of 1933 filing requirements. An Issuer is a corporation that has distributed to the public, securities, registered with the Securities and Exchange Commission.[23]

Norwich Pharmacal order. An order that allows for the discovery of evidence from innocent third parties, such as financial institutions. The principle underlying the order is that if, through no fault of his or her own, a person facilitates the wrongdoing of others, then that person comes under a duty to assist the victim. He or she can assist by giving the victim full information and disclosing the identity of the wrongdoers.

notice. Formal notification to the party that has been sued in a civil case of the fact that the lawsuit has been filed.[5]

objective advisor. Independent, third party who makes recommendations regarding a decision or course of conduct.

occupational fraud. The use of ones' occupation to intentionally misuse or misapply their organizations' assets or information for the direct or indirect benefit to that individual. Occupational fraud can be classified into three main areas of fraud schemes, misappropriation of asset schemes, fraudulent statement schemes, and corruption schemes.

offer of employment. A job offer, typically defining the terms of employment.

Office of Inspector General (OIG). An office that protects the integrity of a corporation. OIG has a responsibility to report program and management problems and recommendations to correct them both to the Secretary and to the Congress. OIG's duties are carried out through a nationwide network of audits, investigations, evaluations, and other mission related functions performed by OIG components.

Office of the General Counsel. A diverse legal practice, attorneys supervise the development of the Department of Commerce's legislative and regulatory programs, defend decisions of commerce officials against judicial challenge, and advise agency officials on personnel, procurement, and budget matters.

offline storage. The storage used for disaster recovery or archiving that must be made available through human intervention. Backup tapes are typically used for offline storage.

ontology. Involves an analysis conducted soon after data is first loaded to the review platform, for the purpose of evaluating the collection of electronic evidence to determine potentially relevant information that may drive case strategy, such as key topics or themes of the case, dates and amounts, specific vocabulary and jargon, and people.

open-source information. Information derived from public sources which now includes the enormous and growing repository of online data, including search engines, Web logs (blogs), and Web sites.

Organization for Economic Co-operation and Development (OECD) Convention on Combating Bribery of Foreign Public Officials in International Business Transactions. An organization that establishes legally binding standards to criminalize bribery of foreign public officials in international business transactions and provides for a host of related measures that make this effective.[19]

Organization of Economic Co-operation and Development (OECD). An organization that brings together the governments of countries committed to democracy and the market economy from around the world to support sustainable economic growth, boost employment, raise living standards, maintain financial stability, assist other countries' economic development, and contribute to growth in world trade. The organization provides a setting where governments compare policy experiences, seek answers to common problems, identify good practice, and coordinate domestic and international policies.[19]

orientation program. A program typically attended by a new employee after the offer of employment is accepted. This session is designed to assist new employees in adjusting to their jobs and work environment and they can become better acclimated into the culture within an organization.

parallel investigations. Investigations that occur when multiple civil regulatory and criminal law enforcement authorities simultaneously initiate proceedings that relate to the same facts or overlapping targets.[21]

parallel proceeding. Situations where both criminal and civil investigations and cases are in progress at the same time. An example would be when a trustee is conducting an adversary proceeding to recover property, while there is a criminal investigation of the debtor for bankruptcy fraud involving concealment of the same asset.[29]

pay and return scheme. Schemes frequently carried out by using the invoices of legitimate, third party vendors who are not a part of the fraud scheme. In these cases, the perpetrator is an internal employee who intentionally mishandles payments owed to legitimate vendors. There are different versions of the scheme

generally used: double paying invoices, paying incorrect vendors, and vendor overpayment.

personal share (or home directory). A portion of the server's disk storage that has been allocated for file storage. A personal share or home directory is used by a specific custodian.

petty cash. Typically a small amount of cash that is kept at the organization to be used for small miscellaneous types of expenditures. When theft of petty cash occurs it would be classified as a misappropriation of asset type fraud scheme.

plaintiff. A person who brings an action; the party who complains or sues in a civil action.[5]

playbook. A predetermined set of criteria that helps decision makers sort through the available information in a more objective way. This set of predeveloped criteria greatly enhances the consistency and speed of the initial response to an allegation of fraud.

portable document format (PDF). A file format created by Adobe Systems in 1993 for document exchange. PDF is used for representing two-dimensional documents in a manner independent of the application software, hardware, and operating system.

practitioner. Someone who practices a learned profession.[17]

preissuance reviewer. A person who reads the report or work products and summary memorandum, refers to the engagement letter to confirm the scope of services provided, and discusses significant matters with the engagement partner.

preliminary loss estimate. Initial estimate of a business' insured losses after reinsurance recoveries and net of reinstatement premiums.

preliminary work plan. A plan that will set the overarching objective and divide the tasks into manageable work streams.

preservation. The process that begins with notification to custodians that they must preserve ESI in their custody or control, which is a process known as a legal hold.

preservation notice. A communication that suspends the normal disposition or processing of records.

preservation plan. A process or methodology that an organization will create so that, in the event of a need to preserve necessary documents, the organization has a plan in place that explains the technique(s), including schedules for preservation actions, quality assurance testing, backups, and so on, and instructions for documentation that will be followed.

privacy statutes. The expectation that confidential personal information is disclosed in a private place and will not be disclosed to third parties.

private branch exchange (PBX). A private switching system, usually located on a customer's premises with an attendant console. It is connected to a common group of lines from one or more central offices to provide service to a number of individual phones.[14]

privileged. Information that is not subject to disclosure in a court of law. Intended to protect an individual's ability to access the justice system by encouraging complete disclosure to legal advisers without the fear that any disclosure of those communications may prejudice the client in the future. Investigative findings commissioned by legal advisors to provide advice to their clients also may be privileged.

privileged work products. The work product of an attorney is not discoverable unless the court determines that denial of discovery will unfairly prejudice the party seeking discovery. The actual work of the investigation can be apportioned among the company, attorneys, accountants, and other specialists in any way that is appropriate, as long as the attorney directs the work and the work is conducted in the context of assisting the attorney in rendering legal advice.

processing. The stage at which data may be filtered for content.

procurement fraud. Classified as a corruption type of fraud scheme and includes cost and labor mischarging, defective pricing, defective parts, price fixing, bid rigging, and product substitution.

profiled. To look for clusters of similar variables, for example, by location, by frequency, by product type, and so on, so that a predictive model can be built to monitor for risks.

Project Management Institute (PMI). The world's leading not-for-profit association for the project management profession. PMI advocates project, program and portfolio management that can enhance and accelerate organizational change.

project planning. The planning process that encompasses a range of activities related to scope, schedule, cost, quality, staffing, communication, risk, and procurement that are used to develop a project management plan and manage the project.

proof of loss. Documentation or declaration given to insurer by policyholder stating or substantiating insured loss.

proprietary data. Data that is privately and exclusively owned and may be protected by secrecy or law.

Public Company Accounting Oversight Board (PCAOB). A private sector, nonprofit corporation, created by the Sarbanes-Oxley Act of 2002, to oversee the auditors of public companies in order to protect the interests of investors and further the public interest in the preparation of informative, fair, and independent audit reports.

public disclosure. The notes that investigation team uses to report its findings to the appropriate party, such as directors, legal counsel, and oversight bodies.

public records. Records that include any document filed or recorded by a public agency in a public office that the general public has a right to examine. Historically stored in hard copy, public record information now is widely available on searchable computer databases.

quality assurance partner (independent review partner). A partner of the accounting firm other than the engagement partner that will function as a pre-issuance reviewer.

quality assurance program. A program to ensure the quality of the work products that are submitted to the client and external parties.

Racketeering and Influencing Corrupt Organizations Act (RICO). Part of the Organized Crime Control Act of 1970. The goal of the act was to punish and deter organized and organizational crime.

receivership. A court action that places property under the control of a receiver during litigation so that it can be preserved for the benefit of all. When a trustee or liquidator has been appointed, he or she has the legal authority to further the investigation by recovering assets or compelling witnesses to provide information. Trustees, liquidators, or receivers also have broad powers to control the business; investigate missing assets, and distribute the assets.

records management program. A planned, coordinated set of policies, procedures, and activities needed to manage an agency's recorded information. The program encompasses the creation, maintenance and use, and disposition of records, regardless of media. Essential elements include issuing up-to-date program directives, properly training those responsible for implementation, publicizing the program, and carefully evaluating the results to ensure adequacy, effectiveness, and efficiency.[2]

regulators. Subsystem or independent group that determines and maintains the operating parameters of a system or activity.

regulatory investigation. An internal investigation conducted by a company on behalf of a government regulatory agency such as the SEC or DOJ. The regulatory agency, such as the SEC and DOJ, would then leverage the company's fact finding results before proceeding with their own course of action.

regulatory officials. The officials in charge of implementing regulatory procedures by making sure law and policies are followed. These officials could include SEC enforcement lawyers and accountants, DOJ lawyers, FBI agents, and IRS agents.

regulatory safe harbor. The attempt by a regulatory agency to potentially reduce or eliminate an organizations' liability under the law, on the condition that the organization performed its actions in good faith. The regulatory agency may have a standard policy for fielding requests, for voluntary self-reporting companies, or providing avenues to lessen sanctions if the company's full cooperation so warrants.

relational database. A type of database that supports very efficient analysis of structured data.

remote access technologies. Provides the ability to connect to the network from a distant location, for example those employees who work from home or travel extensively. The ability to access the system from a remote location typically requires a computer, a modem, and remote access software to allow the computer to dial into the network over a telephone line, cable, or satellite service.

report database. A collection of data organized for rapid search and retrieval.

request list. A list submitted to the client asking for certain types of information and documentation believed to be relevant to the investigation, based upon information known at that time.

rescission action. To abrogate (a contract) and restore the parties to the positions they would have occupied had there been no contract.[17]

residual data. Data that has been deleted or is no longer active on a computer system and is no longer visible using the application with which the original file was created. For example, documents may be recovered from a hard drive stored in a networked office printer.

respondent. The party that responds to a claim filed in court against them by a plaintiff. A term used in arbitration for the defendant.

restitution order. Remedies intended to reverse unjust enrichment and prevent a wrongdoer from profiting from the crime provided by criminal courts.

resulting events. Events that arise as a consequence, effect, or conclusion.

revenue recognition review. In the context of an investigation into a revenue recognition issue, a review of

keywords such as accelerate, big bath, cookie jar, stretch, gap, pull-in, and close the gap, can be used to determine how prevalent this issue was in the emails and other documents used to review during the investigation.

revenue recognition schemes. Schemes that seek to increase the amount of revenue recognized or accelerate the timing of the revenue recognition. These types of fraud would be classified as fraudulent statement schemes.

review protocol. The procedure to identify key e-mails and associated documents of interest in the investigation.

rider. Additional insurance coverage provided for something that is not specifically covered by the primary policy that is in place.

risk criteria. Objective criteria used to help in assessing incoming reports of matters potentially requiring investigation.

rollover approach. Quantifies a misstatement based on the amount of the error originating in the current year income statement. This approach ignores the effects of correcting the portion of the current year balance sheet misstatement that originated in prior years (that is, it ignores the carryover impact of prior year misstatements).

Rule 26. A regulation that requires that the expert report state all the opinions and the basis for them.

rules based queries. When using analytics, these queries rely heavily on the individual performing the analytic test, to ask questions of the data based on what is known currently about the data.

sales pursuit cycle. The time and effort that it takes to secure a contract which often represents a significant amount of revenue to the proposing companies.

sanctions. The detriment, loss of reward, or coercive intervention annexed to a violation of a law as a means of enforcing the law.[17]

Sarbanes-Oxley Act of 2002 (SOX). An act to protect investors by improving the accuracy and reliability of corporate disclosures made pursuant to the securities laws, and for other purposes.

SAS. An acronym for *Statement on Auditing Standards*, which are issued by the Auditing Standards Board (ASB) of the AICPA.

scienter. The misrepresentation or omission is intended to deceive or defraud investors.[30]

search warrant. A written order issued by a judge that directs a law enforcement officer to search a specific area for a particular piece of evidence.[5]

Securities and Exchange Act of 1934. The act that empowers the SEC with broad authority over all aspects of the securities industry. This includes the power to register, regulate, and oversee brokerage firms, transfer agents, and clearing agencies as well as the nation's securities self regulatory organizations (SROs).

Securities and Exchange Commission (SEC). The mission of the SEC is to protect investors, maintain fair, orderly, and efficient markets, and facilitate capital formation. Congress—during the peak year of the Depression—passed the Securities Act of 1933. This law, together with the Securities Exchange Act of 1934, created the SEC, which was designed to restore investor confidence in our capital markets by providing investors and the markets with more reliable information and clear rules of honest dealing.

Securities and Exchange Commission Staff Accounting Bulletin (SEC SAB) No. 99, *Materiality.* This SAB expresses the views of the staff that exclusive reliance on certain quantitative benchmarks to assess materiality in preparing financial statements and performing audits of those financial statements is inappropriate; misstatements are not immaterial simply because they fall beneath a numerical threshold.

Serious Organised Crime Agency (SOCA). An executive non-departmental public body sponsored by, but operationally independent from, the Home Office. SOCA is an intelligence-led agency with law enforcement powers and harm reduction responsibilities.

server. A computer in a network that is used to provide services (as access to files or shared peripherals or the routing of e-mail) to other computers in the network.[17]

severity of impact. A rating used to determine the magnitude of a fraud that has occurred, such as the following: high equals a $2 million dollar loss. The impact can describe both the loss of actual dollars or the effect on qualitative factors such as brand and reputation, or both, which are hard to quantify with a specific dollar amount.

shadow investigation. An investigation that independently assesses whether the audit committee's findings, actions, and recommendations are appropriate.

share. A portion of the file server's disk storage that has been allocated for file storage.

side A coverage. Typically provides coverage directly to the directors and officers for loss—including defense costs—resulting from claims made against the, for their wrongful acts.

side agreements. Agreements made outside of publicly known contracts.

side B coverage. Reimburses a corporation for its loss where the corporation indemnifies its directors and officers for claims against them.

side C coverage. Optional coverage that protects the corporation against securities claims or other special types of claims not covered by general liability policies.

signatories. Signer with another or other.[17]

site visit. Going to a client location and evaluating processes to gain access to hard copy and relevant documents.

skimming. The theft of all or a portion of the cash receipts of a business at a particular point of sale or other point where cash or payments enter a business. These schemes are "off-book" frauds, meaning that the money is stolen before it is recorded in the accounts of the victim organization.

slush funds. Off-book cash that is maintained and can be used for illicit purposes such as corruption or for the personal benefit of those company representatives generating and maintaining the funds. These funds are frequently built from the improper conversion of a company's cash.

special committee. A committee formed by the board of directors when allegations of potential financial statement fraud first surface. The committee is formed to evaluate the veracity of the allegations and lead the related investigation.

spokesperson. A person designated to respond to media requests and coverage.[17]

spoliation. The intentional destruction, mutilation, alteration, or concealment of evidence, usually a document.

SPSS. Predictive analytics software used by companies to anticipate change, manage both daily operations and special initiatives more effectively, and realize positive, measurable benefits.

Staff Accounting Bulletin (SAB) No. 104, *Revenue Recognition.* Issued in 2004, the prevailing accounting guidance related to revenue recognition. Generally, SAB 104 requires that 4 requirements must be met to recognize revenue, including persuasive evidence of an arrangement, delivery has occurred or services have been rendered, seller's price to buyer is fixed and determinable, and collectability is reasonably assured.

stakeholders. May include shareholders, directors, management, suppliers, and others within an organization who have interest in the success of an organization in delivering intended results, objectives, and maintaining the viability of the organization's products and/or services.

Statement on Auditing Standards (SAS) No. 1, *Codification of Accounting Standards and Procedures.* The AICPA professional standard that states that it is management's responsibility "to design and implement programs and controls to prevent, deter, and detect fraud."

SAS No. 54, *Illegal Acts by Clients.* This statement prescribes the nature and extent of the consideration an independent auditor should give to the possibility of illegal acts by a client in an audit of financial statements in accordance with generally accepted auditing standards. The statement also provides guidance on the auditor's responsibilities when a possible illegal act is detected.

SAS No. 99, *Consideration of Fraud in a Financial Statement Audit.* An auditing statement issued by Auditing Standards Board of the American Institute of Certified Public Accountants in October 2002. SAS No. 99 requires the auditor to gather information necessary to assess the potential risk of fraud in two areas: financial reporting, and the misappropriation of assets.

Statements on Standards for Consulting Services (SSCSs). SSCS supersedes the Statements on Standards for Management Advisory Services and provides standards of practice for a broad range of professional services, including, but not limited to, consulting services, management advisory services, business advisory services, or management services.

structured ESI. Contained in databases, such as financial or accounting databases (that is, general ledger, accounts payable, and payroll) and other databases.

subpoena. A writ commanding a person designated in it to appear in court under a penalty for failure.

subrogation. The right of the carrier to be put in the position of the insured in order to pursue recovery from third parties who may be legally responsible to the insured for the loss paid by the insurer.

summary memorandum. A comprehensive record or written statement.

Surety & Fidelity Association of America (SFAA). The U.S.-based organization that comprises insurance companies that underwrite surety and fidelity bonds. Such bonds are intended to facilitate commerce, enhance economic development, and protect consumers and policyholders from a variety of risks.

sweep. A search for offline media, such as backup tapes pulled out of rotation, hard drives, and other magnetic media. A sweep may require the development of a questionnaire that the company implements on its own regarding these media, or it may involve technology advisors performing a physical sweep (walk-through and collection of media).

systems administrators. Database server administrators, e-mail server administrators, network specialists, and desktop application support personnel who have a specific expertise but are typically not trained in forensic disciplines.

tax-deductible expenses. An item or expense subtracted from adjusted gross income to reduce the amount of income subject to tax.

technical advisors. People who assist with the collection and management of electronic evidence.

The IT Governance Institute (ITGI). Established in 1998 in recognition of the increasing criticality of information technology to enterprise success.

third party claims. A claim by the respondent against a party not already named in the proceeding.

tied-out. A process that includes either by footnote or cross reference all the support for each of the statements, data, or assumptions has been agreed to supporting documentation.

tone at the top. Leadership personnel who set an example through actions and communications. The tone at the top is the message disseminating from the very top of the organization to the bottom.

transactional documents. Documents created by organizations through their financial computing system.

transactional systems. A system that processes the data from financial transactions in a database system.

Transparency International. The global civil society organization leading the fight against corruption, brings people together in a powerful worldwide coalition to end the devastating impact of corruption on men, women and children around the world. Their mission is to create change towards a world free of corruption.

Transparency International's Corruption Perception Index. The index provides an overview of how the perceived level of corruption in a particular country compares with other countries.

U.S. Attorney General. The Judiciary Act of 1789 created the Office of the Attorney General which evolved over the years into the head of the DOJ and chief law enforcement officer of the federal government. The Attorney General represents the U.S. in legal matters generally and gives advice and opinions to the President and to the heads of the executive departments of the government when so requested.

U.S.–European Union (EU) Safe Harbor Framework.
The framework that would prohibit the transfer of personal data to non-EU nations that do not meet the EU's "adequacy" standard for privacy protection. While the U.S. and the European Union share the goal of enhancing privacy protection for their citizens, the United States takes a different approach to privacy from that taken by the European Union.[31]

U.S. Federal Sentencing Guidelines for Organizations. An organization created in 2001 with the guidelines to govern the imposition of sentences by federal judges on organizational defendants. The guidelines impose harsh penalties upon organizations whose employees or other agents have committed federal crimes. Penalties include restitution, remedial orders, community service, and substantial fines, based upon a point system for determining severity of offense.

U.S.–Swiss Safe Harbor Framework. The framework that simplifies the transfer of personal data by Swiss firms to American companies that self-certify to the U.S. Department of Commerce. In addition to administrative simplifications for businesses, the bilateral data protection framework will also strengthen the data protection rights of those concerned with respect to these companies.[31]

unicode. A unique number for every character, no matter what the platform, no matter what the program, no matter what the language. The code enables a single software product or a single Web site to be targeted across multiple platforms, languages and countries without re-engineering. It allows data to be transported through many different systems without corruption.[32]

Uniform Foreign-Country Money Judgment Recognition Act. Provided for enforcement of foreign country judgments in a state court in the United States. The 1962 Uniform Foreign Money-Judgments Recognition act has been enacted in 32 states.

United Nations Convention against Corruption (UNCAC). The convention promotes and strengthens measures to prevent and combat corruption more efficiently and effectively.

United Nations Convention against Illicit Traffic in Narcotic Drugs and Psychotropic Substances. A convention that focuses on providing comprehensive measures against drug trafficking but includes provisions against money laundering and provides for international cooperation, including aspects of the transfer of proceedings of profits.

United Nations Convention against Transnational Organized Crime. The purpose of this convention is to promote cooperation to prevent and combat transnational organized crime more effectively.[20]

unstructured ESI. A centralized system of managing telephone messages for a large group of people. The term is also used more broadly, to denote any system of conveying voice message, including the answering machine.

Upjohn warnings. Also known as "Corporate Miranda," contains the following elements: (1) the attorney represents the corporation and not the individual employee; (2) the interview is covered by the attorney-client privilege, which belongs to and is controlled by the company, not the individual employee; and (3) the company may decide, in its sole discretion, whether to waive the privilege and disclose information from the interview to third parties, including the government.[18]

USA PATRIOT Act. The act is an enhanced law enforcement investigatory tool for responding to terrorist financing that has provided significant impetus to global AML initiatives.

victim. One that is acted on and adversely affected by a force or agent.[17]

voluntary disclosure. A disclosure issue concerning whether the company should self report to the government. Self disclosure avoids the risk of involuntary disclosure by third parties, such as government investigations or whistleblowers. If the government discovers that the company knew about the issue and did not raise it with the government, the punishment meted out by the government could be more severe.

waived. To relinquish voluntarily (as a legal right).[17]

waiver. The act of intentionally relinquishing or abandoning a known right, claim, or privilege.

whistleblower. An employee who exercises from speech rights to challenge corporate and government abuses of power that betray the public trust.[33]

whitewash. When the composition of the board consists of mainly company executives during an investigation which leads to allegations of bias.

work product doctrine. Under this doctrine, government investigators are typically not entitled to obtain work product materials (that is, materials generated or prepared by counsel in anticipation of litigation or that reflect an attorney's independent thought process, counsel's legal analysis, and the efforts of counsel in anticipation of litigation).

working paper. Records kept by the auditor of the procedures applied, the tests performed, the information obtained, and the pertinent conclusions reached in the course of the audit and any records developed by a CPA during an audit.[3]

World Bank Group. A lending institution whose aim is to help integrate developing and transition economies with the global economy, and reduce poverty by promoting economic growth. The bank lends for policy reforms and development projects and policy advice, and offers technical assistance and nonlending services to its 181 member countries.[19]

Glossary Key

1. *12 Key Standards and Self-Assessments,* "The Financial Action Task Force's 40 Recommendations on Money Laundering and 9 Special Recommendations on Terrorist Financing." www.treas.gov/offices/international-affairs/standards/code09.shtml (accessed July 27, 2009).

2. *A Federal Records Management Glossary.* National Archives and Records Administration, 1993.

3. *Accounting Terminology Guide,* www.nysscpa.org/glossary (accessed July 27, 2009).

4. *APEC Privacy Framework.* APEC Secretariat, 2005.

5. *Common Legal Terms.* www.uscourts.gov/understand03/content_9_0.html (accessed July 27, 2009).

6. *Control Objectives for Information and related Technology 4.1.* IT Governance Institute, 2007.

7. *Description of Coverage for Mercantile and Governmental Entities.* www.surety.org/scontent.cfm?lid=4&catid=2&spid=19 (accessed July 27, 2009).

8. *DSC Risk Management Manual of Examination Polices.* Federal Deposit Insurance Corporation, 2004.

9. *Employee Benefits Security Administration Enforcement Manual.* United States Department of Labor, 2009.

10. FASB. FASB Statement No. 2, *Accounting for Research and Development Costs.* Financial Accounting Standards Board, October 1974.

11. FASB. FASB Statement No. 5, *Accounting for Contingencies.* Financial Accounting Standards Board, March 1975.

12. FASB. FASB Statement No. 154, *Accounting Changes and Error Corrections—a replacement of APB Opinion No. 20 and FASB Statement No. 3.* Financial Accounting Standards Board, May 2005.

13. *Form K-8.* U.S. Securities and Exchange Commission. www.sec.gov/answers/form8k.htm (accessed July 27, 2009).

14. *Internal Revenue Manual.* (2.13.3.3) Chapter 13 "Enterprise Networks" Section 3 "Voice Premise Communications." Internal Revenue Service, 2006.

15. *Legal Dictionary.* www.legal-dictionary.org/ (accessed July 27, 2009).

16. Marmor, Randall, and John Tomaine. *Commercial Crime Policy,* 2nd ed. American Bar Association, 2004.

17. *Merriam-Webster Online,* www.merriam-webster.com/dictionary (accessed July 27, 2009).

18. Murphey, Paul B. and Lucian E. Dervan. *Attorney-Client Privilege & Employee Interviews in Internal Investigations.* Contemporary Legal Note Series No. 49, March 2006. Washington Legal Foundation.

19. *OECD Glossary of Statistical Terms,* www.oecd.org/glossary (accessed July 27, 2009).

20. *Protocol to Prevent, Suppress, and Punish Trafficking in Persons, Especially Women and Children, Supplementing the United Nations Convention Against Transnational Organized Crime.* Article 2 "Statement of Purpose," United Nations, 2000.

21. Rao, Pravin B. "Dealing with Parallel Investigations." *Criminal Justice Section Newsletter* 17, no. 1 (2008).

22. Schott, Paul Allan. *Reference Guide to Anti-Money Laundering and Combating the Financing of Terrorism,* 2nd ed. The International Bank for Reconstruction and Development/The World Bank/The International Monetary Fund, 2006.

23. Securities and Exchange Commission. 17 CFR Part 230 (Release No. 33-7541;S7-14-98). RIN: 3235-AH35. "Revision of Rule 504 of Regulation D, The 'Seed Capital' Exemption."

24. *Statistical Briefing Book.* U.S. Department of Justice. www.ojjdp.ncjrs.gov/ojstatbb/glossary.html (accessed July 27, 2009).

25. The University of Cincinnati College. *Securities Lawyer Deskbook.* University of Cincinnati, 1998.

26. Title 18 "Crimes and Criminal Procedure," Part 1, Chapter 47, § 1001(a).

27. Title 18 "Crimes and Criminal Procedure," Part 1, Chapter 96, § 1968(a).

28. Title 28 "Appendix," *Federal Rules of Civil Procedure,* Part 5, § 26(a).

29. *United States Trustee Manual.* U.S. Department of Justice, 1998.

30. Weil, Wagner, and Frank. *Litigation Services Handbook: The Role of the Financial Expert* 3rd ed. Wiley, 2001.

31. *Welcome to Safe Harbor,* www.export.gov/safeharbor (accessed July 27, 2009).

32. *What is Unicode?* www.unicode.org/standard/WhatIsUnicode.html (accessed July 27, 2009).

33. *What is a Whistleblower?,* www.whistleblower.org/template/page.cfm?page_id=118 (accessed July 27, 2009).